ANTIQUE PORCELAIN DIGEST

1. MEISSEN. APOSTLE PETER. Modeled by Kändler, possibly as an experimental piece from which the larger series was copied. Superbly modeled. Trimmed in purple and gold. c. 1735. 8″ h.

Mr. and Mrs. G. Ryland Scott Collection.

ANTIQUE
PORCELAIN DIGEST

BY

CLEO M. SCOTT

AND

G. RYLAND SCOTT, JR.

With over Seven Hundred and Fifty specimens Illustrated
of which One Hundred and Six are in Color

THE CERAMIC BOOK COMPANY
NEWPORT · MON · ENGLAND

FIRST PUBLISHED IN 1961

Process Engraving by E. Stephens, Newport, Mon.

PRINTED AND PRODUCED IN GREAT BRITAIN BY
HARDING AND CURTIS LTD
BATH, SOMERSET

DEDICATED

TO

OUR CHILDREN AND GRANDCHILDREN

FOREWORD

In publishing the book *Antique Porcelain Digest*, the authors, Mr. and Mrs. G. Ryland Scott, have filled a much needed vacancy on the bookshelf of the ceramic collector.

The many volumes published some 25 to 40 years ago, although, if available, fundamentally still of great value, have become obsolete in many respects owing to more recent discoveries, some of which have completely changed our conceptions in many directions. To the collector in the United States, very little information printed in English was available.

The re-issue of the late W. B. Honey's book "Dresden China" in 1946, printed in the United States, brought the first English text book to American collectors and was of great value. It dealt, however, only with Meissen porcelain and brought an English version of the book by Ernst Zimmermann, published in 1926. George W. Ware's book, "German and Austrian Porcelain" published in 1956, the first publication by an American author, became of great interest to the beginner-collector but was limited to the factories of these two countries.

Mr. and Mrs. Scott's new book, for the first time brings concise and up-to-date information covering the entire range of porcelain ceramics as viewed by an American author. Their great knowledge and experience as collectors of many years is brought out to great advantage to the reader. On the occasion of numerous "porcelain study trips" to Europe during the past ten years, they not only had the advantage of being able to augment their own considerable collections, but had the opportunity to visit all of the major European public collections, discussing specimens with the Keepers of Ceramics and also viewing many important private collections. The many notes they made during these visits have been successfully incorporated in their book.

During the past fifteen post-war years, owing to the increased interest in collecting 18th century porcelains, many new theories and facts have been brought out through intensive research on the part of collectors, and bulletins of the various Ceramic Circles of all countries have greatly assisted in adding to our knowledge. The authors have made excellent use of these findings, which is reflected throughout the book.

Of additional importance is the fact that most of the extensive material used for illustrations has not been previously published. It represents specimens mainly from collections in the United States and should thus be of interest to European collectors.

RALPH H. WARK.

Hendersonville,
North Carolina, U.S.A.
1960.

INTRODUCTION

During the past decade my wife and I have frequently been asked the question: "Where can we buy a book that will give us the essential information about old porcelain and yet will not require too much time to read?" The further inquiry usually followed: "Why don't you write such a book?" As a result of these questions we gave the matter serious consideration, which revealed that while a number of excellent books were available dealing with individual factories and others with certain countries, none seemed to fill the need or serve the purpose that we had in mind. Few books dealing with German or French factories had been published in English. Many of the existing books on porcelain had been written many years ago and in some cases were now out of print. Considerable new information was available as a result of the research of the several Ceramic Circles. We had ourselves collected much new material through travel, study, and experience in connection with putting together our own collection. We accordingly decided to write a book which would supply what seemed to us the principal need in the literature of antique porcelain: an up-to-date digest beginning with the Chinese but dealing mainly with the best periods of the European factories, that is from 1710 to 1820.

We take considerable pride in the many excellent illustrations which we present, many of them not previously published. For some of these we are indebted to the great museums of the world and for many others to individual collectors, particularly in this country. As a matter of convenience and with we hope pardonable pride, we have shown a number of illustrations from the collection that we have had the pleasure of putting together, and for this we ask the reader's indulgence. For the benefit of those who will not find time to read the digest, we have added at the end of most chapters a condensed statement, giving the principal characteristics and marks. We realize that a cross-index has advantages to the serious student, yet even after consulting the indexes of other books we have often found difficulty in finding the desired information without recourse to tediously searching through many pages before finding the one or ones we sought. In our book therefore, we decided not to have an index but to include in the table of contents a rather detailed list of subjects as they appear in the book along with page references. We trust that the reader will have no difficulty in finding quickly any desired subject. With the exception of the frontispiece all photographs are in the back of the book, beginning with the color plates and following with the black-and-white ones in the same order of topics as in the text. Detailed descriptions will be found immediately preceding the plates.

*   *   *

On behalf of my wife and myself I wish to thank the Museums and private collectors who have so generously permitted us to illustrate this book with examples from their collections.

Detailed acknowledgements will be found in the descriptions which immediately precede the illustrations, and condensed acknowledgements under the respective illustrations themselves.

Many of the illustrations shown in this book are accompanied with no attribution; where this occurs the specimens are from a collection put together by my wife Cleo Meador Scott and myself over a period of a quarter of a century and now located in the porcelain room of the Brooks Memorial Art Gallery, Memphis, Tennessee.

This collection is the property of the authors and their children and grand-children: Mrs. Cleo Scott Allen of St. Louis, Missouri, and her three children, Robert Holt Allen, George Sewell Allen and Betty Vincent Allen; and George Ryland Scott III and his children, Charles Ryland Scott and Barbara Marie Scott of Atlanta, Georgia.

Mr. Ralph Wark has read and criticized the section on Meissen porcelain and Mr. Kildare S. Meager of Swansea, Wales, has read and criticized the section on Welsh porcelain. Mr. W. D. John has read all of the manuscript and has supervised the overall format to insure the same high standard attained in the many books that he has either written or published. Dr. John Quincy Wolf, head of the English Department of Southwestern University, Memphis, Tennessee, and his wife Bess M. Wolf, have not only read but corrected the entire manuscript. To all of these good friends we extend our heartfelt thanks, for without their help this book could never have been written.

Finally, we wish to thank all the learned authors from whose books much of the information has come and in this group we include the members of the several Ceramic Circles who have provided the research necessary to learn the facts. We refer the readers to our selective bibliography and say very frankly that any real student or advanced collector must of necessity read the books listed in order to learn the full story of the many factories that we have here attempted to cover as fully as the limited space would permit.

GEORGE RYLAND SCOTT, JR.

Scottswood,
Germantown, Tennessee, U.S.A.
1960.

CONTENTS

CHAPTER 1
ORIENTAL PORCELAIN

CHAPTER 2
GERMAN AND AUSTRIAN PORCELAIN

CHAPTER 3
SCANDINAVIAN, SWISS AND OTHER CONTINENTAL FACTORIES (1758-1800)

CHAPTER 4
ITALIAN PORCELAIN (1575-1800)

CHAPTER 5
FRENCH PORCELAIN (1673-1800)

CHAPTER 6
ENGLISH PORCELAIN

CHAPTER 7
AMERICAN PORCELAIN

Antique Porcelain Digest

Antique Porcelain Digest

GENERAL INFORMATION

Before discussing the various types of porcelain treated in this book, it may be well to give a few definitions that are already well known to the serious collector.

CERAMIC ART

The ceramic art extends back many centuries before the Christian era and has been defined as "the art of molding, modeling and baking clay." It may be divided roughly into porcelain and pottery. Porcelain, whether fine or commonplace, antique or modern, is always translucent, or when held in front of an incandescent lamp, light can be seen through it. On the contrary, pottery, whether faience or common earthenware, is always opaque and no light can be seen through it no matter how intense the beam. A question frequently asked is: what is the difference between porcelain and china? There is, of course, no difference, as porcelain is called china because the Chinese invented it.

Three different basic types of porcelain have been produced, as follows: 1. True, or hard-paste. 2. Artificial, or soft-paste. 3. Bone china.

TRUE OR HARD-PASTE PORCELAIN

This is the type made by the Chinese, made at the Meissen and other German and Austrian factories, also the French factories after 1769 and the Plymouth-Bristol factories in England. Its principal ingredients are kaolin clay and feldspar. The former is the final residue of granite which has decomposed for centuries. It is infusible and will resist the extreme heat of the kiln which, in some cases, reaches 3000 degrees fahrenheit. The latter, also called china stone, is fusible and will melt readily in the kiln. The Chinese liken the kaolin clay to the bones in the human body and the china stone to the flesh. When these two substances have been fired together in the kiln, "biscuit" porcelain results. As the feldspar melts, it covers the small grains of the kaolin clay, thus permitting light to pass through and giving the translucency so much desired. The biscuit is now covered with the glaze, which is composed of the china stone only. The Chinese usually gave only one deep firing after the glaze had been applied to the sun-baked biscuit. The European factories used two hard firings, one to the biscuit, and a second only slightly less intense after the glaze was added. After this stage all of the factories used the same process. The enamel colors were added and the object again put in the kiln at a considerably lower temperature than during the previous firings; after which the gold was applied and fixed in the kiln at a still lower temperature. Chinese porcelain was baked at a somewhat lower heat than that made in Europe.

ARTIFICIAL OR SOFT-PASTE PORCELAIN

Failing to discover the secret of making true porcelain, some of the early Continental factories partially solved the problem by using glass and ordinary clay to produce the second type mentioned above. The soft-paste lacked many of the practical advantages of the hard, yet it possessed a warmth and beauty not possible to obtain with true porcelain. The enamel paints and gold used in the decoration melted more deeply into the glaze of the soft-paste porcelain, while remaining on the surface of the hard-paste porcelain.

BONE CHINA

The Bow factory in England was the first to discover the benefits to be attained by using calcined bone ash in the production of porcelain. It was not until the start of the nineteenth century, however, that Josiah Spode invented his new formulae for making bone china, which revolutionized the manufacturing processes. The composition comprised equal parts of china clay, china stone, and bone ash. This was a very practical porcelain but lacked much of the beauty of the other two. The soft-pastes can be readily cut with a tempered file, the hard-pastes will resist the file, whereas bone china can be cut, but with some effort. As bone china came after the eighteenth century, we are little concerned with it in this volume.

CHAPTER 1

ORIENTAL PORCELAIN

CHINESE PORCELAIN

In approaching even a digest of Chinese porcelain, one is immediately conscious of the enormity of the task. Were it not for the works of such authorities as S. W. Bushell and R. L. Hobson, to name only two of many, the attempt to give a brief resumé would not have been made, and this book would have started with the occidental porcelain factories, founded centuries after porcelain had been evolved and produced in the orient. The reader is urged to study the books on the subject given in the bibliography and to visit museums in Europe, Canada and the United States where magnificent collections put together many years ago may be seen. We wish to call attention to a large collection in Blenheim Palace, near Oxford, the home of the Duke of Marlborough, where may be seen hundreds of pieces of fine quality Blanc-de-Chine, Powder Blue, K'ang Hsi and Famille Verte. The Victoria and Albert, and British Museums are rich in Chinese porcelain, particularly large vases. In Toronto, Canada, will be found a world-renowned collection of ceramics dating back to the earliest period. In the Metropolitan in New York, Walters Museum in Baltimore, the City Art Museum in St. Louis, and in many Continental museums will be found such examples as to leave no question that the Chinese excelled all others.

THE T'ANG DYNASTY (618-907)

The first porcelain was apparently made in the T'ang Dynasty, and Illustration 105 shows a wine cup of this period. Similar ones are in the Röhss Museum in Gothenburg, Sweden. A casual examination of these wine cups would lead the collector to the erroneous conclusion that they are pottery; but when placed in front of a strong light, it will be seen that they are translucent and, therefore, porcelain. The development of porcelain came about gradually during the first few centuries of the Christian era. Pottery was gradually fired at increasing temperatures until it became vitrified and finally, after many stages, it evolved into a white, translucent material—porcelain.

THE SUNG DYNASTY (960-1278)

William Burton, in his book on the subject, says that Sung porcelain is simple, the body never white and occasionally drab, the translucency poor, especially in heavily potted pieces, the glaze imperfect and uneven, and the color decoration secured by the use of colored glazes, never by painting over or under the glaze, as was commonly done in later periods. The four types produced are known as "Ju yao," whose pale green surface was compared to the lightest jade and felt like congealed lard to the touch; "Kuan yao," characterized with a crackled green or blue glaze; "Chün Chou yao," characterized by a blue dappled with purple or plum-colored splotches; and finally, the "Lung Ch'uan yao." This last is the type familiarly known as Celadon. The name was added in the eighteenth century when a French actor appeared in a mantle of grey-green color similar to that found on Sung vases. The decoration was usually lightly incised under the glaze and mostly floral. Illustration 106 is a rice bowl having one of the variations of this color, decorated with incised flowers and having incrustations. Many fine shapes were produced in this period. Illustration 108 shows a pair of figures, Ying Ch'ing ware. In 1126, the factory was moved to Ching-tê-Chên, destined to become, under Imperial patronage, the greatest ceramic center ever established.

THE MING DYNASTY (1368-1644)

This was a period of great importance in the production of porcelain. Blanc-de-Chine continued to be made of fine quality at Fukien, while at Ching-tê-Chên, the colored enamels were made. All the resources of the Emperor, including skilful potters and other artisans, under the control of State officials, produced new styles which were remarkable. The first new technique was the use of raised lines to define different portions of the pattern; the lines were left unglazed and the space within the lines filled in with glaze of different colors, ochre yellow, turquoise blue, purple, and sometimes an opaque white. Contrary to the usual practice, these pieces seem to have been fired twice in the manner later used by the European factories. The "egg shell" pieces disclose the remarkable art of the potters. One method of decorating is known as "rice-grain." About the beginning of the fifteenth century, the production of blue and white wares appeared. This proved to be of great importance and was one of their greatest achievements. By the latter part of the century, the supply of imported Mohammedan blue had failed, and the use of native materials resulted in a lowering of the quality of the product. During the reign of Chêng Tê (1506-22), a further supply of Mohammedan blue was secured, and exceptional pieces were made using two shades of the intense blue with great success. An under-glaze red was perfected at an early date and is quite rare. Later it was replaced by an inferior on-glaze red derived from iron. To the "three-colored" pieces composed of green, purple and yellow, were now added under-glaze blue and the on-glaze red, for what is called the "five-color" pieces. When the green was vigorous and predominated, it was called "famille verte," which reached its zenith in the K'ang Hsi reign. In addition to the famous under-glaze blue, the "three-color" and the "five-color" decorations many monochrome colors were used during this period and reached a high state of perfection during the following reign of K'ang Hsi. Ming yellows, an Imperial color made only for the Emperor, are famous. Also highly sought after was the ox blood (*sang de boeuf*) and the apple green. We feel that the Ming artist overpainted as a rule, thus losing the effect found later, where the white porcelain is given an important place in the design.

Illustration 109 is a Ginger Jar in Ming blue-and-white. The design illustrates "the hundred antiques." Illustration 110 is one of a pair of early Ming blue-and-white plates. Illustration 111 shows an interesting pair of small Ming bowls decorated in a blue-and-white pattern, later copied at Meissen and there called the "Onion Pattern." The object shown in the design is not an onion but a pomegranate; but this pattern, made at Meissen first around the middle of the eighteenth century, was produced in large quantities in the nineteenth and twentieth centuries and copied profusely by other factories.

Much of the information concerning the products made before the long reign of Wan Li (1573-1619), during the great Ming Dynasty (1368-1644 A.D.), are revealed in translations of the writings of eminent Chinese authors. The lack of examples of the two greatest periods of the Ming Dynasty, viz. the Hsüan Tê period (1426-1435) and the Ch'êng Hua period (1465-1487), make it most difficult to give a true picture of the products made at that time. Fortunately, we have in the great collections of Europe and America, many examples of the Wan Li period and the succeeding ones. Illustrations 114, 115 and 116 show three such pieces.

It will be understood that there existed many factories devoting their entire time to the production of porcelain for the Emperor and his court; such pieces are known as Imperial porcelain, and the information contained in the ancient Chinese writings refer exclusively to such pieces. There existed, however, other factories devoted to the manufacture of porcelain for private use, and little information is available as to their products, so we can but surmise that they followed closely those made at the Imperial potteries and were in all probability not quite so fine.

R. L. Hobson (*Chinese Pottery and Porcelain*, 1915) in referring to the products of the Hsüan Tê period, says that a fine blue-and-white as well as polychrome painted porcelains were made. Under-glaze red and crackle were also produced. This red was called "ape's blood," and is excessively rare even in China. The blue-and-white of this period was the finest ever made and authentic specimens are virtually un-procurable. Five colors: turquoise, yellow, crimson, red brown, and black were used. Painting in on-glaze enamels was practised in this period to a limited extent, and the enamels were thickly applied. In the next period it reached perfection. cf. Illustration 117.

As stated in the Ch'êng Hua period, the enamel colors were thin and were delicately applied. This period shares the honors of the Ming dynasty with its predecessor, as stated. It would seem that, in addition to the blue-and-white, both three-color and five-color pieces were made certainly during the Ming Dynasty. The Ch'êng Hua mark is one of the commonest found on Chinese porcelain, but there are no genuine examples in Western collections. The Wan Li specimens referred to found in European collections are, for the most part, in blue and white.

THE TECHNIQUE OF MING PORCELAIN

The bulk of the materials comprising the two important elements, kaolin (or porcelain earth) and porcelain stone were found in abundance in the districts surrounding Ching-tê-Chên, where the factories were located. The china stone was pounded and purified in mills worked by the water power of the mountains, arriving at Ching-tê-Chên in the form of briquettes. Hence the name PETUNTSE, which was applied to it. Neither time nor toil was spared in the preparation of Imperial porcelains, and it is said that the vessels were allowed to dry for a year. It was not the usual custom with Chinese potters to harden the ware with a slight preliminary firing before proceeding to decorate and apply the glaze, and consequently such processes as under-glaze painting in blue, embossing, etc., were undergone while the body was still relatively soft and required exceedingly careful handling. The glaze was applied in several ways, by dipping in a tub of glazing liquid, by painting the glaze on with a brush, or by blowing it through a bamboo tube, the end of which was covered with a piece of tightly stretched gauze. One of the last operations was the finishing of the foot, which was hollowed out and trimmed, and the mark added (if it was to be in blue as was usually the case), and covered with a spray of glaze. To the connoisseur, the finish of the foot is full of meaning. It is here that he gets a glimpse of the body which emerges at the raw edge of the rim, and by feeling it, he can tell whether the material is finely levigated or coarsely grained. The foot-rim of the Ming porcelains is plainly finished without the beading or grooves of the K'ang Hsi wares, which were evidently designed to fit on a stand; and the raw edge discloses an area which is almost always of fine white texture and close grain (often almost unctuous to the touch), though the actual surface generally assumes a brownish tinge in the heat of the kiln. A little sand or grit adhering to the foot-rim and radiating lines under the base caused by a jerky movement of the lathe, are signs of hasty finish, which occur not infrequently on the export wares. So the Chinese collector attaches great importance to the bottoms and feet which can testify to the fashion of the firing.

Ming glazes at the early period were thick and solid and have been likened to "massed lard." This is due to successive coatings of glaze to ensure a perfect covering

[5]

for the body and also accounted for the undulating appearance of the surface called "grains of millet," an effect much prized by the Chinese connoisseur, who also called it "chicken skin" or "orange peel". The porcelain glaze is rarely dead white, and in the Ming period it was greenish, as indeed it was in most Chinese glazes. The shapes are too numerous to note here and were taken from metal forms, certainly in the case of the more elaborate ones, where they displayed great skill.

Ming washes were laid on in "flat" white, while the K'ang Hsi were "marbled." Some of the Ming colors were blue under-glaze, red sang-de-boeuf, peach bloom, pea green or celadon, lustrous brown, turquoise and yellow. Another group applied to the biscuit and fired in a temperate part of the kiln are known as "the three colors," viz., green, yellow, and aubergine. They had great translucency. Finally there might be a mixture of enamel over-glazes with the under-glaze blue. Gilding was used throughout the Ming Dynasty.

THE PORCELAIN OF TÊ-HUA IN FUKIEN PROVINCE

The well-known *blanc-de-chine*, made at Tê-hua in the southern province of Fukien, was in the seventeenth and eighteenth centuries, the chief porcelain made in China elsewhere than at Ching-tê-Chên. Though nothing is yet known of the origin of the industry or of its history, it seems certain that it had precursors and that there were porcelain kilns in the province in much earlier times; but even the well-known later wares cannot be classified and dated with any precision. Reign-marks were apparently never used, nor can the color of the glaze, which varies widely, be used to date it, as the different glazes were apparently used at the same time. As the late Mr. W. B. Honey says (*The Ceramic Art of China*, 1945, p. 133): "The colour, for example, which ranges from a cold bluish white through a soft, smoky grey, to a creamy white and pinkish tone, has proved useless for the purpose;" and Mr. Hobson comments: "The glaze varies in tone from ivory or cream white to the colour of skim milk, and its texture may be aptly described by the homely comparison with blanc-mange. When the ivory colour is suffused by a faint rosy tinge, it is specially prized."

Illustration 118, a bottle, decorated with raised prunus (flowering plum), was formerly in the Royal Collection at Dresden, whose mark it carries, and has the prized color referred to above. The late Mr. Honey illustrates at Plate 144, a figure of Kuan-yin, the most popular Buddhist figure in China. This figure, which is in the Victoria and Albert Museum, is 15 inches high. Illustration 123 is an equally important figure showing Kuan-yin (one who hears cries!), the so-called Goddess of Mercy, and her slave boy, who is holding a covered bowl in which is seen a turtle. Most Chinese figures are ceremonial pieces, and this one is no exception. It differs from European figures in that it is not "molded" but "chiseled" out of a piece of clay.

Again quoting from the late Mr. Honey (p. 134) concerning such figures: "The most important specimens of Fukien porcelain are perhaps the Buddhist figures, which have for long been famous. Modelling at once bold and sensitive with a remarkable sense of total rhythm, was helped by a rare quality in the material, which seems to have the property of vitrifying without losing shape. Edges remain sharp, and the most delicate detail is for some reason never lost under the thick glaze covering. The best Fukien figures (Plates 143B and C and 144) may indeed be held to be the finest porcelain figures ever made." Père d'Entrecolles stated that Tê-hua porcelain was never colored, and convincing Chinese decorated specimens of the seventeenth or eighteenth century have never been identified with certainty. The general absence of colored glazes or painting, in spite of the fashions of the time, was perhaps due to a reluctance to disfigure the peculiar beauty of the ware.

Illustration 119 is a laughing Buddha reminiscent of the all-white Böttger pagodas. Illustration 122 is another example of a ceremonial figure. Illustration

120 is a small white vase with incised decoration, and finally, Illustration 121 shows two Foo dogs. All the pieces of blanc-de-chine are believed to be of the seventeenth or eighteenth century, and give some idea of the wide variety of the wares and why they were so popular in Europe and America.

K'ANG HSI REIGN (1662-1723)

The unfavorable political disturbances occurring at the end of the Ming Dynasty and the beginning of the Ch'ing or Manchu Dynasty did not lend themselves to the further development of porcelain manufacture at Ching-tê-Chên. However, in 1662, when the Emperor, K'ang Hsi ascended the throne, all this was changed. During his reign which ended in 1723, and the two succeeding ones, those of Yung Chêng (1723-36) and Ch'ien Lung (1736-96), Chinese porcelain reached technical perfection. The Emperor K'ang Hsi was deeply interested in porcelain, and in 1680, great impetus was given to its production. During his reign the famous "famille verte," predominantly green, came to its fruition. It was also at this time that the rare "famille noire," a black glaze, was applied to the porcelain and usually covered with a thin green lacquer to prevent the black color from peeling. The usual decoration was white enamel lotus, hawthorne or other oriental flowers. Large vases of this design are extremely rare and have sold for as much as $40,000 a pair.

The monochrome colors were a speciality of this period. The color most admired in America was the so-called "peach bloom." S. W. Bushell describes it as follows: "a pale red, becoming pink in some parts, in others, mottled with russet spots, displayed upon a background of light green celadon tint. The last color occasionally comes out more prominently and deepens into clouds of bright apple green tint." A beautiful ox blood red was made, and this, as well as the "peach bloom," have brought extremely high prices, especially in America. The blue-and-white specimens of this period are extremely fine and are characterized by a technical advance, in that a clear and sharp demarkation appears between the blue and the white, whereas Ming pieces have a tendency for the blue to run. The three-and five-colored enamel designs were made, and the new designs left more of the beautiful white undecorated. In other words, the tendency to over-decorate in the Ming Dynasty was corrected. To attempt to enumerate all the products made, including copies of previous times, would be futile. Everything was produced that the fertile Oriental mind could conceive and made superlatively well.

This period to most European collectors was the greatest; modern Chinese collectors likewise appreciate it, and both groups pay high prices for it. Chinese literary opinion gives the preference to the Sung and Ming dynasties. The ox blood red, called by the French *sang de boeuf*, started and finished in this period. Its characteristics were (1) a brilliant red, varying in depth, and sometimes entirely lost in places, but always red and without any of the grey or grey-blue streaks which emerge on the *flambé* red and the modern imitations of it; (2) the faint crackle of the glaze; (3) the stippling of the glaze at the foot-rim. (Illustration 124).

As stated, every kind of color was made at this time; the following are the best known and admired: snake skin green, eel yellow, turquoise, and "spotted yellow" were probably the most beautiful. Monochrome yellow, brown, purple, green, soufflé red, soufflé blue were not far behind. Western collectors have agreed, however, to give the place of honor to the K'ang Hsi blue-and-white. The peculiar virtues of this ware are due to simple causes. Blue was still regarded as the best medium for painted designs, and the demand for it, both in China and abroad was enormous. The body material was formed of carefully selected clay and stone, thoroughly levigated and free from all impurities. No pains were spared in the preparation of the blue pigment which was refined over and over again, until the very quintessence had been extracted from the cobaltiferous ore. So it is little wonder that the blue-and-white of this period was unsurpassed in purity and perfection of the porcelain, in the depth and luster of the blue, and in the subtle harmony between the color and the white porcelain background. Vast quantities were shipped to Europe by the Dutch and the other East India companies. In addition to blue on white, they made white on blue, also in quantity. The prunus has been applied to every conceivable form. One sometimes hears the term soft-paste Chinese porcelain. As a matter of fact, the body is hard, but the designation arose because some of the glazes used were softer than the ordinary glaze as a large amount of lead was introduced. There are numerous instances in the succeeding reigns when even soaprock was used in making the porcelain.

The polychrome color glazes, such as green, turquoise, and aubergine violet, fired in the more temperate parts of the kiln, so popular in the Ming period, virtually ceased in this period. On the other hand, the other three-color group, composed of transparent green, yellow, and aubergine purple glazes, were freely used in this and the Yung Chêng periods in imitation of Ming prototypes; when so found they are technically perfect.

The noblest examples of carefully tracing designs on the biscuit and then applying a transparent glaze are found in the large vases with designs reserved in grounds of green black, yellow, or leaf green. The most noted examples, as stated, will be found where the precious black-ground vases, the "famille noire," as they are called, is encountered. K'ang Hsi was famous for its "famille verte," (Illustration 126, an important pair of vases) which can be distinguished from similar earlier designs by the addition of an over-glaze blue enamel which enhances the brilliance of the color scheme, and at the same time removes the necessity of using under-glaze and over-glaze colors together. A beautiful enamel of violet blue tone is an important factor of the "famille verte" decoration and the merits of a vase or dish are often decided on the purity and brilliance of this color tone. Often, but not invariably, a kind of halo of dull luster is found around the blue enamel. This is interesting in the light of what we will say later when discussing the Nantgarw Welsh porcelain, where under certain circumstances, the same phenomenon exists. Omitting under-glaze blue in describing the K'ang Hsi "famille verte," the colors comprise a dark leaf green, often mottled in appearance, a beautiful light apple green, which is characteristic of these wares, an aubergine color which varies from purple brown to rosy purple, a yellow of varying purity and usually of brownish tone, a green-black formed of the brown black pigment underwashes of transparent green, a blue enamel of violet tone, and the thin iron red. The blue enamel and red are sometimes omitted, leaving a soft harmony of green, aubergine and yellow in which green plays the chief part. A little gilding is often used to heighten parts of the design. Powder blue was an invention of this period, and it is eminently worthy of the homage it has received from collectors and ceramic historians.

As strange as it may seem, the Chinese during this period copied the Japanese or Korean porcelain, erroneously called Imari. The correct name is, of course, Arita Ware, as Imari was the seaport from which it was shipped. As will be seen under the head of Japanese porcelain, this ware may be divided into Kakiemon and Imari styles, the former being the finer of the two types. It was no doubt the success which these wares met in European markets that induced the Chinese to take a lesson from their pupils and to adopt the "Imari" style. At any rate, they did copy all these types, sometimes very closely, sometimes only in part. The Japanese style is unmistakeable to those who have once learned to know its peculiarities, of which masses of blue covered with gilt patterns and the prominence of red and gold are the most conspicuous. The Chinese porcelain is thinner and crisper, its glaze has the smooth oily sheen and faintly greenish tint which are peculiar to Chinese wares, and the raw edge of the base rim is slightly browned. The Japanese porcelain, on the other hand, is whiter in the Kakiemon ware, grayer and coarser in the "Old Imari," and the glaze in both cases has the peculiar bubbled and "muslin-like" texture which is a Japanese characteristic. The Japanese under-glaze blue is dark and muddy in tone, the Chinese bright and purer, and the other colors differ, though not perhaps so emphatically. The iron red of the Chinese, for instance, is thinner and usually lighter in tone than the soft Indian red or thick sealing-wax color of the Japanese, and there is a difference in feeling between the two. The general character of the Chinese "Imari" is that of the K'ang Hsi period, but it was also copied in the succeeding reigns.

Illustration 129 is a small vase decorated in the "five-color" enamel. Illustration 127 is a small bottle having a peach bloom and dragon decor in under-glaze blue and red. The dragon has five claws, which indicates that the piece was made for the Emperor. Four claws were permitted for the children of the Emperor, and three claws for others. Illustration 128 is a Pilgrim bottle of this period. The decor is a dragon, and the colors under-glaze blue and red. Illustration 112 shows the fine quality of the blue-and-white.

YUNG CHÊNG REIGN (1723-36)

The Emperor K'ang Hsi was succeeded by his son, who reigned under the title of Yung Chêng. The interest that he had shown in ceramics as a prince was continued when he mounted the throne. Probably his most important act was to appoint personally, T'ang Ying to the head of the great Ching-tê-Chên factory in 1728. A complete list of the products of the factory is given by R. L. Hobson (*Chinese Pottery and Porcelain*, 1915), pages 223-226.

The ordinary Yung Chêng porcelain differs but little from that of the previous reign, though it tends to assume a whiter appearance, and the green tinge of the glaze is less marked. A change is noticeable in the finish of the base rim of vases and bowls. Bevelling of the edges is less common, and gives place to a rounded or angular finish, the foot-rim being often almost V-shaped; while the slight tinge of brown around the raw edge, which is usual on K'ang Hsi wares, is often entirely absent. The actual potting of the porcelain displays a wonderful degree of manipulative skill, and the forms, though highly finished, are not lacking in vigor. They are, in fact, a happy mean between the strong free lines of the K'ang Hsi and the meticulous finish of the later Ch'ien Lung porcelains. They have been justly described as "extremely refined and elegant."

The Yung Chêng period is not conspicuous for blue-and-white, although it copied Ming specimens. It perfected the "famille rose" colors and other enamel wares. T'ang Ying himself, however, refers to the rose colors as of foreign origin.

The manufacture of eggshell dishes and services with famille rose enamels in the Canton style and with "ruby backs" was in full swing in this period, and the general tendency to label them all Ch'ien Lung errs on the side of excessive caution. The reigns of Yung Chêng and Ch'ien Lung were prolific in monochrome. As for the K'ang Hsi glaze colors, they were practically all now reproduced.

CH'IEN LUNG REIGN (1736-1796)

The brief reign of Yung Chêng was followed by that of his son, who ruled under the title of Ch'ien Lung for a full cycle of sixty years, at the end of which he abdicated in accordance with his vow that he would not outreign his grandfather, K'ang Hsi. He was a devotee of the arts, and they flourished greatly under his long and peaceful sway. He himself was a collector, and he retained the services of T'ang Ying, the most distinguished man who had held the post of head of the Imperial factories.

During this period, Chinese porcelain reaches the high-water mark of technical perfection and the mastery of materials is complete. But, for all that, the art is already in its decline. By the middle of his reign it is already over-ripe, and towards the end it shows sure signs of decay. At its best, the decoration is more ingenious than original and more pretty than artistic. At its worst, it is cloying and tiresome. The ware itself is perfectly refined and pure, but colder than the K'ang Hsi porcelain. The famille rose painting, while unequalled in this period, had been invented in the previous reign. (Illustration 125, Hexagonal Lantern). The painting is dainty and finished, but the broken tints and miniature touches cannot compare in decorative value with the stronger and broader effects of the Ming and K'ang Hsi brushwork. The potting is almost perfect, but the forms are wanting in spontaneity; and the endless imitation of bronze shapes become wearisome.

Speaking generally, the monochrome types in vogue in the previous reigns were now repeated. In the commoner types of Ch'ien Lung blue-and-white, the blue is usually of a dullish indigo tint, wanting in life and fire.

CHINESE LOWESTOFT (ACTUALLY EXPORT WARE)

The use of Western designs on the porcelains of the Ch'ing dynasty, especially in the eighteenth century, attained such large proportions that it must be treated as a class apart. At one time the absurd notion prevailed that this porcelain was the product of a little English factory at Lowestoft which started in 1757 but made mostly blue-and-white porcelain until 1770. This unfortunate misconception is referred to as Chaffers' great blunder. We now know that an enormous trade existed between China and Europe at the time, and there is now little surprise that innumerable orders for table services were sent out to China with armorial and other designs specified for decoration. During the last half of the eighteenth century, European-style flower painting and European border patterns were used by the Chinese decorators, such patterns originating at Meissen and Sèvres. Another group demanding some attention were the "Jesuit" patterns, decorated with subjects bearing on the Christian religion. This export ware was popular in America around the Revolutionary period, and large quantities were brought to England and France, and Holland as well.

Marks on Chinese Porcelain

For a complete treatment on the subject, see the chapter in volume one of R. L. Hobson's book (1915). The following is taken in part from it. The custom of placing marks on porcelain originated with the Chinese. The mark is usually painted on the base with a brush, and blue is the commonest medium; red and other on-glaze colors are chiefly found on relatively modern "famille rose" specimens. During the K'ang Hsi period, most of the porcelain that was marked carried the Hsüan Tê and Ch'êng Hua marks rather than the K'ang Hsi mark. Quite often, the presence of the K'ang Hsi mark on porcelain of the period will indicate a fake. The Japanese have used extensively the Chia Ching and Wan Li marks on forgeries of the Ming period. In the year 1677 the potters at Ching-tê Chên were forbidden to use the period-name of the Emperor. It is on this account that we find conventional marks inside the double ring which was usually occupied by the *nien hao*, a common practice in the K'ang Hsi period. In many cases, the rings were left empty. Whereas Ming marks are common on K'ang Hsi, the K'ang Hsi mark itself is comparatively rare, except on specimens which must belong to the later years of the reign. It is freely used on quite modern wares. Yung Chêng and Ch'ien Lung pieces when marked are usually but not always authentic. The marks on Imperial porcelain are carefully executed and except in cases of deliberate forgery are authentic. In fact, a well-written mark is almost as certain a sign of Imperial ware as the five-claw dragon itself. At the private factories, the marks were often carelessly, even illegibly printed, and probably little trouble was taken with this part of the decoration except on the choicer specimens. On a large proportion of the private wares, the mark was omitted altogether. The marks on Chinese porcelain may conveniently be grouped under the following headings; (1) date marks; (2) hall marks; (3) potters' names and factory marks; (4) marks of dedication, felicitation, commendation, etc.

Finally, it must be said that all Chinese marks must be treated with great caution. In fact it is safer to regard them merely as secondary evidence, first basing one's judgment on the paste and glaze, the style of decoration, and the quality of the colors. The one exception, as stated, is in connection with Imperial porcelain.

Illustration 131 is an example of export ware made for the French, and the fish design has been said to indicate that it was made for Madame Pompadour, but this is probably untrue. Illustration 130, a tea caddy, is a typical example of an armorial decoration, probably for the English trade. Illustration 132 is an export ware cream jug and is part of a tea service that was sold at Leeds, England, more than a century ago. It was described in the old catalogue as English Lowestoft. The gold decoration was probably added at the Derby factory, as each piece has the number "2" in gold at the foot-rim. The Derby factory did not make the under-glaze blue and white, as explained in our chapter on Derby, but purchased export ware and, after adding the gold, sold it to the trade as its own. The numeral "2" was assigned to James Stables, one of Derby's best gold decorators. Such practices lent color to the claim made by Chaffers that this export ware was made at Lowestoft. As a matter of fact, the placing of the numeral on the underside of the foot-rim of this service (which was a peculiarity of Lowestoft) makes it not unreasonable to say that it may, in fact, have had the gold numeral put on there, as the old catalogue states. It is therefore possible that a very small fraction of "Lowestoft porcelain" (Chinese export ware) may have been decorated at Lowestoft.

JAPANESE OR KOREAN PORCELAIN

Naturally, the early interest in porcelain came to Japan from the Chinese, and in 1513, we find Gorodayu Shonsui, of Ise, returning from a five-year visit to the Chinese state factories of Ching-tê-Chên. He established a pottery in the province of Hizen, and his first productions were made from Chinese models. Gradually factories increased in the neighborhood of the seaport of Imari from which some of its products took their name. We refer to them as "Old Japan."

We are here particularly interested in the porcelain produced at Arita, province of Hizen, in Japan (Korea) around the middle of the seventeenth century, which was exported extensively by the Dutch traders in competition with the export ware of China. The Dutch enjoyed the privilege of a trading station on the island of Deshima, after the less politic Portuguese had been driven out of Nagasaki in 1632. We are especially interested in this porcelain as it, and not the Chinese as many think, was the inspiration for the porcelain designs at Meissen, St. Cloud, Chantilly, Chelsea, Bow and Worcester.

This porcelain so extensively copied was of two general types, as follows: (1) Kakiemon; (2) Imari. The first and finest was of a very distinctive style of decoration, which is traditionally supposed to have been started by a potter named Kakiemon, who, with another man of Arita, learned the secret of enameling on porcelain from a Chinese merchant about the year 1646. This type is distinguished by slight but artistic decoration in vivid enamels of the "famille verte" supplemented by gilding and occasionally by under-glaze blue. Favorite designs are a banded hedge, prunus tree, a Chinese boy, and a tiger or phoenix; two quails in millet beside a flowering prunus; simple flowering sprays or branches coiled in circular medallions; or only a few scattered blossoms. Whatever the nature of the design, it was artistically displayed, and in such a manner as to enhance without concealing the fine white porcelain.

The second type was made entirely for the European trade, and it is distinguished by large masses of dark, cloudy blue, set off by a soft Indian red and gilding. These colors are supplemented by touches of green, yellow, and aubergine enamels, and occasionally by a brownish black. The ware itself is heavy, coarse, and grayish, but its rough aspect is well concealed by irregular and confused designs of asymmetrical panels surrounded by mixed brocade patterns. The panels often contain Chinese figures, phoenixes, lions, floral designs of chrysanthemums, peony and prunus, a basket of flowers, rough landscapes, or garden views. They are medleys of half-Chinese, half-Japanese motives, a riot of incoherent patterns, but not without broad decorative effect, thanks to the bold masses of red, blue and gold. There is a finer and more Japanese variety of this same group, distinguished by free use of chrysanthemum rosettes, and the Imperial kiri, and by panels of diaper pattern and floral designs alternating and counterchanged in color, the grounds now red, now blue and now gold. The same color scheme prevailed in this sub-group, and the dark blue was usually netted over with gold designs.

Illustration 133 shows an early Wine Pot of the thirteenth-fourteenth century. Illustrations 134, 136, 137 and 138 show the Japanese "Kakiemon" patterns of 1650-1700, and Illustrations 135, 139 and 148 show "Imari" patterns of the same period, which were so generally copied by the Europeans.

CHAPTER 2

GERMAN AND AUSTRIAN PORCELAIN

THE MEISSEN FACTORY

The study of Meissen porcelain is generally divided into the following periods: (1) Böttger Stoneware and Porcelain (1709-1719); (2) Meissen under Augustus the Strong (1720-1733); (3) Meissen under Count Brühl (1733-1756). While it is true that Augustus the Strong played a major part in its progress until his death in 1733, and that Count Brühl did much to further its development thereafter, we prefer here to divide it into three periods, named after the men whose artistic creations are responsible for its great achievements: (1) The Böttger Period (1709-1719); (2) The Herold Period (1720-1735); (3) The Kändler Period (1735-1750). This porcelain is erroneously referred to in America and England as "Dresden" and in France as "Saxe."

THE BÖTTGER PERIOD (1709-1719)

The boast of a boy still in his teens that he could turn base metal into gold gave to Saxony the distinction of being the birthplace in Europe of true or hard-paste porcelain. This boy was Johann Friedrich Böttger (1682-1719) who gave early promise of becoming a great chemist. Taking up alchemy in its many fantastic branches, he came to believe that he possessed, or could discover, the secret of making gold from base metals. Mysterious reports reached King Frederick I of Prussia that Böttger had actually achieved this miracle, and he was commanded to appear before the King and demonstrate his magical powers. Böttger, alarmed at the possible consequences of his failure to produce gold for an extravagant King, fled to Saxony in 1701, only to be arrested by Augustus the Strong, Elector of Saxony and King of Poland, who also had heard of the gold-making alchemist, and who ordered him to demonstrate his powers. He was held a virtual prisoner in Dresden, where he was subsidized and ordered to produce gold. This, of course, he was unable to do; in 1703 he tried to escape and the following year was placed under the supervision of E. W. Tschirnhausen, a Saxon nobleman, to continue his chemical researches. By 1705 he had exhausted the patience of the King and was imprisoned in the Albrechtsburg fortress at Meissen, twelve miles from Dresden. In September 1707, he was brought back to Dresden to work in a new laboratory for porcelain research under the supervision of Tschirnhausen, and there the two men worked together in an effort to produce not gold, but porcelain. Tschirnhausen had made a survey in 1694 of the mineral wealth of the country and set up works for polishing agate and manufacturing glass. He had also conceived the ambition to make porcelain in Saxony. The purchase of Chinese porcelain by the King is said to have almost bankrupted the country. In July 1708, a start was made on the construction of a factory in Dresden Neustadt, and Tschirnhausen was made Privy Counsellor and Director, which titles he refused to use until his researches had been successfully concluded. Three months later he died. Böttger continued to experiment alone and on March 20th 1709, reported that he could now make "good white porcelain, together with the finest glaze and appropriate painting in such perfection as to equal, if not surpass, the Indian." This date thus takes rank for the invention, or more properly, re-invention of true, or hard-paste porcelain. On January 23rd, 1710, a patent was issued announcing the establishment of the Royal Saxon Porcelain Manufacture, and on March 7th the same year, it was housed in the Albrechtsburg fortress at Meissen. At the Leipzig Easter Fair 1710, some experimental pieces were shown.

It would be unfair to give full credit to Böttger for the re-discovery of true porcelain, for it is certain that Tschirnhausen contributed; but the final success did not come until after his death. It was not until the Leipzig Easter Fair 1713, that the technical difficulties had been sufficiently overcome to permit the new factory to offer pieces for sale. One of the difficulties was that the clay secured from Colditz shrank too much in the kiln. For a time, the Colditz clay was used in a mixture with a better clay discovered at Aue, and later named after the owner of the property "Schnorr's white earth." The Colditz clay was finally given up entirely in 1717 and only the "Schnorr" clay used. Alterations in the kilns also improved the porcelain manufacture.

BÖTTGER'S RED STONEWARE

In his historic report to the King in March 1709, Böttger had made reference to his discovery of another product called "red stoneware." It was again mentioned in the establishment decree of January 1710, and at the Leipzig Easter Fair of that year was offered for sale. This was the principal product of the factory for the first five years, but how much was made after that time is not known. The late Mr. W. B. Honey, Keeper of the Department of Ceramics in the Victoria and Albert Museum, in commenting on this ware says, (*Dresden China*, 1954, page 51) "The manufacture of the red stoneware offered none of the problems that attended the porcelain, and the foundation-year of the factory (1710) already saw it made in quantity. The material was indeed a noble one, of quite exceptional fineness of grain and as a rule so intensely hard that it could be engraved and polished on the glass-engraver's wheel. This process in fact, became its characteristic mode of decoration. Its sensuous beauty of substance, it may be said, can be fully appreciated only when a piece is handled. Its colour (due of course to an oxide of iron in the clay) varied with the firing, and in the uncertain heat of Böttger's primitive kiln this variation was considerable. Light firing or a cooler position in the kiln usually gave a bright red, even inclining to orange-vermilion; the more usual and most desired color was a dark red-brown; over-firing gave a very dark brown or grey-black, for which the meaningless name 'iron porcelain' is still current." The earliest shapes were taken directly from Chinese pieces. Figures such as those of Augustus the Strong and from the Italian Comedy, and pagodas later found in the white Böttger porcelain were made. Also much useful ware, such as tea-pots, tea-caddies, coffee-pots, eagle tea-pots, and octagonal sugar boxes were first made in the red stoneware. Illustrations 102, 141 and 142 are some of the finest known specimens of this ware, while Illustration 145 is one of the earliest and probably copied directly from a Chinese sample. When the ware was not of a good color, it was customary to coat it with black and decorate it. Many fine examples are found decorated in this manner. It is important for collectors to realize that this product is extremely hard and a fine Swiss file will not scratch it. Many fakes exist and products of other factories resemble it, but they can always be detected by the lack of hardness. Bayreuth made much similar ware. A rival factory was established at Plaue but its products are not as fine as red stoneware and, like the Bayreuth ware which was first made in 1730, are not so hard. Much applied decoration is found on the red stoneware and on the Böttger white porcelain.

BÖTTGER'S PORCELAIN

Reverting now to the porcelain made during the Böttger period, we find few figures except pagodas, other than those made in red stoneware and referred to above. Illustration 305A indicates one of the pagoda figures and Illustrations 149 to 162 show specimens from the unique collection of Mr. Siegfried Kramarsky. The greater part of the products were useful and the choicest of them are adaptations of the silver shapes of Johann Jacob Irminger, the King's silversmith. The porcelain is more varied in form than the stoneware however, and comprised all sorts of vessels for the tea table: coffee-pots; tankards; sugar boxes, vases, bottles and beakers, and cups and saucers, but not plates. Applied masks, acanthus, little sprays of roses, vines or bay leaves were characteristic decorations. The Böttger paste, unlike the Chinese, used as the fusible element alabaster instead of feldspar. The porcelain has a distinctly yellowish or smoky tone, due probably to the presence of iron and titanium as impurities in the material. The glaze is sometimes hazy and has minute bubbles. It is brownish by transmitted light and rarely has moons or even tears caused by large pieces or aggregations of frit and showing round spots or cuts of higher translucency by transmitted light. This formula continued to be used, modified to a more or less extent, as late as 1725.

Illustrations 143, 144 and 147 show three specimens of Böttger white porcelain. The earliest piece is the tea bowl and saucer (dated c. 1713) which have an applied decoration of rose and bay leaves. W. B. Honey (*Dresden China*) illustrates a similar one from the Victoria and Albert Museum, Plate VII-b. The second is a teapot of the same shape as shown in the red stoneware. The decoration is an applied basket of fruit, etc., dating about 1715. The third is a coffee-pot decorated with applied acanthus leaves and having a crossed swords mark, probably dated c. 1724. The factory was therefore still using the Böttger formula, probably in modified form, in 1724, at which time most of its products were probably of entirely different paste and glaze.

Illustration 167 shows a style popular during the Böttger period, consisting of a molded strawberry design around the outside of the tea bowl and saucer. Such pieces are frequently touched up in gold to highlight them. The porcelain here is of the creamy Böttger type and the saucer is not marked. On the other hand, the cup which appears to belong to the saucer, has a crossed swords mark of the earliest type in blue under the glaze, but it is placed at the foot-rim and not in the center of the bottom, as was done after 1724. The combination of Böttger porcelain and oddly-placed swords mark enable us to date the cup, with some accuracy, as 1722-23, probably an experimental piece. In 1722 the question of a factory mark was first considered, and at that time Steinbrück proposed the use of crossed swords as the factory mark. But the King decided in favor of the KPM mark, and it was adopted in 1723 and was used in 1723-24 only on teapots and sugar dishes, and in 1724 the crossed swords replaced it. It may be supposed that in proposing the crossed swords mark, Steinbrück would have had a few experimental pieces to demonstrate his suggestion. This may be one of such pieces, and the absence of a mark on the saucer would seem to bear this out. A few other specimens exist with the swords mark similarly placed, so that such pieces are among the first to be marked with the crossed swords. Illustration 90 is an early shape taken from the Chinese. This teapot has an early swords mark of 1724. The porcelain is from the Böttger formula. The raised oriental flower and bird design picked out with gold was characteristic of the Böttger period. In addition to the factory decoration, it also has a Hausmaler decoration added to the lid as well as to the pot, consisting of garden scenes in black and Pomeranian red monochrome by an unknown decorator. (The Hausmaler were independent painters who procured porcelain in the white and decorated it as they chose). Illustration 163 is of unusual interest because of the embossed emblem of the King and is from the collection of Dr. Hans Syz.

After the death of Böttger in 1719, the factory was reorganized with Steinbrück as Administrator, and Nehmitz, Köhler and Schuberth as "arcanists." The use of alabaster was partially replaced by a felspathic stone. This was a great improvement, and as soon as Johann Gregor Herold arrived in 1720, he made extensive experiments to provide a suitable white glaze for his colorful paintings. E. Zimmermann (*Meissner Porzellan*, 1926) shows a number of incised and impressed marks that are found on early Meissen porcelain, which he calls paste marks. He thinks they were used during the 1720's in an effort to produce a white and brilliant paste and glaze. It is certain that many different formulae were tried and, as a result, the beautiful brilliant white paste and glaze were finally produced. The green translucency is believed to result from the addition of a small quantity of cobalt blue, which combined with the yellow iron oxide present in the clay creating the green color seen by transmitted light and resulting in the fine white surface so much desired at the time. This process was also used later at other factories on the Continent and in England. The green color by transmitted light and the moons are quite pronounced in pieces heavily potted in early Herold porcelain, becoming less prominent as we reach the 1730's. By 1760 when processes and clay with less impurity had been evolved, the moons, tears and green translucency completely disappeared. The collector should realize that where this had occurred, the desirability of the piece concerned is greatly diminished.

Illustration 169 depicts an eagle teapot, which shape was also made in the red stoneware. The eagle is decorated in silver, long since oxidized to a black tone. The other decoration is in the gold chinoiserie (pseudo-Chinese figures) about which so much difference of opinion exists. Such figures are known to have been closely copied from engravings by Martin Engelbrecht in 1719 at Augsburg. The gold of this teapot is of the thin type believed by the more experienced collectors to be factory work. If factory work, it was probably done after the arrival of Herold, as he introduced the style there of chinoiserie decoration; but this is not necessarily so, as gold painters were at the factory (Funcke, for instance) during Böttger's lifetime. We have no proof that he painted chinoiseries. Illustration 168 shows a handleless beaker cup and saucer falling into the same category. Illustrations 166 and 165 show a teapot and a tea bowl and saucer from the von Born collection, also falling into this class. Illustration 170 shows a tea bowl and saucer of different shape. The bowl is fluted and the chinoiseries (on the inside of both cup and saucer), are decorated with a heavier gold and in a manner that suggests the work of a Hausmaler. The saucer has an S in luster which Honey ascribes to the hand of Seuter. This attribution advanced by the late Mr. Honey in his book *Dresden China* is not accepted by such authorities as G. E. Pazaurek, who says the records show that the white undecorated pieces had these marks on them when they left the Meissen factory. This view is shared by many authorities today.

During the lifetime of Böttger, the factory was unsuccessful in its efforts to produce a suitable under-glaze blue so much desired by the King. Upon the death of Böttger and the reorganization of the factory, a new and larger kiln was built and, as has been pointed out, feldspar was substituted for alabaster as the fusible element. Both were a great help to Köhler in his efforts to produce the under-glaze blue. By the time of the arrival of Herold, in April of 1720, Köhler had perfected a good blue-and-white, and this was the only color fired in the kiln that the factory had produced before Herold's arrival. It is true that the two beaker cups which were presented to the King are decorated in polychrome colors, but they were cold painted. Böttger made an important contribution in the discovery of a luster, or mother-of-pearl paint, which was used to good account by Herold when he reached the factory, in combination with his own palette. After 1725 these luster paints were not usually so intense as formerly but continued to be used until 1735, when they were discontinued.

JOHANN GREGOR HEROLD AT MEISSEN

The King, in order to protect the secrets of his famous porcelain factory, kept not only Böttger, but the other employees, as virtual prisoners in the factory. True, he let Böttger have anything he wanted short of his freedom. It was in part due to this treatment and directly to over-drinking, that Böttger was brought to his grave at the age of thirty-seven. One of Böttger's associates was Conrad Hunger, a gold Hausmaler, who decorated Meissen porcelain in a unique manner. In 1717 he left Dresden at the suggestion of the Austrian representative and joined with Du Paquier in the formation of the Du Paquier factory in Vienna. While he was not an employee at Meissen, he had secured much information from Böttger and he claimed to have the "arcanum." It transpired however, that while he did have a great deal of information, he could not produce a satisfactory porcelain. Recourse was had to the Meissen factory, and this time, January 1719, Samuel Stölzel, kiln-master and arcanist for six years and considered one of Meissen's best craftsmen deserted Meissen and fled to Vienna for a promised yearly salary of one thousand florins. As his desertion was to help establish the first rival factory, it was a blow to the King. While at Vienna, Stölzel came in contact with Johann Gregor Herold, a man employed by Hunger to decorate the porcelain which Stölzel was to produce. Recently examined records of the Meissen factory disclose that Herold in 1718 was a painter in the great faience factory of Strasburg and that, in 1719, he was a painter of wall paper in Vienna. Early in the same year (1719) he was employed by Hunger as the decorator for the Du Paquier factory. Stölzel was not satisfied with his employment, reputedly because he did not get the thousand florins he had been promised. In any event, the recently available records of the Meissen factory disclose that on April 12th, 1720, Stölzel arrived at Freiberg with the intention of proceeding to Dresden, and that he had the painter, Herold, with him. The records further show that they arrived at Meissen on April 20th, 1720, and after displaying to the Commission the specimens brought with them from Vienna, were received with open arms. Stölzel was given his former job as kilnmaster and arcanist, and Herold was put in charge of the decorations. As no enamel painters were there, Herold did all of the painting himself until he could train apprentices to assist him. In a very interesting record brought to light in 1959 and printed here as Appendix No. 3, Herold says, "When in 1720 I first came to the factory from Vienna, I found no painters employed at all. I had to do all the painting and decorating alone. Shortly after my arrival, I took into service a young apprentice by the name of Heintze, who has now developed into one of my best painters." This was written on February 24th, 1731, and from this authentic report, we can now for the first time positively attribute decorations made during the first few years of the Meissen factory to the hand of Herold. Some of these attributions had previously been questioned. One reason for this doubt was that the decorations of the factory during that early period were so many and so varied that it did not seem possible that one decorator could have done them all. But it must be remembered that Herold was a master draughtsman who could copy any style of which he had an etching or print, and that by rearrangement and combination, he could create what seemed to be many new styles. He was also a talented artist and creator of styles. Certainly it was a great and very important day for the Meissen factory when Herold was entrusted with its decorations. In the July 1959 issue of *Mitteilungsblatt* (Swiss Ceramic Circle), we find certain important data furnished by Mr. Otto Walcha, presently in charge of Archives at the Meissen Factory. It is from this source that we are able for the first time to disclose the early experience of Herold. The following quotation regarding his arrival at Meissen is from the same source: "Upon his arrival at Meissen on May 14, 1720, however, he was most cordially welcomed by the Commission, since it had become of vital importance to the factory to secure the services of an experienced painter. The sample porcelains he submitted which he had brought along from Vienna were greatly admired, and he was employed and paid for his work by the piece . . . Herold's first work was the painting of a service decorated in red camaieu (July 19, 1720). Prior to that date, however, he already painted individual pieces in red and blue . . . September 9, 1720—he is given 147 copper etchings as samples . . . On November 25, 1720, Herold is requested to paint as many pieces as possible, copying the oriental style." The only other new item is that the first assistant to Herold was not Christoph Horn as has been supposed, but John Casper Ripp who came from Delft and was a master in blue. Among the other first assistants was Mehlhorn, who was also a painter in blue. After the death of Köhler, we find another blue painter, Johann Kretschmar, who worked at Meissen from 1726 to 1752.

DECORATIONS BY HEROLD'S OWN HAND

It can now be quite reliably stated that all polychrome or enamel painted specimens of good quality decorated during the years 1720-1723 inclusive were the personal work of Herold. It is further believed that most of the work so painted before the adoption of the crossed swords as a factory mark are likely to be by his hand.

Among such pieces fall the genre landscape paintings, in which the early palette brought from Vienna is used. The colors are in the pastel shades rather than in the more intense colors appearing around 1724 and used exclusively after about 1725. Illustration 93 is a bouillon cup of early shape and without a mark. It has the finest genre landscape painting that it has been the pleasure of the authors to see. The scenes have an extreme depth and the effect of the sun's rays is breath-taking. This method of painting the sun's rays has long been considered an attribute of Herold's among collectors. Illustration 91 is a waste bowl in the same style, including in the landscape hunters on horseback, animals, etc. It is picked out in red only and, of course, has no mark. The inside of the bowl has a landscape in the red camaieu, similar to the service referred to in the records of the factory quoted above as being Herold's first service, painted in July 1720. Illustration 182 is a three-footed cream pot and cover decorated in the early genre landscape. The beauty of these paintings compares favorably with that of the finest oil paintings.

While the use of fantastic animals became popular in the seventeen thirties, and in the past has been ascribed to Adam Friedrich Löwenfinck, it is believed that Herold himself painted the first ones adopted from oriental originals, and that the later ones were copied from his designs and varied to suit the period. Illustration 97 is apparently a unique piece in the form of an extremely large chocolate pot. The paste and glaze are identical with that of the period of the early twenties. The decoration includes almost every color found in the early palette of Herold and, in addition, the early intense luster and mother-of-pearl effects invented by Böttger.

POLYCHROME CHINOISERIES

We now come to the most important decoration used by Herold for his own work and later, by the other Meissen decorators in quantity until 1730, when it was gradually superseded by the harbor scenes, a modification of this style. It will be remembered that the factory records relate that Herold in September 1720 was given 147 copper etchings, and in November of the same year was requested to paint as many oriental styles as he could. The exact nature of the copper etchings is not disclosed, but it is certain that Herold derived much of this style from Nieuhof's *Embassy to the Grand Tartar Cham* (published in 1669) and similar sources. He was certainly inspired by the Dutch travel books as has been shown by Ernst Zimmermann and G. W. Schulz. The July 1957, No. 39 issue of the *Keramik-Freunde der Schweiz* may be consulted for reproductions of etchings used by Herold and for sketches that Herold made from them for use as designs for his porcelains. Also shown in this issue are examples of Meissen porcelain so decorated. Chinoiseries are not copies of Oriental life and custom, but rather what the Occidental mind erroneously conceived them to be. The first design, possibly as early as 1722 and maybe earlier, included a group of very tall Chinese men and women, framed with a cartouche consisting of a band of the Köhler blue and an outline of gold enclosing it; to this is added Böttger luster, and the frame thus formed is picked out in the early Eisenrot scroll work. Illustrations 99 and 190 show two tankards so decorated. The picture shown was painted by Gregor Herold from his own sketch copied from the earlier etching, all shown in the publication referred to above. These tankards were made before the mark was used. While the usual design made and painted by Herold showed the Chinamen with faces filled in with flesh colors, it is nevertheless believed that he painted the fine tankard given here as Illustration 100. This is also a piece without a mark and thus falls into the category definitely ascribed to Herold's own hand, as no other painters were at Meissen to paint it. (The reader should bear in mind the fact that no porcelain painters were available because no porcelain had been decorated with enamel paints fixed in the kiln before 1719, when a small number of such pieces were painted by Herold at the Du Paquier factory at Vienna). This tankard is unique also in that it has a diaper at the top and bottom of Lambrequin design and in the under-glaze blue of Köhler. The decoration shows the Chinese Emperor and Empress seated at a drum type table having tea. The remainder of the decoration includes a typical Chinese rock design and Indian flowers and insects. The faces here are outlined only in the early red. The use of intense Böttger luster also indicates early decoration. Somewhat similar decoration, as regards the outline of the faces is usually ascribed to Ehrenfried Stadler, who came from Delft to the factory in 1723 at the age of twenty-one as an assistant to Herold. Since he had painted only pottery before reaching Meissen, we do not believe that he could have produced such fine work at the time. A signed Stadler piece is shown on Plates 46 and 47 of *Veb Verlag Der Kunst, Dresden.*

Tea services were popular, and Herold personally decorated many of them in polychrome chinoiserie between 1722 and 1724. Up to 1723, as has been said, the Meissen factory had no factory mark; it was during the years 1723 and 1724 that it was decided to mark the teapots and octagonal sugar boxes, and these two shapes only, with the KPM mark. Therefore, it is pieces having such marks or having no marks at all which we can ascribe with certainty as Herold's own work. Illustration 92 is of a tea bowl and saucer without mark and, from the decoration, dated about 1722. Unlike the slightly later pieces, it is painted on one side of the cup only. The Chinaman is of large proportions and is shown with the Emperor and Empress seated, and consequently, only half of the figure, which is rare and considered one of the earliest known types of chinoiserie. Illustrations 89 and 181 show two tea bowls and saucers, both made before the mark was used and dating about 1723; these are the type which Herold painted.

Turning now to another shape found in the tea services, Illustration 98 is a hexagonal tea caddy. The shape here shown has six concave edges, dividing the caddy into as many panels. Similar shapes were known in Böttger red stoneware and porcelain and represent the earliest form used. The decoration in polychrome chinoiserie is a single large figure in each panel, five showing the Emperor in different costumes, and the sixth, the Empress. It dates about 1722. Illustrations 171, 174 and 191 show four similar caddies, except here the edges are convex, a slightly later shape, and the Chinamen, while of large size are not quite so tall as those on the one just mentioned. These were painted by Herold about 1723 and are not marked. Still another shape noted in tea services is that of Illustration 172, an octagonal sugar box, having the rare KPF mark and decorated in polychrome chinoiserie, painted by Herold during the first few months of 1723 or possibly as early as 1722, when the experimental crossed swords mark was tried. Illustration 96, an octagonal sugar box, has the KPM mark, and, in addition, a crossed swords mark, both in blue under-glaze, and a gold No. 55 on box and lid. It was painted by the hand of Herold. Finally, the teapots themselves also had the KPM mark. Illustration 70, a masked head teapot decorated by Herold in polychrome chinoiserie, has the KPM mark in under-glaze blue and in addition a crossed swords mark in blue enamel over the glaze. The pot and cover each have the gold number 20. In explanation of the over-glaze blue enamel swords mark, it may be surmised that the piece was made and glazed in 1724 or earlier, but not decorated until 1725. When taken out of stock to be decorated, and the piece lacked the necessary swords mark, the decorator was instructed to add the over-glaze blue marking. The directive regarding marking all pieces with the swords mark from late 1724 on could have been carried out in the case of such a piece in no other way.

Illustration 71 is of a coffee-pot of the period of 1723-24 and as such, would not have a mark. It does, however, have the gold number 14 on the pot as well as on the cover. The gold number stands for identification, in all probability of the gold painter who had to account for all the gold given to him by Herold. For this reason when he decorated all pieces of a service, he would put his gold number on them, including lids. Since the gold work had to be of the same quality and style throughout, it was always one and the same painter who did the gold work on a complete service. We do not know the identity of the gold painters, though these numbers make it possible for us today to recognize that the individual pieces belong to an original set. Thus, if the lid of a piece carries another number than the bottom, it is a substitute for a lost lid, which is quite a common occurrence.

While Herold concentrated most of his work on the type of chinoiserie described above, he did decorate some sets in a different style. Illustration 88 is a teapot of quite different shape from the one noted above, although it also has a masked spout. The figures in the decoration are large in size but are "Turks" and not Far Eastern subjects. The painting is exceptionally fine and was done by Herold himself. The mark is KPM and probably was executed in 1723. Each of the examples shown encloses the decoration in a cartouche, which became virtually the equivalent of a signature for Herold after he reached Meissen; he used no cartouche at Vienna. Böttger's luster and gold are included and finally picked out in Eisenrot. In general, but not invariably, the pieces decorated in polychrome chinoiserie up to 1724 are picked out in red only; from 1725 to 1735, purple and red are used together on the same piece; and finally, from 1735 to 1740, purple only is used. Gold only was used in 1735. From around 1740, we find a gold band outlined in black. By 1725, but not before, gold was used in the decoration.

Illustrations 95 and 177 show a rather unusual pair of tea bowls and saucers of small size. The decoration is finely executed, probably by Herold himself. The swords are of the earliest type, dating c. 1724. Instead of the usual cartouche to outline the decoration, the saucers enclose between one red circle at the outer edge and two red circles of smaller diameter, Oriental scroll work extending around the circumference and about $\frac{3}{4}$ inch wide. Within this border is framed unusually fine chinoiserie. The saucers are $4\frac{1}{2}$ inches in diameter and have on the bottoms three concentric red circles. The insides of the cups have colorful butterflies at the bottom, and starting at the rim, a band of colorful scroll work, extending down $\frac{3}{4}$ inch. The outside of the cups has a continuous chinoiserie decoration. The colors comprise a very brilliant red, yellow, blue, purple and gold. In addition to these colors, we find a deep brown which when held at an angle reveals the finest early Böttger luster. The writers have never encountered similar specimens. Illustration 72 is an oval sugar box, which shape followed the octagonal ones, It is ornamented in the chinoiserie motif with the decoration continuous around the box as well as the lid. Wide bands of gold surmounted by the typical green band enclose the figures. The mark is the crossed swords and, in addition, the box and the lid have the gold number 20.

As previously pointed out the Meissen factory copied most of its Oriental designs from the seventeenth century Japanese. The "famille verte" of the Chinese K'ang Hsi was an exception. Meissen specimens, painted however in this style, are quite rare. We illustrate here three such pieces as Illustrations 231, 238 and 249.

KAKIEMON DECORATIONS

It has already been pointed out that Herold brought to Meissen a palette comprising a wide variety of enamel colors which could be fired in the kiln. They had, however, a tendency to peel off, and Herold, in conjunction with the chemists who were available at Meissen, began at once to correct this fault. As a result, after several years he produced a new palette range more intense and practical than the pastel colors brought from Vienna. Included in this new palette was a splendid iron red, at times almost fiery in tone; a strong rose-purple; a luminous turquoise or sea green; and a clear and usually slightly yellowish leaf green. One enamel color alone remained for a time unsatisfactory. This was the blue, which was especially desired in perfection for copying the porcelain of Japan or Korea, in the style created by Sakaida Kakiemon. This color was available together with a new range of delicate tones, especially suited for exact reproductions of Kakiemon, not later than 1728, and possibly slightly earlier. Before a satisfactory enamel color was available, under-glaze blue was substituted.

Illustration 195 shows a very early example of the Kakiemon design. It is a little octagonal tea bowl and saucer, with decoration of flowering prunus tree with an under-glaze blue trunk; a small bird in flight is in the same under-glaze blue. Adding to the interest of this piece is the caduceus mark, also in under-glaze blue, and, in addition, the engraved Jöhanneum mark, showing that it was formerly in the collection of Augustus the Strong. The early design and mark indicate a date c. 1723. Illustration 193 is a waste bowl of rather rare design, known as "Chinesische Blumen" and having an early swords mark; we date it about 1725. A covered bouillon from the same service is in the Ralph Wark collection in Hendersonville, North Carolina. Illustration 196 is of an early masked type teapot with the KPM mark, and it is decorated very sparsely in the Kakiemon style comprising mostly Indian flowers. It dates at 1723 or 1724, probably the former. Illustration 81 is an early Kakiemon tea service having the swords mark of 1724. It comprises a teapot, cream jug, sugar in the form of a Chinese rice bowl, and four tea bowls and saucers. The decoration includes a Chinese bird, rock garden, Indian flowers, etc. The reds are of the intense early color, and the use of yellow in the decoration, particularly on the birds, is unusual. The blue is under-glaze, as the enamel blue needed had not been perfected. Illustrations 235 and 236 show a large hot water or coffee-pot and a tea bowl and saucer. These are also in the Kakiemon style and represent two of the many similar styles made between 1725 and 1730. They have the swords mark and are probably several years later than the tea set. The Kakiemon designs perfected by Herold cover a large and important class, and W. B. Honey says that in addition to the plum tree growing among stylized rocks, etc., he also painted designs having rat-like and fantastic animals; birds with long curved or spiky tails, a curious banded hedge looking like a wheatsheaf; peony, chrysanthemum, and other flowers; vine branches with berries most beautifully rendered, with some floral diapers; figure subjects of playing children, including the famous incident Ssüma-Kuang and the fish bowl, which was interpreted at Chelsea as "Hob-in-the-Well."

Illustrations 199 and 200 show two "Red Dragon" plates; the larger of the two was formerly in the Lord Fisher collection and has a caduceus mark in under-glaze blue. The early intense red and the mark indicate a date of 1723. Some authorities consider that the caduceus mark was used only on pieces intended for the Turkish market, the Turks thinking that the crossed swords mark was a Christian emblem.

The Festive Publication to Commemorate the 200*th Jubilee* of the Meissen factory, issued in 1910, contains the interesting story that Augustus the Strong made a tour of the factory in 1728 and when he saw pieces such as the one shown as Illustration 200, he so admired them that he gave orders to discontinue their production for the trade and ordered a complete service for his Dresden Palace. Such a service was made and we show the other Red Dragon plate, Illustration 199, which is from this service; it has the mark KHC in crimson, which stands for "Royal Court Pantry," at Dresden, and was made 1730-34. The Red Dragon style later became very popular and was reproduced in quantity by the factory up to recent times. Illustration 201 shows a large plate, probably from one of the first Kakiemon dinner services made for the King. It is known as the "Yellow Lion," although it is in fact a tiger with bamboos and a plum tree. It was made about 1728, and this specimen has, in addition to the usual crossed swords found on all pieces after 1725, a KHCW which was the mark put on pieces made for the Warsaw Palace. Illustration 202 is one of a pair of plates known as "Tiger und Bambus." These plates were decorated probably around 1728. Each plate has a swords mark in blue enamel over the glaze, as well as the so-called Jöhanneum mark. The practice of referring to the inventory marks of the Royal collection in the Japanese Palace in Dresden, as Jöhanneum marks, is incorrect, as the Jöhanneum was not established until about 1876, at which time the Royal collection, which had been stored in boxes in the basement of the Japanese Palace were unpacked and put on display in an old riding stable and called at that time and since the Jöhanneum. W. B. Honey and others say that no wholly satisfactory reason for the over-glaze mark has been ascribed. The present authors consider the reason is quite plain, especially with reference to plates like those shown here. The shape is from early Chinese models and the porcelain of a type made before 1724. It seems quite logical, therefore, that such plates had been made before the order to mark each piece was issued, and these plates were taken out of the store room about 1728, and after they were decorated, the over-glaze enamel mark was added, as in no other way could they be marked. Illustrations 197 and 198 indicate another famous Kakiemon design popular at the period, variously known as the "Flying Dog" or "Fox," but in reality a squirrel. Shown here is a large platter and a cream jug. They date about 1730. Illustration 194 is an octagonal tea caddy having one of the Kakiemon designs which was much copied at the Bow and other English factories and again at the early French factories. The Oriental tree and the two quaint partridges present one of the finest adaptations of the art of Sakaida Kakiemon. Illustration 85 shows a pair of condiment jugs which are extremely rare. The design is oriental and most pleasing, particularly when decorated, as in this instance, in the early red and under-glaze blue of Köhler. The shapes are quite attractive, one having an animal's head as a spout, the other a large lip. The high dome lids are interesting. After inspecting nearly every museum in Europe, we can recall that only the David's Museum in Copenhagen has an early pair. The Jägerhof Museum in Düsseldorf (the collection of Dr. Erich Schneider), has a pair similar in size to those shown here, but of later decoration. The Vienna Museum has three such pieces, but the period is about 1735, whereas those shown here are of the period of 1724. Illustration 188 is a most interesting example from the Ralph Wark collection, the decoration by Stadler, c. 1725.

From the above, it will be seen that the Kakiemon designs played a very important part, as did all types of Oriental styles, in decorations of the Meissen factory, and that, while Meissen appropriated the decoration, it also modified and changed it to suit its purpose. Many of the other factories then copied the Meissen copies.

GROUND COLORS (UNDER-GLAZE AND OVER-GLAZE)

In the early years of the Meissen factory, King Augustus greatly favored the blue-and-white and colored grounds. The failure to produce the former for long or in quantity, was a great disappointment to him. The latter, however, were made in great quantity and variety, beginning around 1725 or shortly thereafter. Köhler with the assistance of Mehlhorn, produced a satisfactory under-glaze blue from about 1720 until Köhler's death in 1725. Herold relates in his report of 1731 that while Köhler imparted his secret to him on his death bed, he was unable to produce it. It was not until 1732 that a fair under-glaze blue was produced, and not until modern times that a wholly satisfactory one was made. Illustration 203 shows a large vase in the collection of Mrs. C. B. Stout of Memphis having the Köhler blue. This vase has the AR mark and is rare. Illustration 205 shows a pair of Meissen vases decorated in under-glaze-blue by David Köhler in 1720. We represent two of a set of four marked 1-4 and embossed with "K," possibly trial pieces: from the collection of Mr. R. H. Wark, the other two in the collections of Dr. E. Schneider, Düsseldorf and of Dr. Siegfried Ducret, Zürich. Illustration 73, a Meissen coffee-pot, has the Köhler under-glaze blue and is unusual in that the cartouche lacks the outline which is ordinarily used with such designs. Again, the mark is of an unusual shape, the points of the swords making an angle of far more than 90 degrees. This shape seems to occur only on pieces made in 1724. Illustration 148 is of an extremely rare small tea bowl decorated in Köhler under-glaze blue. This was undoubtedly an experimental piece made about 1720 in an attempt to produce what the Chinese called "cracked ice." The crackle is entirely under the glaze and produces a pleasing effect. Why it was not made later is not known—probably because of the difficulty of production. It has pseudo-Chinese symbols in under-glaze blue as its mark which is recorded in Willy Doenges' *Meissner Porzellan* (1921), page 161, illustration 22, and was formerly in the Royal Saxon collection. The dead-leaf brown glaze was perfected as early as 1720 by Samuel Stölzel, and continued to be used on useful wares until about 1730. Illustration 214 also shows such a piece.

The King was insistent that Herold perfect his colored enamel over-glazes, especially the yellow, which in China was an Imperial color. Hannover pictures a group of such ground pieces, previously found in the Schlossmuseum at Berlin and the Dresden collection and dated 1726 and 1727. The Meissen factory produced a pale biscuit color; clear and deep yellow; three shades of leaf or emerald green; olive green; sea green; pale grey and lilac; a soft "clair de Lune," pale lavender; and a deep crimson purple; a warm lilac blue; a light, true apple green; and a rouge-de-fer, also called "eisenrot," which sometimes became smoked in firing. No other factory made such a wide and varied assortment of color. We illustrate as No. 179 a beaker cup and saucer, decorated around 1721-23 with Herold painted chinoiseries, on an unusual "mottled blue" under-glaze, from the collection of Mrs. C. B. Stout. Another one is in the Ralph Wark collection. Illustration 253 is a teapot having a rare "Blue céleste" ground color, from the Ralph Wark collection. Illustration 254 shows an invalid cup and saucer, the paste is a pale lavender all the way through, with the handle, spout and a raised AR in white porcelain. This most unusual specimen is from the collection of Mrs. Henry C. Isaacson, Sr. of Seattle. A few other rare shades not often encountered and made probably on an experimental basis will be mentioned in connection with the illustrations. Illustration 76 is a small coffee-pot or milk jug and is an example of the pale lavender mentioned above. It will be noted that the lighter the purple, the earlier the piece. Later pieces are dark; also the cartouche is not outlined. Illustration 75 shows a cream jug in the rare powder blue, or as W. B. Honey describes it, a "warm lilac-blue." So far as we know, there are only seven pieces extant, all from the same service. Illustration 74 shows a two-handled chocolate cup in the deep crimson-purple. The decoration on this cup is one of the finest that we have seen and probably represents the best work of Johann Georg Heintze. Illustration 211 is of another piece in the purple or mauve color. It dates around 1740 as it was not until about this date that German flowers came into use. It is an unusually shaped covered bouillon, the stand being of the trembleuse type. Illustrations 208 and 209 show a small turquoise blue dish and also a small tea caddy with sloping shoulders in the same color. Illustration 215 is of a large coffee-pot in the olive green color. Illustration 210 shows a cup and saucer in the apple green fond. Illustrations 213 and 79 show a rectangular tea caddy, and a chocolate cup and saucer, both in the yellow fond. Here the yellow is at its very best. It is of the earliest period and superbly decorated. Illustration 207 is a tea bowl of extremely pale shade. The saucer, which was not born with the cup, illustrates the pale "biscuit color." Illustration 212 is of a three-footed yellow creamer from the A. Chevèt collection. The decoration is of the period of 1740.

AR VASES

Probably around 1723, another mark was used to designate unusually fine vases intended for the King's Japanese Palace or to be given by him to important personages. The large under-glaze blue vase referred to above is an early example. However, most of the vases, usually in sets of three, five or seven, were in the fond colors, or in fine Kakiemon style decoration. Illustration 216 indicates the latter type and now in the Smithsonian Institution in Washington, D.C. The mark is a monogram capital AR in under-glaze blue under the base. Only three such vases in a black ground are known. A pair is in the Irwin Untermyer collection in New York and illustrated as Plates 71 and 72 in his *Meissen Catalogue*. The other one is also exceptionally fine and is here shown as Illustration 218. It is a part of the well known Kocher collection, now in the *Berne Historical Museum*, in Berne, Switzerland. The decoration of this vase is surely by the hand of Gregor Herold. Illustration 80 shows one of a pair of AR vases in colour. The yellow ground is the intense "egg yolk," typical of the period. The decoration is in purple monochrome and depicts landscapes in early Watteau style. Illustration 217 shows a fine AR vase decorated with Oriental figures and flowers, 1725-30 (courtesy The Detroit Institute of Arts). Illustration 219 shows a rare pair of AR vases 28 inches high, with Oriental flowers and insects painted in polychrome colors directly on the rouge-de-fer-(iron-red) ground, 1730-40 (courtesy The Metropolitan Museum of Art, New York). At the Stadtmuseum in Meissen will be found an AR vase finely decorated with chinoiseries and in addition to the AR mark it has: *J. G. Höroldt fec. Meissen 17 Augusti* 1726.

SCHWARZLOT DECORATIONS

A favorite form of decoration on Du Paquier porcelain was a black monochrome known as Schwarzlot. Chinese porcelain, as well as glass painted in Bohemia, used the black monochrome. The Meissen factory did not use it to any great extent, but some extremely fine examples do exist. Illustration 221 is of a tea bowl and saucer of early shape, the latter having three concentric red circles under the bottom, usually associated with an early period. Also, we here again find the early swords mark on the saucer, not at the center, but near the foot-rim. This could indicate a date for the porcelain of 1722-23. The decoration is entirely in black monochrome, or Schwarzlot, and one view depicts chinoiseries, the other Occidental personages. The cartouche has the early copper luster and is picked out in dark puce only. It is interesting that every piece of Schwarzlot that we have seen is picked out in dark purple. This is not thought to have the usual meaning, i.e., that the piece should be dated c. 1735. The porcelain and decoration here are early. Illustrations 220 and 223 show two beaker-shaped chocolate cups with saucers, the cups having two handles. These pieces are not from the same service, as may be seen by the gold marks. The cartouches are unusual in that they are oval rather than round. This is probably because of the beaker shape of the cups. The decoration in each case represents a quay or harbor scene, usually associated with the period 1730-35. One of the cups includes in the decoration a large round building. On the saucer is a tree referred to as a pine in Mr. Ralph H. Wark's article in the *Keramik-Freunde der Schweiz* of April 1956, Illustration 34, in which he discusses at length his theory concerning the work of von Löwenfinck. He cites the large round house and the pine tree as two characteristics of this painter's work. These paintings are beautifully executed and could very readily be by his hand. Löwenfinck is known to have used the monochrome black in his work, as is shown by a signed piece. Also shown as Illustration 222 is a milk jug beautifully decorated in Schwarzlot, depicting landscapes and Korean flowers. The spout and handle are decorated with a reddish-purple stippling in a most unusual manner. In addition to the black monochrome, the artist has introduced a light purple and a light blue to highlight the buildings, ships, and clouds. This is unique so far as we know.

THE MOST IMPORTANT MEISSEN PAINTERS

The most important painter at the Meissen factory was Johann Gregor Herold, who as head of the factory for over 50 years exercised the most profound influence on its style of painting and decoration. He is undoubtedly responsible for most of the styles painted there. As the production of polychrome enamel painted ware increased, Herold was forced to devote more and more of his time to the administrative work and thus found it essential to have assistants. He had either to secure painters who had had experience in painting on faience or to train apprentices with no previous experience in painting of any kind. From his report he seemed to prefer the latter. No porcelain painters were available, for Meissen was the first factory outside of the Orient to make true porcelain and no enamel painting to be baked in the kiln had been done at Meissen before Herold came there in 1720.

By 1725 he had at least two good assistant painters who had obtained their experience in faience factories in all probability. The first one was Johann Ehrenfried Stadler, and the other Christian Friedrich Herold, the latter possibly a relative. In addition to these two assistants, there were two apprentices who had joined the factory in 1720 when Herold arrived. They were Johann Christoph Horn and Johann Georg Heintze.

The Meissen factory would not permit its painters to sign their work. The reason was to give the factory prominence and in all probability so that Herold himself, as its head, would get all of the credit. For this reason it has been and still is very difficult to say with certainty who painted the many fine services and other ware that the factory produced over a period of 40 years. Fortunately there do exist a few signed pieces that at least make it possible to draw certain conclusions. Before the second World War there existed a fine AR vase that was signed by Gregor Herold himself. Unfortunately, this vase was destroyed. There exist a number of signed pieces bearing the name of Christian Friedrich Herold, Carl Heinrich Keil and others, which for a long time were thought to be their work and signed by them. Today, however, it has been recognized that these pieces are in fact the personal work of Johann Gregor Herold and were in all probability presentation pieces of Herold, and he placed the name of the recipient on the object. In the case of Keil and Herold, both relatives of Gregor Herold, the objects were tankards, the Keil one formerly in the Gustave von Gerhardt collection, the Christian Herold one in the Erich von Goldschmidt-Rothschild collection.

On the other hand, there exist pieces actually signed by Christian Friedrich Herold, Johann Georg Heintze and Bonaventura Gottlieb Haeuer. The first-named comprise snuff-boxes, dated 1730 and 1735 and some enamel work done on copper as "homework." Of the second we have a copper plaque decorated in enamel colors showing the Albrechtsburg at Meissen, bearing the signature of Heintze and the date

1734. Of the painter Haeuer quite a few pieces from a tea-service decorated with "Silver Miners" are known to exist. Such signed pieces are very rare and in our judgement only the pieces signed by Gregor Herold are factory decorations and those only as presentation pieces. The other exception would be where a plaque of a new design was created and was to be used as a copy by the other painters. Such a piece is Illustration 226 in the Ralph Wark collection. As will be seen in the following discussion, the signatures attributed to Löwenfinck while at Meissen were in every case concealed ones.

Adam Friedrich Von Löwenfinck (1727-1736)

In 1727 Herold engaged a boy 12 years old as an apprentice who was destined to become the most controversial painter ever to work at the factory. This boy's name was Adam Friedrich von Löwenfinck. He served his apprenticeship as a flower painter and became a regular member of Herold's staff in 1734, and he fled the factory in 1736. Neither Herold nor the factory records have anything good to say about him and yet paintings that have been attributed to his hand over the years have been sought after by collectors and highly treasured by them. It is thought by many that because of his great talent, Herold was jealous of him and this may very well be true. Strangely enough, his name was at an early period connected with the painting of fable animals, which was somewhat unusual in view of his apprenticeship as a flower painter. The late Mr. W. B. Honey refers to certain obscure marks, such as a tiny "LF" written on a leaf of an AR vase at the Berlin Schlossmuseum, which was considered a concealed signature of Löwenfinck. Other similar examples with "VL" are noted. Finally, the well known authority Schnorr von Carolsfeld in preparing the catalogue (1925) for the Fritz Buckhardt collection found the letters L and F on the boots of an Oriental figure painted on a tankard. He pronounced this the signature of Löwenfinck and proceeded to ascribe like decorations to his hand. For many years no one questioned his attributions. As the tankard was exceptionally well-decorated the fame of Löwenfinck spread.

In 1949, however, the German authority Konrad Hüeseler published a paper in which he discredited the work of Löwenfinck. This was followed in 1950 by a paper signed Louis Levin which completely discredited him as a painter. As a result of these disparaging papers and the thirty-year controversy that had gone on about this little known painter, Mr. Ralph H. Wark, of Hendersonville, North Carolina, a well known collector of Meissen porcelain, decided to make an exhaustive study of the matter and the result of his research was made known in a very comprehensive article which appeared in the Bulletin No. 34 of the Swiss Ceramic Circle, April 1956. His article related his extensive research covering a period of eight years. Space here will not permit more than a brief reference to his article which completely changed the opinions held up to this time by most of the experts.

Mr. Wark carefully reviewed the existing specimens of faience that were signed either in full or by initials and which were clearly the work of Löwenfinck after he left the Meissen factory. This study revealed that on a Höchst faience vase which Mr. Wark purchased, the signature was "A.F.v.L.f.(ecit)." He further found on a Bayreuth faience tankard the signature of F.v.L. These signatures were of course in no sense concealed ones as no necessity for concealment existed at those factories. Mr. Wark then made a discovery that he considered most important. He had previously purchased a number of pieces of Meissen porcelain from a dinner service made for the second Earl of Jersey. Among these pieces was a beautifully decorated tankard and on this tankard he found a concealed signature which he read as F.v.L. From this discovery, Mr. Wark concluded that the entire dinner service was by the hand of Löwenfinck to whom he also attributes another large service characterized by a black-and-gold border, known as the "Fable Animal Service," and still a third one, decorated with fable animals and having a basket weave border. These attributions are made as a result of similarity of design and style. They have been generally accepted by many dealers and collectors and pieces from these services bring high prices on today's markets. Illustration 227 shows the tankard with the concealed signature.

The Jersey service has three distinct types of decoration as follows: 1. Chinamen in silhouette. 2. Chinamen in landscapes. 3. Chinamen and Europeans together in landscape. Mr. Wark points to this as showing the versatility of Löwenfinck, but as only the first type is shown on the signed piece there is always the possibility that more than one decorator worked on this service, as in fact was the usual custom at the factory. Illustrations 227, 228, 229 and 230 show the different types of decoration in the Jersey service.

Mr. Wark places much importance on a letter discovered by the late Kurt Röeder, written from Bayreuth by Löwenfinck to Damian Pflug, a commissioner of the Meissen factory. Mr. Wark points out that this letter says that Löwenfinck while at Meissen made *drawings* and *designs* himself, which were copied in poor work by other painters there. Mr. Wark says: "This proves to us that he made his own designs, and thus the Jersey service showing some decorations where there are Chinese figures plus European figures placed in European styled landscapes indicate *his personal drawing*, since there exist no Oriental samples of this type of decoration, nor are there any European etchings known of this type, which he could have copied. Thus, this also proves that all the Jersey pieces with their three different kinds of decorations were painted by him, not that part of the service was done by someone else."

Mr. Wark further comments on this letter written by Löwenfinck: "Since he says that other painters copied very poorly his work, that accounts for a number of pieces, up to now thought to be his and which are of such lesser quality. Since others painted his designs, there must exist such pieces. Therefore, I discredit some of them and say they are by these other painters."

While the letter in question is a *self-serving declaration*, never given much credence in a court of law, it may very well explain many questions that have in the past confused the experts.

The following illustrations are some of the types previously attributed to Löwenfinck and they may very readily be his work. Illustration 86 is an octagonal deep dish, the shape and size of which is exactly the same as the ones in the Jersey service and having the same incised potter's mark on the bottom of the base. The decoration here includes a Japanese bird and Oriental flowers. It is a fine example of the Kakiemon style; this plate was attributed to the hand of Löwenfinck by the late Mr. W. B. Honey. Illustration 78 shows an important punch bowl and cover, identical in shape and size with one in the famous Jagd service made for the King. Both bowls are decorated in the intense yellow fond color, and while this one has the fable animals as further decoration, the one in the Jagd service has only sprays of Indian Blumen as a decoration. We attribute the decoration to the hand of Löwenfinck, as well as Illustration 243, a sugar dish decorated with fable animals having spindley legs and sprightly movement, in the past associated with his work.

DUTCH HARBOR OR QUAI SCENES

These were probably the best loved of all the styles created at the Meissen factory. While they are chinoiserie in a sense, still they are never referred to as such but are variously called "Harbor Scenes," "Dutch Harbor," "Quai Scenes" or "River Scenes." They were the natural outgrowth of the general change in public taste, which had become tired of the predominantly Oriental influence in Art. The development is first noticed by paintings of Christian Friedrich Herold, who places mainly Turks but also Chinamen into European scenes, which then become completely European with sailors and merchants clothed in flowing Dutch costumes. But with the less important size of the figures represented, it became necessary to devise a more important background, and in due time there evolved elaborate landscapes, landing stages, and shipping motifs, including feathery trees, or harbors with the sky patterned with masts and rigging. While this style was not fully developed until 1730, a few primitive European landscapes appear in the early twenties and continued to be done occasionally. Such pieces were within feathery scroll work picked out in red only, just as were the chinoiseries.

While the harbor scenes may have been the natural outgrowth of the chinoiserie, they were undoubtedly influenced by some Augsburg engravings of Italian port scenes by Melchior Kysell, published in 1682.

Pazaurek has attributed the development of this style, that is the harbor scenes, to the Meissen painter, J. G. Heintze. To support this opinion, he shows a signed plaque in enamel on copper in the Landes-Gewerbemuseum, at Stuttgart, which is dated 1734. It is painted in purple monochrome with a view of the Albrechtsburg at Meissen, showing the bridge over the Elbe, with small figures, trees, and shipping, treated in much the same way as on a great deal of the porcelain of this period. Other plaques are known, such as the one shown, Illustration 226, by Heintze—1740. Heintze is also credited with the mannerism of writing a date with the post-horn on a milestone or similar object in the scene. Many pieces have been so attributed to him.

Another well-recognized group believe that C. F. Herold, a relative of Johann, created the style or at least developed it. There can be little question, however, that more than one painter is responsible for its creation or development, and we may feel quite sure that J. G. Herold had a part in it as in most every style developed at the factory. The harbor scenes are shown to fine advantage in connection with the fond or ground colors, and many of the illustrations shown here under the heading of fond are in this style. Of like interest are the monochrome decorated pieces already referred to, which also are frequently so decorated.

Illustrations 69 and 233 show two covered bouillons and stands. The first is a very early specimen, around 1725, probably decorated by C. F. Herold. The colors are in the early palette, and it is picked out in the red only, a sign of early decoration date. The other dates around 1730. Illustration 68 shows a beaker decorated in the style of Christian Frederich Herold. It has a continuous decoration of harbor scenes, including ten men in colorful costumes, three of them in a small boat; a larger boat is nearby, and a castle is in the distance. Further around, we see an island with a large ship and some smaller ones near it. Seven men of different nationalities and stations in life complete the picture. A beautifully painted sky is overhead, surmounted with an elaborate gold scroll design. The lower part of the beaker is divided into eight panels by wide gold bands. Each panel is decorated with a harbor scene painted entirely in monochrome. Every other panel is in orange, and the alternate ones are in puce or lavender. On the bottom are the swords mark and the gold number 7. Illustration 232 is of an early small beaker decorated in harbor scenes.

Illustration 67 exhibits a teapot with a masked head and decorated in the style attributed to C. F. Herold. It has the gold number 55. Illustration 239 shows a tea and coffee service painted in the Dutch harbor and landscape style of the period of 1730, having the cartouche picked out in red with a little puce added. The mark appearing on each piece is the gold letter "ii." The decoration is in the style of C. F. Herold, but was in all probability painted by several different artists. The service comprises: coffee pot with lid, waste bowl, teapot with masked spout and without lid, cream jug and lid, rectangular tea caddy and matching lid, three tea bowls and five saucers. Illustration 176 shows an oval sugar box painted in a continuous harbor scene. The lid is similarly decorated and, in addition, has six small vignettes in puce monochrome, and a dog finial in white and gold. The gold mark is 4, and the swords mark is of the period 1725; the painting is probably by Heintze

It will be seen from the above descriptions that a wide field was opened for the Meissen artists under J. G. Herold and that they took advantage of the opportunity.

MEISSEN DINNER SERVICES

Up to the period of 1725, the factory had been busy primarily with the production of tea services, and it was not until after this date that the production of dinner services came into vogue. When visiting the famous Blenheim Palace in England in 1957, we saw a large collection of a Meissen service, which was there represented as having been a present from Augustus the Strong in 1720 to the Third Duke of Marlborough. As the porcelain had the basket weave border called early ozier which was introduced about 1733 (the basket weave was copied from the Chinese), we realized that the date of the gift was in error. The design actually was one of the early molded designs that Kändler created in an attempt to get away from the plain flat surfaces on which Herold had insisted. The decoration included Indian flowers, a flying dragon, and a Phoenix bird, the dragon being the symbol of the Chinese Emperor, and the phoenix, the Empress. Pieces such as the "Nut Bowl," Illustration 225 and a large platter, Illustration 224, are from this service. Count Sulkowsky was so pleased with the design that the factory made him a large service in 1737 using the identical design, with the exception that the dragon and phoenix bird were omitted, and in their place, the Count's Coat-of-Arms was painted.

The most famous of the services made by the factory, however, was one made for Count Brühl. It was started in 1737, and finished in 1741. It comprised 1,600 pieces which remained intact until the Second World War. The molding of this service was quite elaborate, using for its principal motif two swans, and it is familiarly known as "The Swan Service." Some of the pieces are formed with fully molded swans, and each piece has the coat-of-arms of Count Brühl. (Illustration 247, one of a pair from the City Art Gallery, St. Louis, Missouri) Many fakes are found in the market and the molds have been used to reproduce the shapes which have been sold in undecorated condition. Some pieces have also been decorated in recent times. One test for authenticity is to see if the coat-of-arms on plates and platters is set at about a forty-five degree angle, when the swans are in the upright position; and if not, one may be sure that the piece is a fake. Illustrations 184 and 185 show a plate from this service and a tea bowl.

Illustration 244 shows a deep Meissen bowl and cover, from an early dinner service. Similar pieces from this same service are in the Jägerhof Museum in Düsseldorf. It is the "Lambrequin Pattern" of Japanese origin, or "Imari" style. The decor is primarily red and under-glaze blue, and dates 1725-30. Illustration 246 is from Dr. Schneider's collection, at Düsseldorf.

Illustration 186 shows another famous service known as the "Count of Munich" service. It was probably made about 1740, and the decoration consists of a very elaborate coat-of-arms which, in the case of the plate shown here, covers the entire center surface, and the border is in the basket weave. The Russian Government in 1959 returned 500 cases of porcelain formerly in the Jöhanneum collection, and one of the pieces was a large and extremely elaborate centerpiece from this same service.

About 1740, the use of the Deutsche Blumen or naturalistic flowers came into vogue, and it was this style which became well known in England and America as "Dresden." Illustration 252 shows one of three charming examples of cups and saucers painted in this manner.

The Meissen factory had no regard for the independent painters, but nevertheless, a good deal of the Meissen porcelain in its undecorated state got into their hands and was, in many cases, so beautifully and unusually decorated that today any good collection should have at least a few pieces. The prices frequently exceed that paid for comparable factory work. The best Hausmaler were from Augsburg, Bohemia, and Silesia. For a comprehensive discussion of this matter, see the books on the subject by G. E. Pazaurek. Illustration 242 shows a type of such work frequently found on the market today. There were eight of these beaker two handled chocolate cups and saucers in the original leather case, with under-glaze blue decoration of rock and Chinese bird pattern of the period of c. 1725. The original blue decoration has been covered, more or less, with gold thought to have been added by the Hausmaler, F. J. Ferner, some twenty years later and now worn off in places, creating a very colorful effect. Illustration 241 is a plate in the distinctive style of the Hausmaler Mayer of Pressnitz. Beside the main groups there were isolated artists working on their own account and one of these was Canon August Ernst Otto von dem Busch of Hildesheim who spent his holidays in 1750-75 engraving designs on white porcelain with a diamond-point and coloring them black. Birds, flowers and landscapes with monuments were his favorite subjects. Illustration 192 depicts two views of a bodkin holder with silver mounting from the collection of Dr. A. J. Mourot which seems to be a unique design.

THE KÄNDLER, OR PLASTIC, PERIOD

While it is true that Count Brühl was at least the nominal head of the factory after the death of Augustus the Strong, and that he supported Kändler fully in his work, Herold was, and remained, in full charge of the operation of the factory and must have had a part in the decoration of the figures. Yet it is to Johann Joachim Kändler that we must give the credit for the remarkable figures produced from 1735 to 1750, which did so much to make the factory famous and which brought its golden age to a close.

The late Mr. W. B. Honey in his authoritative book *Dresden China* has this to say: "to Kändler will always stand the credit of first discovering a European porcelain style in figure-modeling which should exploit the plasticity and shining whiteness of the paste and the brilliant reflections of the glaze, and set them off by full-toned audacious color. In modeling these figures, Kändler showed himself the first European artist to understand that the glazed surface of the glittering white porcelain, and the powerful colors at his command, could be used to enhance the effect of turbulent force in the modeling. Unlike his predecessors, he was prepared to model his figures boldly, with deep hollows for dense shadow, and strong projections which took advantage of what may be called the nervously plastic quality in porcelain, which can be made alive to the finger tips. It is no short-coming in this art of porcelain that parts should project in a precarious way. One of its paradoxical charms lies in the fact that it can be so modeled, with a fragile tremulous sort of delicacy."

Kändler was basically a baroque modeler, and while later he modified his style so as not to be completely out of step with the advent of the rococo, yet his great love remained with the baroque. Many of his figures were made as table decorations to replace the sugar or wax ones used on the great festive boards of the time. His designs were made not for the common people, but for the amusement of a frivolous court, and the cost prevented their general use. The court of Augustus derived its tastes largely from the French, which set the style for the extravagant living of the time. Louis XV and his grandfather Louis XIV were lovers of porcelain and made its production and use a part of their frivolous existence. The styles produced in the figurines, therefore, very naturally reflected this sumptuous pageantry. Masquerades, operas, tournaments, and elaborately dressed hunting parties were a part of the Saxon court life, and so it is little wonder that we find many of Kändler's finest figures revolving around the Italian Comedy. The reason for its popularity is found in the fact that the figures were made to please a frivolous and fun-loving court, which adored masquerades and the theater. They loved to live in a world of make-believe.

The earlier figures, such as the pagodas, Callot dwarfs and a few others with a decided oriental origin and a baroque style, are usually attributed to Georg Fritzsche, who came to the factory in 1712, but is not believed to have been regularly employed. Illustration 164 is an example from the collection of Dr. A. J. Mourot. Johann Christoph Ludwig von Lücke made some models in 1728-29, but few piecies of his are known. We shall discuss later the modelers Eberlein and Reinicke, who were Kändler's assistants. His immediate predecessor was a baroque sculptor named Johann Gottlob Kirchner. The King since 1721 had been occupied with the furnishing of the "Japanese Palace," which was not merely to house his fabulous collection of porcelains but was to have chandeliers and other decorations all in porcelain. In 1727, it was decided to furnish the palace with figures, birds and animals, all of life size. This would require the services of an original modeler, and the King at this time employed Johann Gottlob Kirchner, brother of the Court Sculptor, to do this work. After a year, during which time he proved to be inefficient and frivolous, Kirchner was dismissed, and Johann Christoph Ludwig von Lücke, an ivory-carver of repute, in 1728 was put in his place with the title of Modell-meister. After six months, he was likewise dismissed; and for a year, no one was employed. Kirchner was brought back in 1730 and worked on large animals, vases, and the Apostles. By this time, the Palace building had been enlarged, and it was planned to furnish a chapel with reliefs on the walls, a pulpit, altar, organ pipes, and twelve nearly life-sized figures of the Apostles, all in porcelain. To help him with this work, the King in 1731 appointed another young sculptor who became the greatest of all Meissen modelers, Johann Joachim Kändler. From this time on, the two young sculptors worked together. When the King died in 1733, Kirchner was finally dismissed and Kändler, who had the full confidence of Count Brühl, was put in charge of all modeling work and was given the title Modell-meister, formerly held by Kirchner. This title he held for forty years.

It soon became evident that porcelain was not a satisfactory medium with which to make the life-sized figures of personages, animals and birds, and this work was discontinued. But a number of them were made; in addition to the life-sized figures in the Dresden Museum, examples are to be found in other museums. In 1957, the authors saw in the Grand Salon of Longleat, ancestral home of the Marquess of Bath, a large number of life sized birds and animals. According to the guide at the Salon, they were pottery door stops. But strangely enough, they were rare porcelains, the only ones remaining in the house, which is now opened to the general public.

After the death of the King, Kändler created the fine dinner services with the plastic motif about which we have already spoken. At the same time, he made the first small figures which were destined to become so famous. His co-sculptor and rival, Kirchner, belonged to the baroque movement, peculiar to Dresden, and while there can be little doubt that Kändler was the more talented, especially in the use of porcelain as a medium, Kirchner did not lack qualifications for creating a meritorious plastic style. Among other items created by him we find clock cases, a magnificent well-fountain with supporting figures, a number of primitive animals, and a superbly executed statue of the Apostle Peter, as well as a sixteen-inch statue of Augustus the Strong.

KÄNDLER FIGURES

Coming now to the figures made by Kändler after the death of the King in 1733, we find him modeling the same figures in small size that had given so much trouble in the large. These included birds, animals, and Apostles. Color Illustration 1 depicts a unique statue of St. Peter, superbly modeled, with the hem of his mantle decorated in deep purple and the edges outlined in gold. It is believed that it was this model that suggested the set made for the Empress Wilhelmina Amalia of Austria, mother-in-law of Augustus III.

Kändler modeled many fine birds, and some outstanding examples will be seen in *Meissen and other Continental Porcelain*, in which those in the superb collection of Mr. Irwin Untermyer are illustrated. Illustration 298 and 299 here, show two Hoopoes from this collection; one bird is attributed to Kändler, 1736, and the other to J. G. Ehder, 1741.

In 1735, Kändler produced his first Italian Comedy figure, a seated Harlequin playing a bagpipe. Illustrations 6, 286 and 288 show three versions of this figure, the first is believed to date 1735, and the other two slightly later. Note the protrusion of the feet and legs in the first one, and the absence of decoration on the base, indicative of early pieces. In 1736, Kändler modeled the Beggar Man and the Beggar Woman Playing the Hurdy-Gurdy. W. B. Honey illustrates the Beggar Man, Plate 39, from the Lord Fisher collection. Colored illustrations 2 and 3 show both models. Note here the early base with the feet and leg protruding, and the simplicity. They were re-modeled later in larger size. Also in 1736 came the first version of "Pantaloon and Columbine," the "Court Jester Schindler," and a "Standing Hussar Playing Bagpipes." It was also in this year that the first crinoline group appeared, known as the "Lovers with a Birdcage." (See Illustration 276.)

While Kändler was modeling these figures in his spare time taken from his work on the big and elaborate dinner services mentioned above, his assistant, Johann Friedrich Eberlein, was in 1735-36, modeling two figures representing a new concept of Chinese sitting on cushions on four-sided pedestals; and the "Dutch Dancers," better known as the "Tyrolese Dancers," later copied with such success by English factories. By 1740, figures had so captured the taste of the public that they were made in great quantity and are considered the best products of the factory. Kändler's figures of this, his best period, showed the strong rhythmic movement and clear composition for which he is famous. When we combine these qualities with the brilliant glaze and the rich intense colors which characterized them, it is little wonder that the critics agree that these figures have never been equaled by any other factory. Up to 1740, the figures were single ones for the most part, and the groups in all their glory followed and reached their zenith by 1750; after which new styles with pastel colors and rocaille bases became popular. During the best period, we rarely find two figures decorated exactly alike. Powerful reds and yellows, and a strong intense black are characteristic. These, however, were only a few of the colors encountered. What part Herold played in the decoration is not known.

Before naming the more famous creations, it may be well to say a word about the Meissen figures in general. A characteristic of the early ones is that the bases are small and unimportant. They were not at first intended as a part of the beauty of the design, but merely as a means of support. Note how in so many of the early examples the feet and legs extend well beyond the confines of the base. In some of the early crinolines, the lady's skirt completely covers it. Later, the bases became progressively larger and, whereas in the earliest ones no decoration is found, now we find in addition to the early molded design, a few painted flowers. Then a few applied flowers were added, and those of rather large size; and finally came smaller applied flowers in greater profusion and design. About 1745 to 1750, the rocaille, or rococo base came into style, and became a part of the picture. This tendency reached its climax in Victorian times when the frame became as important as the picture. The underside of the base was usually flat and unglazed.

Early colors were ground from mineral earths, and once one has seen them, one need not be misled by nineteenth century reproductions. By around 1800, chrome had been invented and was generally substituted for the more costly colors used during the eighteenth century. It is also helpful for collectors to study styles in connection with the clothes, hats, and hair dress of the several periods. Should a figure, for instance, show a lady with Victorian dress or hair style, then it will at once be plain that it is not of the eighteenth century.

Something should be said here regarding the construction of figurines, as it requires the services of a number of skilled workmen, any of whom could destroy the artistic beauty of the figure. First we require a sculptor known as a modeler, who creates the figure, usually in wax. Then the original wax model is turned over to a molder, or "repairer," as he was called, who after due consideration, cuts the original model into as many parts as his judgment dictates; after a plaster of Paris mold is made for each piece, and the parts have been molded in biscuit porcelain, they are assembled and held together by a slip, or thick glaze. Finally they are fired in the kiln. It will be seen that the repairer played a very important part, as he could mar the beauty of the figure by failing to do his job well. When it is realized that the figures shrank about one-eighth in size in the kiln, and had a tendency under the intense heat to warp, we can appreciate the skill required in his task. When the repairer has finished assembling his parts, such items as hats, ribbons, shoes, etc., were molded by hand and applied to the piece before the first deep firing, after which the figure was in what is known as the "biscuit" form. It was then dipped in the glaze and again fired, after which the enamel decoration was added and fixed in a muffle-kiln at a lower temperature. Finally, the gold was applied and once again the piece was fired, this time at a still lower heat. It is apparent that the kilnmaster could ruin the work of his fellow workers. The molds produce the best specimens when the outlines are sharp. After a limited number of pieces have been made, the edges of the molds wear to such an extent that new ones must be made if production of this item is to continue. This accounts for the fact that all figures from the same mold are not equally good, and also, to some extent, for the fact that so few of the early figures remain today.

JOHANN FRIEDRICH EBERLEIN

Eberlein came to the factory in 1735 and was a great help to Kändler. It is sometimes hard to distinguish his work. There are certain figures, however, having distinctive oriental style, such as those he modeled in 1735-36, that are his sole work. Illustrations 260 and 262 show two such figures modeled by him in 1740. They are "Fall" and "Winter" from a set of the seasons. "Fall" in particular is extremely well modeled. A characteristic of Eberlein's work is that the model's eyes are slanted in an oriental manner and the noses are of a pronounced Roman type. Illustration 293 is also a specimen of his work.

PETER REINICKE

In 1743, Peter Reinicke became an assistant to Kändler, and he so closely copied his master's work that it is hard to distinguish it from that of Kändler. The folk-type figures of Illustration 265 "Turkish Woman Mandolin Player" was modeled by him in 1744.

FOLK TYPE FIGURES

The "Beggar Musicians," and the "Tyrolese Dancers" were the forerunners of a folk type, also suggested by the Cris de Paris, engraved by Comte de Caylus. Illustrations 264 and 11 show the "Map Salesman" and the "Print Salesman," both made around 1740. Illustrations 9 and 15 show two figures of the same type and period; "The Pipe Smoker" and "Standing Hurdy Gurdy Player." The latter is exceptionally good. Falling into the same general class are Illustrations 273, 275, 272, 267, 266, 268, 274 and 14, "Clothes Presser," "Fish Saleswoman," "Dancer in Country Costume," "Walking Gardener," "Sitting Male Gardener," "Sitting Woman Gardener," "The Coppersmith," and finally a particularly fine figure known as the "Drunken Farmer." The latter figure was modeled 1735-40, and similar examples are found in the sales catalogues of the well known Feist and Gerhart collections. Finally, Kändler modeled a series of Silver Miners; several are undoubtedly modeled after Augustus himself. One of such pieces is depicted in Illustration 263.

ITALIAN COMEDY FIGURES INCLUDING HARLEQUINS

Of all the figures by Kändler, none can surpass those modeled after the Italian Comedy. Sometime between 1735 and 1740, he created a series of twelve single Harlequins, eleven men and one woman, which are considered among his best work. Colored Illustration 13 shows an outstanding member of this group, known as the "Grimacing Harlequin." Illustrations 291, 283, 284 and 285 portray other fine examples. W. B. Honey makes this sharp comment on the Harlequins, and has this to say: "The baroque force shown in the great animal figures is here concentrated in a few inches of violent movement, and these grimacing Harlequins seem to be the embodiment of all that ribald mockery of human respectability and pretentiousness in which according to one definition all comedy consists." About 1740 Kändler modeled one of his best group Harlequin figures, known as "The Indiscreet Harlequin," shown here as Colored Illustration 8. This must have been one of the first from this mold, as the features are so sharp and the decoration so fine as to make it one of the best specimens extant.

Falling into this category of Italian Comedy Figures, we see here (Colored Illustration 4) an important one, known as "Scaramouche and Columbine" and dated c. 1744. A group of small single figures, also from the Italian Comedy are shown in Illustrations 10, 5, 7, 271 and 12: "Pantaloon," "Columbine," "The Capitan," (the last two attributed to Reinicke) "Boy as Harlequin," and "Africa." The last is an unusual figure and may be connected with the others, of about the same size and period, or more probably it is from a series of the Continents not well known.

CRINOLINES

The groups of ladies in crinoline skirts and their lovers are not all of equal merit but they did provide a foil for the colorful decorations of the period. The first and probably the best, the "Passionate Lovers with a Birdcage," is here illustrated as 276, from the Morgan collection, now in Wadsworth Atheneum at Hartford, Connecticut (by whose courtesy we show many examples here). Less than year later, 1737, Kändler modeled a seated lady with an immense spreading skirt, whose hand a lover is kissing, while she takes a cup from an attendant black boy holding a tray. Illustration 279 shows this figure, certainly one of his best. Another of his more famous compositions, represents a gallant in a dressing-gown kissing his hand to a lady who wears a crinoline skirt and holds a fan. We illustrate it here mounted on an ormolu base, as Illustration 277, and it, as well as Illustration 280, known as "The Lovers," is from the Morgan collection. Another outstanding example of a crinoline depicted as lovers, is Illustration 278, known as the "Spanish Lovers." It was modeled in 1741 by Kändler and is from the Ralph Wark collection. Illustration 281 from the Morgan collection is known as the "Heart Seller," and is in reality one of the many variations of the "Lady with the Chocolate Cup."

Illustration 294, the "Ardent Lovers" and Illustration 295 the "Chinese Lovers," are examples of lovers not in crinoline, from the collection of Mrs. C. B. Stout: Illustration 293 "Harlequin and Columbine Dancing" and 296 "Mockery of Old Age," from the same collection as well as Illustration 297, a Derby counterpart. Illustration 292 is known as the "Turk with Jumping Horse" and is one of a number of fine examples owned by the Antiquarian Society of Memphis, now on permanent loan to the Brooks Memorial Art Gallery, Memphis, Tennessee.

Kändler modeled the Seasons, Continents, etc. Illustration 282 shows two of the Continents, America and Africa. This is the large series and the finest, although several sets were modeled within a year of each other. "Africa" here was modeled by Kändler in 1745, and "America" was modeled by Eberlein, also in 1745. The records show that Reinicke modeled "America" also in 1745.

Kändler also modeled many mythological figures. Illustration 261 shows "Rape of the Sabine." Illustration 287 shows "Psyche and Cupid" modeled about 1740-45. Illustration 289 shows the "Naked Centaur" modeled 1745-50. Illustration 290 is superbly modeled (c. 1750) and the paste and glaze are of the finest. It represents "The Arts." The base of this figure, and of the Centaur, illustrates the rocaille or rococo base now becoming popular.

The early figures had the swords mark on the unglazed base, and in many cases, it disappeared in the kiln. Around 1745 the factory started to use a small mark under the glaze on the edge of the base.

LARGE FIGURES

In 1737, Augustus III commissioned Kändler to make an Altar garniture consisting of the twelve Apostles together with six single candle holders, a large crucifix, a credenz-plate with two pitchers for wine and water, a holy-water font, bell and chalice. From specimens still preserved today we see that actually three sets of these Apostles and candlesticks bearing the Austrian Imperial coat-of-arms were made. The original set, owing to the death of the Empress was never delivered to the court; however, a few years later a set was sent to the Empress Maria Theresa. Eight of the Apostles of this set are still preserved at Vienna, the remaining ones to make a dozen are duplicates. Actually only one complete set is still intact. That set with six additional candlesticks is on display at Biltmore House, the Asheville, North Carolina Estate of the late George Vanderbilt. Illustration 255 shows this complete set, and we are indebted to Mr. G. H. V. Cecil, grandson of the original owner for its use here.

The Seattle Museum of Art owns eleven Apostles but no candlesticks. The missing Apostle is James the Lesser. In addition to these three sets some single Apostle figures still exist in various private collections.

Much later, in 1772, Kändler again modeled a new set of Apostles and the Altar garniture pieces. This was a commission from Pope Clemens XIV, who died, however, before it was completed. His successor, Pope Pius VI had it enlarged and it was delivered to Rome in 1775. It then is supposed to have been made a gift from the Pope to the Duke of Bridgewater in 1796 and thus came to England. Inherited by the present Lord Ellesmere it was disposed at Christie's in London, in 1959, to the Antique Porcelain Company. All of the above sets were decorated in gold and white with colors only for the coat-of-arms. The single figure of St. Peter shown here as the Frontispiece is in polychrome as will be seen from the illustration.

Late in the century, possibly 1790-1800, another all-white casting was made of the twelve Apostles which today are in the possession of Mr. Creighton, Ft. Lauderdale, Florida. Strangely enough, this set also came from England.

Also among the large figures is one of Schmiedel, Illustration 257, modeled by Kändler c. 1737 and 256, depicting Fröhlich modeled 1728-29 by Lücke, by courtesy of the Detroit Institute of Arts. Likewise between 1738 and 1745 Kändler and Reinicke modeled a number of busts in half-size of Emperors and Saints. Illustration 258 shows one of these, from the collection of Mrs. C. B. Stout, of Memphis, Tennessee, who has six in her collection. The one shown here is St. Thomas, modeled in 1743. Illustration 259 shows a figure modeled by Kändler, representing Augustus the Strong, by courtesy of the City Art Museum, St. Louis, Missouri.

FAKES, FORGERIES AND HAUSMALER

As early as 1723, as we have seen, the Meissen factory adopted a mark to protect itself from the Hausmaler, or outside decorators, who had secured the Meissen porcelain, usually of the Böttger period, in undecorated condition. Today such wares are not considered forgeries but constitute a class that is much sought after by collectors. They usually had a distinctive style of decoration of their own and did not, as a rule, attempt to copy factory decoration.

During the nineteenth and twentieth centuries, when the price for old porcelain both useful ware and figurines, reached such high levels, many fakes and forgeries were made. One of the most notorious forgers was Samson of Paris, who forged every kind of porcelain, and his pieces are dangerous because he was quite skilful. Samson himself contended that he did not try to mislead people and pointed to the fact that, when he created a Meissen reproduction he added to the crossed swords mark a capital "S" between the hilts, to show that it was a Samson copy. After his death, his heirs in carrying on this work were not so scrupulous. The paste, glaze, and colors of his work will not usually deceive an experienced collector.

Additional forgeries to guard against are vases and other useful ware made in the nineteenth century in Dresden by Frau Wolfsohn and marked AR. This famous mark, already referred to, was not used at Meissen after about 1735 or a little later. Wolfson at first purchased seconds from the Meissen factory and later made porcelain and decorated it in the style of Meissen and added the "AR" as her trade mark. For a quarter of a century this practice went on, but finally the Meissen factory brought suit and stopped her from using it. After that date she adopted a crown "D" as her factory mark, and her ware is called "Crown Dresden." It will deceive only the inexperienced collector. Meyers und Sohn also used the swords mark with an "M" between the hilts, and many small factories of the late nineteenth and early twentieth centuries used marks that looked something like the crossed swords mark. For a list of such factories, one may consult *German and Austrian Porcelain*, 1953, by George W. Ware. None of these should create difficulties for an experienced collector.

A more dangerous type of fake was made at Potschappel by Carl Thieme. He made some copies of Kändler figures that were good enough to deceive certain dealers, who thought them originals. The figures were carefully made and included "Crinolines" and "Harlequins" of the best period. The lot sold for £50,000. In 1909, suit was brought to recover that sum and, with the testimony of Professor Brinckmann, Director of the Hamburg Museum, and Frederick Litchfield, a noted authority, the money was recovered. In 1957 in Munich, we saw for sale gold and polychrome chinoiseries in the antique shops that were still being made at Meissen. They would not victimize an experienced collector, but they would the beginner.

In general, there are ways of distinguishing the genuine from the false. The fakes and modern Meissen are not as hard as the old pieces. By transmitted light, they are clear white, with no "moons" or "tears." The wares of the Herold period of Meissen should show green translucency and should have "moons" and "tears," especially in heavily potted pieces. The later colors are derivatives of chrome invented about 1800 and are not so intense or so colorful as those ground from minerals in the eighteenth century. The figures of the eighteenth century always had brown or black eyes, whereas those of the nineteenth century frequently are blue.

Yet another way to detect fakes purporting to be finely decorated pieces of the Herold Period is as follows:

With Herold chinoiserie painting of the early period, 1720 to 1724 before the piece carried a swords mark, there should be no gold within the scene, highlighting pleats in clothes or on flowers, attributes etc. When a decoration with chinoiserie has a swords mark, there should be gold within the scene. At the same time any cartouche used in this connection should then also have purple as well as gold and red in the scrollwork. Before the swords the scrollwork should be in red alone with gold and luster when used.

The forger, however, will nearly always make the mistake of using no gold, but purple and red in the scrolls. Or if he has a piece with swords and decorated in polychrome chinoiserie, he will make the mistake of omitting the gold in the figures and thereby making it possible for the advanced collector or reliable dealer to detect the fake.

CHARACTERISTICS OF THE BEST PERIOD OF MEISSEN (1709-1750)

1. Red stoneware is extremely hard.
2. Böttger porcelain is distinctly yellowish with smoky tone.
3. Böttger porcelain is brownish by transmitted light and has no "moons" or "tears."
4. Böttger porcelain is never decorated with baked enamel paint.
5. Böttger porcelain decoration is usually applied or molded.
6. All Meissen porcelain is hard-paste and will resist a file.
7. Good under-glaze blue only 1720-25. Fair after 1732. Herold period glaze, brilliant white, not always the same, however.
8. Herold porcelain "moons" and "tears," and green by transmitted light, especially in heavily potted pieces, becoming not so green with only "tears" after 1735.
9. Palette of pastel shades 1720-23 or 1724, brilliant and intense after these dates until 1750.
10. The cartouches picked out in red only during early period up to about 1724; red and purple 1725-35; puce only 1735-40; gold band with black border 1740; gold band only, 1735, on fond pieces; naturalistic flowers, 1740.
11. Large Chinamen, all fine decoration, 1720-24, painted by J. G. Herold.
12. No mark until 1722. Only teapots and sugar boxes marked MPM and KPF 1722; KPM 1723 and 1724; crossed swords mark on all pieces after 1724; caduceus and AR marks beginning 1723.

VIENNA PORCELAIN

The second in point of time among the European factories to make true porcelain was that of Vienna. Its history may logically be divided into two periods, one during the time it was under private ownership, and the other while it was a State factory.

DU PAQUIER PERIOD, 1718-1744

The Du Paquier factory started in 1718 as a private concern under the direction of Claude Innocent Du Paquier, who together with certain associates was granted a patent giving them exclusive rights to produce porcelain in Austria. For our purpose, it will be necessary to refer to only one of the original associate founders of the factory, Christoph Hunger. Count von Virmont, the Austrian representative in Dresden persuaded him to go to Vienna in 1717. Although not an employee of the Meissen factory, Hunger was nevertheless a close friend of Böttger, who in all probability divulged to him many of the closely guarded secrets of the factory, probably while intoxicated. Hunger represented himself as having the arcanum and a knowledge of the operation of the kilns. That he did not have all the knowledge that he claimed was realized when it became necessary for Vienna to secure the services of an employee of the Meissen factory before any satisfactory porcelain could be made. Hunger's previous experience had been largely as a gold decorator.

Regarding Du Paquier, who was the driving influence during this entire first period, little is known except that he was a gentleman who, since the year 1705 had held the office of a Hofkriegsratagent at the court of the Emperor Charles VI in Vienna. This title was not so important as the high-sounding name would imply. It merely meant that he was the representative of a commander of the Emperor's forces to look after his interests in his absence. While he is described as of Dutch origin, he was actually born in the German town of Trier. He occupied himself over a period of years in an attempt to produce porcelain, but without any financial assistance from the State; eventually he was forced to obtain the secret from Meissen. Nothing of importance was produced so far as the records show until 1719, when the Meissen arcanist Stölzel arrived.

Mr. J. F. Hayward in his excellent book *Viennese Porcelain of the Du Paquier Period,* 1952, has covered the subject thoroughly, and those desiring a more detailed account of this subject are urged to read it. We here draw extensively from it.

Mr. Hayward in Plate I, illustrates the first piece of Du Paquier porcelain of which there is a record. It is a two-handled beaker chocolate cup and trembleuse type saucer, undecorated, now in the Hamburg Museum, and dated 1719. This is undoubtedly an experimental piece, as inscribed in the paste of the cup is "Gott allein die Ehre und sonst keinen mehr." The cup is further inscribed with the initials J. M. K., and the date is repeated on the underside of the saucer. The inscription on the lower line has been interpreted "3 Mai 1719" or "3 Martz 1719." The cup is greenish in tone, whereas the saucer is white, probably the work of Stölzel. The only other known dated piece was a beaker cup, formerly in the Berlin Kunstgewerbe, which was decorated in polychrome enamel, the decoration including Japanese foliage and birds, and bearing on the base, lightly fired in black, the date, "20 August 1719." This cup is illustrated by K. Berling as an experimental piece. Unfortunately it has been destroyed, and so no marked piece in a decorated condition is available for comparison with early specimens that exist today. This is most unfortunate, as it necessitates that conclusions be drawn without a marked piece for comparison.

Two important events happened in 1719. One was the arrival, early in the year, of Stölzel from Meissen, and the other the hiring of the decorator Gregor Herold by Hunger at about the same time. Samuel Stölzel was the best qualified arcanist at the Meissen factory. As no satisfactory porcelain had been made before his arrival, his coming was a most important event. With his experience and suitable materials, the production of good porcelain and the potting of desired shapes should have presented no problem, as such work had been done by Stölzel while he was still at Meissen. We may divide early Du Paquier porcelain into three groups as follows: (1) that made with native clays before the arrival of Stölzel; (2) that made after his arrival, with native clays; (3) that made after his arrival, with Schnorr clay. The first is quite opaque and has a yellow brown color both by direct and transmitted light; it also has "moons" or large "tears." In fact the paste and glaze are so poor that one readily understands why the services of Stölzel were so urgently required. Illustration 311 shows a cup and saucer of this type. The decoration is in the Japanese style; the polychrome enamels are of the bright pastel shades indicative of the period of 1719 and the dry enamel has a decided tendency to peel off. In addition to the above, the decoration is placed on a *mat* that is "mottled" or "stippled" in a manner peculiar to the work done during the first few years after Herold reached Meissen. Illustration 312 from the Wark collection shows the same style in a KPF teapot painted by Herold at Meissen 1722. While this Du Paquier cup and saucer are not marked, except with the single "thumb" scratches, it is certainly a documentary specimen of the year 1719 and was painted by Herold at Vienna.

The second type has a yellowish color by direct and transmitted light, but more nearly resembles Böttger porcelain, except that "tears," which are not present in Böttger, are noted here. Illustration 309, an octagonal sugar box, is an example of this type.

The third type has a grayish-white tone, is green by transmitted light, and frequently has "moons" and/or "tears." This kind is more nearly like the Meissen made from feldspar, yet it is readily distinguishable from it. An authority on the subject has said that if a Meissen cup is set by the side of a Du Paquier one, the latter looks almost as though it needed washing. Some pieces, however, are quite well done. As in all types of porcelain, there is quite a variation, and only years of experience will enable one to distinguish in some cases. Illustration 310, another octagonal sugar box, is an example of this last type.

The second great event in 1719 was the arrival of Gregor Herold, who after 1720, for a period of more than fifty years managed the Meissen factory and was easily its most outstanding painter. Information just recently come to light from the archives of the factory, shows that Herold was a decorator at the great Strasburg faience factory in 1718, and was a wallpaper decorator at the time Hunger brought him to Vienna. He was born in Jena and was twenty-three years old when he came to Vienna in 1719. Illustrations 59, 60, 62, 63, 64, 307, 308, 309, 310 and 311 show examples believed to have been painted by Gregor Herold in 1719 while still in Vienna. Some of these are beyond question the type of pieces taken by Herold and Stölzel to Meissen in 1720 which caused the officials of the Meissen factory to restore Stölzel to his high place as arcanist and to turn the decorations of the factory over to the unknown Herold, who remained director of decorations for more than fifty years. Special attention is directed to Illustration 60. This cup and saucer is decorated in the classical style that was used by Herold at Meissen and was certainly painted by him at Vienna. It was thus expertized by the late Dr. E. W. Braun, one of the all-time great authorities on Vienna porcelain. Illustration 59 is one of a pair of cups and saucers that also fall into this same category, and Illustration 62, a trembleuse saucer and beaker cup painted in monochrome red could quite well have been one of the pieces taken to Meissen. This cup and saucer are also shown in the catalogue of the renowned Carl Mayer collection, and is there dated 1720 by Dr. Otto von Falke and J. Folnesics. Illustration 63 is a beaker cup and saucer decorated in much the same style as the dated one now destroyed.

Hunger also left the factory in Vienna in 1720 and founded the Vezzi factory in Venice, more about which will be detailed later under the heading "Italian Porcelain." The fact that he was able to do so would seem to substantiate his claims to have the arcanum, or probably he learned it from Stölzel while at Vienna. This last assumption would seem logical, as Du Paquier was able to make porcelain after the departure of Stölzel.

According to the records, the Du Paquier factory was compelled to close for a while after losing its technical staff. We know that in 1723 Du Paquier was attempting to sell the factory. There has been a tendency by most authorities not to accept the idea that well potted and finely decorated pieces can possibly be the work of Stölzel and Herold at Vienna at 1719. With this conclusion we wish to disagree. To date all such pieces 1720-25 is illogical, for as shown above, a whole year was at the disposal of the top arcanist from Meissen in which to continue to do what he had already done for many years at Meissen. The experienced decorator, Gregor Herold, at the age of twenty-three had a whole year to produce decorations similar to the ones he had already made at Strasburg and elsewhere. With the long hours that employees worked at that period much could have been and undoubtedly was accomplished, and Stölzel, it must be remembered, had been promised the princely salary of 1,000 florins a year. We again call attention to the specimens illustrated here, and to the fact that the potting is good and the colors and decorations excellent and, in most cases, in the same style used by Herold as soon as he reached Meissen but never found at Vienna after he departed.

Now in addition to what has been said about the factory during the two or three years after the departure of these men, let us also examine what was produced there. J. F. Hayward, after illustrating the marked undecorated piece, shows as his Plate 2a, a specimen from the British Museum which is dated "Vienne 12 Julii 1721." It is a flower vase of a form copied from Dutch faience. He says concerning it: "It is of particular interest, since it is the earliest dated piece known to have been made after Du Paquier had lost his two technicians, Hunger and Stölzel. Its form is striking, for it derives beyond a doubt from the familiar Dutch tulip vase. Indeed, its Dutch form has prompted one commentator on the subject to suggest that Du Paquier must have had recourse to Dutch workmen after the departure of his kilnmaster . . . The ungainly shape and uncertain potting mark this piece out as a primitive, and show that in 1721 the Vienna factory was in these respects still far behind Meissen standards. A glance at this vase explains the serious loss experienced by Du Paquier through the desertion of Stölzel, Herold and Hunger . . . It has a coarseness that recalls the Delft original which it copies. Its form has also been somewhat distorted in the firing. This piece cannot be claimed as an example of rapid progress in the factory, but in view of the difficulties already related, this is not altogether surprising." The cups and saucers shown on Plate 3: a, b, and c are there dated 1720-25. Mr. Hayward in commenting on 3a, says: "In Plate 3a, is illustrated a chocolate-cup with cover and saucer which is only slightly later than the 1719 cup and saucer in the Hamburg Museum. It is decorated with floral designs in a faint purple monochrome. The potting is weak, the cup being oval rather than circular in section. There are faults in the paste, and the glaze has not run evenly, with the result that it is very thin in parts and too thick in others. It resembles the 1719 cup and saucer in shape except that the handles are not of Meissen form, and that instead of being fluted, the sides are gadrooned. The decoration of Oriental flower sprays is painted with considerable uncertainty, one might almost say, incompetence. One hesitates to associate the name of Herold with such primitive painting, and I think that such pieces were decorated after Stölzel and Herold had left Vienna."

The above quotation would seem to conclusively prove that (1) While Stölzel and Herold were at the factory, the potting and the decoration were excellent. (2) As soon as they left, both the potting and the decoration became bad. This seems to prove that our illustrations shown here, having all of the attributes of the first and none of the second, are marked as the work of Stölzel and Herold at Vienna.

By 1725, a range of enamel colors had been developed, iron-red (which lacks the fiery tone of Meissen), green, purple, pink, yellow, and blue—in fact, almost the complete palette of the factory during its quarter of a century of life. The colors are delicate, almost pastel in tone, and contrast with the immensely strong baroque colors which were by this time developed at Meissen. The factory copied the Japanese designs, and Illustration 314a is a good example of the "Imari". (Compare with its Meissen counterpart, Illustration 246).

Schwarzlot was used extensively at Vienna from the earliest period and Illustration 309 shows the early type which had a sombre gray tone. Later it was more intense and high-lighted with gold and also monochrome colors. It was not used to any great extent at Meissen. Gold played a minor part in the decorations of Du Paquier, but decorations in monochrome colors were a favorite form of decoration. Silver, rarely used at Meissen, probably because of the unavoidable oxidation of the silver, was employed to a considerable extent in Vienna. Illustration 305 shows such a decoration, long since turned black. Chinoiseries, which played such an important part in the decorations at Meissen after the arrival of Herold, were not characteristic of the early production at Vienna, certainly not after the departure of Herold. The chinoiseries that we do find, painted either by the artist of the factory, or by the Hausmaler decorators, are not in the style of Herold. Mr. Hayward says that there is nothing intrinsically improbable in the suggestion that Herold, who introduced chinoiseries at Meissen, first developed them at Vienna. The Meissen Commission's report to the King, at the time that Herold first arrived at Meissen, indicate clearly that some of the pieces presented were in this style. A characteristic difference between the Herold chinoiseries at Meissen and the earlier ones at Vienna is pointed out by J. F. Hayward when he says: "Characteristic of the early Vienna chinoiserie decoration is the distribution of the figures over the whole surface of the piece without the confinement of a frame of scrollwork." The Meissen chinoiseries were set up within a cartouche and later reserved in white panels against a colored ground.

LAUB-UND BANDELWERK

While, as stated above, the early chinoiseries and other decorations at the Du Paquier factory did not have a frame for the picture as was customary at Meissen, we find that during the period of 1725-35 a very distinctive frame was developed which is characteristic of Vienna and has received the name of "Laub-und Bandel-werk." In commenting on the development of this baroque ornament, Mr. Hayward says: "The Du Paquier foliate strapwork ornament, splendid in general effect and yet composed in detail of the most delicately and exquisitely drawn scrolls and straps in iron-red, a soft-purple, blue and green, can without exaggeration be described as the most handsome and, I think, one of the most fitting forms of porcelain decoration that was ever achieved in eighteenth-century Europe. Though intended originally to serve as a border ornament only, and though doubtless seen at its best in this form (Plate 36), the Du Paquier strapwork could be so varied as to provide an answer to every problem of ornament. In its more ambitious forms, it covers the porcelain with a delicate web of color that stands up brilliantly from the white ground, enhancing the surface qualities of the material. Though ornament of this type is familiar enough on contemporary silver, and indeed in the whole field of applied art, it does not appear in a similar form on Meissen porcelain, and this fact in particular confirms my contention that most of the Du Paquier ornament was developed independently of Meissen. Elaborate foliate cartouches do indeed usually surround the figure subjects of Meissen chinoiseries, but these bear little resemblance to the Vienna ornament; firstly, because they are more light and feathery than the dignified Vienna strapwork, and secondly, because they are only intended to provide a rich frame for some figure subject and have no independent significance. In Vienna, strapwork was, on the other hand, not exclusively treated as a subsidiary ornament, but was formed into decorative compositions which had their own independent existence (Plate 34a and b)." We show here as Illustrations 313, 313a and 314, unusually fine examples of this style of ornamentation.

The figure subjects of this period were landscapes, biblical scenes, mythological subjects, putto subjects, hunting scenes and figure subjects in contemporary costume. They were usually executed in monochrome, even if enclosed within a cartouche of polychrome scrollwork. The favorite colors were puce, schwarzlot, high-lighted with purple and orange monochrome, without any gold whatever. The flower decoration, "Deutsche blumen," was outstanding for its colorful effects.

In the Oest Museum, Vienna, will be noted an unusually large collection of Du Paquier porcelains and also Vienna porcelain. A complete room from the palace of Count Dubsky at Bruin will here be seen, all in Du Paquier porcelain. The mantel, walls, fireplace, furniture, chandeliers and the space around the frieze are decorated with fifteen-hundred-and-seventy panels of porcelain, none of it marked. Innumerable porcelain vases, tea and chocolate cups, etc., are also used as decoration.

The factory also made a number of large dinner services. Illustration 316 shows probably the earliest, made for Prince Rohan, and Illustration 315 is quite similar. The most important one is known as the Jagd Service and is now in the Oest Museum. It was originally ordered for the use of the Austrian Imperial Court by the Emperor Charles VI (1685-1740) and was subsequently presented by the Empress Maria Theresa (1740-80) to the monastery of Sankt Blasien. It eventually came to the Corinthian monastery of Sankt Paul im Lavanttal, whence it was acquired for the Vienna Museum. Other similar services are known and described by J. F. Hayward and he dates the Jagd Service as not earlier than 1730-35. The Vienna Museum describes the service as the earliest made at the factory, but it does not hazard a guess as to the date. In general the decoration comprises animal subjects painted in schwarzlot, the borders in schwarzlot and gold. The border is very finely executed with a precision that is conspicuous by its absence among the early schwarzlot specimens. The same applies to the hunting subjects which occupy the central panels of the big dishes of the service; they are decorated in quite a different technique from the earlier pieces, which were painted in a free manner with a full brush. The design here was applied by means of hatching and shading as in an engraving, with the exception that the instrument used to apply the color had a blunter point. An unusual feature also is the complete absence of the trellis motif, which is otherwise an almost indispensable element of the later Du Paquier border designs.

In the absence of factory records, it is hard to be sure concerning the artists of the factory. It is believed that much of the decoration was done by Hausmaler and also by the regular painters who took undecorated pieces home and there decorated, and in many cases, sold them. It is certain that no set designs then in vogue at Meissen were practised here. In fact, one of the great charms noted in the decorations found on the porcelains produced at Vienna, is the complete absence of set design. As so much doubt and uncertainty exist as to the artists at Du Paquier, we must refer the reader to Mr. Hayward's book; but he appears rather averse to attribute anything definitely to any one artist except in the few cases where signed pieces are in existence, and even in those cases, he points out that as they are signed, and as the factory did not permit its painters to sign their work, such pieces were in all probability decorated outside the factory. The late Dr. E. W. Braun has made a few attributions, as has Gustave E. Pazaurek in his books on 'Hausmalerei.' But the truth of the matter is that no one can say with any degree of certainty which artists decorated at the Du Paquier factory, or what each painted even if he did work there. K. W. Anreiter, Anton F. J. Schulz, Joseph Philip Danhoffer, Christian Frey, Jakob Helchis, C. F. von Wolfburg, and the famous hausmaler Ignaz Bottengruber who, whether he worked there or not, certainly decorated many pieces of Vienna porcelain, and saw his style copied frequently on Du Paquier by other artists who may have worked there, all of whom certainly had some connection with the Vienna factory. Another well known group of Hausmaler who did not work at the Vienna factory but who surely decorated much of its porcelain were the Preusslers.

The production of independent figure sculpture was very limited at Du Paquier (Illustration 317 from the collection of Dr. Hans Syz is an interesting exception). However, a considerable proportion of Vienna porcelain during the baroque period was decorated with plastic ornament. This frequently consisted of standing figures sculptured and set upon some appropriate part of the object in question. These figures, rendered in the shape of naturalistic or fantastic animals, human beings, busts, Hermes and the like, have quite characteristic forms which bear slight relationship to the achievement of contemporary sculptors. There is no trace of the strong movement, wind-tossed draperies, and dramatic gestures that are regular features of Kändler's figures. J. Folnesics' introduction to the catalogue of the Mayer collection of

Viennese porcelain says that these figures resemble the creations of the confectioner, and it is quite possible that Du Paquier employed such people. It will be remembered that it was the function of the confectioner from the sixteenth until well on into the eighteenth century to provide table decorations in the form of figures and other conceits made of wax, sugar and tragacanth and the like for festive occasions of every kind, and especially for wedding feasts.

As previously stated, the Du Paquier factory did not mark its products. Certain potters' marks are, however, sometimes found only lightly incised, and it is easy to miss them if one does not look closely. The most frequently used marks are either a roughly incised vertical stroke, possibly intended to represent the number 1, or a Z which may be intended to represent the number 2. The figure 3 and, according to Braun, the figure 4, are also known, but are certainly far rarer than the 1 and 2. Occasionally initials, presumably those of the decorator, will be found painted over the glaze. Again the enamel colors seem to lie on the surface, which had a tendency to make them flake. This was true particularly in the early period. It was noted by Hauptmann Kühn that the foot rim of Du Paquier porcelain is frequently left very rough, just like the edges of common potters' clay, and it will be frequently so noted.

THE ROYAL VIENNA FACTORY (1744-1864)

Early in the year 1744, on the expiration of the Imperial patent, Du Paquier decided that it was impossible for him to carry on the work, and he therefore offered the factory to the State for purchase. The Empress Maria Theresa accepted his offer on the terms he had suggested, and took over the factory, the stock, and sufficient raw material supplies to last for four years, valued in all at 55,000 gulden. In return, the State agreed to pay off all creditors and to pay Du Paquier a salary of 15,000 florins a year to manage the factory. While the contract provided that he would remain as a manager Du Paquier applied for a pension in the same year and died on the 27th of December 1751.

Assured of Imperial protection, aided by good employees of every kind, the State factory now began to flourish under the directorship of Mayerhofer. A new deposit of kaolin clay was discovered at this time in Hungary which was superior to that formerly used, and a decree was issued that every article from that time on must be marked. As already mentioned, Du Paquier was never marked; now Vienna porcelain was always marked. The mark was the Bindenschild, or arms of the House of Austria, familiarly called today the "beehive" mark. From 1744 to 1749, the mark was painted as a rule in iron-red, purple or black but was also impressed or incised in the paste in a more or less irregular form. From 1749 to 1827, the mark was painted in under-glaze blue, for the first thirty or forty years somewhat slantways, rather large and in thick strokes. Between about 1770 and 1810 it became smaller, and at the same time symmetrically rounded in shape. After that, it was for a time long and narrow, and in the 1820's it was almost triangular. In 1827, the blue mark was superseded by the uncolored impressed mark which was now reinstated in a more regular shape than before. In 1783 impressed year-marks were introduced, the years prior to 1800 being indicated by the last two figures of their date, for example 86 for 1786; after 1800 by the last three figures, thus; 806 for 1806, etc. It must be pointed out that these marks point only to the date the porcelain was made and that it could have been decorated later. Also it must be noted that during the nineteenth and twentieth centuries, the marks were faked by other factories, (see *German and Austrian Porcelain*, by George W. Ware).

Every endeavor was now made to secure the most artistic talent and to introduce new models and colors, all in the rising Rococo taste. From Meissen came Christian Daniel Busch, who, however, soon went on to Nymphenburg. More successful was the importation of Johann Gottfried Klinger, also a Meissen painter, who remained in Vienna for over thirty years. A skilful chief painter was obtained in the person of Johann Sigismund Fischer, and a distinguished model-master was procured from the Vienna Academy, namely, Johann Joseph Niedermeyer (working from 1747 to 1784). Lastly, in 1750, a skilful but restless modeler was obtained in Ludwig Lücke, who, however, the very next year offered his services to Fürstenberg, and in 1752 turned up in Copenhagen like the incorrigible vagrant potter that he was.

The Europeanized chinoiseries, also those of Jean Pillement, for instance, still lived on in the factory, and were only superseded about 1770-80 by a new sort of Oriental style, an imitation of lacquer painting with Chinese motifs in gold in slight relief on a black or vermilion ground. The day of the great baroque scrolls was now past, and the black decoration was restricted to small, slight border ornament. During the next few years, the factory followed in almost every sphere the originals created by Meissen, and also continued to procure some of its best artistic talent from that source, including Philipp Ernst Schindler, to whom are ascribed its finest figure paintings of the period 1750-1760; these comprise scenes of gallantry after Watteau, cavalry skirmishes after Rugendas, and peasant subjects after Teniers.

Interest was now also awakened in figure-modeling like that of the Saxon factory. While during the Du Paquier period figure-modeling played a small part, now independent and group figures became important. Unfortunately, very few of the Viennese porcelain figures of the Rococo period can be ascribed to any particular artist. The work of Niedermeyer is better known. Its style lies in the innocent and untroubled air of the figures, in their light, as it were, slightly dancing movement and in the amiable smile of their little round heads. These are qualities more or less common to them all, whether they represent types from the street or from pastoral life, from the salon or the Court. The earliest figures followed the Meissen colors, but quickly developed a delicate, and by some thought insipid, coloring of their own. The style of the day, however, in all factories was to turn from the strong baroque colors to the softer pastel tones. The dominant hues at Vienna became a series of reds and browns in combinations with a pale violet, a light copper-green, a black, a yellow and gold. The Vienna bases of pancake form now assumed the peculiarity of being encircled either by a wavy acanthus stem in gold, or by a frieze of pendant gilt tongue motifs, also described as "cresting." Of these two modes of decoration the latter appears to be somewhat the older.

By 1760 there was a tendency away from the Rococo at Meissen and towards the influence of Sèvres, which by this time was taking the lead from Meissen, which had suffered badly from the effects of the Seven Years War. This tendency towards Sèvres was heightened by the union between the Austrian and French courts in the person of Marie Antoinette.

Despite the splendid success of the factory, by 1784 it was brought to the verge of bankruptcy and offered for sale by the State. No purchaser was found, but it was saved when Konrad von Sorgenthal assumed the directorship of the factory, a position which he held with distinction from 1784 to 1805. This period is thought by some to have been its golden age.

Niedermeyer was still the chief modeler, and other artists from the Academy of Arts were active. The finest representative of this level of culture is the sculptor, Anton Grassi, who was working at the factory as early as 1778, though it was only on the death of Niedermeyer in 1784, when he was made chief of the modeling department, that he had full scope to set the mark of his taste upon its productions.

Typical of the Vienna figures are Illustrations 319 and 320 from the series known as the Arts. One of the figures, representing Geography, includes two children, one looking into space with the help of a telescope and the other deep in the study of a map. The other figure is a representation of Music showing a child playing a flute. In each of the figures a very colorful monkey is included. They date about 1765, and the decoration is in the soft pastel tones of the period. Similar figures are shown in the Carl Mayer collection. Illustration 325 is a rather unusual one, representing Romulus and Remus, and was modeled by Niedermeyer about 1760. Illustrations 323, 322, 321 and 324 are the work of Niedermeyer around 1760 and are known as the "Wigmaker," the "Hairdresser," the "Tailor," and the "Personal Guard of Maria Theresa." We here show Illustration 326 known as the "Faint" and Illustration 327 known as the "Polish Musical Family," modeled around 1780, by Anton Grassi.

CHARACTERISTICS OF DU PAQUIER PORCELAIN

1. The porcelain before Stölzel, brownish both to the eye and by transmitted light; after Stölzel in 1719 either creamy to the eye or by transmitted light; or green by transmitted light and gray-white to the eye, both kinds made contemporaneously.

2. "Moons" and "tears," usually found in all types.

3. No factory marks; a lightly incised 1 or 2 frequently encountered, rarely 3 or 4; these probably potters' marks.

4. Enamel colors, pastel shades in early period had tendency to peel off as did the gold. Enamel at all periods had tendency to lie on surface.

5. No cartouches used to frame chinoiseries.

6. "Laub-und Bandelwerk," a beautiful foliated strapwork intended originally as border, characteristic of this factory; introduced 1725-35.

7. Schwarzlot and other monochromes usual type decoration, gold sparingly used but silver frequently.

8. Little known about artists; paintings fresh as no set types prescribed by the factory.

9. Four principal styles of decoration; chinoiseries in Herold style, only while he was there, or Japanese designs; "Laub-und Bandelwerk;" motives frequently in schwarzlot; German flowers, putti, etc.

10. Pieces decorated by Hausmaler.

CHARACTERISTICS OF ROYAL VIENNA PORCELAIN

1. Nearly always marked with the shield of Austria.

2. Copied Meissen in the early period, later Sèvres.

3. From 1783, date numerals impressed or incised.

4. Europeanized chinoiseries continued until 1770, then gave way to imitations of Chinese paintings on lacquer. The great baroque scroll work was then over.

5. By 1760, tendency was away from the Rococo and towards the Neo-Classical.

6. While few figures were made at Du Paquier, many were made after 1760 at Vienna; many of the finest up to 1784 were by Niedermeyer and after that date by Anton Grassi.

THE SIX MAJOR GERMAN FACTORIES
(after MEISSEN)

The following six important German porcelain manufactories came into operation mainly as the result of the activity of absconding artists, workmen and arcanists from the Vienna factory.

1. Höchst (1746-1796), arcanist Johann Benckgraff.
2. Fürstenberg (1753-1859), arcanist Benckgraff. Private ownership after 1859.

3. Nymphenburg (1753-present), arcanist J. J. Ringler.
4. Wegely (1752-1757); Gotzkowsky (1761-1763); Berlin (1763-present), arcanist Benckgraff.
5. Frankenthal (1755-1799), arcanists J. J. Ringler and Joseph Hannong.
6. Ludwigsburg (1758-1824), arcanist J. J. Ringler.

We have seen that the Meissen deserter Stölzel made available to Vienna his knowledge of the arcanum as well as the equally important knowledge of how to construct and operate the kilns for making porcelain. When he in turn took to Meissen with him the gifted Vienna painter Gregor Herold, he fully repaid this debt. It must also be remembered that it was renegade arcanists from Vienna and not Meissen, who spread the knowledge of porcelain production to the six factories above, as well as to other lesser ones. Ringler's associate at Höchst, Johann Benckgraff, sold the arcanum or secret of porcelain, first in 1752 to Wegely (later Berlin) and in 1753 to Fürstenberg, where he died in the same year. Ringler went on to sell the secret to the others.

HÖCHST (1746-1796)

The first in point of age of these six factories was Höchst. We here again encounter the controversial Meissen painter Adam Friedrich von Löwenfinck, who ten years earlier had fled from the Meissen factory, gone to Bayreuth, Fulda, and possibly to the French factory of Chantilly. Now we find him in company with two Frankfurt merchants applying to the Elector of Mainz in 1746 for the privilege of carrying on a porcelain factory at Höchst. E. Hannover says that Löwenfinck had been forced to leave Meissen on account of debts and fraudulent transactions; nevertheless, he and his syndicate were granted the privilege requested for a period of fifty years, and in addition the right of using the wheel from the Electoral Arms as a factory mark. Soon, however, strife arose among the directors of the factory, and in 1749 Löwenfinck was obliged to resign, after which he sought a new refuge in Strasburg.

His successor as arcanist was the renegade migrant Johann Benckgraff, who we will see hurriedly left Höchst in 1753 for Fürstenberg, after previously selling his secret process, his kiln model, and himself to the Duke of Brunswick for a fee of 200 guilders. It was not until 1765 that the factory was restored to a sound footing. The next and last Elector of Mainz, Friedrich Karl Joseph took a keen interest in the factory, but the shareholders exploited it, and in 1778 he was forced to take it over. This did not help matters financially, however, and in 1796 the factory was closed and its effects sold two years later at public auction to Daniel Ernst Müller at Damm who made figures from the old molds and added a D to the mark. In addition, many such figures were made of faience, and today a new firm is producing porcelain ones in some quantity. No one with experience should be misled by either kind; but, sad to say, this is not the case with the old ones.

The Höchst mark, a wheel with six (occasionally five) spokes, occurs on pieces up to about 1770, with or without an Electoral hat above it, sometimes impressed in the paste, sometimes painted over the glaze in black, brown, purple, iron-red or gold. From 1770 it is found almost exclusively in under-glaze blue. The early pieces are marked with a red wheel only, on top of the glaze. E. Hannover calls attention to pieces with the monograms of Löwenfinck and Zeschinger; the former, strangely enough, in the light of Ralph H. Wark's research, is *A.L.* and not *F.v.L.*

In services and single pieces of useful ware Höchst produced practically nothing that had not been already modeled at Meissen. Probably the most characteristic decoration of this factory was the use of a purple approaching carmine, usually in landscapes in monochrome. Illustration 400 depicts such a piece. This factory copied from Meissen chinoiseries, "Indian" and "German" flowers, "Mosaik" patterns and others. Illustration 401 shows an example of the early "German" flower painting at its best.

While Höchst is not noted for its useful ware, it has been thought by some authorities to rank third among the German factories in the excellence of figures. Some uncertainty exists as to the identity of the modeler of certain early pieces. Illustration 328 for example, is thought to have been modeled by Simon Feilner, who made similar pieces at Fürstenberg. This figure has the red wheel mark and dates c. 1755. In W. B. Honey's *German Porcelain*, 1947, is shown as Plate 32 a Höchst figure of the same date and general style of setting. Honey attributes it probably to the modeler J. F. Lück, who also modeled similar specimens at Ludwigsburg and Frankenthal. It will be noted, however, that the figures in the Lück piece have round chubby faces, quite unlike the one shown here.

Nos. 332 to 333e illustrate twelve figures representing Italian Comedy characters and probably modeled by Simon Feilner, 1750-53. (In the collection of Mr. and Mrs. Edward M. Pfleuger of New York.)

Illustration 18 shows a miniature figure of Columbine from the Italian Comedy. The size is unusual for this factory. The mark is a red wheel and we date the piece c. 1755. E. Hannover refers to a group of miniature figures from the Italian Comedy as having the initials of Löwenfinck or Zeschinger on them. He illustrates as No. 252, a figure of Columbine dated 1746-1749 in the Kaiser Fredrich Museum, Berlin. The piece shown here may be of the same period and date. Illustrations 17 and 19 in color (Boys playing with Goat and Violin) are also shown in Kurt Röder's book and are there dated 1755. They are charming figures.

From 1762 to 1766, Laurentius Russinger was master-modeler at the factory, and the porcelain modeling of that time exhibits, both in style and in regard to its coloring, some kinship with the productions of Frankenthal under J. A. Hannong. This may be explained by the fact that the modeler Johann Friedrich Lück spent some time at Höchst before going to Frankenthal in 1758. Russinger departed in 1767 for Pfalz-Zweibrücken. So it will be seen that good traditions for porcelain modeling were already in existence when the sculptor Johann Peter Melchior arrived in 1767 at the age of twenty-five. He had already had some experience as a sculptor for in 1769 the Berlin factory tried to secure his services. It is not surprising therefore that in 1770 he was made Court Sculptor and about this period created his most important figures. He later became master-modeler at Frankenthal.

A reaction had by this date set in against the Rococo style, and so Melchior created one of his own and thus became an artist of importance; beyond question he played the leading part in making the figures of this factory famous. He found a new expression of all the phenomena of life in so far as children are concerned and his works are fresh and as a rule distinguished by a multitude of lively traits which make them the finest products of his hand. They are also free from the unnatural style of the previous period. Illustration 342, known as the "Beggar Musicians" is of the period of 1768 and is from the collection of Mrs. C. B. Stout, which is one of the most comprehensive collections of Höchst in private ownership today. Illustration 337 (seated girl) is also of the period 1768, and Illustration 329 is known as the "Chinese Emperor." Colored Illustrations 21, 22 and 23 (two Sultans and a Sultana) are of the period 1770 and certainly represent some of Melchior's best work. One of the Sultans has a green robe which is quite unusual as Melchior seemed to prefer the color pink. Illustrations 330 and 331, "The Disturbed Sleeper" and "Children at Play," are among his best known pieces (c. 1770), and Illustrations 334, 335, 336, 338 and 339 (five in all) are also typical of his style; the boy eating an apple is unusual in that his coat is of a blue color not often found in such figures.

FÜRSTENBERG (1753-1859; (private ownership 1859 to present day))

The Fürstenberg factory was founded by the reckless Duke Karl I of Brunswick, with the technical assistance of the Vienna arcanist Johann Benckgraff, the painter Zeschinger, and the master-modeler Simon Feilner, all from Höchst. The early table wares and vases are remarkable for delicate Rococo patterns in relief, due probably to the necessity to cover up imperfections in the porcelain. The paste and glaze materials came from far away Passau, and the early products were dull in color and frequently marred by impurities. After 1770 the quality was greatly improved. Though after this period an admirable palette of enamel colors, including rich blackish-green and purple, a clear yellow and a warm brown with rich gilding, was freely used, collectors have not been too interested in it. Many modelers were employed, including Johann Christoph Rombrich (1758-1794), Anton Karl Luplau (1778-1804), and P. Hendler; nevertheless the production of figures was limited, primarily because of difficulties in manipulating the paste. In addition to the list of modelers the records show that the following decorators were employed: Andreas Oest, Johann Heinrich Eisenträger, C. G. Albert, Christ Luplau, Johann Friedrich Weitsch, and Heinrich Christian Brüning.

Probably the best figures made, in addition to the Italian Comedy figures by Feilner, were smaller versions of these figures by Rombrich and his assistants and some fine minature models, three of which we here show as Illustrations 365, 366 and 367; they date c. 1770. (For Italian Comedy figures, see Otto Blohm catalogue).

The factory mark, a capital F in script, is painted in blue under the glaze on most items. These marks have been copied on modern fakes but are not identical. For a comparison see page 107 of *German and Austrian Porcelain*, 1953 by George Ware.

NYMPHENBURG (1747 to present day)

The Bavarian Elector Maximilian III Joseph, who married the granddaughter of Augustus the Strong, like so many other German princes of the eighteenth century, regarded the possession of a porcelain factory as almost indispensable to his estate. He therefore lent a willing ear when a Munich potter Niedermayer offered to establish a factory, and provided him in 1747 with a site in the suburbs of Munich. General production did not begin until 1753 in spite of the presence of three workmen from Vienna, and it was not until the arrival of Joseph Jakob Ringler that production got under way. He was discharged, however, in 1757, and became director at Ludwigsburg in 1758. In 1761, the factory was moved to the Nymphenburg Palace grounds in Munich, where it is still operating under private ownership of the Bäuml family and where many of the old forms of figures are reproduced today.

By 1765 Nymphenburg had taken its place among the major factories, with three hundred men on its payroll. Difficulties came, however, with the general economic troubles of the early 'seventies and the death of Maximilian III Joseph in 1777. His successor was a relative, Elector Karl Theodor, who was no stranger to the manufacture of porcelain, since he owned the thriving Frankenthal factory, which he favored over Nymphenburg. When he died, however, in 1799, Maximilian IV Joseph closed the Frankenthal factory and combined it with that of Nymphenburg.

The porcelain of the best period is consistently white and fine-grained, though the glaze occasionally inclines to a green or grey where pooled in the hollows. The table-wares of the early period were admirable, showing an airy Rococo style recalling the contemporary architecture of the Nymphenburg palaces. Naturalistic flowers, fruits, birds, and figures in landscapes in the style of Nilson and Teniers, were done in the Meissen manner, but with a distinctive treatment of the foreground. All show a sensitive touch and fine color; a warm red was used for the face, and a soft green monochrome was sometimes employed. The lacework borders in gilt, pink, and pale blue enamel are also very good. Illustration 456 shows the useful ware of the best period.

This factory, however, owed its great renown almost exclusively to its plastic work, or, more correctly, to a single artist who was, in one sense, the greatest master of porcelain modeling the world has yet seen. Compared with Kändler, the mightiest and most prolific of all, Franz Anton Bustelli, is, it is true, but a minor spirit, narrowly limited in taste and style. In contrast to Kändler, Bustelli knew how to express himself in plastic formulas so well adapted to, and compatible with, the very nature of porcelain that they would be unthinkable in any other material, and today appear, alone of their kind, as having lasting vitality.

Bustelli for barely ten years (1754-1763) worked in the service of Bavaria. In commenting on this great artist, who died in 1763, it has been said that he appeared without warning from the unknown, wrought wondrously for a decade, and then returned from whence he came, leaving behind him no record of himself except in the creations of his hand and soul. This much is certain, however, that his style was not developed out of nothing, any more than that of any other great artist. Bustelli created single figures or groups in which elegance appears innate, inasmuch as they represent the gentlefolk of his own time, with their good manners or their graceful mannerisms. Some of his figures represent a gentleman kissing the lady's fingers, a lady flirting half hidden by her fan, a lady taking a few dance steps or running from a dog which has fixed its teeth in her dress and has torn a rent in it. In all of these it is the momentary play of feature, and even more the spontaneous movement which has interested Bustelli. Of groups consisting of several figures he produced only a few. Evidently, it was the single figure or the group of two figures in which the movement of the one forms a single unit with that of the other, that chiefly attracted him. To sum up his style in a single word we have only to say *movement*.

Of all his figures certainly the ones most admired today are his single figures of the Italian Comedy. He is supposed to have made a set of sixteen. Nine of these in color will be found in the Munich Museum and eight also in color will be found in the superb Kocher collection in the Berne Historical Museum in Berne, Switzerland, who have been kind enough to permit us to show here six of his most important pieces, Illustrations 356 to 361. As will be seen, four of them are actresses from the Italian Comedy in the persons of Columbine, Isabella, Arlequina, and Lalage; and the other two represent actors Octavio and Mezzetino. Not only are the grace, charm and movement of these figures breath-taking, but the paste, glaze, and colors are so fine that once one has had the great privilege of seeing them, one will never be deceived by later reproductions. (Six such figures in the late 1950's brought $100,000 in the London auction rooms).

Many charming figures were left white, and the "repairer," P. A. Seefried (1756-1766 and 1768-1810), who assembled the figures during Bustelli's lifetime, continued to do so after his death in 1763. The later ones, even when made from the original molds, may be recognized by the expert. More of the later ones are to be found in the white and it is thought that new molds in the style of Bustelli were later made. Many of all types will be found in the great Museum in Munich, where the later ones are captioned as "in the style" of Bustelli and the original early ones are designated as "by Bustelli."

After the death of Bustelli in 1763, a Bohemian, Dominikus Jacob Auliczek (born 1734), became master-modeler at the Nymphenburg factory. He had behind him a long academic training as a sculptor when he came to Munich in 1762, and found plenty to do, first as successor to Bustelli, later with commissions for a series of statues for the palace park at Nymphenburg. Both these and the figures of gods, allegories of the elements, the Continents, etc., which he executed during the next few years for the factory itself, show that he belonged to the academic eclectics of the age, who were well up in anatomy and other branches of knowledge which porcelain did not call for, but were unacquainted with all its special requirements. Illustration 362 shows Asia, from a series of the Continents, and depicts St. Simon Stylites, in a manner quite typical of Auliczek's art.

WEGELY, GOTZKOWSKY AND BERLIN (1752 to present day)

These three factories are here treated together, since the second grew out of the first, and the third out of the second. Frederick the Great was no different from the other kings of the eighteenth century in owning a porcelain collection and wanting to own a factory for producing it. Illustration 118 shows a fine specimen of blanc-de-chine that was in his collection before finding its way into the Royal Collection in Dresden. So when in 1752 Wilhelm Kaspar Wegely, a wool merchant, offered to start a factory in Berlin with the assistance of Johann Benckgraff, the Vienna arcanist, he received every encouragement from the King in the way of privileges and com-modious premises. At the outbreak of the Seven Years War, Wegely hoped to secure workmen and models from Meissen. But Frederick, dissatisfied with Wegely's porcelain, planned himself to start a new factory with Meissen help. Wegely there-fore closed his factory in 1757.

Wegely's porcelain was white and of good quality, made from the same clay as Meissen (Aue), but its exceedingly hard body and glaze gave trouble with the enamels, and unpainted specimens form a large part of the surviving pieces. His head modeler was Ernst Heinrich Reichardt and his chief painter Isaac-Jacques Clauce from Meissen. His tableware followed Meissen and had no great distinction, frequently using Watteau subjects in purple monochrome. On the whole, however, the figure repertory of this factory is different from that of Meissen and has a great deal of character. Reichardt is presumed to have been the modeler. His figures are unassuming, consisting mostly of bourgeois peasants and artisans, gardeners, hunters, and their womenfolk. They have a certain directness of observation and freshness in execution. Illustration 377 shows a gardener in color and is certainly well done. For the most part, however, they are plain white, and when painted the colors are strong and pure, with unbroken tints, like those of Meissen at its best period.

Wegely's mark is a W written in four strokes, generally painted in under-glaze blue, more rarely impressed or incised. We find on his porcelain, in addition (and on the figures almost regularly), three numerals impressed with stamps; the upper-most one apparently refers to the paste used, the lowest to the model. No one has yet been able to explain the significance of the figure in the middle, which is often 90.

When the Wegely factory closed in 1757, Frederick the Great was not yet ready to establish a factory of his own. In 1761 a Prussian financier named Gotzkowsky bought the secret of porcelain from Reichardt, who had been with Wegely, and started a factory in Berlin with the help of artists from Meissen, including F. E. Meyer, who became chief modeler, and the painters Carl W. Bohme, J. B. Borrmann, and K. J. C. Klipfel, as well as the miniaturist I. J. Clauce, formerly at Wegely. The paste was yellowish-grey, but the quality was reasonably good. While few pieces are known today, a considerable quantity of useful ware was made. Illustration 383 shows a cup and saucer of this period and the decoration is in a puce monochrome. The mark is a script G, which is found on these examples. The factory was sold to the King in 1763 and has remained state property to the present day.

Frederick the Great above all else wanted to make Berlin porcelain equal or superior to that of Meissen, which factory during the Seven Years War he had done so much to ruin. As neither Wegely nor Gotzkowsky was able to achieve this end he tried his own hand at the task. Georg Grieninger was made director of the royal Berlin factory in 1763 and served in this capacity until his death in 1798, but King Frederick himself was the actual manager of the factory and was therefore responsible for its financial and artistic achievements and failures. The best period was from 1763 to the death of Frederick in 1786. He placed large orders with the factory for important services for his palaces. These are in fact among its best work. The porcelain was at first made from the Passau clay and was then creamy in tone. From 1765-1770, however, Silesian and Prussian clay gave it a cold white color. The predilection at Berlin for a dominant note among the colors led naturally to a marked tendency towards painting *en camaieu*, or with a single color, or with two at the most, such as iron-red and gold, or pink and gray, which combination was a peculiarity of the factory.

Frederick the Great had hoped and believed that his porcelain factory was in every way the equal of Meissen. Again and again he expressed himself to this effect, when sending gifts of his porcelain to relatives or to friendly princes. But, however great the merit of his factory in its best years, its contribution to art can never be compared with that of Meissen. Quite apart from the great debt it owed to Meissen, it was poor indeed by comparison.

Of its plastic work as represented by its figures and groups it again fell short not only of Meissen, but likewise of other German factories. Friedrich Elias Meyer was the master-modeler and did most of the work, or at least was responsible for the designs. His younger brother, Wilhelm Christian Meyer, who was associated with the factory from 1766, was a more accomplished modeler than his brother. We owe to him, besides a long series of figures of children with allegorical significance, a series of Muses and other mythological figures and allegorical groups, which like the apotheosis of 1770 relating to the marriage of the Dauphin and Marie Antoinette, are indeed more French than German in style, but, on the other hand, fine and distinguished in taste. Illustrations 374 and 375 show two children modeled by him from a series of the Twelve Months.

FRANKENTHAL (1755-1799)

Paul Anton Hannong, who at the time was operating a faience factory at Strasburg, began operations at Frankenthal in 1755. With the help of the arcanist J. J. Ringler he had started to make hard-paste porcelain at Strasburg but had been stopped by the French authorities because the State, in the interest of the monopoly for the Vincennes factory, forbade other factories to decorate their wares. The Elector Karl Theodor was delighted to have the porcelain factory and gave Hannong the privilege of establishing it at Frankenthal near Mannheim. The factory was operated by Hannong's two sons in turn as the father remained at Strasburg. Upon Karl's death in 1757 his brother, a modeler, ran the business until 1759 when he purchased it from his father. He sold it to the Elector in 1762, who employed Adam Bergdoll as director until 1775, in which year Simon Feilner replaced him. Feilner had served rather prominently as modeler with other major factories. Following the French wars the factory was confiscated in 1795 and leased to Peter van Recum. It was closed in 1799 when its best artists and workmen went to Nymphenburg. Some of its models were purchased by Nymphenburg, which reproduced some of the figures.

The Frankenthal paste from 1755-1775, made from Passau clay, was white, smooth, excellent in quality, and the glaze was nearly opaque. Illustration 396 shows a bowl of the early period. At times the paste resembled the French and English soft-paste. Illustration 341 shows a gravy boat having the Karl Theodor mark. Both paste and glaze are actually fairly soft to the file and except for the mark could be taken for English Chelsea. Illustration 389 is one of a pair of cups decorated in the style of Watteau, with the Karl Theodor mark; again we note the fine opaque glaze having the appearance of soft-paste; however, in this case the porcelain is quite hard to the file. It was the opinion of W. B. Honey that at their best the "Frankenthal tableware and vases were beautifully finished and were often painted with elaborate figure-subjects of a kind seldom attempted elsewhere in Germany, as well as in versions of the more ordinary Meissen styles. Three artists are known by their signed pieces: Jacob Winterstein (1758-1781) painted subjects after David Teniers amongst others, Jakob Osterspei (1759-1782) mythological scenes. The decorative designs are remarkable for chintz-patterns and gilt-striped grounds; trellis and other diapers show a fondness for crimson and green in combination. Cabaret sets were a favorite form, comprising teapot and teacups, cream-jug and sugar basin, on a lozenge-shaped tray." The influence of Sèvres, always in evidence, became stronger in the last period of the factory, with *oeil-de-perdrix* styles and exotic birds in panels. The factory closed before the Empire style became popular. During its best period it was influenced by the Rococo and later by the Neo-Classic.

Like the other South German factories its greatest claim to fame rests with its plastic art. According to E. Hannover, "the porcelain figures of Frankenthal appear to be highly valued among collectors, though not in the same degree as those of Meissen. Even Konrad Link does not, of course occupy a position like Bustelli, not to speak of the modelers of less importance who worked at the Palatine factory." However, this factory did make more than eight hundred figures and six hundred different items were on exhibition in Munich in 1909. It produced more figures than any other establishment in the same period. Hannong's first master-modeler, Johann Wilhelm Lanz (1755-1761), made highly creditable figures under the influence of Meissen models. Illustration 348 shows the "Sitting Cello Player," modeled by Lanz in 1755. It has the Lion mark and impressed PH (this piece was expertized by the late Dr. E. W. Braun.). Lanz's successor, Johann Friedrich Lück (1758-1764), who had previously worked at Meissen and Höchst, as George Ware says, modeled "similar but more elaborate and fashionable figures with rounder cheeks and a slight air of stiffness."

In 1762 when Karl Theodor acquired the factory, he employed court sculptor Konrad Link, who created classical and allegorical subjects, portrait-busts and other figures of high merit, some in attractive colors, and some in white. Illustration 354 shows a figure modeled by his hand, from the Seasons series, and Illustration 447 shows a fine pair representing two of the twelve months. Karl Gottlieb Lück succeeded him in 1766 and was responsible for the production (1760-1775) of large quantities of small figures and groups. Frankenthal figures enjoyed their golden age during this fifteen-year period. Illustration 350 shows one of his more pretentious figures known as "Shepherd and Shepherdess." Illustrations 343 to 346 show an outstanding group of Chinese musicians; Illustrations 347 and 349 show other Chinese figures. Illustration 352 shows a sculptor, and Illustration 351 represents "Boy Feeding Lamb." Also by the same hand are Winter and Summer from the Four Seasons, Illustrations 353 and 355. Lück was succeeded by Adam Bauer (1775-1779), and he in turn by Johann Peter Melchior, who had gained distinction at Höchst, but served at Frankenthal until 1793 without surpassing the work of his distinguished predecessors. The last master-modeler of Frankenthal was Landolin Ohmacht, who followed Melchior. While the figures of Frankenthal are highly valued by collectors, they are not considered comparable with those created by Kändler and Bustelli.

The marks of the factory at the earliest period were the letters PH for Paul Hannong, and under-glaze blue lion, or a lozenge-shield. Under Karl Theodor, 1762-1795, the mark is CT, his initials (Charles T.) beneath a crown. The old Frankenthal marks of Karl Theodor also carry numerals showing the year of production. When Nymphenburg reproduces these figures it adds the impressed shield of Nymphenburg so as not to mislead anyone.

LUDWIGSBURG (1758-1824)

Karl Eugen, the "free-spending and luxury-loving" Duke of Württemberg, like other rulers of the day, wanted a porcelain factory of his own. In 1758 he secured the services of that roving arcanist from Vienna, J. J. Ringler, and contrary to his previous behavior, Ringler remained director for forty years. The return of the court to Stuttgart in 1775 and the Duke's death in 1793 marked the stages in its decline. In vain did Elector Frederick, afterward king of Württemberg, try to revive the factory; but by 1824 it was, of necessity, closed.

It was found necessary to transport the clay from near Passau, which was a considerable distance away, and in spite of the proficiency of Ringler the porcelain produced at this factory was rarely white, but more often smoky-hued or yellowish-gray. A variety of table wares were produced with rocaille ornament in relief. During the best period, 1758-1770, the Rococo style was used, and a basket-weave pattern known as "osier" was usual. Illustration 394 shows a typical teapot decorated with a landscape in purple monochrome and showing the characteristic pair of C's overlapped back to back with a crown, in under-glaze blue. The paste has a soft yellow or creamy tone. From 1770 the styles became Neo-Classical and finally Empire.

Again we find the figures the preference of the Duke and the principal interest of the factory. A great many models were made, and it is not easy to assign them to particular artists. According to Adolf Brüning, the early designs were copied from Meissen counterparts in the Duke's collection. Be that as it may, the factory also produced many original models that showed imagination and inspiration, probably provided by the great luxury of the Ludwigsburg court. Gottlieb Friedrich Riedel, who had worked at Meissen and other major factories, was the chief designer of all types of porcelain, 1759-1779. Johann Göz was at the factory briefly (1759-1762), and the court sculptors, Ferretti and Lejeune, are credited with modeling for the factory at intervals, 1762-1767; likewise, a repairer under Riedel, 1762-1767, Jean-Jacques Louis of Namur is thought to have modeled a series of animals and lively dancing figures with Rococo bases. He may very well be responsible for the delightful diminutive groups, including the so-called "Venetian Fair" figures, which were suggested by the Duke himself, who in 1767 had visited Venice. These groups in some cases compare favorably with the best figures produced by any of the South German factories. Illustrations 363 and 364 are known as the "Apple Vendor" and the "Turnip Vendor." Dr. E. W. Braun dated these figures as among the earliest produced at the factory but would not hazard an opinion as to the modeler. Illustrations 371 and 372 are known as the "Man with Turkey" and the "Woman with Turkey"; the latter is shown by O. Wanner-Brandt in *Alt Ludwigsburg* (1906) in Fig. 281. The late Dr. E. W. Braun also places the date of these as among the factory's earliest products, but fails to name the modeler except to remark "Modeler of Folk Type." These figures as was the case of the preceding two have the crossed C's and coronet as a mark in under-glaze blue. Illustrations 369 and 368 of "Shepherd" and "Shepherdess" date about 1765-1770, and are shown as Nos. 249 and 250 by Leo Balet in his *Ludwigsburger Porzellan*. Again Dr. Braun does not assign a modeler. The six figures illustrated are very typical of early Ludwigsburg, and while some of the bases are in the rocaille style, the figures have none of the carefree exuberance of the Rococo, but are certainly in the Baroque style. The figures usually have a certain character about them that makes them noteworthy and easily attributed to this factory, even if we cannot be sure of the name of the modeler.

We now come to an entirely different group of figures, and in connection with them we have no difficulty in naming the modeler. In 1764 the famous court sculptor Johann Christian Wilhelm Beyer was placed in charge of the modeling, and immediately made his influence felt upon the style prevailing at Ludwigsburg. His style was Rococo and classical, and he had a preference for large figures. The great variety of his figures includes fishermen, singers, wine drinkers, classical characters, musicians, fortune tellers; some exceptionally fine figures based on ancient mythology are shown by E. Hannover. Illustration 373 shows one of his best and is known as "Satyr and Bachante" or "Bacchus and Woman." Dr. Braun dates the figure 1765 and names Beyer as the modeler. Illustration 370 is known as "Hunting Group," is dated 1765 and is probably by Beyer. Later figures are of little interest to collectors, probably because Beyer left Ludwigsburg in 1767.

THE LESSER GERMAN FACTORIES

Fulda 1764-1790.
Ansbach 1758-1860.
Kelsterbach 1761-1802.
Ottweiler 1763-1775.
Cassel 1766-1788.
Gutenbrunn (Pfalz-Zweibrücken) 1767-1775.
Wurzburg 1775-1780.

NOTE: See *German and Austrian Porcelain*, by George W. Ware for the names of about twenty more factories; also for nineteenth and twentieth century factories and their additional marks.

Space will not permit even a digest of these factories; however, it may be said that they created many figures and some useful wares of much artistic value. Fulda figures in particular are quite collectable, as are many others. Illustration 16 shows a figure known as "Turk," modeled in 1760 after a French engraving by Ferriol, by the Ansbach factory. Illustration 386 shows a well decorated cup and saucer with the name of the factory which made it, Pfalz-Zweibrücken, in under-glaze blue and Illustration 378 shows a typical Gera figure, known as the "Hun Family." The porcelain is yellow but the modeling is fairly good. It has an under-glaze G mark. Wallendorf is another of these factories and at one period made some fine useful ware as shown by Illustration 340 from the collection of Mrs. H. C. Isaacson Sr. Among the best of the figures made in Thuringia were those of Kloster Veilsdorf. An example is Illustration 376 from the Italian Comedy, "Mezzetino as a Painter."

The Thuringian factories are similar to the English Staffordshire ones in that both were strictly commercial, catering to the middle and peasant class. Seven of these factories were owned by the Greiner family. The Gera factory started in 1763 and has continued to operate to the present day. Fuel and kaolin clay were plentiful in Thuringia.

CHAPTER 3

SCANDINAVIAN, SWISS AND OTHER CONTINENTAL FACTORIES

THE COPENHAGEN FACTORY

The Danish author, Emil Hannover, in his authoritative *Pottery and Porcelain* introduces the subject of the porcelain of his native country with this statement: "And now we come to the old royal Copenhagen factory, which naturally must lie particularly near to the heart of the Danish writer. Whilst it would, of course, be out of place here to write its final monograph, which still remains to be done, we may perhaps allow it a somewhat disproportionate amount of space." He then proceeds to discuss in great detail for more than fifty pages the history of this factory. In finally summing up its accomplishments, he has not let his love of the Danish porcelain affect his good judgment. He says: "Danish collectors seem to be even more interested in the purely plastic productions of the factory, its many groups and figures, than in the old Copenhagen tea sets, vases, flowerpots, mugs, inkstands, etc., and as a rule, without sufficient reason. For, though the most artistic of the Copenhagen 'useful' porcelain of the eighteenth century will bear comparison with corresponding German ware of the same period, and the same applies to many of the plastic-architectural decorative pieces, the Copenhagen groups and figures are, as a rule, stiff, awkward and devoid of grace; with few exceptions they are far inferior not only to those of Meissen, but even to many of the minor German factories."

The first attempts to found a porcelain factory at Copenhagen are shrouded in mystery. There is some evidence that Mehlhorn from Meissen established a factory in 1756. About 1760, a Frenchman named Louis Fournier was making soft-paste there, but his work was short-lived. A hard-paste factory was established by a chemist named Müller in 1772. It was not a commercial success, and so in 1775 the State took over the factory. In 1853 Bing and Grondahl started another factory, specializing in modern porcelain; although tourists seem to be interested, it certainly is of little interest to collectors. The factory mark is known as the three wavy lines, indicating the three belts of sea which divide the islands of Zealand and Funen from Jutland.

MARIEBERG

Swedish porcelain is confined to three classes made at Marieberg; a soft artificial ware resembling French Mennecy, made about 1770 and marked MB in monogram; true porcelain marked with the three crowns of Sweden, about 1780; and a hybrid porcelain, also marked with the three crowns and in addition the emblem of the royal house of Vasa. The industry seems to have come to an end in 1782. It is true that Jean E. L. Ehrenreich applied to the Swedish Government as early as 1758 for the privilege of making true porcelain and did some experimenting with it. Marieberg faience is, of course, well known.

The painted porcelain of this factory is usually tastefully executed, and E. Hannover considers it greatly superior to the plastic productions made there. These figures include some of the well known characters from the Italian Comedy and mythological beings, but for the most part, they consist of subjects from daily life. When executed in soft-paste, the figures have a certain charm. They are for the most part unpainted but are not infrequently found with a polychrome decoration, generally restricted to a dotting of the dresses with spots of different colors. The eyes are so executed as to give them unusual prominence.

ZÜRICH

The Zürich Porcelain and Faience Factory founded in 1763 and situated at Schören near Bendlikon was conceived by a number of Zürich men, among them the famous poet and painter, Solomon Gessner. Compared with the many earlier European factories founded and subsidized by the nobility, Zürich was a stock issuing company with the aim of giving work to many needy citizens. Its first Director was Adam Spengler, a native of Schaffhausen. Production was started late in 1764 with sales beginning in 1765. Solomon Gessner furnished many of the drawings for the landscape paintings on table ware and even did some of the decorating himself. Sales could not keep up with production, however, and in 1791 it was decided to dissolve the company. In 1793, a former employee, Matthias Nehracher, a son-in-law of Spengler, took over the factory.

At the beginning it produced some good soft-paste porcelain, a fact which seems strange, since at that time the formula for producing hard-paste porcelain was well known. The latter product during the factory's prime (1775-1790) distinguishes itself for its fine cream color.

The groups and single figures produced by Zürich follow the lines of other European factories. We find, to some extent, very charming Shepherds, Gardeners, Street Criers, and Mariners, and also single figures or groups of everyday folk. The most important modelers of the factory were Valentin Sonnenschein and Jacob Spengler, the son of the factory's Director. Jacob Spengler left in 1790 for the Derby factory, becoming one of its best modelers.

Zürich porcelain itself often shows impurities in the paste and firing cracks. As a mark, the letter Z in under-glaze blue is used. Many of the figures, however, carry no marking.

After the death of Nehracher, Hans Jacob Nägeli took over the factory in 1803. Today there still operates in the same buildings a pottery plant. An excellent account of the manufactory and its varied productions is given in *Die Zürcher Porzellanmanufaktur* recently published by Dr. Siegfried Ducret of Zürich. Illustrations 379 to 382 show figures made at this factory and they are all from the collection of Dr. Siegfred Ducret.

NYON

A small manufactory was established here towards the end of the eighteenth century by a French flower-painter named Maubrée, who had left the royal works at Sèvres. The paste is of good quality, the paintings generally floral, carefully executed, and the general character of the productions is that of hard-paste Sèvres. The mark is a fish in under-glaze blue. Illustration 392 shows an unusually fine plateau with cremiers, decorated in the typical floral style, and each piece carrying the fish mark. This example is from the collection of Mr. and Mrs. L. B. Dow, Jr. of Memphis, Tennessee.

While none of the factories mentioned above are considered outstanding by connoisseurs in other countries, this cannot be said of the collectors in the respective countries where the factories exist. The well known adage "A prophet is not without honor except in his own country" does not apply here. When in Scandinavia or

Switzerland, the scarcity of its own early porcelain and the price asked when a piece is found indicate that in the opinion of the natives their porcelain ranks with the best.

OTHER MISCELLANEOUS CONTINENTAL FACTORIES

An Imperial Russian porcelain factory was established at St. Petersburg by Christoph Konrad Hunger who had managed the Vezzi factory for five years in Venice after leaving Vienna in 1720, where he had assisted Du Paquier in establishing a factory. Little was accomplished under him however, though some progress was made in 1753 and in 1763 the factory became commercial. Nothing of special interest to collectors was produced here. The mark was the Russian eagle and the initials of the successive rulers, the paste was hard and the decorations followed Meissen.

There were a number of factories in the Netherlands and Belgium that made porcelain, such as Amstel (1764-1810), Weesp (1764-1771) and Oude Loosdrecht (1771-1784). Illustration 399 shows a cup and saucer from the last-named factory, carrying the mark and decorated after a Meissen original. A factory was started at the Hague (1775-1785) by the Viennese Anton Leichner. While this factory had a short life, it made some creditable hard-paste. The mark is of a stork holding a fish in its beak; if genuine, it should be in under-glaze blue. The borders of the few fine table services made at this factory are decorated with a beautiful *bleu de roi* color with fine gilding. A service of this kind is preserved in Buckingham Palace. Illustration 385 shows a cup from the Hague factory decorated in this manner.

CHAPTER 4

ITALIAN PORCELAIN

The late Mr. W. B. Honey aptly stated the situation regarding Italian porcelain in his Foreword to the recent book on the subject by Mr. Arthur Lane, when he remarked: "The neglect of Italian porcelain by students of art history in view of the importance of the wares in the evolution of European porcelain is a piece of irony. No study adequate to the importance of the wares has ever been published, and a full survey has long been overdue." Mr. Lane, Keeper of the Department of Ceramics in the Victoria and Albert Museum, has done much to clarify the situation, and we here draw extensively from his book *Italian Porcelain*, 1954. We heartily recommend it to those desiring more information than it is possible for us to give here.

Italian porcelain, with the possible exception of Capo-di-Monte, falls far short of the perfection attained in Germany and France. There were no native deposits of china clay for making hard-paste, yet Capo-di-Monte made a frit porcelain of exceptionally fine quality, and its productions as well as those of certain other Italian factories did have a refreshing character of their own.

MEDICI PORCELAIN

With the Medici porcelain, Italy anticipated by more than a century any other successful attempt to make soft-paste porcelain in Europe, and for even a greater span, the successful efforts of the Meissen factory to make hard-paste porcelain. While the products of this factory hardly come within the scope of collectors today, a word about it is necessary.

Since Venice was famous for its glass, it is not strange that Venetians should have thought that a combination of clay and glass was the proper formula. The serious manufacture of porcelain lasted only from its discovery about 1575 until the death of Francesco I, in 1587, and only about 50 pieces are known today. As pointed out by Mr. Lane (page 4), "almost all Medici porcelain betrays its experimental character by some technical defect. The white material is rather thickly potted and apt to sag out of shape; it is translucent, and can have a yellow or greyish cast. The thick, glutinous glaze may be clear or hazy with minute bubbles, and often has a wide crackle. It leaves bare the edge of the foot-rim and sometimes misses small spots on the surface, where the paste turns pink. Occasionally the blue painting is deep and rich, with purple outlines; more often it tends to gray." The painted designs fall roughly into two classes: those borrowed from the maiolica painters and those of an orential character. Some of the examples are without a mark. Some have the six balls of the Medici arms; some dated in the period 1577-87 have as a mark the dome of Sta. Maria del Fiore, the Cathedral of Florence, with or without the letter "F." Mr. Lane in his book illustrates some eight interesting specimens of this soft-paste porcelain, one of them in the Metropolitan Museum, of New York.

THE VEZZI FACTORY, VENICE

The earliest factory in Italy producing hard-paste or true porcelain was the Vezzi factory in Venice. The prosperous goldsmiths, Francesco and Guiseppe Vezzi, in 1716 offered the State 100,000 ducats for patents of nobility. In 1720, Vezzi began making porcelain with the assistance of Konrad Hunger, who had been a partner of

Du Paquier at Vienna. Hunger had apparently secured his knowledge of the arcanum from Böttger at Meissen. It is believed that Vezzi began making porcelain with the help of Hunger in 1720, and that Hunger remained until 1725 when he returned to Meissen and informed the Commissioners there that the Venetian factory depended on the clay imported from Aue in Saxony for its existence. In 1728 the Saxon authorities forbad the export of this clay.

The Vezzi factory in its seven years existence, 1720-27, made remarkable progress. The best pieces bear comparison with the contemporary wares of Meissen and Vienna. Though it varies considerably, the material is always a true hard-paste porcelain of German type; indeed, students of German porcelain sometimes attribute to Vezzi pieces which they find difficult to place elsewhere. According to E. Hannover, who is in most cases quite reliable, "We on our part are inclined to believe that the factory of Vezzi did not mark its porcelain as long as Hunger was in its service, and that, therefore, all unmarked hard porcelain resembling early Vienna or decorated with leafy scrollwork and Chinese or European figures or harbor-scenes in the style of Herold, or which is in the shapes used by Böttger, belongs to the years 1720-25 (Hunger period); all pieces marked with the name of Venice in all forms or abbreviations, date from the time between 1725 and 1740."

Mr. Lane seems to completely discount this theory and shows that the factory closed in 1727 and that most of the porcelain produced while Hunger was at the factory was marked. "Identification of Vezzi porcelain," he says, "is usually easy, as most pieces bear a factory mark 'Venezia' written in full or in the abbreviations 'Vena.' 'Va,' in under-glaze blue, in gold, or in enamel colors (usually red). The painted mark is often accompanied by capital letters or figures of unknown meaning scratched in the paste." To support his statements, Mr. Lane has produced many examples so marked.

E. Hannover illustrates in Fig. 556 an octagonal sugar box, which is unmarked, as an example of the Vezzi factory. Shown here as Illustration 310 is a Du Paquier piece painted by Gregor Herold, although this piece could be a specimen of Hunger's work at Venice.

LATER VENETIAN FACTORIES

The N. F. Hewelcke factory (1758-63) and several factories at Este from 1781 need not be discussed here. The Cozzi Venice factory obtained an exclusive privilege from the Senate in August, 1765, for the manufacture of porcelain. A workman named Pietro Lorenzi from the Le Nove factory brought the secret of the arcanum, but returned to Le Nove the next year. This factory and that of Le Nove produced porcelain during the same period, and the paste of the two factories is virtually indistinguishable. They are both slightly gray with a wet-looking glaze that develops a brownish tone where it lies thick. The colors used at both factories are virtually the same.

The output of the Cozzi factory was large. The factory mark was a large anchor, boldly drawn in iron-red, and is almost invariably present on Cozzi table wares. Illustration 405 shows a tureen, cover, stand, and the original spoon having this mark: An almost identical specimen is in the collection of Mrs. Neil McDougal, of Seattle. Illustrations 395, 406 and 459 are other typical examples shown. This factory closed in 1812.

The Le Nove factory started in 1762 and closed in 1825. Pasquale Antonibon, the proprietor of a flourishing maiolica factory, began building a kiln for porcelain at the end of 1752. With him was Sigismund Fischer of Dresden, who moved to Capo di Monte in 1754. Le Nove was noted for tooled gilding of a very high quality. Illustration 404 is an example of this work. The factory mark was a star with six points, usually in red or gold. It consists of crossed strokes and does not have a solid center like the star-mark of Doccia. Most of the figures are unmarked, and the same is true of many of the tablewares, but on the latter a scratched "N" appears. Le Nove has remained an important center of the ceramic industry till the present day.

In north-west Italy, a factory was started at Vinovo (1776-1820), but its products are not of such a character as to justify recording here.

DOCCIA

The Marchese Carlo Ginori created a porcelain factory at Doccia near Florence in 1735 which has continued to the present day. It remained under the control of the Ginori family until 1896. From then till the present time it has been incorporated with the Società Ceramica Richard of Milan under the name of Richard-Ginori. Experiments with Italian clays apparently began in 1735, with Gaspare Bruschi as chief modeler, and Carlo Ginori directing the experiments to obtain a satisfactory paste. By 1740 enough progress had been made to enable him to obtain a privilege for making porcelain in Tuscany, with sales starting in 1746.

Mr. Lane in *Italian Porcelain* says (pages 33-34): The factory-mark of a star, taken from the Ginori arms, apparently came into use only towards the end of the eighteenth century. It is found in various colors, and has a more solid center than the star used at Le Nove, except when it appears in the form of crossed triangles. Ginori, or Gi impressed, are mid-nineteenth century marks, as is the crowned "N" sometimes found on the so-called "Capo di Monte" reproductions. It is fairly easy to identify most Doccia porcelain by the material. The so-called *masso bastardo* used from the beginning is hybrid hard-paste, more distinctly gray than any other Italian porcelain. It readily develops fire cracks, and marks of turning are often visible on shaped vessels; the porcelain looks and feels rough. The glaze lacks brilliance, has a sticky, smeared appearance, and on early pieces often shows a pronounced green or yellow tinge. As compared to Doccia, both Cozzi Venice and Le Nove are more glassy and brilliant. From 1770-90 the Doccia glaze was often made opaque and sometimes dead white, probably by an admixture of tin oxide. A finer and more translucent cold white paste was adopted towards the end of the eighteenth century for wares of the best quality.

The earliest useful wares made between 1740 and 1757 were baroque in style, with heavy handles, snake-like spouts, and handleless tall cups and saucers, as well as dishes with deeply molded wavy edges.

Illustration 408 is of a rather fine tureen from the best period and now in the collection of Mrs. H. C. Isaacson, Sr., in Seattle, Washington. Illustration 403 shows a cup and saucer in the style of Herold; the luster is in enamel. Doccia also made some unusual pieces with double walls, the outer ones pierced and decorated in relief. Such a specimen will be seen in the British Museum. The 1757 inventory indicates that much early ware was decorated in under-glaze blue. As a matter of fact, a considerable quantity of useful wares was made during the last quarter of the eighteenth century on a white ground with Italian peasants, landscapes in medallions, and views of towns and buildings with a deep blue band in under-glaze to relieve the border. Illustration 407 shows such a piece. This factory, while commercially successful, has never attained any high esteem with collectors, partially due to the poor quality of its paste and glaze, and partially to the fact that in its production it gave more attention to its commercial success than it did to the creation of distinctive forms.

Doccia made many figures both large and small, and Illustration 449 is a kneeling woman, from the collection of Mrs. W. S. Harnan, and is a fine example in white. The more popular and less pretentious models have large clumsy hands, small heads with receding brows and chins; iron-red stippling for flesh tones, especially noticeable where the color frequently runs between the fingers, giving a very unpleasant effect. The colors are garish, and this, coupled with the typical *masso bastardo* paste makes them anything but appealing. Doccia made a number of life-size figures, which like those made at Meissen, would have been more appropriate if the medium had been marble or bronze.

[60]

Mr. Lane says in his book, *Italian Porcelain* (p. 40, footnote 1) that "Morazzoni illustrates twenty-one Doccia pieces as Capodimonte and nine as Venice (Cozzi). In Eisner de Eisenhof's book on Capodimonte, five Doccia items are illustrated, and in E. Hannover's *Pottery and Porcelain, Vol. III* (English edition, 1925), all eight illustrations of Capodimonte actually represent Doccia porcelain."

An entirely erroneous conception exists in this country about certain figures and useful wares marked with the crowned "N." This mark was never used at Capo di Monte. It was first used by the Royal Naples factory around the end of the eighteenth century. It is found extensively today on porcelain sold to the beginner as Capo di Monte and is the mark of mid-nineteenth century fakes made by the Ginori factory; even cruder pieces of relief-ware have been made in Paris and Germany (by Ernst Bohne and Sons of Rudolstadt and others).

The Capo di Monte factory (1743-59); Buen Retiro (1760-1808); and the Naples, Royal Factory (1771-1806) are treated here together, as the Bourbon factories. It should be emphasized, however, that while Capo di Monte and Buen Retiro had the same management, same workmen, and even the same materials (certainly at the early period of Buen Retiro), the Naples Royal Factory was quite distinct.

THE CAPO DI MONTE FACTORY

When in 1734, Charles of Bourbon became King of Naples, he built the Capo di Monte Palace and later started the porcelain factory of the same name. He took a personal interest in the factory which was undoubtedly spurred on as a result of his marriage to Maria Amalia Christiana, the daughter of Augustus the Strong of Meissen fame. It is said that she brought as a dowry seventeen porcelain table services.

Charles built his factory on the grounds of Capo di Monte located just outside of Naples in 1743 where it was operated under his close personal supervision until 1759 when he became Charles III of Spain, whereupon he moved his factory including the workmen and equipment to Spain, where the factory was called Buen Retiro. It operated there until 1808. For the first ten years after the transfer, it is quite difficult to distinguish its products from those made at Capo di Monte as the management, workmen and materials were identical at each plant. Each factory during the periods mentioned used the same mark which was the Bourbon fleur-de-lis.

We can, however, to some extent, distinguish between them by studying the style and their intended use. The Capo di Monte factory up to 1757, created almost entirely baroque figures and useful wares, while on the contrary, the Buen Retiro factory produced in the first ten years of its existence objects mainly in the Rococo style and very little, if any, useful wares. After the early period, the Buen Retiro factory used Spanish clays in its products, and these may readily be detected by the yellow color not present at either factory when the Italian clay was in use. The products of the Naples factory on the other hand, are largely in the Neo-Classic style. The Naples factory until late in the century used the monogram "FRF," painted in blue, red, or black enamel under a crown. The late mark was an "N" under a crown, painted in under-glaze blue or stamped in the paste. This is the mark that has caused so much confusion. The paste of Capo di Monte was invariably a soft frit, as was that of Buen Retiro for the first ten years. The Naples factory at first made both hard and soft-paste, but later only hard-paste.

Giuseppe Gricci was chief modeler throughout the life of the factory at Capo di Monte and later at Buen Retiro. He was indeed a very gifted artist. Giovanni Caselli directed the painters until his death in 1752. The Saxon, Johann Sigismund Fischer, worked as a leading painter from 1754 until his sudden death in 1758. Luigi Restile succeeded him as chief painter, but refused to follow the factory to Spain.

Records of the Capo di Monte factory show that productions were put on sale there between 1743 and 1745. It will be noted here that no porcelain was offered for sale at Buen Retiro until around 1788 when King Charles III decided to do so. The principal articles offered for sale at this early period by Capo di Monte were snuff boxes, cane handles, and tea services. This factory like many others produced *blanc-de-chine* (Fukien) porcelain with applied prunus-sprays. Illustration 397 shows a pair of early beaker cups and saucers in this style. The cups are without handles, and the porcelain is very white and translucent; both cups and saucers have the fleur-de-lis mark in under-glaze blue.

Mr. Lane says (p. 47) that: "The Archives are so explicit about the painted designs on the earliest useful wares that these can be readily identified in existing examples of perhaps slightly later date. The painter, Giuseppe della Torre specialized in tea services with battles, seascapes, landscapes, figure subjects and cupids. At first, these were painted only in monochrome blue, violet, black, crimson and red. Figure subjects with 'arabesques in gold' are already mentioned in 1745, and this class probably includes both the garden parties in contemporary dress, and the idyllic scenes of classical nymphs and deities." Illustration 398 shows a tall beaker cup without handles and a saucer, each bearing the fleur-de-lis mark in under-glaze blue, which are in all probability from the period of 1750 and possibly by the hand of Giuseppe della Torre. It will be noted that the composition of the tree on this saucer is almost identical with the one shown by Mr. Lane as "B" in Plate 66. This may, of course, be early Buen Retiro, but as we know, this factory made little, if any, useful ware.

"The Capo di Monte material is a beautiful soft-paste 'frit' porcelain, usually pure white, and highly translucent . . . The glaze fits closely, is lustrous without being too glassy, and often 'misses' under the foot, where the factory mark of a fleur-de-lis in under-glaze blue is almost invariably present . . . The material has better plastic qualities than any French soft-paste, the cups and saucers being made very thin; but in the larger pieces, the walls are thick . . . The earliest cups have no handles." All shapes so far mentioned are quite free from any suggestion of the Rococo style; their affinities are with the German late baroque. When, however, the Portici porcelain room was created, 1757-59, the Rococo was adopted and remained in great favor during the first decade after the factory was transferred to Spain. While it is difficult to say whether pieces decorated in the Rococo were made at one place or another, it will be remembered that the Spanish factory at this time was not interested in making useful wares and did not offer anything for sale.

Mr. Lane points out that "certain mannerisms of Capo di Monte painting deserve notice (whether on figures or useful wares). The colors are usually stippled on, or in the case of flowers, drawn in very fine hair lines. Flesh tones are often shaded in violet; and on polychrome pieces, there are almost always clouds in violet and pale orange-red. The coloring generally is soft and harmonious." The gilt border patterns are to some extent like the Vienna *Laub und Bandelwerk*. The gold is laid on thickly and is apt to wear off. (Buen Retiro figures are rarely stippled).

As mentioned by Mr. Lane, archives of the factory describe a number of figure groups modeled by Guiseppe Gricci between 1743-45 as follows; a Pantaloon group of two figures; a group of three figures; Pulcinella; Madonna della Pieta; St. Sebastian; Immaculate Conception, Bacchus, shepherd with she-goat; poor people; woman spinning and various animals. "This is, naturally, not a complete list, for many must have been made after 1745, but it indicates that Gricci's range of subjects was wide, and justifies the ascription to him of a series of figures which are among the most attractive in the whole range of European porcelain." The marks when present are either impressed or painted in under-glaze blue. These figures are untouched by the Rococo style, and were probably made between 1743-1756. Mr. Lane shows quite a number of such figures and also adds that "Gricci's power as a more serious sculptor is seen in a very remarkable large group, about 21 inches high, of the Virgin Mary bending over the dead Christ, with a separate figure of St. John standing on the same rocky base." It is emotionally Baroque in feeling. Illustration 101 is a remarkable example of Gricci's work. It depicts Orpheus playing to the animals and is certainly one of the finest figures in existence, not only of Capo di Monte but of any European factory. It is shown here in color from the front as well as the back, and so far as we know, this figure has not been heretofore illustrated. It is about 15 inches high and has the fleur-de-lis mark in under-glaze blue under the base of the plinth, which is an integral part of the figure. The modeling is in the Baroque style; the paste and glaze as well as the stippling are in the best tradition of this factory. Illustration 20 shows Summer from a series of the Four Seasons, which seems to have been a favorite subject at all of the European factories. The mark is a fleur-de-lis impressed in the base. The color and stippling, as well as the paste and glaze, are typical of this factory.

Commenting on the work of Guiseppe Gricci, we here quote a few excerpts from *Capo di Monte and Buen Retiro Porcelains*, 1955, by Alice W. Frothingham: "Some idea of his versatility can be formed after reading the records of production at the Capo di Monte factory. The works noted as by him range from the insignificant to the impressive, from the serious to the frivolous . . . At the same time he worked on busts and medallion portraits of the King and the Queen, on popular types and animals, and on figures of classical mythology and the Christian religion."

The great masterpiece of the Capo di Monte factory, according to Mr. Lane, is the "Porcelain Room" erected in the Royal Villa at Portici between 1757 and 1759. In his opinion, this room surpasses the early Vienna porcelain room constructed for Count Dubsky at Brunn about 1730, to which we previously referred under Vienna porcelain. "So perfect is the technique, in spite of the large scale, that a visitor who sees this room (it may now be seen in the Palace of Capo di Monte) for the first time is obliged to re-adjust his whole conception of porcelain as a decorative medium. Giuseppe Gricci and his brother Stefano were the modelers; Fischer and Luigi Restile the painters." While the decoration was in the Rococo, this spirit had not reached its zenith, and it remained for these same sculptors at Buen Retiro to decorate the Aranjuez Palace in a greatly different spirit. The two palaces were decorated in an Oriental style in each case, but Miss Frothingham, in referring to the two palaces, says: "At Aranjuez the Oriental composition show little of the restraint of those modeled earlier at the Capo di Monte factory. Indeed, in a flamboyant burst of full-blown Rococo exuberance, the human figures, animals, birds, insects, fruit and flowers run riot across the walls and the ceiling . . . Added to the activity of these scenes, there is noticeable a liveliness of facial expression and posture, as in the chinoiseries of Boucher. Contrasting with the placidity of the Capo di Monte figures, the faces are gay with laughter, the gestures free with the natural twist of bodies and the vivacious tilt of heads."

We agree with Mr. Lane when he says that Capo di Monte richly deserves its reputation as the most distinguished Italian factory. In artistic quality its useful wares and figures stand high among the eighteenth-century porcelain factories of Europe.

BUEN RETIRO FACTORY

King Charles III built a new factory in the grounds of the Buen Retiro Palace in Madrid which was ready in 1760, and he also undertook the decoration of the Palace of Aranjuez at the enormous cost of 571,555 Spanish reales. Conspicuously painted on a vase in relief is the signature 'JOSEPH GRICCI DELINEA^{IT} ET SCUL^{IT} 1763.' The work was probably completed in 1765. In the Royal Palace at Madrid will be found a porcelain room, smaller and quite different in its cold Neo-Classical style from the one at Aranjuez.

After 1770, a great deal of trouble was encountered with the paste and glaze, which it may be presumed was no longer brought from Naples. From 1780 a hard-paste was made and entwined "C's" under a crown was used as a factory mark. Illustration 402 shows a typical Buen Retiro specimen of the latter work of the factory; we need not further comment.

The authors spent some time in Spain in 1960 and found no Buen Retiro porcelain for sale. Aside from the Palaces already referred to, the most important collection remaining is the "Osma Collection, Instituto de Don Juan," 43 Fortuney Street, Madrid: there, will be seen more than fifty pieces of Buen Retiro, of which about half are figures. Some are large in size and the paste and glaze vary from white to cream to brown. Most of them carry the blue under-glaze Fleur-de-lis mark. None has any stippling which is so characteristic of Capo di Monte and only one has a Rococo base.

NAPLES ROYAL FACTORY

Ferdinand IV of Naples ruled from 1759 to 1825. He decreed the revival of a Royal porcelain factory in 1771, and a new factory, built near the Royal Palace at Portici, was ready in 1773. The composition of the paste was entrusted to Gaetano Fucci, an old Capo di Monte hand; Francesco Celebrano, was chief modeler until 1781; and the painters included Antonio Coiffi, who had worked at Capo di Monte and Maria Grue. The factory was small and of little importance until 1779 when Domenico Venuti raised it to some importance and gave it its typically Neo-Classical stamp. It made many large services. The mark, as previously stated, was "FRF" under a crown, and the paste, soft and glassy. After 1782, the porcelain was opaque tin-glazed and later a pure white. The chief concern of collectors is to remember that it was this factory, and not Capo di Monte that at one stage, even though a late one, used the crowned "N" as a mark, which has been subsequently copied by fakers, to mislead the unwary. To those students who wish a more complete picture and history of this as well as the Buen Retiro factories, we recommend once again *Italian Porcelain* by Arthur Lane.

CHARACTERISTICS

1. Medici porcelain, first in Europe, soft-paste. To be studied only in the museums.

2. Vezzi Venice, hard-paste, 1720-27, usually marked.

3. Cozzi, hard-paste, usually marked with large red anchor.

4. Le Nove similar, contemporaneous with Cozzi, hard-paste; when marked, a star is used; noted for fine tooled gilding.

5. Doccia too commercial for collectors; still in existence; in nineteenth century sold products as Capo di Monte, later used mark of Naples factory, crowned "N" to mislead purchasers. Readily distinguished by poor gray paste, known as *masso bastardo*. Nineteenth century, used a star as mark when crowned "N" absent.

6. Capo di Monte exceptionally fine white translucent frit porcelain, usually marked fleur-de-lis under-glaze, but figures sometimes with same mark impressed; style almost always Baroque; fine coloring, noted for stippling; useful ware made for sale; also noted for exceptional figures modeled by Gricci in baroque style; life of factory 1743-59.

7. Buen Retiro, 1760-1808, paste and glaze like Capo di Monte, 1760-70; style usually Rococo; made little if any useful wares; none for sale until 1788; later periods paste yellow due to use of Spanish clay, marks until late in century same as Capo di Monte, then entwined "C" with a crown, at which time paste hard. Stippling on figures rarely used.

8. Naples Royal factory had small output until 1779; mark "FRF" under a crown until end of the century when crowned "N" used; soft-paste until late in century; Neo-Classical style employed.

CHAPTER 5

FRENCH PORCELAIN

Porcelain, as has been previously noted, was invented by the Chinese many centuries before the Europeans discovered the secret. At Meissen, we have seen, Böttger re-invented porcelain at the end of the first decade of the eighteenth century, and this factory was responsible for its marked success for the next forty years or until the middle of that century. In each case, however, it was "pâte dure" or hard-paste and not "pâte tendre" or soft-paste porcelain that was made.

We have also seen that in 1575 the Medici factory at Florence made for the first time a sort of "pâte tendre"; however, this may be considered as a kind of experiment that failed to succeed, since for a century following no such porcelain was made. It therefore can be said that a French factory was the earliest to produce the "pâte tendre" at Rouen in 1673, and other French factories carried on the production of this kind of artificial porcelain exclusively for the next three-quarters of a century. During this period only soft-paste was made, and around the middle of the eighteenth century, the English factories joined in its production. "Pâte dure" or hard porcelain was not made in France until 1769, and while some fine quality porcelain was made with this medium, it was the "pâte tendre" that established the French porcelains among the most highly prized by collectors of any European type.

It must be remembered that the French Court during the eighteenth century was the style and cultural center of Europe, and the luxury-loving aristocrats of all the other countries revolved around it. As an example, at the Court of Augustus the Strong only French was spoken. Before the turn of the seventeenth century late Baroque or Louis Quatorze was the vogue. The historic *lambrequin* style was used on the earliest porcelains, which when combined with the perfectly proportioned shapes and sympathetic material, gave distinction to the early porcelains of Rouen and St. Cloud. The greatest claim to fame, however, was in connection with the Rococo style which the French created, even though it was not applied to its porcelain with such extravagance as in the French ormolu and furniture. The Louis Quinze porcelain has a measured wildness, tempered to the flowing grace and supple rhythm noted in all French porcelain down to the time the Classical styles were adopted there. The Rococo was contemporary with the rise of the Vincennes and Sèvres factories, and by the middle of the eighteenth century, its influence gradually made itself felt all over Europe in forms and subjects of decorations, and especially in the adoption of biscuit as a medium for figures; and with the triumph of the Sèvres styles, the German Rococo in porcelain and German leadership in the art came to an end. The most important contributions towards this leadership were the paintings of Francois Boucher, the inventive genius of Jean Hellot, the wise and far-seeing direction of Jean-Jacques Bachelier, the fine taste and enthusiasm of Madame de Pompadour and their effect on Louis XV.

ROUEN

Whereas the records show that as early as 1664 Louis XIV granted Claude Reverend, a merchant and citizen of Paris, a monopoly to manufacture and import porcelain for fifty years, no pieces have been positively identified, and it is believed that he was merely a dealer. In the Sèvres museum will be seen two specimens marked "A.P." with a star, and there called Rouen. While the "P" might very readily stand for Poterat, the "A" is not easily explained, as the founder of the Rouen factory was Louis and his father Edme. A close examination of these pieces will disclose that the paste has a decided yellow cast not found on other examples of Rouen but usually associated with the later St. Cloud factory. Some authorities suggest that perhaps these few marked pieces may be experimental ones made by Reverend, but there is no proof that he ever established a factory.

In 1673 we reach sure ground as Louis Poterat, a faience-maker of St. Sever, near Rouen, applied for and was granted an exclusive monopoly for the fabrication of plates and dishes, pots, and vases of porcelain like that of China, and of faience after the Dutch fashion, for the period of thirty years. It is strange that no mention was made of the privilege granted to Reverend just nine years earlier. After the death of Louis Poterat in 1696, his brother closed the factory and relinquished his porcelain rights. During the twenty-three years of its existence this factory made a limited quantity of useful wares, of which some fifty examples are known today. They include flower-pots, salt cellars, and cups and saucers, nearly always decorated in blue only, and always in the French style of the reign of Louis XIV, strangely enough never inspired by Chinese design.

Mr. E. S. Auscher, who was "Chef de Fabrication" at the Sèvres factory from 1879 to 1889, in *French Porcelain*, 1905, one of the few authoritative books on the subject found in English, as translated and edited by William Burton, F.C.S., says: "For a long time the beautiful Rouen porcelains made by the Poterats were over-looked, or confounded with those made shortly afterwards at St. Cloud, though nowadays one wonders that this should have been the case, as there are essential differences between them." He then proceeds to give essential differences. As his opinions have been extensively accepted and repeated in most English books, we would like to correct what we believe is a fallacy in his principal identification. He says: "Finally, the blue colour is darker and more intense, *while the manner in which it has been applied bespeaks still more strongly the hand of the faience-maker. In our opinion, the blue of the Rouen porcelain has been painted on the 'raw' glaze exactly as was the custom in the manufacture of faience while, on the contrary, the blue on the St. Cloud porcelain is distinctly under the glaze, and appears to have been painted on the unfired body, or on the 'biscuit', and fixed to it by a low fire before putting on the glaze."* We accordingly examined several pieces in our collection; those in the Decorative Arts section of the Louvre; those at the Sèvres Museum, and we found it most difficult to say whether the blue had been applied under or over the glaze, because the glaze of both Rouen and St. Cloud are so soft that even applied over the glaze it sank into the glaze in firing. However, in examining an important specimen in the British Museum, we were thrilled to see that at certain points near the base, the glaze failed to reach it, and we could without difficulty say that certainly in this instance, the blue was in fact under the glaze. The piece in question was labelled Rouen and had all of the other attributes of this factory. Later, in Paris, we had an opportunity to examine a specimen of reputed Rouen in the hands of an outstanding dealer in early French porcelain, and fortunately for our purpose, this piece had been very recently broken in half, which gave an excellent opportunity to see if the blue decoration was under or over the glaze. Like the piece in the British Museum, it was under the glaze. We since have obtained the opinion of several experts on the subject, and they all agree that the blue of Rouen like that of St. Cloud is always under the glaze.

This important discovery leaves the identification on a more difficult basis. With the other differences enumerated by E. S. Auscher we quite agree, and we will here quote him. Commenting on an example of Rouen, he says: "On comparing such a piece as this with any piece bearing the mark 'St. Cloud' we shall be struck, in the first place, with the nature of the paste, which is less amber-colored than the latter, and indeed possesses a slightly greenish tone. The glaze, too, is less vitreous, and is again of a very pale sea-green tint rather than what one would describe as the 'ivory' tint of St. Cloud." He further says that the blue decoration of Rouen is often darker and somewhat grayer than that used elsewhere. We have found that the seventeenth century St. Cloud bearing the "Sun" mark is not nearly so amber in color as the eighteenth century porcelain bearing the "St. Cloud" mark in some form. Illustration 409 shows an important specimen, a jug or ewer, of undoubted Rouen, from the Morgan collection now in the Metropolitan Museum of Art. Illustration 413 shows a trembleuse cup and saucer not marked and believed to be Rouen: Illustration 43 shows a knife and fork, either Rouen or seventeenth century St. Cloud.

ROUEN CHARACTERISTICS

1. Soft-paste.
2. Unmarked.
3. Decoration blue under the glaze.
4. French style decoration, usually "lambrequin."
5. Very translucent and greenish-yellow by transmitted light.
6. Paste and glaze gray-green.
7. Blue darker as a rule than others.
8. Few pieces known.

ST. CLOUD

The first enduring establishment for producing "pâte tendre" porcelain was started at St. Cloud not later than 1696, and an exclusive privilege was granted to the family of Chicanneau by Louis XIV. We may surmise that Chicanneau, a clever man, had in all probability secured the secrets of manufacture from Poterat and may have experimented (and probably did so) with its manufacture before the above date. In any event, the first documentary date connected with St. Cloud porcelain was the letters-patent dated 1696 and issued by Louis XIV to "Barbe Coudray, the widow of Pierre Chicanneau, and to Jean-Baptiste, Pierre and Genevieve Chicanneau, brothers and sisters, children of the mentioned Coudray and the mentioned Pierre Chicanneau, and undertakers of the faience and porcelain works established at St. Cloud." It further stated that the children had arrived at the point of making porcelain of perfect quality before 1696. The patent further said that Poterat had never carried the production to perfection, and that since his death his family had made no porcelain and therefore the new patent would not injure the heirs of Poterat.

We have little information in French memoirs concerning the early production of the factory. Strangely enough, we have to rely on the account of a journey to Paris in the year 1698 of an Englishman, Dr. Martin Lister (afterwards physician to Queen Anne), who accompanied the Duke of Portland to Paris and remained there some time while the treaty of Ryswick was negotiated. In writing an account of his trip he said: "I saw the potterie of St. Cloud, with which I was marvellously well pleased, for I confess I could not distinguish betwixt the pots made there and the finest China ware I ever saw. It will, I know, be easily granted me that the painting may be better designed and finisht because our men are far better masters of that art than the Chinese; but the glazing came not in the least behind theirs, not for whiteness, nor the smoothness of running without bubbles. Again, the inward substance and matter of pots was, to me, the very same, hard and firm as marble, and the self-same grain on this side vitrification. Farther, the transparency of the pots the very same . . . They sold these pots at St. Cloud at excessive rates, and for their ordinary chocolate cups askt crowns a-piece."

The chateau of St. Cloud belonged to the Duc d'Orleans, a patron of the Arts, and it lies on the road from Paris to Versailles and would therefore attract the notice of the great Lords attending the court. *Le Mercure Galant*, October, 1700, gives an account of a visit of Madame la Duchesse de Bourgogne as follows: "I have forgotten to write to you that the Duchesse de Bourgogne, when she had passed through St. Cloud and turned along the riverside to visit Madame la Duchesse de Guiche, made her carriage stop at the door of the house where the MM. Chicanneau have had established for some years now a manufactory of fine porcelains, which without doubt has not its like in all Europe. The princess found pleasure in seeing several pieces of very good shape made on the wheel. She saw some others painted in patterns that were more regular and better done than those of the Indian porcelain. Then she went to see the faiences being made in the manufactory, and afterwards MM. Chicanneau conducted her into the office, where she saw quantities of fine and beautiful porcelains in their perfection, with which she was so pleased that she promised to come again. She did not leave without shewing her satisfaction by the gratuities she gave the workmen."

The privilege granted to the factory in 1712 extended for ten years, and in the new grant the name Henri Trou appears. He was Usher of the Antechamber to the Duc d'Orleans and had married the widow of the elder Chicanneau. The factory was apparently carried on with marked success, as we find that in 1722, the privilege was extended to the heirs of Chicanneau and Trou for a further period of twenty years. This third grant was probably due to the influence of the Duc d'Orleans, who was now Regent of France and who was himself greatly interested in the production of porcelain. The factory was apparently destroyed by fire in 1773 and not rebuilt.

The appearance of St. Cloud porcelain is very characteristic. The paste is yellowish, particularly during the eighteenth century. That made during the seventeenth century and having the sun mark is more nearly like the Rouen paste. It has a fine grain and the glaze is clear and brilliant, with few bubbles and rarely blisters. It is greenish-yellow by transmitted light and extremely translucent. It may be said that when examining "pâte dure" or hard-paste, you can see light through it; but when examining "pâte tendre" or soft-paste you look through the porcelain, almost as you would look through a window, and this is particularly true of St. Cloud porcelain.

Most of the products of the factory are small in size, comprising jars for *pot-pourri*, soap dishes, powder boxes, jars for pomade and other articles for the toilet table, three-lobed salt cellars, mustard pots, cruets for oil and vinegar, cups with trembleuse saucers, labels for wine bottles and other trifles for the dining table, and finally knobs for canes, snuff boxes, and other personal requisites. Among the few larger pieces flower pots (cachepots) are the most numerous. In the Decorative Arts Section of the Louvre in Paris may be found a large collection of St. Cloud.

In general one may divide the products of the factory into those decorated in under-glaze blue only, those entirely in white and those in polychrome colors. Those in the first class are the earliest, and these are almost always marked. From 1698 (or maybe slightly earlier) to 1712, the mark is a sun either incised or in under-glaze blue. Louis XIV liked to speak of himself as "Le Roi Soleil" (the sun king). Another early mark was "St. C" and from 1724 the letter "T" was added for Trou. Illustration 412 shows one of a pair of cups and trembleuse saucers having the sun mark. The porcelain and the potting are superb, and the decoration is the typical *lambrequin* style. The second class are copies of the popular Fukien blanc-de-chine. Illustration 410 shows the type, also a cup with a trembleuse saucer. The cup has a handle and is not of the beaker shape as was the previous illustration. The potting is here much heavier and the paste more amber in color. It probably dates c. 1720. This piece is unmarked and strangely enough such pieces are rarely if ever marked. The decoration is the flowering plum branches or prunus which was so popular. The third class, or those decorated in polychrome colors, are frequently copied from the porcelains of China and Japan. Gilding is rarely found on St. Cloud porcelain. We cannot wonder that forms as well as the decorations were copied from Oriental counterparts, as all of the beverages for which many of the shapes were designed were of recent importation from the Orient: Chocolate was first imported in 1651, and its use did not become general until the reign of Louis XV; tea made its first appearance in 1652 and coffee came from Mocha and became common in 1670. Along with the new beverages came teapots, coffee-pots and cups and saucers of true Oriental styles, and these were very naturally copied by the potters of St. Cloud and of other European factories. The polychrome pieces like the all-white ones are seldom if ever marked. Why this was true is hard to explain. Illustration 41 shows a cane handle, crudely decorated with chinoiseries in polychrome colors. A few fine figures were also made, and Illustrations 416 and 417 from the R. Thornton Wilson collection now at the Metropolitan Museum in New York, shows a pair of unusually fine figures of Chinamen in brilliant polychrome colors.

St. Cloud porcelain is rarely copied. A few pieces of Tournai porcelain are known bearing the false mark "s$\overset{+}{\underset{T}{c}}$." Some few pieces are known with certain letters that may be from an offshoot of the factory in Faubourg St. Honoré and Faubourg St. Antoine in Paris. It is also known that a porcelain factory was started at Lille about 1711 by two faience makers Dorez and Pélissier, but little is known of such products.

St. Cloud Characteristics

1. Soft-paste.
2. Seventeenth century, sun mark.
3. 1700-24, mark is St. Cloud.
4. 1724-73, St. Cloud + Trou.
5. 1696-1712, blue decoration only, always under-glaze.
6. French designs, usually "lambrequin."
7. Nearly always marked.
8. 1712-73, white like Fukien or polychrome decorated, Oriental style, almost never marked.
9. Sun marked pieces quite like Rouen.
10. Blue usually not quite so dark.
11. Very translucent and greenish-yellow by transmitted light.
12. White pieces not nearly so white as Vincennes.
13. Colored figures rare.

CHANTILLY

From an artistic point of view, certainly one of the most important of the early French factories was that of Chantilly. An interesting feature of the history of early European porcelain factories was the patronage of the great nobles, princes, and kings of the different realms. As we have seen, the Duc d'Orleans was the patron of the St. Cloud factory, and as the Regent of France, he was instrumental in securing exclusive rights to this factory as long as he lived. Another great personage provided the funds to carry on the work started in 1725 by Ciquaire Cirou at Chantilly. The Prince de Condé, known as Monsieur le Duc, the princely owner of the magnificent domain of Chantilly, only after the death of the Duc d'Orleans in 1735 was able to secure letters-patent for Cirou to produce porcelain like that of the Japanese. This privilege was for a period of twenty years, and covered fine porcelains of all kinds and colors in imitation of Japanese, reserving, however, the rights of the heirs of Chicanneau.

At this period the Prince de Condé was collecting with avidity specimens of early Japanese Arita wares, Imari, and more especially Kakiemon, after the style created by the famous potter of the same name. This porcelain was produced in the province of Hizen in the second half of the seventeenth century, and we illustrate several pieces from the Franks' collection, now in the British Museum. In these charming designs, ornamental sprays, branches, and flowers are distributed in an artistic way across the plates or other pieces of ware, interlacing, and sometimes enclosing quaint figures of the ibis, partridge, or quail, or drawings of fabulous animals. These dainty Kakiemon patterns, painted in brilliant touches of red, yellow and blue, enhanced with a little gold, on a white porcelain of unequaled quality and finish, became the rage of the period all over Europe. Not only were they copied or adapted at Chantilly, but they made their way to all the French, English, and German factories. At Chantilly, the beautiful opaque tin glaze surpassed that of the Japanese from which it was copied. This glaze resembled that of the faience-makers and was rendered milky-white and opaque by the addition of oxide of tin. It was this use of a stanniferous glaze which gives such a distinct aspect to the early Chantilly porcelain. The factory continued to produce porcelain until the Revolution of 1789. Around the middle of the century, when the Vincennes factory and that of Mennecy began to give real competition, the Chantilly factory changed its paste and glaze to a more transparent one to meet the competition. This porcelain does not compare with that made at the early period.

Illustration 26 shows a melon teapot in color and is very characteristic of the best period of the factory. The decoration is unusually fine, possibly by the hand of von Löwenfinck who went to Chantilly after he left Meissen. Illustrations 28, 414, 454 and 455 show other excellent examples of this factory: Illustration 454 is from the collection of Mrs. Creighton; Illustration 455 from that of Mrs. Nichols, both of Seattle, Washington. Illustration 27 shows a cane handle with chinoiserie decor. While there are not a great many polychrome-decorated Chantilly figures known today compared with those of the Mennecy factory we are able to show here in color as Illustrations 24 and 25, two figures of the Seasons, decorated with the Hizen colors on a tin glaze porcelain. It is interesting to note here that the brothers DuBois, who founded the factory at Vincennes, were employed at Chantilly about 1735.

CHANTILLY CHARACTERISTICS

1. Soft-paste.
2. 1725-50, opaque tin glaze.
3. Mark above dates is red hunting horn; Japanese decoration.
4. 1750-89, porcelain as to paste, glaze, and decoration copied Sèvres.
5. Mark at that time hunting horn in blue.
6. White in style of Fukien popular.
7. Colored figures rare.

MENNECY

The factory at Mennecy-Villeroy, about 18 miles south of Paris, as in the case of the previous factories, owed its existence to the protection of a distinguished patron, the Sieur de Villeroy. He owned a small faience factory, and it was there that Barbin created and developed, about the year 1735, a manufacture of soft porcelain, without having obtained the necessary authorization by letters-patent, which shows how powerful must have been his protector. In 1748 Barbin applied for permission to establish a kiln in Paris, but this privilege was refused because His Majesty the King had granted it to Charles Adam. Barbin moved his factory to Mennecy in 1748, in order to receive the protection of the Duc de Villeroy. It was stipulated that he must not employ any workmen who had worked at Vincennes, neither must he copy nor imitate the productions of that royal factory. About 1766 the directorate passed to Messrs. Jacques and Jullien of the Sceaux factory, who continued the works until 1773, when they were removed to Bourg la Reine. The works were closed in 1806.

The Mennecy paste is beautifully soft and has the appearance of ivory; it is quite similar to the Fukien blanc-de-chine of the best period. After 1750, the paste was changed in an effort to copy Vincennes, which was much whiter, and it lost its original beauty. Its birds and flowers were charmingly executed. The absence of gilding is the result of the rigid monopoly given to Adam of the Vincennes factory, and therefore we find the edges of pieces finished with a blue, yellow or pink line of color. Decoration in rose color was specially favored, and the earlier specimens so decorated may almost be said to be characteristic of its wares. Polychrome decoration was largely used; its flowers painted in yellow, blue, rose, and lilac were especially fine. The lids of tea and coffee-pots frequently end in flowers, which are finely modeled and carefully picked out in colors.

Mennecy featured vertical rather than flat pieces, so plates and dishes are rare. On the other hand, Mennecy figures are very much sought after. They are extremely colorful and are present in greater quantity than those of St. Cloud or Chantilly, which are quite rare and are usually not so colorful. Illustration 418 is a close-up view of a Mennecy group (R. Thornton Wilson collection): Illustration 419 is a grotesque (Morgan collection) and Illustration 451 is a figure from the collection of Mrs. Creighton, of Seattle. This factory also made biscuit figures and also figures in the white glaze only. Illustrations 420 and 421 show a pair of such figures as children representing the arts. The porcelain is quite like the finest Fukien blanc-de-chine. Color Illustration 40 is of a sugar basin decorated with the rare bird design. This mold was made later at Bourg la Reine and illustrated in color by Auscher and also by Hannover. The present one is Mennecy and carries the impressed "D.V." mark. Illustrations 415 and 411 show a characteristic teapot and a mustard pot. Color Illustration 42 shows a milk jug and cover decorated in the rose monochrome for which Mennecy is famous: Illustration 453 is from the collection of Mrs. Stoddard and Illustration 458 that of Mrs. Nichols, both of Seattle, Washington. All of these pieces have the "D.V." mark, which was the factory mark, either scratched or in enamel and date about 1750.

MENNECY CHARACTERISTICS

1. Soft-paste
2. 1735-48, rarely marked.
3. Factory moved to Mennecy, 1748; then marked "D.V." impressed or painted, until 1806.
4. Porcelain paste and glaze like finest period Fukien or appearance of old ivory.
5. Many fine white and polychrome figures.
6. Sèvres styles; also Oriental.
7. No gold used in the decorations as result of edict prohibiting its use; monochrome colors substituted, particularly rose, which is like a trade mark of this factory.
8. Vertical rather than flat pieces.
9. Bird designs in polychrome colors unusually fine; but rare.

VINCENNES

In 1738 two brothers named DuBois, one a sculptor and the other a painter, who had surreptitiously learned the secrets of making porcelain from the factory at Chantilly, where they had been employed and discharged, went to Vincennes and had little difficulty in obtaining there an interview with Orry de Fulvy, brother of the Comptroller-General of the finances of the kingdom, who obtained for them the necessary privileges and the patronage of the King of France. They were provided with capital and the use of a riding-school at the palace of Vincennes in which to carry on their experiments. By 1740 they had achieved some success and were joined by a man named Gravant, who is also supposed to have secured some secrets as to the method of producing porcelain. Old manuscripts disclose that the production was not entirely a success, as five-sixths of the pieces were lost in the firing. The DuBois brothers were either discharged or surreptitiously departed, leaving behind debts of 50,000 livres and all of their materials. This was a great blow to Orry de Fulvy, but fortunately Francois Gravant, who had made copies secretly of all of the notes relating to the composition of the paste and the method of firing, persuaded Fulvy to permit him to carry on the work. He secured workers from Chantilly and by 1745 had been able to produce a beautiful white porcelain.

On July 24th, 1745, a privilege was granted to a company formed for the purpose of porcelain manufacture and a patent was issued in the name of Charles Adams for a period of thirty years. Larger quarters were provided and capital of 90,000 livres, later increased to 250,000 livres, was made available. A clerk from the office of taxes, named Boileau, a clever administrator, became managing clerk. The celebrated chemist and academician Hellot conducted the chemical operations; the modeling was superintended by Duplessis, a goldsmith and sculptor; while an artist named Bachelier, and an enameler to the King, named Mathieu, directed the painting and decorating. The secret of applying gold to porcelain was bought for a large sum from the Benedictine friar, Hippolyte, of the Abbey of St. Martin des Champs. By 1750 the finances were again insufficient, and the King made a new effort to place the factory on a sound basis. The capital was increased to 550,000 livres. A hundred workers had been employed by this time, and the production had been restricted almost exclusively to making imitations of natural flowers, which were greatly in demand. They were furnished with leaves in lacquered metal and set on wire stems, being then bound together in bouquets in vases. To show her father, the King of Poland, that the Vincennes factory compared favorably with the one at Meissen, the Crown Princess chose in proof a vase mounted in ormulu with two flanking figures and an enormous bouquet of flowers containing 480 blooms. It is also recorded that on one occasion the art-loving Madame de Pompadour entertained the King in her winter garden, where she had placed large quantities of porcelain flowers and by the addition of suitable perfumes had created the effect of having flowers of all kinds in the middle of the winter season. It is said that the King was much impressed and became even more interested in the Vincennes porcelain factory.

The unexpected death in 1750 of the minister, and in 1751 of the manager de Fulvy again led to a reconstruction of the syndicate that the de Fulvys had founded. From 1753 the King became a shareholder to the extent of one-fourth of the capital which had now become 800,000 livres, and the factory was granted permission to style itself *Manufacture royal de porcelaine de France*, and to mark its products with two intertwined "L's." The question of the factory mark will be discussed later. The privilege was taken from Charles Adam, who had apparently acted for the old syndicate, and reissued to Eloi Brichard, and by this change the factory became a royal manufactory. Wide powers were granted him to inspect other potteries, and severe penalties were leveled against anyone attempting to compete with the royal factory. From 1753 to 1756, the Vincennes factory was a royal manufactory and produced the finest porcelains ever made in France and possibly anywhere else. In 1756, the premises at Vincennes had become inadequate, and as there were obvious advantages in having a new factory situated near the Court, the choice fell upon Sèvres, midway between Paris and Versailles, and in the immediate neighborhood of the palace of Bellevue, which Madame de Pompadour had built three years before. While the old factory was soon forgotten, and the world knows so well the name of Sèvres, few have heard that of Vincennes. Yet it is to the Vincennes period that we owe those specimens which show the French *pâte tendre* in all its grace and freshness. In comparing the large and important vases of the Sèvres period such as Illustrations 430 and 431 shown here with the Vincennes less pretentious ones, E. Hannover says: "What is known of these vases from the collections at Windsor Castle and Buckingham Palace, the Wallace Collection in London, and the collections of the Rothschild family in England and in Paris, makes it hard to understand the unbounded admiration for them; only their rarity can explain the fact that the French should feel the lack of them in the public collections of Paris as an ever-open wound; for as a matter of fact, the many smaller and less pretentious specimens in Paris, and especially at the Sèvres Museum, give a far richer and more favorable impression of the art of French porcelain during its first years at Vincennes."

We may best sum up the qualities of early Vincennes in the whiteness of its paste and the simplicity of its decorations. The flowers are very simply painted, without dark outlines or pronounced shading; the birds vigorous but slender. Of the more ordinary china-ware were plates, cups and saucers, bowls, jugs, oval and round sugar basins, butter dishes, mustard and jam pots, watering-pots, candlesticks, snuff boxes, flower holders, and cheese dishes. A very few figures were made painted in clear or opaque enamels. Such a figure may be seen in the Museum at Sèvres. Strangely enough, the outstanding color is the *jaune jonquille,* and this seems to be the only example of this very rare color to be found there. No examples are to be found at the Decorative Arts Museum in Paris. Illustrations 424 and 425 show an extremely rare pair of Vincennes figures in color, modeled by Blondeau and dated 1753, from the Metropolitan Museum, the gift of Mr. R. Thornton Wilson.

Illustration 422 shows a pair of important pot-pourri vases with cupids on the rocky bases. The porcelain and the glaze are extremely white and brilliant, qualities which distinguish it from any other porcelain. While such groups and figures were apparently designed primarily to be executed in "biscuit" they are found, as in this case, covered with a clear, white transparent glaze. Sketches of this pair are in the archives of the Louvre in the handwriting of Madame de Pompadour, who made the sketches of what she desired. These are probably by the celebrated sculptor La Rue and from every point of view are among the finest products of the factory. Illustration 423 shows one of the finest examples of the "biscuit" figures and is known as the "Harvester." A similar figure and its companion were included in the "Art Treasures Exhibition, New York, June 1955," and there described as follows: "Pair of Vincennes figures of Harvesters, modeled by Bondeau, c. 1750. Boy with a sickle and girl with sheaves of wheat in her apron . . . after Francois Boucher, and the only known examples. From the collection of the Comte de Chavagnac."

The ground colors, which the Meissen factory had produced in the middle twenties, became the distinctive excellence of Vincennes and Sèvres. As a result of the soft-paste and glaze of Vincennes and Sèvres, these ground colors reached the height of perfection. Nowhere else did the *bleu royal* or *bleu-de-roi* attain such depth and power as here, where it was invented by Hellot in 1749, superseding the *gros bleu*; no other establishment succeeded in producing a turquoise, or *bleu turquin,* of such perfection on the beautiful glaze of Vincennes as did Hellot in 1752. In contradistinction to the *bleu-de-roi*, it may be pointed out that this turquoise was an enamel color placed on the already fired glaze. Illustration 39 shows an example of the *bleu-de-roi* and Illustration 31 shows the turquoise of this period, the sugar box being a part of the Governor Harrison service. It is somewhat darker and richer than that of the Sèvres period. A beautiful green was first produced in 1756, the last year of the Vincennes factory, and it is much superior to that evolved at Sèvres. Colored Illustration 38 shows an example having the date letter "D." The turquoise example has the royal cypher without a date letter, and the *bleu-de-roi* cup and saucer have the date letter "B" for 1754 and the mark of the decorator Mutel. The rarest of all the colors produced during the Vincennes period about 1753 was the *jaune jonquille*, which is a soft, beautiful yellow of pure quality with no green in the the yellow. It was apparently hard to make as it was, so far as we know, used only for about four years. Only a few examples are known and these are all decorated by the famous painter Vieillard in combination with his rendition of Boucher children in monochrome blue enamel. We are fortunate in being able to illustrate them here. The earliest examples and the only ones that we know of having the date letter "A" are Illustration 427 depicting a sugar bowl and cover in the Victoria and Albert Museum, and Colored Illustration 30 a conserve pot, cover and stand in the authors' collection. The ground color is the typical "canary yellow," the cartouche is a single gold line, the decoration is in monochrome blue enamel only, the figures are children after Boucher, depicted without clothes and the sugar dish has under the base the royal cypher, the date letter "A" and in addition the mark of Vieillard. The conserve pot is similarly decorated, and in addition the tray or stand is of the trembleuse type, decorated with doves and sheaths of arrows. It has the date letter "A" and the mark of Vieillard under the base of the barrel and also under the base of the tray. It is believed these are the only examples in existence, yet it must be acknowledged that other examples may exist in private collections or may appear in the future. Illustration 426 is of a cup in the Victoria and Albert Museum and is certainly of about the same period. It lacks the date letter, and the child is clothed. Illustration 429 shows specimens in the Wadsworth Atheneum at Hartford, Connecticut, and are from the J. Pierpont Morgan collection. There are six pieces in all, four of which are illustrated here. The tea set has a tray, teapot, creamer, and sugar bowl, also a cup and saucer and bon-bon dish, not shown. None of them have a date letter, only the royal cypher and the mark of Vieillard. When these pieces were exhibited by the Metropolitan Museum some years ago, the date was given as c. 1755. The decoration is much more sophisticated on these than on the ones dated 1753. The children are fully clothed, and the cartouche is quite elaborate, indicating the slightly later work of Vieillard. The creamer is the only piece with no mark at all. Illustration 38, mentioned above with the date letter "D," has the mark of Vieillard, and also shows an elaborate cartouche and a more sophisticated rendition of the Boucher children; in this case, however, the painting is in polychrome colors (the date 1756 was the last year of the Vincennes factory).

Though the Vieillard specimens in monochrome blue enamel on the *jaune jonquille* ground are superb, they are not his only achievements of great merit. He also painted some outstanding pieces in the monochrome blue on the white ground. Colored Illustration 29 shows the only piece that we have seen bearing the date letter "A" for 1753 and the mark of Vieillard. The decoration seems even finer and the white ground is of the finest quality Vincennes pâte tendre. It will be noted that also in this case, as in the other two pieces bearing the date letter "A," the children have no clothes and are superbly drawn. If the children were clothed and framed, Vieillard could be accused of having "gilded the lily." Illustration 428 shows a teapot decorated by Vieillard in blue monochrome on a white ground. This example is in the Victoria and Albert Museum. The date letter here is "B" for 1754, the children are clothed, and the picture is enclosed in an elaborate gold cartouche. Illustrations 452 and 460 are specimens from the collection of Mrs. W. L. Harnan of Seattle.

Before passing to the productions made at Sèvres, it may be well to say a few words about the marks of the factory during both periods. Some authorities state that the royal cypher was used in a few cases before 1753, and that when this was so, of course, no date letter was added, but that in some cases a dot or dots were used. The noted French authority, E. S. Auscher, previously referred to, has this to say: "It seems probable that no definite mark was used during the early years of the undertaking, but a few pieces have been met with which from their early style should be attributed to this period, although they bear the two interwoven "L's" of the later period. Sometimes the two letters stand by themselves, with a point in the middle." In any event, one must exercise great care in making such attributions. It would seem strange that the King would have specifically granted the privilege to use the royal cypher in 1753, when the factory was made a royal one, if the mark was already in use. Many pieces of Sèvres porcelain dating as late as 1780 carry the royal cypher without a date letter. One can say with certainty that the date letter was frequently omitted. In the Wallace Collection, London, many examples will be found of important pieces of *rose Pompadour*, which was not made before 1757, marked with the cypher and bearing no date letter. This is likewise true of other colors introduced after 1753, and it is also true of many pieces of pâte dure, which were, of course, not made before 1769. On the other hand, the presence of a date letter assures one that it was placed on the piece by the decorator himself after he had completed his work. This is not true of Meissen and many other porcelains, on which the mark was placed under the glaze at the time the porcelain was made and which may have been decorated many years later; this is well worth remembering by the collector.

VINCENNES CHARACTERISTICS

1. Soft-paste.

2. Before 1750 few examples except figures with white glaze only and individual porcelain flowers.

3. Royal cypher without date letter rarely, if ever, used before 1753. Then "A" as indication of 1753, etc. Unfortunately, not always do we find date letter. "D" for 1756 last date for Vincennes.

4. When color was under glaze, mark was also, and then indicated only date of porcelain, not decoration. Otherwise date indicated date of decoration and was applied by artist; can be relied upon.

5. 1745-50 a few figures were modeled by Blondeau or La Rue with white glaze only. These are exceptionally white and very fine. A very few were polychrome decorated. Biscuit figures 1750-56 modeled by Blondeau were exceptionally fine. All Vincennes figures of soft-paste.

6. Color ground of this period exceptional. *Bleu-de-roi* 1749, *bleu turquin* 1752, rarest of all—*jaune jonquille* 1753 or possibly earlier, deep green 1756. All invented by Hellot.

7. While objects not so large as those of Sèvres, considered finer from standpoint of connoisseur.

8. Use of monochrome blue as a decoration invented by Vieillard 1753. All specimens Vincennes rare and expensive, but worth the cost.

SÈVRES PÂTE TENDRE

From 1756 to 1769 the world famous Sèvres pâte tendre was made at the new factory, to which the great wealth of Louis XV was available and which produced the fabulous porcelains of that period. The finest painters, sculptors and chemists were brought together at Sèvres. One has only to visit the Wallace Collection in London (to name but one) to realize the remarkable excellence of the products during this period. Many new colors were now introduced, but none have received the acclaim that has been given the *rose Pompadour*, erroneously referred to in England sometimes as *rose du Barry*. The new color was first made in 1757 and some authorities say it was the work of "Xramet," but certainly Hellot had some claim to its discovery as its use ceased upon his death in 1766. This color has been extensively copied but never equalled, and to the connoisseur its "opaque" beauty is unmistakable. In addition to the important shapes produced during this period, the flower painting and above all the gold work were superb. The gold was laid on thickly and then burnished and tooled in a manner not practised elsewhere. The greatest artist in the gold work was Le Guay, who was at the factory from 1749 to 1796. His mark is found in company with the most renowned painters and frequently alone where the gold work is superb.

In 1759 the King, at the instigation of Madame de Pompadour, decided to take over the factory, and its existence was thus for the time assured. A large staff of sculptors set to work, with Bachelier as artistic director of the entire institution, Falconet as chief of the figure modeling department, and Duplessis as head of the remaining modeling shops. Even greater, however, was the staff of painters, some of whose works can be identified by the marks they used. E. Hannover in his *European Porcelain* volume gives at length the names of the principal artists of the Vincennes and Sèvres factories and what they painted. Of the subjects painted, flowers and fruits were the motifs most frequently used. The number of bird painters, on the other hand, number but a few in comparison, and the explanation is that only the artists who painted birds without flowers and not birds in combination with flowers, which are by far the commoner type, are so listed. Similarly, the group of landscape painters must be regarded as proportionately larger than appears in the lists. Vieillard, one of the greatest artists of the factory, was quite as much a landscape painter as a figure painter; in many of his decorations the figures are merely accessory to the landscape. He was undoubtedly the creator of the style of painting in monochrome blue enamel which, either on the white grounds and particularly on the *jaune jonquille* grounds, constitutes some of the most excellent decoration of the factory. Among the more noted artists in figure painting were Dodin and Morin; in the painting of birds Aloncle, Chappuis aîné and Evans; and flowers Micaud, Leve aîné, Méreaud aîné, Nöel, Taillandier, Tandart, and Thévenet père.

Most of the specimens made during this great period appear to have been intended for the King's service, for the furnishing of the royal palaces of Versailles, the Trianon, Marly, Bellevue, Meudon, St. Germain, and Fontainebleau. The King also used them as presents for his relatives, his friends, his courtiers, and his ambassadors. They were also made use of as diplomatic presents, sometimes perhaps as diplomatic bribes. Like Louis XIV, Louis XV was obliged to send all his silver to the mint twice during periods of national distress, and the courtiers became quite accustomed to the use of porcelain; thus Sèvres profited by the deplorable state of the country's finances. In addition to the dinner services of simple or elaborate form in the style of Duplessis and the small tea and coffee services, the trays, the sugar basins, and the milk pots which are so vastly admired today, we find an enormous production of vases, designed by architects and sculptors of eminence, the importance and beauty of which astound us today.

W. B. Honey in his *European Ceramic Art* sums up the situation well when he says: "Figures were, of course, required and were at first enameled in colors like the German. The thought of monumental sculpture soon intruded, however; color was abandoned and Bachelier, perhaps as early as 1750, conceived the notion of dispensing with glaze to produce a material more nearly resembling marble, and with this anticipation of the Neo-Classical all the peculiar advantages of porcelain were unfortunately renounced. But the white glazed figures made in the space of a few years before the final establishment of biscuit stand at the summit of achievement in European porcelain-figure modeling. Some were made by Louis-Felix de la Rue, others by Blondeau. Many of the best are anonymous, but the influence of Boucher is over all . . . Eventually, with the appointment in 1757 of Etienne-Maurice Falconet, the porcelain figure was thought to be at last raised to the level of true sculpture, but in fact, lost its individuality . . . But the innumerable models made under the direction of Falconet's successors, Le Riche and Boizot have in the majority of cases ceased to be specifically porcelain, and the excellence of their sculptured originals cannot avail them. In style they belong to a new age, foreshadowed in the work of Falconet himself . . . These are the first landmarks in the Classical revival, and the Rococo, which had never been extravagantly adopted, even at Vincennes, now fades into the graceful early French variety of the Neo-Classical inexactly known as the *Louis Seize* style.

Other indications of a loss of "porcelain-sense" are not lacking. Already in the 1760's is to be noted a tendency to give the material a richly wrought character as of jewelry, with more elaborate gilt patterns and diapers and reticulated colored grounds. As time passed this tendency became more pronounced, and the pictorial painting, becoming more elaborate, was mistakenly allowed to cover the whole surface of the beautiful white porcelain. Alternatively, diapers of small sprigs or garlands of flowers delicately but conventionally painted, set another fashion for the contemporary factories. By 1775, the forms of the sumptuous vases had hardened to a metallic symmetry, and thenceforward the Sèvres factory ceased to be of creative importance, though for a long time it was as prosperous as ever. Its classical style lacked the authority of Wedgwood, to whom the leadership must be assigned in this later period, and it is rather on account of the fresh and spontaneous work of the "fifties" and "sixties" that the Sèvres porcelain takes its high rank among the ceramic wares of Europe."

We show here three of the most important pâte tendre examples from the Wallace Collection as Illustrations 430, 431 and 432. Two of these pieces, the candlestick vase and *vaisseau à mât* are there thought to date 1756 and 1757 respectively; however, they have no date letter. Similar vase modelings will be found at the former home of the Rothschilds, Waddesdon Manor, now under the National Trust, some 40 miles from London. Here they are dated 1762 and 1761. The elephant-head candlestick vase is said to have been modeled by Duplessis and painted by Dodin; the other example is thought also to have been modeled by Duplessis, and the bird paintings are attributed to Aloncle. Why such important pieces are not dated or marked by the decorator is difficult to explain. The third piece, a pot-pourri vase, is dated 1757, but here again the painter's mark is absent. Illustration 437 shows a sugar basin decorated with flowers on a turquoise ground and bearing within the royal cypher the date letter "F" for 1758. Illustration 37, a cup and saucer having a combination of yellow and green and in addition the *oeil-de-perdrix* pattern so popular at the time, shown here in color. The mark is the royal cypher without a date letter, but as the colors are those used in 1757, we believe this example to be of that date. Illustrations 434 and 435 depict two important vases, c. 1758, from the Metropolitan Museum of Art, New York. Illustration 32 shows a cup and saucer of the famous *rose Pompadour* ground, and Illustration 433 shows a garniture from the R. Thornton Wilson Collection (1757-63) in this color. Illustration 33 is also a cup and saucer and is quite an outstanding example of the flower painting of Micaud and the gold work of LeGuay. There was no finer work done at the factory than that of these two artists. The date letter is "H" for 1761. The ground is the royal blue. It may be well to point out that the *bleu-de-roi* of the Vincennes period has a somewhat mottled appearance, whereas that of the Sèvres period does not. The reason is that at Vincennes the blue which was placed under the white glaze was applied with a brush, while later at Sèvres it was made uniform by applying it as a powder. Colored Illustrations 36 and 35 a cup and saucer and a platter, were decorated by Vieillard and show his skill as a painter of landscapes as well as figures, the cup and saucer, 1761, and the oval dish, 1765, all having the Sèvres *bleu-de-roi* ground. Colored Illustration 34 is a large beaker chocolate cup and trembleuse saucer, decorated with exotic birds by Evans and Aloncle, and having the date letter 1763, *bleu-de-roi ground* and *oeil-de-perdrix* pattern.

SÈVRES PÂTE DURE

About 1770 Sèvres for the first time produced hard-paste. For a while the factory continued to make soft-paste as well, but soon it was found that the pâte dure could be produced more cheaply, and the beautiful pâte tendre was no longer made. Collectors know that when a piece of Sèvres has a date letter before 1770, it is pâte tendre, but if the date letter is after 1770, it may be either.

It will be remembered that in 1753 Paul Hannong offered the secrets of hard-paste to Boileau, who is reputed to have treated him very badly. But, it would seem that it was the failure of Macquer to find suitable kaolin clay on French soil rather than the lack of knowledge as to how to make it that delayed its appearance in France for so long. Finally in 1768, extensive pure deposits were discovered at St. Yrieix, near Limoges, and in 1769 the State acquired them. It was not until about 1772 that production of pâte dure was under way in any quantity, and even then less of it was made than of the soft-paste. The hard porcelain frequently has a royal crown above the cypher. As stated, the mark on the pâte tendre was on top of the glaze, though an exception occurs when an under-glaze color was used, in which case the mark was under the glaze, as was the ground color. The mark on the hard porcelain was under the glaze, and it must be remembered that in such cases, the mark does not necessarily indicate the date of the decoration but only the date when the porcelain was made. Sèvres biscuit has no factory mark until after 1860, but at times a molder's mark appears. No mark should be treated with more caution than that of Sèvres for none has been more abused, since Sèvres has at all times offered the forger a higher profit than any other porcelain. Least dangerous are absolute forgeries, the most innocuous of these having year-marks belonging to the period of soft porcelain, though the material in them is hard. Very often we find on these articles the year mark "A" for 1753, showing that the forger well knew that Vincennes porcelain is even more valuable than Sèvres and stopped at nothing in order to give his product the appearance of being as old as possible. Earlier forgeries of this sort are betrayed by the use of a painter's mark of a well known flower painter on a piece with figure decoration, or by the use of a date letter earlier than the period of the painter. Very often, however, these counterfeits are so contrived that neither paste nor marks betray them, being covered with one or the other of the famous ground colors and mounted in ormolu, so that it is difficult or impossible to check the marks, if any such are there at all. In this category belong, for instance, the large vases and dishes, or even table-tops with paintings after Watteau, or of the French kings with their ladies, which all visitors to Paris should recollect and which are designed to entrap the tourist. Experienced collectors can readily see that these pieces with their inferior painting and even worse ormolu are not eighteenth century. Not many fakes are found today in soft porcelain; however they were made in considerable numbers at St. Amand-les-Eaux between 1815 and 1877. The gilding on true soft Sèvres porcelain is laid on thickly and deeply chased or etched with a fixed nail, whereas in imitations it is treated with an agate, which gives a smoother and thinner effect. Some dangerous forgeries were made in England at the Coalport factory in imitation of the color grounds. The Minton factory also made some excellent copies, not with the intent to deceive, as it placed its own mark on those pieces; but in many instances the forger has removed them and substituted the Sèvres mark. Other reproductions were made at Madeley in England by Thomas Martin Randall, who produced in 1830-40 an artificial porcelain which he succeeded in covering with a turquoise ground like that of Sèvres. He also was one of those who purchased slightly decorated Sèvres porcelain and added important decoration. This practice is known as *clobbering* and is by far the most difficult to detect, as the piece has the old paste and glaze and the correct mark. Other French factories, including Tournay and St. Amand-les-Eaux, made soft-paste porcelain and copied the royal factory mark, and much of their undecorated porcelain fell into the hands of the home decorators, as in fact did much undecorated Sèvres. In Hungary, Fischer of Herend successfully copied Sèvres.

Genuine Sèvres plates, cups and saucers frequently have a little round hole drilled in the foot-rim, by which they were hung during the second firing in the muffle kiln. When this hole is lacking, the piece is subject to suspicion. The hole, however, should be carefully examined, since the faker knowing that such a hole should be present, will drill one in the piece. If it is faked, the hole will be free of glaze, but if genuine it will contain glaze to some extent. It will also be remembered that chrome colors were not invented until 1804, and therefore if the decoration has a chrome green, recognizable by a warm yellowish tone, and particularly if it lacks the slight iridescence which generally accompanies the copper-green, the specimen was manifestly not decorated in the eighteenth century. Again, refired gold loses some of its brilliance, and the porcelain itself frequently shows yellowish stains and small black spots. Finally, it should be added that the newer ground colors generally differ more or less from the older ones of Sèvres. The *turquois* is, as a rule, too green—the *rose Pompadour* too transparent or muddy. All "jeweled porcelain" with date marks prior to 1780 are false, certainly in so far as the jeweled decoration is concerned, as this style was not originated until that date. It is well to remember that only a very few Vincennes or Sèvres figures were made with a glaze or were decorated. As regards hard French porcelain, not very much has been counterfeited on account of its lesser value. The beginning collector should therefore realize that many dangers are present in buying old Sèvres porcelain; however, the satisfaction of owning a genuine piece would seem to warrant a certain degree of risk. Reputable dealers are the answer, if one can afford to pay the price. Illustrations 436, 438, 439, 442, 443 and 444 show examples of pâte dure.

SÈVRES CHARACTERISTICS

1. Soft-paste 1756-69; 1770 to end of century both soft and hard-paste made, the soft gradually becoming scarcer after 1770.

2. Marks, royal cypher usually with date letter "E" for 1757 and so on, but sometimes not dated.

3. Period 1757-69 golden period of Sèvres referred to as pâte tendre.

4. Important vases found in this period.

5. Most important new color *rose Pompadour*, made only from 1757 to 1766, when Hellot, noted chemist, died. Copied afterwards but never equaled.

6. Frequently faked.

7. Exceptionally fine decorations and superb gold work.

8. Gold heavily applied and design put on with a nail.

9. Plates and dishes etc. should have a small round hole in the foot-rim and should have some glaze in this hole to be genuine.

10. Several English factories copied Sèvres, but not hard to identify. Most dangerous fakes use genuine porcelain but add important decoration.

11. While useful ware nearly always marked, figures never marked.

12. Jeweled decoration first used 1780, so pieces with earlier date marks fakes.

13. Check (for fakes) period decorator worked at factory with the date mark; also type of decorating he did.

14. Watch for poor ormolu and chrome colors as fakes.

PARIS OR OLD PARIS

While this porcelain is far less collectable than that previously described, much of it came to America during a period of twenty years before and twenty years after the end of the eighteenth century, to say nothing of the large quantity that has been brought in at a very much later date. In the U.S.A., it is referred to generally as Old Paris, even though for the most part it is not old at all.

In 1959 a very interesting paper on this subject was given in Memphis by Mrs. Carrington Jones, past president of the Memphis Antiquarian Society. She said among other things that "Old Paris is not like Vincennes or Sèvres, the product of one factory with one mark. It is from the little factories that furnished a retreat for disgruntled or runaway workers, who for one reason or another detached themselves from the Sèvres factory. It is the grouping of all the little or big, successful or unsuccessful, good or bad, producers of hard-paste porcelain in the city of Paris since the time that hard-paste was known in France in 1769. It was the expression in French porcelain of the rising democracy against absolute monarchy. In spite of edicts, many little bootleg factories sprang up all over Paris, and in nearly every case were protected by rich noblemen who wanted to have their own factory in spite of the King. Even the Queen was not excluded from such a group."

No attempt will be made here to cover the subject. We show as Illustrations 441, 445 and 446 such pieces. It will be understood that many other small factories existed throughout France.

TOURNAY, SCEAUX, BOURG-LA-REINE, ORLEANS, BRANCAS-LAURAGUAIS, ARRAS AND SAINT-AMAND-LES EAUX

The new collector is advised to consult such books as *French Porcelain*, by E. S. Auscher, and *European Porcelain*, by E. Hannover about these factories, as space will not permit nor their importance justify inclusion here. Illustrations 407A and 457 are examples of Bourg-La-Reine (collection of Mrs. Stoddard of Seattle). An exception will be made in the case of Tournay.

This factory was established in 1750 by F. J. Peterinck and the business was so successful by 1762 that 250 workers were employed. It will be remembered that at the time it was under the domination of the French crown. At first it followed Meissen shapes but soon it copied Sèvres, and the "ribbon," "oeil-de-perdrix," exotic birds, and little landscapes became its chief designs. Such porcelains were marked with crossed swords and with four crosses. Illustration 391 shows a piece so marked.

Tournay made some excellent white figures. Illustrations 508 and 511 are probably the work of this factory, although they bear a close resemblance to some of the mysterious "Girl-in-a-Swing" English figures. The French artist Duvivier of Chelsea and Derby fame worked at this factory.

E. Hannover, in commenting on the factory says: "In his work on the factory of Peterinck—a valuable book—Soil de Moriamé has registered and reproduced a number of these plastic pieces, but seems too much to have taken as his starting point the dangerous theory of Ujfalvy, that all figures in soft-paste without a mark are from Tournay (or England). To Tournay however, may doubtless be ascribed certain groups of kindred style, especially a little series of the pastoral type, with a tree as the center of the group. For these, however, we must refer the reader to the illustrations in the work mentioned." This factory is supposed to have made many pieces and sold them as Sèvres. One thing is certain, that the factory made a great deal of porcelain in soft-paste, and that much of it is of fine quality, but there is also a marked tendency to assign to this factory much that it did not produce.

CHAPTER 6

ENGLISH PORCELAIN

The principal English factories started around the middle of the eighteenth century. It will be remembered that 1756 was the date of the beginning of the Seven Years War and the decline in the leadership of the Meissen factory. In 1753 Louis XV took over the Vincennes factory and made it the Royal Factory and in 1756 moved it to Sèvres. In short, there was much widespread activity in the European porcelain manufactories as the English, French, and other factories made their bids to rival the great factory at Meissen. The English factories copied Oriental, French and Meissen models, and in some cases the English designs were copied from Oriental copies made at the Meissen factory. Just as the French factories were noted for their pâte tendre, or soft-paste, so, for the most part, were the English factories. The only exceptions were Plymouth, Bristol and New Hall, which will be discussed a little later. The English factories differed from those of Meissen, Vincennes, and Sèvres in that they had no Royal prince or emperor to provide the necessary funds for carrying on the work of the factory. They were strictly commercial ventures, and they had to make their way without any contribution from the Crown. They did, however, enjoy the patronage of many English aristocrats who were interested in porcelain and were willing to pay high prices for fine pieces.

CHELSEA

As Chelsea was undoubtedly the most celebrated English factory, it would seem proper to commence with it. Its early history is shrouded in some mystery, and we cannot say with certainty whether it was started earlier than Bow. Both were located in or near London. Three names have been associated with its beginning: Nicholas Sprimont, to whom its later success was undoubtedly due, was recorded as a goldsmith of Soho in the records of the Guild in 1742; Charles Gouyn was a silversmith of Soho (both men were of French extraction); Thomas Briand was the third man.

The *Daily Advertiser*, March 8th 1749, says: "Mr. Sprimont takes the Liberty to acquaint the Publick, that the favourable Reception and general Approbation his China-Ware has met with, makes it necessary for him to suspend all further Sale thereof at his Ware-house after Tomorrow, that he may have Time to make a sufficient Quantity of such Things he has observed to be most agreeable to the Taste of those who have done him the Honour to look at his Performance . . . He also gives Notice, that he has no Sort of Connexion with, nor for a considerable Time past has put any of his Ware into that Shop in St. James's Street, which was the Chelsea China Warehouse." In reply to the above advertisement inserted by Sprimont, we find an advertisement by S. Stables, the owner of the Chelsea China Warehouse in St. James's Street referred to in the Sprimont advertisement, in which he says he was supplied by none other than Charles Gouyn, late proprietor and chief manufacturer of the Chelsea House. This advertisement appeared in the *General Advertiser* of January 29th 1750. From the above, it may be inferred that the partnership between Sprimont and Gouyn did not last very long and was terminated with some bitterness. Gouyn's name is not heard of later, so his real contribution, if any, will remain in doubt. The third man, Thomas Briand, is thought by some to have associated with the factory because of records found in the original *Journal Book* of the Royal Society, under date February 10th, 1742-43. The record states: "Mr. Bryand, a Stranger, that was present, shew'd the Society several Specimens of a sort of fine white Ware made here by himself from native materials of our own Country, which appear'd to be in all respects as good as any of the finest Porcelane or China ware; and he said it was much preferable for its fineness to the ware of Dresden, and seem'd to answer the Character of the true Japan . . . Thanks were ordered for this communication." A further record at the Royal Society shows that "Mr. Thomas Bryand" attended the meeting as a visitor through the introduction of the Secretary, Dr. Cromwell Mortimer, who lived in Chelsea.

From the above we may surmise that this man was the actual founder of Chelsea in 1742 or before. Its founding could have been similar to that of Worcester whose success was based on early experiments of Lund. Briand, on the other hand, may have experimented at this date in connection with some factory unknown today. Who is well-informed enough to say? However, we can safely state that Chelsea porcelain was made during the early 1740's and that its success was primarily due to Nicholas Sprimont. The known specimens that fix a date of manufacture are the Goat and Bee Jugs on which have been scratched in the paste before firing, a triangle, the word "Chelsea," and the date 1745. One such Jug seems to have a date of 1743, though there is some controversy about whether the date on this jug is in reality 1743.

THE TRIANGLE PERIOD (1745-1750)

Coffee-pots and jugs, for some unknown reason, were made only during this period (see *Daily Advertiser* 1749, and references to Excavations below). Practically all specimens are based on silver counterparts and when marked have an incised triangle, sometimes with the word Chelsea and a date added. The porcelain was very translucent with tears shown by transmitted light. Volume I, Transactions 3, the *English Ceramic Circle* contains a splendid paper by Mr. O. Glendenning and Mrs. Donald MacAlister covering fully the early history of the Chelsea factory, and including illustrations. Transactions 3 of the same publication carries an article on the excavations on the site of the old factory. They are well worth reading.

While the Goat and Bee jugs, with incised dates under the base have made it possible to date the early products of the factory, there is no question that many of them in museums and private collections are reproductions, made at the Coalport and other factories during the early part of the nineteenth century. The fact that so many are preserved today, of itself, would make them suspect. Dr. F. Severne Mackenna in his first Chelsea book has attempted to set up standards by which the sheep can be separated from the goats. He says the genuine ones must have short stumpy horns, long manes, and extremely small tails which turn upwards. The bee must be small and fine (not a fat bumble), and the flowers must have petals which are convex. The base must be unglazed, and the handle thin and free of clumsiness.

Equally celebrated are the crayfish salts and the beaker cups. Colored Illustration 46 shows one of these rare cups. It is of a beaker, inverted bell shape, formed of overlapping leaves, taken from a silver counterpart. The decoration is in the Kakiemon style showing a red tiger, and the extremely bright colors are in the Hizen manner. It has a very distinguished history, having been originally in the collection of Disraeli, the great Prime Minister of Great Britain, then passing to the collection of Mr. Bemrose and finally to that of Dr. F. S. MacKenna. It is illustrated in the book of permanent examples of the English Ceramic Circle and is now in the authors' collection. Figures from this period are exceptionally rare. Illustration 461 from the Sigmund Katz collection is shown here.

THE RAISED ANCHOR PERIOD (1750-52)

There is no hard and fast demarcation between this and the succeeding Red Anchor Period. The mark was an Anchor, sometimes in red, upon a raised disk applied to the piece. The porcelain is noticeably heavier than previously. Here we find large "moons," which have become known as "Chelsea Moons." Not many vases or figures, except those of birds are found, and these form a large and important part of the production. Illustrations 463 to 466, 469, 470 and 473 are examples of the finest ones made, though the first two are Red Anchor (c. 1755). They were taken from George Edward's *Natural History of Uncommon Birds*. Illustration 474 is from this History. The Chelsea ones are famous and quite expensive. Illustrations 592 and 593 show interesting figures of Dwarfs from the Schreiber Collection. The man is Raised Anchor, and is marked with an anchor in relief painted in red; the date is about 1750. The woman is Red Anchor and is marked with the usual small red anchor and dates about 1755. On the other hand, animals are much less numerous; pug dogs are encountered most often and domestic animals occasionally. Some figures of the Italian Comedy and copies of Meissen models are known, but rare. Illustrations 485, 486 and 487 are fine specimens from the Boston Museum of Fine Arts. Fabled animal decoration is found, but not in such number and variety as later. Generally, but not invariably, no clouds are depicted, and the animals do not have "red toungs" as in the next period. The painting is more subdued and the animals have lumpy joints. The rocks are always obliquely cross hatched. The animals are frequently spotted, and the scene usually is enclosed with a double circle, red inside and black outside. No one can say for certain who painted these fabled animals. The majority opinion favors Lefèbre and Duvivier. J. H. O'Neale and John Donaldson, outside decorators, are known to have painted such work at a later date. Colored Illustration 47 shows a Raised Anchor platter and Illustration 491 an octagonal deep bowl known as "Hob in the Well' Illustration 462 is a rare and unusual one dating at the end of the raised anchor period and is from the unusually fine collection of Mrs. Sigmund Katz.

THE RED ANCHOR PERIOD (1753-1758)

The Red Anchor paste and glaze are somewhat similar to those of the Raised Anchor except that the glaze is thinner and therefore lighter in weight. Moons are still present, but not so large nor so many as previously. We now have some crazing of the glaze, but not to the marked extent found in the later Gold Anchor period. We also encounter a number of "thumb" or "patch marks," widely thought to occur only on Derby. They are the result of placing the object on small pieces of clay when it is fired in the kiln, and are considered typical of Derby. The most distinguishing marks, however, of this time (found also occasionally on Raised Anchor pieces) are the "spurs" or "stilts" usually three in number, found on the base. They result from the piece being placed on round pieces of clay in the kiln and, after firing, a part of the stilt adhering to the object. Similar spurs are sometimes found on early Bow pieces, but they are usually rectangular or oval in shape and not round. In the case of blown glass, they are called "pontils." Domestic ware can be divided into dinner, dessert and tea services. Here again, we find the strange and unexplainable absence of coffee-pots. Teapots are plentiful, and coffee cups are found. (We find the same absence of coffee-pots in Nantgarw porcelain in the early part of the nineteenth century, yet, then again, the English preferred tea). The designs are usually restrained. Botanical specimens known as "Sir Hans Sloane's plants" are much sought after. By far the most numerous are bouquets of scattered flowers copied from Meissen. Neither bird painting nor ground colors were used to any great extent. Mazarin blue is sometimes found, but it came into general use with the

Gold Anchor pieces. Gold is rarely found, and some writers say not at all. No transfer printing was used as the glaze was too soft to make it practical; the same also applies to blue-and-white. Molded animals and plants were used on tureens which were made in quantities and bring high prices today. Few vases are found until the next period, when they became the principal work of the factory.

We now come to the articles which made Red Anchor famous, the excellent figures. There is no aspect of collecting English porcelain more interesting than that connected with Red Anchor figures. Half a century ago, they were little appreciated. Today, they have reached their height of appreciation. They are more sought after and bring higher prices than any other English porcelain figures. As a class, they are undoubtedly unsurpassed by other English figures and compare favorably with the Meissen ones modeled by the great Kändler. Reasons for their popularity are that they have been brilliantly modeled on unobstrusive bases, the material is very suitable, and they are tastefully decorated. In the main, they are of medium size, and this adds to their simple beauty.

Of the figures modeled, those from the Italian Comedy are among the best. The 1755 sales catalogue of the Chelsea factory listed 72 such figures, including: Harlequin, Pantaloon, Mezzetino, Scaramouche, Columbine, The Doctor, The Lawyer, and The Capitan. Also oriental subjects, classical and mythological personages are found, such as: Gods, Goddesses, Mars, Venus, Diana, Mercury, Jupiter, Juno and Minerva; also the Rape of a Sabine, River Gods, and religious figures, the Seasons, the Senses, the Continents, Science and Art, and Artisans. A few animals were also made. We are indeed fortunate to be privileged to illustrate so many important specimens from collections both public and private in this country and in addition examples from the renowned collection of Lady Charlotte Schreiber (Illustrations 597, 603, 604, 606, 607, 609, 610, 611, 612 and 613 which are all from the latter and dated c. 1755) now in the Victoria and Albert Museum in London.

Illustrations 49, 488, 490 and 546 are examples of useful ware of this period. Illustrations 477 to 481 are Italian Comedy figures from the Boston Museum of Fine Arts. Illustrations 482 and 483, River Gods, are from the same collection. Illustration 475, after the Meissen Monkey Band, is from Colonial Williamsburg, rich in fine examples as is the Boston Museum. Illustration 500, "Tyrolese Dancers," from a Meissen model, and Illustration 476, Perfume Pot, are from the Victoria and Albert Museum. Illustrations 501 and 502 are of examples from the collection of Mrs. Wendell Black, and Illustrations 494 and 495 are from the collection of Mrs. C. B. Stout.

CHELSEA TOYS

Miniature figures famous the world over, under the name of Chelsea toys, were first introduced at this time. Some of the finest ones were made during the Red Anchor period, while the remainder of this large and popular type were produced during the Gold Anchor era. For a complete understanding of this kind of figure, we must refer you to G. E. Bryant's *Chelsea Porcelain Toys*, published in 1925, where the matter is fully covered.

Fable animal paintings were largely the work of O'Neale. Much of the information as to what was made at Chelsea is gained from the sales catalogues, which fortunately are still available. They cover the dates 1755 to 1784, the Red Anchor, Gold Anchor and Chelsea-Derby periods.

The mark used during 1753-58 was a small well-drawn anchor in red, from which the period derived its name. It was usually placed on top of the base of figures, and hardly ever under it. On the other hand, on useful wares, it was placed under the base at the foot-rim. It will be well for the collector to remember this, as fake pieces usually place the mark under the base on figures, and at the center on useful ware, instead of at the foot-rim. Towards the end of the Red Anchor period, and sometimes on into the Gold Anchor, we find the anchor of a considerably larger size used and the color a brown, or brownish-red. It is at that time placed under the base at the center.

Many advanced collectors in recent years have become interested in chemical analysis as a means of determining the maker of English porcelain. The following table shows the changes in the formula of the paste during the four periods of Chelsea's brief history.

Typical analysis of the different periods of Chelsea

	Triangle	Raised Anchor	Red Anchor	Gold Anchor
Silica	70.2	64.74	69.1	45.52
Alumina	.95	6.00	5.9	12.06
Lime	14.00	25.00	20.5	26.00
Phos. Acid	—	.23	—	14.27
Magnesia	1.48	Trace	.71	—
Lead Oxide	7.43	.55	—	—
Potash and Soda	5.61	4.40	3.99	.73

NOTE.—Worcester shows 4% lime, Longton Hall 9%, Bow 24% to 28%, and Derby 24%. Note also that Triangle Period Chelsea has a large percentage of lead and that the other periods of Chelsea have practically none. The Gold Anchor Chelsea has 36% bone ash, offset by reduction of silica and alumina. For those wishing additional data along this line, see the *Burlington Magazine*, Sept. and Oct. 1927, Sept. 1928, and April 1929; also *English Ceramic Circle*, Vol. I, No. 4, 1937.

Another device used by some advanced collectors is the ultra-violet ray lamp. It is, however, of questionable value to anyone except experts. Such machines are quite valuable to the collector to determine quickly and accurately restorations, etc. When purchasing expensive figures, it is an essential piece of equipment.

THE GOLD ANCHOR PERIOD (1758-70)

This period starts when Sprimont resumed production and continues until the factory was purchased by William Duesbury and operated as a separate factory but under the same ownership as Derby. During Sprimont's illness (1756-58), many of his workmen went to the Bow factory, located also in the outskirts of London. When the factory resumed operation, many of these workmen returned. They evidently brought with them knowledge concerning the advantages to be gained by the use of calcined bone ash then used at Bow, but not heretofore used at Chelsea. It was a great help in the practical production of porcelain. When the bone ash was added, the "moons" disappeared from Chelsea.

An examination of Gold Anchor porcelain discloses a clear, fine white paste seen through a thick glassy glaze, which has a marked tendency to craze and to collect in thick pools in depressed areas. Where the glaze collected, it has a faint yellow-green tinge. The porcelain of this period is easily scratched, and the bases were invariably ground, so that the object would present a flat surface, which would otherwise be warped. The paste so exposed is of a gray-brown color and has a granular structure that feels almost "greasy" to the touch. The translucency varies from piece to piece, and heavily potted ones are almost opaque. The tea and coffee services on the other hand, are usually very translucent, and the paste shows a clear, creamy green tint, unmarked by any blemish of opacity. Chelsea china must always remain especially distinguished among the earliest English potteries for the exceptional quality of its paste and glaze. It is pâte tendre in the truest sense of the word. The body is of a delightful milky white with a close sugary fracture, not very resonant; but what appeals most, perhaps, to the senses of the discriminating connoisseur is the glaze. On the best Chelsea pieces, it is almost sensuous in its softness and luscious richness, and there is no doubt at all that the exceptional brilliance of Chelsea coloring is largely due to the peculiar sympathy between color and glaze.

Whereas seldom is gold found during earlier periods, now we find it used profusely. It was at this time too, that the ground colors came into their own. Claret was the most famous, followed by mazarin blue and pea green. Such pieces are noted for the fine gold work found usually as a part of the decoration. It was of a very high quality, and engraved designs in the gold were exquisite and only surpassed by similar work at Vincennes, and at Sèvres during the early years of that factory. The designs on useful ware, and particularly on the fine vases, are unexcelled. They consist of flowers, figures, and fantastic birds of exceptional merit. Just as the figures were the outstanding work of the Red Anchor period, so now the fine vases are the glory of the Gold Anchor. Nothing like them has been made before or since. They show a profusion of applied rococo loops and scrolls. The covers and necks are frequently pierced. By the end of the period, the designs became more restrained. These garnitures were usually grouped in pairs, threes, fives and sevens. The decorations were, in many cases, after Rubens, Teniers, Boucher, Watteau and Pillement. Few were from the Italian Comedy. Ground colors and profuse use of gold played a big part in the decoration.

The figures were in marked contrast to those of the Red Anchor era, which were subdued in color and without gold. Now they became most elaborate and gold was used profusely. They are larger in size and more ambitious in form and, frequently, are posed against elaborate backgrounds of verdure and flowers. Such backgrounds were called "bocages." The Italian Comedy figures so popular during the previous period are now seldom found, and comparatively few mythological figures are known. On the other hand, the Chelsea toys found in the previous period were continued in large quantities. Such pieces are interesting and desirable collector's items. They frequently have mottoes painted on them, and nearly always in French. Oddly enough, the spelling is so poor as to indicate that they were copied from a list by painters who had no knowledge of the language.

While previously Meissen was the principal influence, now we find that Sèvres has taken the leadership in useful wares. As the Sèvres factory made no figures except the all-white in either glazed or biscuit, Meissen continued to set the style in this field.

In the sales catalogues of 1763, we find that 325 lots were sold during a six-day period. The mention of ground colors is interesting. Sixteen times pea green is mentioned; mazarin blue 25 times; crimson 2; rose 3, and yellow 1. The crimson and rose referred to are different shades of the famous "claret" in which Chelsea excels, which color varies greatly in intensity. A few birds are referred to, and frequent reference is made to "chased gold" decoration, not flat brush work as at Worcester, but raised and chased like Sèvres. Chelsea, was noted for a dark blue, improperly called mazarine. But of all the colors made there, the one that was the most famous was the crimson ground known as "claret." This color ground was undoubtedly made at Chelsea as a result of the introduction at Sèvres by Xramet in 1757 of the world famous *rose Pompadour*, which was not made there after 1766. Nicholas Sprimont was not a man to remain uninfluenced by the success of this new color at Sèvres; hence in 1760, he introduced claret at Chelsea. As late as the sale of 1768, it was referred to as "Pompadour Sets." It was difficult and expensive to make and never reached the excellence of *rose Pompadour*, but it had a peculiar warmth which is most attractive to all who love color as a form of decoration. It was made from gold combined with tin, as all such rose colors are, and that it was expensive is manifestly suggested by the fact that it was almost invariably used upon wares which are finely painted and richly gilded. Such a piece is Colored Illustration 48, a small pomade jar with cover. It is decorated with the beautifully raised gold similar to that made at the Vincennes and early Sèvres factories. This specimen is also remarkable in the fact that the painting is clearly of French origin and was, in all probability, painted by an itinerant French artist associated at one time with the Chelsea factory. Fig. 537 is another example.

As illustrating the vases referred to we are privileged to present three of the finest with claret colored ground with panels in reserve from the famous Jones Collection, now in the Victoria and Albert Museum. They are shown here as Illustrations 505, 506 and 507. We likewise show two pot-pourri vases from the same collection decorated with gilding on a mazarin-blue ground; all five of these vases carry the gold anchor mark. The last two are here shown as Illustrations 503 and 504. Illustrations 653 and 654 show a set of Muses, from the collection of Mr. and Mrs. Bertrand Cohn, of Memphis, Tennessee. We also show five figures probably produced near the end of the period. Illustrations 497 and 499 are from the collection of Mrs. C. M. Gooch, of Memphis, Tennessee. Illustration 515 represents the Goddess Juno from ancient mythology, while Illustrations 517 and 518 show a fisherman holding a net and a woman with a basket of fish. These two figures also show the popular bocages of the period.

The life of the Chelsea factory, as such, extends over a period of barely twenty-five years (1745-69), yet in that short space, we find the whole gamut of the potter's art played upon, and from a beginning necessarily primitive and experimental, it rose to the production of works of art quite capable of holding their own beside the state-aided manufacturers of the Continent.

GIRL IN A SWING

Certain white figures have caused a great deal of controversy in England, and have been given the name "Girl in a Swing." The name above was used because one of the figures is a girl in a swing, shown here as Illustration 513. The chemical analysis of such pieces does not point to any known factory. They have as much as 16% in lead content. Some authorities think they are experimental pieces of Chelsea, made during the transition from the Triangle to the Raised Anchor period. Others say that probably some workmen from Staffordshire started a factory that failed. The authors suggest a possible connection with Thomas Briand. The English Ceramic Circle has passed on certain pieces as belonging to this legendary class, and such specimens bring high prices. Illustration 512 shows another example.

REPRODUCTIONS AND FAKES

The term *reproductions* here means pieces made at a much later date to deliberately deceive the purchaser. By *fakes* we mean genuinely old pieces which were originally undecorated or only slightly decorated but to which decoration has been added later. This practice is known as *clobbering*.

With the exception of the Goat and Bee jugs already referred to, there are no reproductions, so far as we know, of Triangle or Raised Anchor Chelsea. Most reproductions occur in the Gold Anchor category in which there has been extensive faking. As the gold anchor is placed on top of the glaze, it is easy to add. English Coalport, Tournay, and Samson of Paris have copied it extensively. Today the descendents of Samson are producing figures in large quantities, and the mark is a gold anchor. Fortunately, these reproductions are easy to detect by the use of a file. The fakes are either hard porcelain or bone china, which resist the file, while the true Chelsea is always soft-paste, and the file will readily cut it and leave a residue on the file of a substance like powdered chalk.

No faking has been found of Raised Anchor pieces, and rarely of Red Anchor. In Triangle period pieces, however, we find some faking. Usually this takes the form of adding a triangle to the base where none existed, and sometimes the word Chelsea and/or a date. The fake can usually be detected as follows: (1) The line of the incision will be shallow at either end, as compared to the middle. (2) There will be auxiliary scratches in the parallel direction. (3) There will be an absence of ploughed-up edge found in genuine pieces where the mark was made in the raw clay.

Coalport, which made most of the reproductions of Goat and Bee jugs, used a bone china which has no "tears" when examined by transmitted light.

DISTINGUISHING CHARACTERISTICS OF CHELSEA

1. *Triangle Period:* very translucent; by transmitted light "pale misty ivory" color; light tears; molded from silver counterparts; not always marked; usual mark incised triangle, sometimes with word Chelsea and date (on Goat and Bee jugs); rarely a triangle or trident in under-glaze blue; only Goat and Bee jugs reproduced in quantity; and triangle, Chelsea, and date sometimes added to otherwise authentic pieces.

2. *Raised Anchor:* extremely white; like white alabaster by transmitted light; taken from silver originals and more heavily potted; very translucent with many large moons; mark was anchor placed on raised wafer (sometimes the anchor painted red); famous for bird figures; never faked or reproduced.

3. *Red Anchor:* paste soft and creamy with greenish-yellow color by transmitted light (particularly plates); not so white nor so heavily potted as Raised Anchor; moons, but not so large; base of figures usually ground and frequently "patch marks"; round spur marks typical; practically no gold; mark of early period, small well-drawn red anchor over the glaze placed near foot-rim on useful ware, and on top of base in figures; later period, reddish-brown anchor of larger size found on useful ware placed in center under base; figures rarely faked or reproduced, and where useful wares are reproduced, the placing of the mark does not conform to above; figures, especially those of the Italian Comedy, the finest made in England.

4. *Gold Anchor:* addition of bone ash, when thickly potted almost opaque, but when thinly potted, white to pinkish ivory, and very translucent by transmitted light; no moons; paste and glaze "fat" and "unctuous" with greasy feel; strong tendency to craze; extreme rococo style with much gold on both figures and useful ware; bases of figures always ground; gold anchor placed on top of base and over the glaze; color ground on large vases extensively used, claret and mazarine blue the most famous; figures large in size and extremely rococo; bocages much in prominence; bases of figures usually glazed; more reproductions of figures and useful wares than found in any other porcelain with the possible exception of Sèvres.

BOW PORCELAIN

We cannot be sure whether Chelsea or Bow was the first English porcelain factory. Early records are available which show that a royal patent was issued in 1744 to Edward Heylyn and Thomas Frye, apparently for the manufacture of porcelain. The *Reading Journal*, or *Weekly Review*, Monday, December 10 to Monday, December 17, 1744, No. 60, records the following: "On Saturday last a grant passed the great Seal to Edward Heylyn of the Parish of Bow, and Thomas Frye of Westham, Painter, of their new invention of *manufacturing a certain material*, whereby a Ware may be made of the same nature as China."

The Bow factory, which was located in what is now London, received much of its inspiration from Oriental sources and was referred to as "New Canton" or as "Stratford-le-Bow." It also appropriated many of its ideas from Meissen and Sèvres, as did most other English factories.

In 1748, a patent for the manufacture of porcelain was issued to Frye alone, the basis for which was the use of an ingredient never before used in the process, namely, bone ash. Since no mention is made of "Unaker" in this patent, its use is problematical or doubtful. This was a very important discovery, for the use of calcined bones in the mixture proved to be of great practical assistance in the future production of porcelain. The Chelsea factory during the Gold Anchor Period used it, and Spode adopted it about 1800 in about equal proportions with kaolin clay and feldspar (china stone) to create a ware known as "bone china," which is today used in England and elsewhere almost universally. The bone ash makes porcelain more stable and easier to control in the fire.

Though Bow porcelain was long ignored by collectors, it is now much sought after. Its lead glaze, frit paste and delicate coloring produce an effect that has eventually earned appreciation. The unusual combination of pastel colors on Rococo bases gives some of its later figures a most artistic feeling and charm.

In October, 1959, a *Special Exhibition of Documentary Material*, to commemorate the bi-centenary of the retirement of Thomas Frye, manager of the factory and 'inventor and first manufacturer of porcelain in England', was shown at the British Museum in London. This was a most important event, as no authoritative history of the early years of this factory has been written. R. L. S. Bruce-Mitford, Keeper of British and Medieval Antiquities, in a preface to the catalogue, says, "This small but, we believe, significant exhibition is the work of Mr. Hugh Tait, F.S.A., Assistant Keeper in the Department*. Its object is to bring together all the known documentary specimens of Bow porcelain, that is to say, pieces which are dated by their inscriptions, or on other evidence; and to group related pieces of Bow around these fixed points in such a manner as to make it possible for the first time, to see the output of the factory historically." It was our pleasure to view this exhibit, and to those who did not have that privilege we would suggest that they secure a copy of the catalogue in which some 50 photographs of important specimens are included.

Mr. Tait in his introduction says: "The history of the Bow factory and its wares has yet to be written. The actual site of the Bow factory was discovered as long ago as March, 1868, during building operations at Messrs. Bell & Black's match factory in the East End of London on the Essex side of the River Lea at Stratford Langthorne, not at Stratford-le-Bow, which is just across the river in Middlesex—and again in 1921, Mr. Aubrey Toppin, M.V.O., discovered on adjacent land a great quantity of kiln furniture, fragments of porcelain, molds, etc., but still no complete and authoritative monograph has been published." He states further that the earliest dated piece of Bow porcelain is 1750 and it therefore remains an unsolved problem as to what porcelain, if any, was produced from 1744 to 1750. He relates some interesting history concerning Andrew Duché, including a record of the Port of London, the entry dated 1743/4; "Earth unrated: 20 tons?: value £5: imported London from Carolina."

We illustrate here four pieces not included in the British Museum exhibition.

Illustration 519 shows a Bow figure from the collection of Mrs. Sigmund Katz, of Covington, Louisiana. It portrays the Muse Polymnia decorated in enamel colors and gold and inscribed on its back is "Polymnie." It is an important early specimen.

Illustration 521 is a documentary piece and is from the Irwin Untermyer collection. It shows Woodward in all white and under the base is incised the date 1750.

* See "Apollo", Feb., Apr., and June, 1960 for recent articles by Mr. Hugh Tait.

Illustration 520 from the same collection is the companion figure of Kitty Clive.

Illustrations 539 and 657 are Bow plates of the period of 1744-48 from the authors' collection. (For verification see Appendix I).

The earliest recorded reference to an actual piece of Bow porcelain is known as the "Bill of John Taylor," and dated 1749/50. At the exhibit and in the catalogue are shown seven pieces of Bow that were actually dated 1750, either glazed and incised, incised, enameled or marked in under-glaze blue; they are all phosphatic. Three of the seven documentary pieces are figures, one of Kitty Clive, one of Henry Woodward, and the third a figure of a Negress with a Basket. The first two were of the well known actor and actress who played in Garrick's *Lethe*. They are undecorated and the glaze is a creamy-white. The third piece is grayish-white. In addition to these three figures there are four pieces of useful ware also having the date 1750. The first is a shell salt, which like the figures is undecorated. It is creamy-white. Two are inkpots, one decorated in under-glaze blue and the other in enamel. The third is a bowl in under-glaze blue. Mr. Tait asks the question as to what kind of pieces were made experimentally or otherwise before 1750? (See Appendix I for a partial answer). Eight pieces not marked are shown, which, as the glaze is still more primitive, are thought to date between 1748 and 1750. All of these pieces are described as phosphatic: in other words, they contain bone ash. The pieces are all useful ware and they are described as having "grayish-drab body and glaze." His conclusion is as follows: "To determine which figures were produced before 1750 is even more difficult. The high quality of the three figures dated 1750 pre-supposes a previous experimental period, but no figures are known with a 'mushroom-gray or drab' appearance corresponding to the early table ware. The production of enameled figures was still presenting great technical difficulties in 1750, as is evidenced by three figures dated 1750: Kitty Clive and John Woodward . . . which are creamy-white, and the Negress with Basket . . . which is grayish-white, for none is decorated* . . . The sequence of development is likely to have been from 'mushroom-gray' or drab to thick creamy and on to grayish-white in figures as in table ware, and consequently the creamy-white would seem to be the earliest of the surviving figures. This sequence, however, was probably never clear-cut; much overlapping is likely to have ocurred."

Some 150 specimens were on display and in addition kiln furniture, the Bowcock papers and an early account book made this a memorable occasion for anyone interested in this early English factory. The manufactory sometime between 1752 and 1757, was carried on under the firm of Messrs. Crowther & Weatherby. From an announcement in the *London Daily Advertiser and Literary Gazette* of 1751 it appears that George Arnold, a very wealthy man of that day, must have provided the funds for Frye to carry on his work. The records also show that Arnold and Edward Heylyn in 1744 purchased together some property which was probably the seat of the original factory. There can be no doubt that Frye was the driving force until his retirement on account of ill health in 1759. From 1750 to 1759 Bow made its most distinctive contribution to English porcelain. In 1755, sales of china brought £18,115. In 1753 advertisements appeared in the Birmingham *Gazette* for painters in blue-and-white and enamelers. A Boston newspaper in 1754 announced the receipt of a shipment of a "Variety of Bow China, cup and saucers, bowls, etc." Whether such shipments had previously been made is not known, nor do we know whether Andrew Duché had anything to do with it. In 1757 the factory announced the opening of a new warehouse for the convenience of its customers.

Thomas Craft says that when Crowther and Weatherby were at the helm of Bow, the firm employed 300 workmen; some 90 painters and about 200 turners, throwers, etc.; Craft himself was among the number. In October 1762, Weatherby died and Crowther carried on the factory alone. In 1765, John Bowcock died and in 1776

* See our Illustration 519 for a decorated specimen, c. 1750.

Crowther sold the entire concern and its equipment to William Duesbury of Derby, who closed the factory and removed the molds and tools to Derby.

In the final ten years, writes Mr. Tait,"the products of Bow lost their distinctive quality and in their over-decorated, ornate and gilded appearance, as well as in the modeling, they are often slavish copies of the Chelsea-Derby and Worcester factories. In these declining years, however, the technical standard remained high and in the blue-and-white wares the paucity of designs was even occasionally enriched."

The products of the early period prior to 1748 are shrouded in uncertainty. The 1744 patent referred to the use of a certain type of clay secured from the Cherokee Indians of America and there called "Unaker." For a most interesting discussion of this subject, one may consult a recent book by Arthur W. Clement, entitled *Our Pioneer Potters*. In this American book, detailed documentary evidence is given concerning one Andrew Duché, who, with the help of General Oglethorpe, secured some assistance from England for a pottery established in Savannah, Georgia, to make porcelain. The evidence produced shows clearly that Duché was actually in London conferring with the founders of the Bow factory at the time the patent was issued. The exhibition catalogue of the British Museum referred to above also contains much interesting information on this subject.

The life of the Bow factory as recorded by most authorities may be divided into four periods. The first one extends from 1744 to 1748. The British Museum Special Exhibition produced no specimens identified as of this period. The second extends from 1748 to 1754, during which time a very large proportion of bone ash was used and many specimens of the period have been positively identified. Illustrations 471, 472, 484, 492, 493, 524 and 532 are of about the period of 1750; Illustrations 528 and and 529 are of the period of 1752; Illustrations 523, 525, 541, 547 and 572 are of the period of 1755; Illustrations 51, 548, 557 and 531 are of the period of 1760; and Illustrations 527, 530 and 540 are of the period of 1765.

One of the surest means of identifying Bow china is by chemical analysis. The presence of phosphoric acid in appreciable quantity immediately points to Bow after 1748. Of course, as previously stated Chelsea began to use bone ash about 1760. English Lowestoft, which began operations in 1757, followed closely the paste and glaze of Bow and consequently used bone ash, but the glaze at Lowestoft is thinner and so may be identified. After 1776 Derby also used bone ash.

To the second period of Bow may be attributed an important class of figures, the heads of which show a distinctive characteristic in the modeling. They have somewhat receding chins, heavy brows and eyelids. Among the figures of this period are boys and girls with baskets. It will be remembered that Chelsea made only boys, which were fat and on rather more clumsy bases. The Bow boys and girls at first glance look alike. More careful examination discloses that the girls have narrower heads and broad plaits of hair done up at the back of the head, whereas the boys' hair clings in clusters of curls all around the heads. The boys have scarves around the mid-sections tied on the right side, whereas the girls have theirs done up on the left side. At this time also all-white figures were made (see Illustrations 626, 627 and 628 for examples of the boys and girls). An important group of figures produced during the period of 1748-54 has been given the name of the "Muse Family." Some authorities believe that all Bow figures of this type were modeled by one artist. The bases of these early figures were of simple molded or rectangular form. While occasionally a workman's mark, such as the planet or an "F" erroneously attributed to Frye, may be found, there was no factory mark during the early period. The fortunes of the Bow factory advanced as those of Chelsea declined during the frequent illnesses of Sprimont, and they correspondingly went down as those of Chelsea rose.

After 1750, a greenish or greenish-yellow tone is characteristic of Bow paste in much of the useful ware, but the color varies widely. Many pieces are decorated with sprays of plum-blossom in applied relief, copied from Fukien porcelain, and some wasters with this decoration were found during excavations on the factory site in 1867. Bow pieces in the form of shells are numerous and were molded frequently from actual shells. The large ones have a transverse ribbing underneath not found on other eighteenth century china.

With the exception of modeled figures and small statues, the efforts of the proprietors of the Bow factory were generally directed toward the production of articles of use rather than ornament. Very few vases are to be found, and these are of a more or less simple character. Quite a considerable quantity of figures, however, must have been made, and even in these a certain use has been anticipated, for they were in large part intended to be mounted upon ormolu bocages, candelabra, clocks, sconces, etc. The branches of the bocages were ornamented with small porcelain flower heads. For mounting on metal, holes were pierced at the time of manufacture in the sides or back of the bases of many of the figures. Sometimes these holes were square and sometimes triangular in shape. This characteristic is considered to be a mark of Bow figures and is not found on any other English porcelain. Broadly speaking, Bow figures in general are more primitive than those made at Chelsea and are relatively heavy in the hand.

The third period, 1754 to 1760, embraces the years of greatest achievement at Bow. It includes some of the finest porcelain ever made in England. The paste has a warm creamy tone with bright tears and moons by transmitted light. The glaze is rather waxen looking, so soft as to be easily scratched, but of an ivory tone and smoothness. The pure and rich enamel colors include a very distinctive opaque light blue, a strong rose purple, a soft rose pink, and a bright translucent green. The clean strength of the colors and their juxtaposition in bold contrasts give Bow china much of its charm. The gilding in this as in other periods of the factory is not of very high quality but has the soft and rather dull appearance that is so much more pleasant than the brassy gilding of modern times; it was used sparingly and to good effect.

Many attractive figures were made, most of them copied from Meissen counterparts. They were, however, remarkably vivacious and delicately executed. The bases at first were simply molded or of rectangular form, but later a characteristic four-footed pedestal was evolved. Its scroll-work was outlined in the strong crimson purple enamel which is quite peculiar to Bow. In addition to the single hole in the side or back of the base, we find holes in the bottom, which were placed there as vents to let the air escape during firing. (These latter holes are also found in the figures of other factories). Some figures have a "T" or "To" mark on the base, which is supposed to indicate that a mysterious molder or "repairer" known as Mr. Tebo molded or assembled the piece. This mark is also found on Worcester, Plymouth and Bristol figures. While Chelsea also used scroll footings, they were usually merely the ornament of the base. An opaque light gray-blue is found only on Bow.

Some fine garnitures were made around the end of this period. Illustration 531 is an example, comprising three vases, one having a cover surmounted with a typical Bow bird in bright colors. The design of this vase includes a white ground, covered with applied blossoms and leaves in relief, and flanked by two female heads, all brightly painted in enamel colors. Butterflies and insects complete the picture. The other pieces are flower pots of beaker shape and decorated in similar fashion. This design is also found in Chelsea and Derby of about the same period; they were all copies of Meissen models. The leaves on the garniture shown here have veins outlined in black. Later copies did not outline the veins, and this was never done at Derby.

Among the figures made during this period will be found "Pierrot" in yellow, "Harlequin and Columbine," "Negro and Negress," the "Woman in Turkish Costume with the Gallant Kissing her Hand." All of these are in the famous Schreiber Collection in the Victoria and Albert Museum. "A Boy Holding a Bunch of Grapes" is also found there and is marked with a script "D". It was formerly thought to be Derby, but a chemical analysis shows it to have bone ash, and consequently to be Bow.

Figures of birds and animals follow the Meissen and Chelsea fashion, but most Bow birds are wholly fanciful. The famille rose and the "Kakiemon" styles were much used. The Bow "Fat Partridge" is well known and is usually found with a border of iron red transfer. Many plates may be noted in an octagonal form but are sometimes round without the usual foot-rim. This latter form is not found in other English eighteenth century porcelain but it is quite common in Chinese export ware. Other typical shapes are cylindrical mugs with loop handles that join the body almost at the bottom instead of descending to join at a more or less acute angle. Mugs slightly spreading at the base are typical but were made also at other factories; however, the heart-shaped lower termination of the handle is peculiar to Bow. The color was always inclined to run as a result of the softness of the glaze. An occasional feature of Bow bowls is the trace of the second firing in spur marks on the rims.

The fourth and final period was from 1760 to 1776 and at the latter date the factory was purchased by William Duesbury of the Derby china factory. The products in these closing years now show a great falling away from the standard of originality and charm previously reached. The porcelain itself is no longer of fine quality; the paste is often nearly opaque, showing a dusky brownish translucency, and the uneven surface glaze is much disfigured by black specks strongly tinged with blue, apparently an attempt to counteract the former yellowish or ivory tone, which was evidently regarded as a shortcoming. The designs and styles were now copied from Chelsea, perhaps aided by the migration of Chelsea workmen, and for the first time, Bow had a factory mark, the anchor and dagger usually painted in red or brown. We show a marked pair of figures depicting "Fire" and "Water" from the Elements series, Illustrations 527 and 530. They each have the anchor and dagger in red. As will be seen, the bases are of the typical four-footed type peculiar to Bow. After 1765, the figures are quite like the Chelsea ones of the same period. Both Chelsea and Bow figures of this time have the patch or thumb marks on the base which are widely supposed to be an exclusive characteristic of Derby.

Finally, Bow gave up to a large extent the manufacture of tea and coffee services and turned most of its energies to dinner services. The following reasons have been ascribed: (1) inability of Bow porcelain to withstand boiling water; (2) difficulty in working the porcelain body; (3) inability to compete with Worcester, whose porcelain, due to the use of soap-stone, could be made more cheaply and had none of the above disadvantages. An old saying is that you may find a chipped Bow plate but never a cracked one. Worcester, on the other hand, unlike Chelsea and Bow, never crazed.

Some Characteristics of Bow Porcelain

1. Good translucency and greenish-yellow, sometimes with moons by transmitted light in the early period, and poor translucency and brownish color during the later periods.

2. Heaviness in the hand.

3. Bases never ground, patch marks sometimes in late period.

4. Square or triangular holes in side of the base of figures not found in other makes.

5. Four-footed bases with shell scrolls painted in a distinctive rose-purple from 1760.

6. Pure rich enamel colors including an opaque wax-blue gray with decorations in pleasing contrasts.

7. Plates and bowls shaped like oriental ones without a foot-rim.

8. Dull gold not of fine quality but artistically used.

9. Late period paste slightly opaque with blue-gray cast, brown translucency and black specks.

10. No factory marks until 1760; then anchor and dagger in red or brown.

11. Phosphoric acid or bone ash as shown by chemical analysis.

12. Figures have receding chins and heavy eyes and eyelids as a rule.

WORCESTER PORCELAIN

For the real inception of the great English manufactory at Worcester, we must go back a few years to Bristol, for it was there that the Worcester factory was in reality started. Until comparatively recently, no connection was thought to exist between Worcester and a soft-paste factory existing in Bristol and described by Dr. Pocock in 1750 in his letters as making sauce boats in the style of the Chinese and selling them for fifteen shillings the pair. This Bristol porcelain was up to 1950 known to collectors as Lowdin's Bristol soft-paste porcelain. In 1950, Mr. Aubrey J. Toppin, M.V.O., presented a paper to the English Ceramic Circle disclosing his discovery of the proceedings in bankruptcy relating to Richard Holdship, one of the original incorporators of the Worcester factory in 1751, which reveals that:

1. William Miller and Benjamin Lund made porcelain in Bristol for from two to four years before the Worcester factory proper was started. Miller was a banker who put up money, and Lund had been associated with the founders of the Bow factory. Lund had a contract to purchase soaprock to the amount of twenty tons per year from the mine owners in Cornwall. This soaprock, soapstone or steatite, was the most important ingredient used by the Worcester factory to make all of its porcelain up to the end of the Dr. Wall period in 1783.

2. Holdship, one of the fourteen original incorporators of the Worcester factory in 1751, acquired this lease from Lund. He also acted for the Worcester Company in buying out completely the Bristol soft-paste factory from Miller and Lund in 1752. It therefore became apparent that Dr. John Wall and William Davis did not discover a formula for making porcelain as had previously been assumed. They merely bought out the Bristol factory which was a going concern based on the use of soapstone as a principal new ingredient. Its value later was fully justified.

We show as Illustration 582, one of a pair of sauce boats made at the Lund Bristol factory. These sauce boats are finely decorated in bright enamel colors in the oriental style. The late Mr. H. Rissik Marshall in his book *Coloured Worcester Porcelain of the First Period*, 1954, says that a painter was working at the time at the Bristol factory who can only be identified as the "fine brush artist," and it was he who painted the mug shown as Colored Illustration 53. A distinguishing characteristic of the Lund Bristol porcelain is that it is heavily potted and has a decided green color by transmitted light. Illustration 573 shows a cup of unusual oriental shape of this period.

The Worcester factory as such was started in 1751 by Dr. John Wall, a painter of sorts but a medical doctor by profession, together with William Davis, a chemist, and other business men totaling fourteen. There were two Holdships, Richard and Josiah, who played a part in the development of the factory. Although Dr. Wall died in 1776, the Wall Period is regarded as extending to 1783, when Davis died. Thomas Flight, the London agent, bought the factory at that time for his two sons,

Joseph and John. Robert Chamberlain, the head painter, became dissatisfied and in 1783 left the factory with his son, who was also a painter at Worcester, and started a rival factory. At first they merely decorated pieces purchased in the white from Caughley, but later made their own porcelain. The Flights, meanwhile, were joined by Martin Barr and the factory changed its name to Flight and Barr, and at the same time changed its paste and glaze. Later in the nineteenth century, all of the Worcester factories, including Grainger and Co., jointed together and are operating today, making bone china. It became a joint stock company in 1840 called the "Royal Worcester Porcelain Company."

The Worcester products during the Wall Period, with which we are concerned, were almost entirely useful wares. While the paste and glaze had much to recommend them from a practical point of view, they did not compare in beauty with those of either Chelsea or Derby. The superb character of its decorations and its fine gold work were its principal attractions. For many years it was thought that Worcester made no figures. In recent years, however, a few have been identified and, due for the most part to their rarity, bring high prices. Illustration 629 may be such a figure. Many collectors doubted that they were in fact Worcester products, but chemical analysis, however, showed the presence of magnesia in the proportion of 13 per cent. "The Gardener and Companion" in the H. R. Marshall Collection, now in the Ashmolean Museum, and those in the Sigmund Katz Collection are good examples of these Worcester figures. The only other factories to use soaprock to any great extent were Caughley and Liverpool. Robert Podmore was the arcanist at Bristol and later Worcester; still later, he made porcelain at Liverpool for ten years. Some authorities believe that a great deal of porcelain at present attributed to Worcester was in fact made by Podmore at Liverpool.

The Worcester glaze is soft and glassy without the "fatness" which is so noticeable in other soft-paste porcelains. It is not quite so melting as the early Derby glaze nor so glassy as Chelsea. It is even impure and blotchy at times. But it is always regular and perfectly controlled. Worcester never had to be ground on the base like Chelsea and it never crazed. It has a tendency to be dry where not glazed and to have the glaze shrink away at the foot-rim. These characteristics are taken for granted in Worcester identification. The Worcester potting was always good, with neatness of form and finish. If one compares a Worcester teapot with one made at Bow, one's eye will speak for the fine proportions of Worcester and the relative clumsiness of Bow. The potting of the sides of Worcester is uniform, and the foot-rim is sharp cut and not wedge-shaped, as is usual with Bow and Lowestoft. Worcester is never gritty and its color varies from cream-white to blue-white. By transmitted light it is almost invariably green during the Wall Period, and it has no moons. While soapstone continued to be used to some extent after 1783, the paste and glaze then underwent a great change. It lost much of its soft green tinge and became whiter, harder, and more opaque, with a cold, glittering glaze. R. W. Binns, in his *A Century of Potting in the City of Worcester* says that one of Barr's improved pastes was known as the Nantgarw Body. Illustration 588 shows a part of a tea and coffee service as an example of this body. It is extremely fine and, exceptfor being a little harder looking, compares very favorably with that used by Billingsley at Nantgarw, which it must be said was one of the finest ever made anywhere.

While the decorations at Worcester were varied and excellent, in nearly every case they were copied from designs of the Orient, either directly or by way of Meissen or French sources. H. Rissik Marshall, one of the most reliable authorities on Worcester, said at the conclusion of an address to the English Ceramic Circle in 1956: "Lastly, you will see a great deal of blue scale and there, although the origin is Chinese, one can say that no other factory in the world used blue scale to the extent that Worcester did, while the decoration may be European flowers which, while they resemble sometimes those of Meissen, at others look more like Sèvres painting, but in the end are so subtly transmuted that they can be nothing except Worcester; turning to figure painting, one gets the Watteauesque figures and then of course, there are also the individual efforts of O'Neale and Donaldson. As you turn away from the collection, you will realize how Worcester has absorbed all the influences and transmuted them into something essentially its own, virtually original, and entirely delightful."

Turning now to some of the patterns, we find the "Willow," the "Broseley blue dragon," the Meissen bouquets of scattered flowers, exotic birds, the partridge pattern and the fan pattern from Japan. The radiating trellis with pendant green festoons and the ribbon patterns are from Sèvres. The colored grounds for which the factory was justly famous were derived from Meissen and Sèvres. These ranged through deep blue, apple green, yellow, claret, turquoise and a "powder blue" which it hoped would compare favorably with Chinese originals. The panels which break up these gorgeous fields are filled with flowers, birds, insects, landscapes, and figure subjects, almost all of either Oriental or Continental origin. They are frequently found with richly chased gilding copied from the skilful "doreurs" of Sèvres.

Among English factories, Worcester was noted for its gold work. On the other hand, there was little pure white ware, glazed or unglazed, made there, and as stated few figures were made. The reason for the first was that the Worcester glaze was not particularly smooth and fine and therefore had to be decorated. The absence of figures in quantity may be attributed to the lack of plasticity in the paste. Worcester porcelain was liable to collapse in the kiln—which also accounts for the fact that Worcester did not follow Chelsea in the use of rococo shapes. Much of the early porcelain was molded. Blue-and-white useful ware was made in quantity throughout the Wall Period, and Illustrations 544, 563, 567, 575 and 577 are good examples.

We find both Chinese and Japanese influence in the fine enamel painted pieces. The usual colors were bluish-green, pale blue, soft Indian red and pale yellow with touches of gilding chiefly on the red. Slight floral sprays, a fantastic animal or bird beside a flowering plum or a hedge of banded straw, a pair of quail, a Chinese figure, or the like make up the central subject. This class of Old Japan was widely popular throughout Europe. The dainty "Kakiemon" designs were of the finest quality, and later the Imari appeared. (Illustrations 489, 561, 562, 564, 565 and 566 are typical examples, the "Bell Pulls" being very rare). To these must be added the ever popular scale design, of which the blue scale was the most common (cf. Colored Illustrations 52 and 55), but which included powder blue and others. A very frequent style variously called "whorl," "spiral," "Catherine-wheel" or "Queen's" pattern was also popular. Toward the end of the Wall Period, the Japanese influence gave way to the more sumptuous patterns copied from Meissen and Sèvres. The exotic birds, butterflies, rich bouquets of flowers, figure subjects, landscapes, clusters of fruit, and festoons and trellis designs followed the importation of the artists from Chelsea. Illustration 52 has the earliest type of scale and the decoration is exceptionally fine, resembling the work of the "fine brush artist" previously referred to.

Transfer printing from copper plates was brought to Worcester by Robert Hancock in 1756, and Illustration 538 shows an example. (There is some evidence that Sadler at Liverpool first discovered this process in 1752). A great deal of Worcester was decorated in this manner, some of which is signed by the engraver. Hancock left Worcester in 1773 and after that date the quality of the printing degenerated. Transfer printing was used by almost every factory and its main value was low cost of production. A similar process known as bat printing was used when the color was always blue and under the glaze. Still another type of decoration frequently mistaken for transfer was penciling. Black penciling is of Chinese origin, about 1730.

Illustration 586 shows a masked jug with a typical Worcester decoration. Illustration 587 shows a fluted plate also typical of Worcester, Illustration 534 is a scent bottle made at the Grainger Worcester factory and Illustration 559 shows one of a pair of chestnut bowls from the collection of the Antiquarian Society of Memphis, Tennessee. These bowls are of the Wall Period and are of interest because one of the pieces carries the red anchor mark of Chelsea. This piece was probably decorated by a Chelsea workman employed at the time at Worcester. Colored Illustration 54 is known as the "Red Cow" design and some controversy exists today as to whether this may in fact be Liverpool made by Podmore rather than Worcester. Illustration 542 is most interesting as the decoration is copied from the Meissen service known as the "Fable Animal Service," having the black and gold stripe enclosing the design. This is one of the services that Mr. Ralph Wark has ascribed to the hand of the controversial Adam Friedrich v. Löwenfinck, about whom we spoke under the Meissen chapter. This Worcester plate is from the collection of Dr. Hans Syz and was decorated about 1800.

Worcester made many fine vases, and of these the large hexagonal ones in ground colors with birds, etc., are the best and most famous. Yellow ground pieces, even though the ground is not usually of fine quality, are much sought after, chiefly because they are rare. The apple-green is also quite popular, and this color is in a beautiful shade and of good quality. Many of the most beautiful vases were painted by the "outside" decorators, the most famous of whom were Giles, Donaldson, and O'Neale. (Illustrations 550 and 551 show the Fable Animal work of O'Neale, from the collection of Mrs. C. B. Stout). The work of these private decorators stands out in the history of Worcester porcelain. The bird paintings and scale grounds easily excel all other types made there. The birds were sometimes sleek, plump birds or unkempt creatures with small wings and disheveled tails. The Worcester birds are considered by some to be too gaudy. This was due to the use almost exclusively at Worcester of a peculiar dry "lapis lazuli" blue. The best decorations of the period can be accounted for by the presence of the Chelsea painters. Colored Illustrations 55, 56 and 57, are examples, the coffee-pot showing the "ruby" ground probably created to compete with the Chelsea "claret."

One of the most noted services was made after the factory was purchased by Flight. Erroneously called the Lord Nelson Service, it was, in fact, made for the Duke of Clarence, brother of the King, after Queen Charlotte and King George III visited the factory in 1788 and placed the order. It was a large dinner service and was decorated by John Pennington, the best painter then at the factory. As the Duke of Clarence was the Admiral of the Navy, each piece has the picture of "Hope" in different poses, together with ships, anchors, etc., symbolic of the sea. The gold work is of exceptional quality on a rich blue border. This was the first time that Worcester added the crown to the factory mark. Illustration 585 shows one of the pieces from this service. Another design is known as the "Blind Earl's" pattern and was introduced about 1765. This name is erroneously applied, as the Earl of Coventry, to whom the name referred, did not lose his sight until 1780. The design is comprised of raised flowers. Illustration 558 from the J. P. Norfleet collection shows the ones made at the Chamberlain Worcester factory.

The Chamberlain factory painted many bright designs. It also used spiral fluting and gadroon edges in the molded pieces, and produced many services decorated in gold only. Illustration 635 shows a plate from a tea service from the collection of Mr. and Mrs. Dunbar Abston.

Worcester has a large number of workmen's marks of which no record will here be made. The factory marks were as follows: (1) A script "W"; (2) A crescent, probably used more than any other mark; (3) Three, four, five or six Chinese symbols, a "seal" or "fretted square" usually found on pieces decorated in the Oriental style; (4) The crossed swords mark, usually with the numeral "9" added, found on pieces copied from Meissen. All of the Worcester marks are under-glaze blue which makes them more difficult to forge. However, many fakes have been made by such concerns as Samson of Paris. As such pieces are hard-paste, they should be easy to identify. Many fakes are made in Staffordshire, but as these are pottery they should be readily detected. The most dangerous are those pieces of genuine Worcester that are redecorated, or those with slight decoration that are given added treatment. The collector should never buy a piece of claret ground or turquoise without a careful inspection, as most of such pieces offered today are fakes. One should look for black specks and blistering of gold on pieces which have been refired.

SOME DISTINGUISHING CHARACTERISTICS OF WORCESTER

1. "Wall" pieces are green by transmitted light with no moons or tears.
2. The glaze is rather thin and usually a bluish-gray in color. Glaze somewhat like that of Chinese export ware.
3. Mark should be in blue and under the glaze.
4. The base is never ground.
5. The foot-rim is sharply cut and not V-shaped.
6. The potting is always good.
7. The glaze under the base nearly always recedes, leaving a "dry edge."
8. Gold is of fine quality.
9. Glaze never crazes or crackles.
10. Rarely, if ever, found in all-white, glazed or unglazed.
11. Few figures ever made, so one should never buy them except from a reliable dealer.
12. The same holds true for colored ground pieces.

LONGTON HALL PORCELAIN

The Longton Hall factory was established not later than 1750 in Staffordshire, which area was noted for the manufacture of all kinds of pottery in the eighteenth and nineteenth centuries. The Longton Hall factory was hardly heretofore considered as having made a product that was noted for artistic accomplishment. During the 1950's, however, it has attained much more acclaim as a result of the untiring research of a number of English collectors, who have at last cleared up the mystery of when the factory was established, by whom, and when it closed, and have gained a better understanding as to its correct attributions.

Longton Hall was the first Staffordshire factory to make porcelain and for a long period of time its actual existence was almost forgotten. J. E. Nightingale, a noted English writer, re-discovered it in 1881. William Pitt and Simeon Shaw, well known writers on the subject of English ceramics, commented on the factory and later W. Bemrose, following the lead of these writers and that of Ll. Jewitt who laid the foundation for all later studies of English ceramics, published his monograph on Longton Hall in 1906, which was universally recognized as authoritative on the subject until the book on Longton Hall, recently published by Dr. Bernard M. Watney corrected many misconceptions contained in the previous books. It is suggested that those especially interested secure *Longton Hall Porcelain* (1957) which gives in detail all of the information that has been discovered by previous writers, in addition to his own research, including excavations at the site of the old Longton works.

I will quote briefly from the well known and highly regarded *First Century of English Porcelain*, 1906, by W. Moore Binns, as being illustrative of the previous opinions held with regard to the products of this factory: "The porcelain of Longton Hall may be cited as an instance of value attaching to that which can lay little or no claim to beauty, but which is merely uncommon and possessing a history, the details of which are little known." And again in describing Longton Hall vases, he says: "The rococo vases were badly designed, of most uncouth forms, and clumsy scroll work. The potting was heavy and unfinished, the paste common and dirty, the glaze thin and poor. In fact, bad and clumsy potting may be considered a trade mark of Longton Hall, and as very little of it is marked, this feature is looked for by collectors who wish to identify specimens."

After reading the above, one wonders why so many collectors continued to pursue the research. Mr. A. J. B. Kiddell and Mrs. Donald MacAlister contributed some important findings and the latter presented to the English Ceramic Circle a paper describing early groups of white figures, to which she assigned the name the "snow-man group." The excavations of Dr. Watney have confirmed her attribution, and such specimens are today sought after by collectors, and like other Longton Hall specimens, bring high prices on the market. Thus the "ugly duckling" has become the darling of many collectors of early English porcelain. Illustrations 509 and 510 show a pair of such figures from the collection of Mrs. C. B. Stout.

In his book, Dr. Watney tells the story of his years of research to put together the available knowledge on the subject and his rare good fortune to unearth valuable information from old files and records two centuries old in the basement of a firm of button-makers whose name was Firmin. This lead was furnished by the discovery in 1933 by A. J. B. Kiddell of two partners of the Longton Hall factory named Robert Charlesworth and Samuel Firmin. Untold research by Dr. Watney finally resulted in the finding of two original Longton Hall indentures which had remained unrecognized for nearly two hundred years. These documents together with other available information make it quite clear that the factory was established as early as 1750. The indenture of 1753 refers to an earlier one of 1751 between William Jenkinson, William Nicklin and William Littler. The document states that William Jenkinson had obtained the "art secret or mystery" of making porcelain in imitation of china ware and that he had rented the Longton premises from Obadiah Lane some time before 1751. Prior to this first partnership, Jenkinson had established a factory with sufficient output for his porcelain to be mentioned in the first agreement as part of his assets. The name Jenkinson had not been previously associated with Longton Hall. There is certain similarity between this man and Benjamin Lund, already referred to in connection with the first Bristol factory at Lowdin's glasshouse in 1749. It will be recalled that Dr. Pocock referred to such manufactures in his famous letters of the period of 1750. William Littler was twenty-six at the time, and his previous experience was in connection with the manufacture of pottery, particularly salt-glaze pottery, and not porcelain. He was included probably for his general knowledge in the field of ceramic production, and he became and remained the manager of Longton Hall. Evidence available seems to point to the fact that salt-glaze pottery was produced as well as porcelain: the excavations prove this statement.

Many writers included Longton Hall along with Chelsea and Bow as having been acquired by Duesbury and added to his Derby factory. This idea was given attention because of the fact that the records show that a large number of additional workmen were added to the Derby factory in 1758, because Duesbury decorated Longton porcelain in London, and because in 1755 he was living in Longton and decorating porcelain there. Documentary evidence now available shows that the Longton factory closed in 1760. In 1753, William Jenkinson sold his interest mostly to Nathaniel Firmin. The Longton factory would certainly have closed in 1755 but for the addition of Robert Charlesworth as a partner. By May 23rd, 1760, he was convinced that Littler could not make a financial success of the business. Accordingly as Charlesworth was the principal owner at the time, he made an announcement in the *Birmingham Gazette* that he had dissolved the partnership as of that date.

The second announcement came from William Littler and Co., saying it was not in Charlesworth's power to dissolve the partnership without the consent of the other partners. The third announcement came from Samuel Firmin, the other principal owner, saying the partnership had been dissolved. These three important discoveries were made by Mr. Kiddell and published by the English Ceramic Circle. They show that the factory went out of business in 1760, just ten years after its start. On September 8th, 1760 another provincial newspaper announced the closing of the Longton Hall factory and the sale of its assets. The factory stock was to be sold at Salisbury and the advertisement stated that there were upwards of ninety thousand pieces of porcelain to be sold without reserve. That this factory could have such a large inventory is hard to believe. In any event, the production must have been considerable. The question raised about the absence of early Derby may well be indicated here. On the other hand, Dr. Watney says that seventy specimens attributed to Longton Hall by Bemrose are now considered to be either Liverpool or Derby.

Having settled the question as to the founders and proprietors of the factory, when it started and when it closed, Dr. Watney set out to find exactly where it was located, and by excavations on the old site to determine exactly what was made there. Dr. Geoffrey Blake agreed to join in this research. After many interesting experiences they discovered the location of the old factory under the stables at Longton Hall. Dr. Watney has secured much valuable information from the excavations and the work is still being carried forward by the Hanley Museum. Dr. Watney established that small circular spur marks on the base of specimens are indicated by the excavations. He also confirmed Mrs. MacAlister's conclusions regarding the "snow man" pieces. Analysis of specimens found at the old site and of "snow man" series showed that both were low in alumina and high in lead content, together with a lime content of about 14 per cent. This accounts for the glassy nature of the paste. The chemical analysis is quite similar to the so-called "girl-in-a-swing" specimens thought by some to be early Chelsea. The "girl-in-a-swing" pieces, however, have about 5 per cent. to 7 per cent. more lead content. Also found at the old site were a number of fragments of fine salt-glaze, including crabstock handles, colored pieces with patterns on them and examples decorated with brilliant cobalt blue. These pieces prove that Littler manufactured earthenware at Longton as well as porcelain. The largest piece found so far, according to Dr. Watney, is a completely collapsed teapot. Its floral molding is identical with two plates in the Rous Lench collection, on a saucer in the Victoria and Albert Museum, and a teapot in the Fitzwilliam Museum; and all of the three examples referred to are decorated in the Littler blue which has for years been considered a trade mark of Longton Hall. Of great importance was the excavating of a solid tree trunk base for a white glazed figure of a bird of which only the claws remain. It has every appearance of being part of a "snow man" figure, and there is a typical small central hole in the base as well as two "snow man" flowers. Also was found a white glazed figure of a dog decorated with the "snow man" flowers. Towards the end of the life of the factory it has been thought that a polychrome version of a Chinese root and fence pattern was used. Examples of this were also found. A blue-and-white knife handle with a decoration including a tuft of bent-over rushes, long recognized as a Longton peculiarity, was found. Many blue-and-white pieces were dug up matching those in private collections. Both biscuit and glazed wasters of identical shapes and moldings found on the site prove conclusively that certain types, already attributed to Longton on other grounds, were, in fact, made there. Among these types are plates with strawberry moldings, cream-jugs and other shapes with a particular form of basket molding.

For many years three quite different types of figures have confronted the collector, all having the common characteristic of being undecorated. Two of these have now been definitely identified as Derby figures made by Planché and "snow man" figures made at Longton. The third one, previously referred to as the "girl-in-a-swing" is still subject to question as to its attribution. The "snow man" figures differ from the other two in that they are poorly modeled and resemble those in Staffordshire earthenware. They are as a rule molded rather than thrown on the wheel and rosette-like flowers are frequently applied. The glaze is like pure glass and so thickly applied as to obscure the modeling but strangely enough the bases are usually glaze free and sometimes the figures appear to have been ground in a manner similar to that used at Chelsea, and a small conical hole is usual. Unlike the figures, mugs and flat ware, the useful ware was usually glazed under the base, and heavily potted. The early wares showed a greenish-yellow to cloudy-yellow translucency with moons and tears but not to the extent shown in the later period: likewise the stilt marks are broader on the earlier examples than on the later ones.

Dr. Watney says that primitive leaf forms exist in the earliest blue-and-white, and uninhibited painting with Littler's startling ultramarine cobalt sometimes completely covers all but the base of these wares. The strange richness of this ground color was increased by the lavish use of unfired gold to paint not only borders and outline cartouches on the blue ground, but also sprays of flowers in reserve. Much of the unfired gold and enamel has now worn off, leaving an unfinished appearance to the piece. Raised white enamel painted on a background of Littler's blue is typical. Some of the early blue-and-white pieces bear a crossed "L" mark in blue, frequently with a small tail of dots, up to four in number, underneath. Whether the mark was for Littler, Longton, or an attempt to imitate the Vincennes mark is not known.

From 1754 to 1757 was the best period of the factory and a large variety of wares was produced, whose potting and modeling showed a marked improvement over the preceding period, especially the rococo forms. The glassy glaze was very translucent and the color thus shown was opalescent green which tended to disappear in thinly potted pieces. In addition to the Littler blue, an opaque yellow-green, powder blue and a very characteristic mulberry color came into use, as well as an orange-red, opaque blue and on figures a red-brown. The method of painting the eyes of the figures followed the style used at Meissen. The pupils and eyebrows are black, the iris and lashes red and the cheeks heavily tinted red. Quite characteristic is the presence of a "scum" line near the base of useful wares. The characteristic shapes produced included teapots, sauce boats and strawberry plates on which leaf and fruit forms predominated.

Littler concentrated his efforts on making blue-and-white useful wares during the last few years of the factory's existence but he was not successful in saving it, even though he concentrated his efforts on simple forms which were easy and cheap to produce. He did, however, continue to make figures, realizing that they were the best products of the factory. They included personages, mythological figures, the Elements, the Seasons, Dancers and Musicians. Among the last figures produced were the Four Continents, and in them the factory achieved its finest result. Dr. Watney says that an analysis of one of these figures shows that the original formula was still in use and that broken fragments disclose brown or black specks of impurities in the paste. The color now by transmitted light is a dirty brown for figures, and a decided green for useful wares. The Continents were later produced at Plymouth in hard-paste from the same, or at least similar, molds; the Longton figures are completely flat under the bases while the Plymouth ones are hollow.

Illustrations 522 and 526 depict two of the seasons, Spring and Summer. These are certainly conversation pieces and whether they are early Longton Hall or the product of some unknown Staffordshire factory around the turn of the eighteenth century is an open question. The style of the figures represented would suggest the latter. On the other hand, while a casual inspection would lead one to suppose that they were salt-glaze pottery, they are in fact very translucent, and the color so disclosed is green and the paste and glaze very soft. The potting is very poor with many black specks and bubbles in the glaze. There can be no question but that the feeling is distinctly Staffordshire. Littler made salt-glaze at Longton and as a matter of fact his previous experience was with its manufacture. The presence of applied moss to the base may also indicate Longton. The color as shown by an ultra-violet light is consistent with its having a Longton Hall origin. Illustration 631 is likewise an interesting example. The paste and glaze are quite soft and the translucency shows it to be porcelain. It is of course one of the Elements, viz. Water. Similar examples are in the Victoria and Albert Museum, from the Broderip collection, and the late Mr. Honey says they are in the style of Ralph Wood; but may be experimental pieces by Enoch Wood around the end of the eighteenth century. The glaze of these colored figures is quite unlike the previous figures shown here in that they have no appearance of salt-glaze but are creamy and smooth. Illustration 516 shows one of a pair of figure candle holders. These are rare early specimens of Longton Hall, and are in color. The glaze is quite like the "snow man" pieces, in that the glaze is heavily applied and pure glass. This has formed at the end of the fingers and toes in the form of a ball of glass. They have all the other attributes of early Longton Hall. The Derby factory made a similar mold but the figures are quite unlike this pair. They have the "scum" line, yellow-green color, mulberry color, flat ground base, with the small conical hole and the unfired gold decoration. Illustration 50 shows one of a pair of Longton Hall vases. As will be seen, it is clumsily modeled and the potting is poor. The blue ground is in the typical Littler blue with the mottled or streaked effect. It is green by transmitted light with moons, and the clothes of the girl disclose the characteristic mulberry color rarely found, if ever, on other English porcelain. The gold is typical of this factory as are the yellow-green enamel colors. The companion vase has typical Longton Hall birds as part of the decoration. A similar bird rendition will be seen on plate 39 of *Longton Hall Porcelain* by Dr. Watney. Illustration 536 shows a very typical Longton Hall sauceboat. The color by transmitted light is pale-green with moons. Included in the decoration will be found yellow-green and mulberry colors as well as dull gilding of poor quality, all characteristic of this factory. At the foot-rim where the glaze meets the body, there is a dark line like that left by "dirty scum water." Illustration 549 depicts a strawberry plate from the collection of Mrs. C. B. Stout which is characteristic, and Illustration 590 shows a pot-pourri vase from the collection of Colonial Williamsburg, Virginia. This vase exemplifies the product of the factory at its best period.

The collection of Mrs. Sigmund Katz is particularly rich in Longton Hall, and we show as Illustration 589 a figure called the "Goat Herd," and also Illustrations 467 and 468 known as the "Seated Leopard" and the "Crouching Leopard," all of the best period of the factory.

DISTINGUISHING CHARACTERISTICS OF LONGTON HALL

1. Poor potting.

2. Glassy glaze.

3. Green translucency by transmitted light; greenish-yellow during the early period to greenish-brown during the later period.

4. Unusual Littler blue, the streaked effect being due to the fact that it was applied with a brush, giving it somewhat the same effect found in early Vincennes blue.

5. A distinctive if unpleasing yellow-green color.

6. An unusual bright purplish-pink or "mulberry" color not found elsewhere.

7. Green translucency with moons or tears by transmitted light, especially on heavily potted pieces.

8. Characteristic leaf molding.

9. Flat bases with small conical holes in figures sometimes ground and frequently having patch marks.

10. Unusual method of painting the eyes of figures.

11. A characteristic bird used in the decoration.

12. Dull gilding of poor quality, frequently unfired.

13. White enamel and characteristic flower painting.

THE DERBY FACTORY

While in the sale rooms Derby porcelain has never been able to compete with Chelsea, Bow or Worcester, in many respects no other English factory can claim the varied interests, originality of products and truly English style that are found in Derby porcelain, whether figures or useful wares.

Its management was progressive and in its artists and craftsmen, whether it developed them or whether it attracted and absorbed them from elsewhere, it has handed down a list of names which must always take a most prominent place in the history of English ceramics. For fifty years it maintained a standard of English art work of the highest order, justly celebrated for technical excellence, great refinement, and exquisite taste. It absorbed the two great pioneer factories, Chelsea in 1769 and Bow in 1776. Some authorities have stated that it also absorbed the Longton Hall factory, but the latest information seems to point to the fact that this factory simply went out of existence about 1760.

The styles adopted by the Derby craftsmen were undoubtedly influenced by the contemporary silver and furniture and by the styles created by the brothers Adam, Chippendale and Sheraton. Among this long list of artists, no name stands out more prominently than that of William Billingsley referred to elsewhere in detail.

Many eminent English writers have told the story of this factory, and in the course of time, many fallacies have been discarded as the result of the untiring efforts of collectors and other students of Derby. There is some evidence that a French refugee by the name of Planché lived in Derby as early as 1745, and there is ample proof that he made small figures and models of cats, dogs and other animals from 1750-1752. It has also been shown beyond contradiction that in 1751-1752 William Duesbury was working in London as an enameler and that he decorated some of the figures made by Planché. As the enamel on the existing pieces has largely disappeared, it is fair to assume that the process was a cold one (not requiring a kiln); later, however, Duesbury did fire his enamel paint. It is also quite certain that Duesbury decorated Chelsea and Bow porcelain. The documentary evidence shows that he was living in Longton as early as 1755, and that he was decorating Longton Hall porcelain there as his own records show he had done while still in London.

The records are quite clear that John Heath, a banker, and others were making pottery at Cockpit Hill in Derby as early as 1751. There are in existence three jugs somewhat resembling the famous Chelsea Goat and Bee jugs, which have been in the past considered documentary pieces of Derby and proving a date of 1750 for the factory. These famous jugs have the following incised marks under the bottom: "D," "D 1750" and "Derby." No other marks occur on Derby porcelain until the Chelsea factory was purchased in 1769. Mrs. D. MacAlister contributed a very informative paper on the subject to the *English Ceramic Circle, Transactions II,* p.45, in the course of which she points out that the Victoria and Albert, and British Museums made a series of tests on early Derby porcelain which showed it invariably to have a high lead content. These tests show a variation from 2 per cent. to 8 per cent; but the three jugs show no lead content and therefore considerable doubt is cast as to whether they are in fact Derby.

In 1756, we find in the records a contract between Heath, Duesbury, and Planché to enter into a partnership to produce porcelain at Derby. Unfortunately this document was not signed. Some authorities attribute the failure to execute the agreement to the fact that Planché had begun to drink to excess. Be this as it may, we have no record of any further connection between Planché and the Derby factory, which certainly was in existence at about that period. However, we find further evidence of co-operation between Heath and Duesbury. In the same year, 1756, Heath acquired the lease of property in Nottingham Road, which was later Duesbury's factory; furthermore, they jointly acquired the process of printing from Richard Holdship in 1764, by an agreement which mentions printing on china. Again they are mentioned together in legal documents when they acquired the Chelsea factory. From the above, it would seem clear that these men worked for some time together, with Heath furnishing the capital and Duesbury operating the factory.

William Duesbury operated the factory with much success until his death in 1786. He was survived by his son William Duesbury II, who was a worthy successor of his famous father. He carried on the factory with distinction until he died in 1796. In 1795 he had taken into partnership an Irishman named Michael Kean, who had good artistic taste. Kean married the widow of William Duesbury II, and he carried on the business until 1811. We are not concerned with the factory after that date.

Partly as a result of the failure of the Derby factory to mark its figures and partly because collectors preferred to designate the ones in their cabinets as Chelsea or Bow, the question finally arose in ceramic circles as to what had become of the large number of figures that must have been made at Derby. Mr. Bernard Rackham, one of England's most noted experts, published in the *Daily Telegraph* of April 1st, 1925, an article on the subject which completely revised the previous opinions. In the *Burlington Magazine* of December 1926, Mr. Rackham and other experts set forth at length the new theories. Anyone desiring a detailed study is urged to read this most interesting article. A number of his ideas will be found at the end of this chapter under the topic "Ways to distinguish Derby porcelain." Reference is here made to John Halsem's *Old Derby China Factory*, 1876, where is recorded a list of Derby figures and statues from the old price list. It comprises about 400 figures and groups, giving quite an exceptional array.

PLANCHÉ PERIOD (1750-1755)

The first or Planché period extends from about 1750 to 1755. The few examples, several to be found in the Schreiber collection at South Kensington, have a band at the foot-rim bare of glaze. This has resulted in such pieces being referred to as "dry edge." It was caused by a lack of skill of the workmen in dipping the figure in the glaze. Another characteristic of such pieces is the presence of a "funnel-shaped" vent-hole in the base. The glaze is usually milk white.

PALE COLOR PERIOD (1756-1760)

The next period, extending from 1756 to 1760, is referred to as the era of the "pale colored" family. This name has been applied because the palette in use comprised pale or pastel shades. These figures, like the succeeding ones, had as a characteristic the "Patch Marks" or "Thumb Prints." This was the discovery made by Mr. Rackham, who found such marks were made as a result of the manufacturing practice of placing the article on little pieces of clay while it was being baked in the kiln. When the pieces were removed from the kiln, the pieces of clay dropped off, leaving three or four dirty areas. Having discovered these marks on late Derby of unmistakable origin, he drew the conclusion that such marks on the unmarked earlier pieces proved that they were of Derby origin, and further he discovered this practice was a continuing process and that these marks are found on practically all Derby figures, as well as on many vases. These patches do occur, however, occasionally on other porcelain. They occur frequently on Red Anchor Chelsea, occasionally on Gold Anchor Chelsea, and on Longton Hall, but regularly on Derby.

The pale-colored pieces have very little gold, and in this respect they are like the Red Anchor Chelsea. The period from 1760 to 1770 is characterized by a great deal of gold and the colors were bright. The coloring of this period includes a very easily recognized turquoise-green with a tendency to become discolored to a dirty brownish tone. The modeling of heads and the flesh-painting (with bright patches on the cheeks) are also distinctive. In this and subsequent periods, the applied flowers on the bases of the figures sometimes show centers in the form of a bun cut with a cross.

It is not too difficult to distinguish Derby figures of the period 1756-1770 from those of Bow. The Bow figures are heavy in the hand, while the Derby ones are usually lighter. The drapery on the Derby figures is more sharply cut. The Bow figures frequently have at the back of the base a triangular or square hole, whereas the Derby ones never do. On the other hand, the Derby figures nearly always have the "patch" marks on the base, while the Bow ones rarely do. Again a chemical analysis will invariably show bone ash in the composition of Bow and not in Derby of the periods under consideration. Derby, on the other hand, will show a lead content of 2 per cent. to 8 per cent. while Bow will show none. Chelsea of the Red Anchor and Raised Anchor periods likewise has no lead content. Gold Anchor Chelsea contains bone ash and has a soft greenish tone glaze not found on Derby. The Derby glaze, however, is rich and unctuous because of the presence of lead in a relatively large proportion. Despite these differences, it is not always easy to distinguish Derby figures from the Chelsea of the same periods. The Chelsea modeling is more refined, however, and the heads of the Derby figures are usually large and exhibit an apparent stare that is not too pleasing. Pastoral Derby figures having elaborate bocages similar to those made at Chelsea during the Gold Anchor period may sometimes be identified by the presence of very large and button-like flowers. It is not unusual to find areas on early Derby figures where the thick soft glaze has failed to adhere to the biscuit, leaving dry spots, but such are not to be confused with the "dry edges" found on Planché pieces. A spot of this kind will be found on Asia, shown as Illustration 630.

During the period 1756-60, typical subjects were Musicians, Turkish Dancers, Lovers with Clowns, Mythological Characters, Continents, etc., all exhibiting unusual originality. In the period 1760-70 well known subjects also included Milton, Britannia, Shakespeare, Dancers, Peddlers, People with Animals, and the Seasons and Elements.

Referring now to some examples of the foregoing, we find Illustrations 615 and 616 showing a pair of figures of considerable size, probably dating 1756-1760 and certainly of the kind that at one time would have been attributed to Chelsea. One figure, Mars, the God of War, is skilfully modeled and has many characteristics of Chelsea. It is heavy in the hand, has only a small vent hole, the bottom is ground, and there are no "thumb marks." The companion piece represents Minerva, the Goddess of Plenty. Unlike the other piece, it is extremely light in the hand, has a very large vent hole, the base is not ground, and it has the characteristic Derby "patch marks." Neither figure has very much gold and both are decorated with the pale palette of early Derby with the exception of the bodices, which are fish scale and decorated with a claret color, which is typical of Chelsea. The base of each figure is flat and in the early rocaille style. The paste and glaze, however, are like early Derby. The faces do not have the fixed stare found so often in Derby. It will be seen that it is not always easy to distinguish early Derby from Chelsea when no chemical analysis is available.

Illustration 630 depicts an early Derby figure of Asia, one of the Continents series. This figure is typical of the period 1756-60. The colors are pale and the base has the expected "patch marks," and the woman has the typical fixed expression. The camel has a characteristic dry spot on its neck, and no gold except the word Asia is found. Here we have no difficulty is making an attribution to Derby. Illustration 624 is of a small figure of a girl with a basket of flowers. It could well have been Spring, from the Seasons series. The girl has the typical fixed stare, and the base has the "patch marks." Illustrations 623 and 625 show two typical Derby figures of girls with baskets. The decoration in each case is in pale colors, and the bottoms all have the "patch marks" and incised numerals indicating different sizes. They date about 1756-60.

Illustration 632 depicts a Derby figure of Falstaff, which was quite popular at this and other factories. The base is of a fairly early shape and dates about 1765. The colors are not so pale as in the previous ones and more gold is in evidence. The base has the characteristic "patch marks," an incised pattern number, and the incised triangle of Joseph Hill, a "repairer."

TRANSITION PERIOD (1760-70)

During the period of 1760-70 the useful ware was not so numerous nor so fine as in the later periods. Large vases were never a speciality of the factory; only a few, if any, under-glaze blue pieces were made during the early period and in this respect Derby was different from the other English factories with the exception of Chelsea. This was probably due to the excessive softness of the Derby glaze: the blue fired in the glost-oven would have been likely to "flow" or "run." Little if any "old Japan" decoration was used until Bloor's time. The useful wares of the early periods show a link with the figures in the painting of flowers with stalks having a peculiar thread-like appearance; these are found quite early on the costumes of the figures and later on are frequent. Another painter's hand is seen in the very large moths, beetles, and other insects copied, of course, from Meissen, but treated in an individual and distinctive manner. At the British Museum will be found some pierced vases or perfume-pots long regarded as Chelsea. The moths, with typical applied flowers and "dirty turquoise" serve to identify the pieces as Derby. Illustration 595 shows a bowl and cover of the early period and is at Colonial Williamsburg, Virginia. Illustrations 596, 598, 599, 600, 601, 602, 605, 608 and 614, of the period of 1760 show a number of different pieces of useful ware of this factory, which are all in the Schreiber collection now in the Victoria and Albert Museum.

CHELSEA-DERBY PERIOD (1770-1784)

About 1769 Duesbury purchased the Chelsea factory and operated it at its original location for fourteen years. This period is known as Chelsea-Derby. Up to this time no factory mark was used by Duesbury and now, in 1770, he used two marks, one to designate the work done at the Chelsea factory, and the other for work done at Derby. The Chelsea product was marked with a combination of the last Chelsea mark, a gold anchor over the glaze, and a "D" interlaced; whereas Derby ware used a "D" surmounted by a crown in enamel colors, also over the glaze. The enamel color of the mark was usually purple or blue. These marks were probably used up to about 1784 when the Chelsea branch was dismantled and moved to Derby. After this Chelsea-Derby period, there was no reason to use two marks, and as will be seen in the next period, only one mark was used and that designated the period called the Crown-Derby.

Dr. F. Brayshaw Gilhespy in his authoritative book *Crown Derby Porcelain*, recently published, says that Chelsea-Derby may date from 1761 or the later sixties, rather than 1770 as generally supposed. He also points out that there was a tradition that all domestic ware was sent to Derby for decoration. In spite of the fact that only a few Chelsea artists are supposed to have remained at the Chelsea factory after it was taken over by Duesbury, yet a very great deal of the useful ware with the Chelsea-Derby mark is in existence. He notes a piece that is marked with a crown and D which is undoubtedly Chelsea.

We show as Illustration 642 a jug with the Derby "Smith's Blue" and flowers painted in the distinct style of Withers, which has the anchor and "D" mark, which seems to confirm his opinion that no real distinction was made. This may, on the other hand, be the exception which proves the rule. The reasons for the two marks related above would certainly seem logical. We have similar examples where certain rules of the factories were not strictly followed. Thus, at Vincennes in 1753 the King decreed that a date letter was to be added to the royal cypher—"A" to indicate 1753, "B" 1754, etc. However, in spite of the order, we find much pâte dure porcelain of the 1770-80 period having no date letter.

There can be no doubt that Duesbury took full advantage of all information acquired upon his purchase of the Chelsea factory, as to recipes for paste and quality of materials, for certainly most of the products of this period are very fine indeed. It was only surpassed by that of the following or Crown-Derby period, during which the finest useful ware made in England is to be found.

The claret and turquoise ground colors on Derby pieces did not reach the level of quality obtained under the Chelsea management. The Chelsea workman responsible for the claret ground probably went to Worcester and not to Derby. On the Derby porcelain, the color always tends to a brownish tone. The dark mazarin blue gave place to a large extent, towards the end of the Chelsea-Derby period, to an opaque enamel of a much brighter lapis-lazuli color, imitated from the *bleu-de-roi* of Sèvres but distinctive enough to be known as "Derby blue" or "Smith's blue". Though the Sèvres influence is unmistakable, the Derby tableware of the Chelsea-Derby period included some highly creditable work, employing a fine and sympathetic but practical material, decorated in excellent taste. The Derby patterns of this and the succeeding periods created a quite distinct style which was not without influence on other English factories. The swags and festoons, small detached sprigs of flowers, wavy lines and the often very charming monochrome painting of urns, vases and classical figures in gray or crimson monochrome are well represented in the Schreiber Collection and others. The striped and wavy patterns resembling those of contemporary brocades are noteworthy. The Derby pieces can be distinguished from Worcester and others by their color under transmitted light (brownish), by their glaze quality, and by the Derby gilding, which seems to have been applied in a thicker condition, making fine brush strokes difficult.

The earliest of the Derby painters whose names and work are known to us is Edward Withers. This so-called Withers style is marked by a slightly conventionalized manner of outlining the petals of a flower. While (as already stated) very little of the so-called "old Japan" pattern was made during the Chelsea-Derby period, this style first made its appearance there and is shown in the pattern book as No. 3. It was of fine quality and more pleasing than the Japanese export porcelain.

The figures of the Chelsea-Derby period represent a continuation of the earlier tradition of Derby rather than that of Chelsea, though it is not always easy to distinguish between figures made at Chelsea and those made at Derby during this time. While the two marks were used on the useful ware, they were rarely used on the figures. The only mark found on figures of this period was a script "N" or "No." followed by a numeral referring to the Derby price list, and occasionally a reference to the size. The biscuit statues for which the factory was famous began to be made in this period and were similarly marked. Early specimens are found in the famous Schreiber Collection, which is especially rich in Chelsea-Derby.

The Chelsea-Derby figures as a rule are enamelled in insipid weak colors, among them a pale "watery" green and pink, and a rich brown; the "dirty turquoise" of the earlier period is replaced with a pleasant clear color inclining to blue, which was evidently from a Chelsea formula. Illlustration 514 is of a figure probably made at Chelsea. The formal flower-painting on the dresses shows the greatest delicacy and refinement, and the same high quality marks the useful wares of the period, upon which rests the chief claim of Derby to an honorable place among the English china factories.

It was during this era and entirely independent of Chelsea that Derby produced the "Biscuit Porcelain," for which it was justly renowned. It will be observed that at some period of its existence every factory has created a speciality that its competitors could not successfully imitate. With Derby, probably, its most distinguished speciality was biscuit figures. The pâte tendre biscuit figures made at Vincennes from 1750 to 1756 and continued when the factory moved to Sèvres up to about 1769 when pâte dure ones were made were quite different from those made at Derby. No other English factory produced them, and after about 1811, the Derby factory either lost the art, or at best made no satisfactory ones. The "biscuit porcelain" of Derby was first produced about 1770 and was probably an attempt to emulate Carara marble. It gave the modeler an opportunity to finish his work without filling up his details and blunting the anatomy of his figure with the addition of a glaze. After the ordinary glazed figure had been designed and modeled, the creator had nothing further to do with its manufacture, and while the first few figures produced from a mold would perhaps be of good quality and finish, the mold would very soon begin to show signs of wear, and the figures lost definition and delicacy. The coloring of a glazed figure easily hid these blemishes, and without this coloring, many much-admired figures would be exposed to a criticism from which the surface decoration shields them.

The biscuit figures of Derby were designed to stand upon an entirely different plane; they were designed as statuary, and intended to be criticized as such; they were to stand finished without any superimposed colors or gold, such as would give a superficial attraction and disarm criticism; therefore, they would require a treatment more careful in every way than that accorded the ordinary glazed and colored statuettes. The paste of which these biscuit figures were made varies considerably, for while some of them are almost of the tone of a fine white ivory, others are colder in hue, having almost the dead white of Wedgwood's jasper. The latter type were the ones made during the Chelsea-Derby period. The ones made during the next, or Crown-Derby period have an additional charm, as the surface is soft and appears to have been polished. This later technique was probably the invention of Kean and included burning the piece (after it had received its biscuit fire) in a glazed seggar in the glost-oven. The process was somewhat similar to the salt-glaze process, in which a handful of salt was added, which had the effect of adding a thin coating to the otherwise dry surface. It is, however, quite different from the process of adding a glaze as is usually done. The process here used had the tendency to suffuse slightly the surface of the biscuit and give the appearance of the soft "polish" alluded to. It is impossible to believe that these figures were made and finished by the ordinary artisan potter; they were of course molded like the ordinary figures, and it is quite possible that the pieces were taken from the molds and put together in the ordinary way, but the best biscuit figures are not merely *made*, they are *molded*, and with so much delicacy, refinement and feeling, that the finishing work must have been done by the modeler himself before he allowed the piece to pass to the fire, where, for good or for ill, as a thing of beauty, or as a lamentable mediocrity, its fate would be sealed and its character be rendered unchangeable. While the pâte tendre figures of Vincennes and Sèvres have much beauty, they lack the infinite fine detail found on Derby.

The earliest known modeler of biscuit was Pierre Stephan, who came to the factory in 1770. His best known work was a set of the Elements: Earth, Air, Fire, and Water. These were mentioned in the Derby price list and offered for sale in 1772, according to a reference in Chaffers. Stephan later went to work for Wedgwood. Two of the Earth and Water figures are in the Herbert Allen collection. The great amount of detail work found on this series is almost beyond belief. Incised under the bases will be found "No. 48," which is the pattern number, and also an incised triangle, which was the mark of the "repairer," Joseph Hill. It was, of course, the duty of the repairer to make the figures after the "Sculptor" or "modeler," (Stephan in this case) had made the model. Hurlbutt says that Joseph Hill was the earliest and finest repairer at Derby and was apprenticed to William Duesbury I.

Among the best modelers was the temperamental John James Spengler, a Swiss, son of Adam Spengler, director of the Zürich porcelain factory. He worked at Derby during the last decade of the eighteenth century. Some of his creations were the Russian Shepherd group, No. 387; two pair of female figures with dead birds, No. 363; Nos. 11, 37, 373 and 381 figures unnamed; the Diana, No. 3012-1901 (Victoria and Albert Museum), and his finest work is considered as the three groups: Bacchantes Adorning Pan, Graces Distressing Cupid, and Virgins Awakening Cupid. These groups were based on paintings by Angelica Kaufmann, the first two engraved by Bartolozzi, the other by W. Wynne Rylands in a print published in 1776. These carry the impressed pattern numbers under the base, as well as the repairer's mark, which in this case is a star for Isaac Farnsworth.

Attention is here invited to Illustrations 617 to 620, showing a rare early set of the Elements. They carry under the base the Derby mark of a "D" surmounted by a crown, which is significant as it was the mark used during this period to distinguish work done at the Derby works from that done at Chelsea under Derby ownership. This mark would tend to confirm the statement previously made that the biscuit figures had no connection with Chelsea, but were the original creation of Derby. In addition, we find No. 48, which is the pattern mark, and a triangle which as previously explained, was the repairer's mark used by Joseph Hill. The "sculptors" or "modelers" marks, never appear on the biscuit figures. What must strike the connoisseur most forcibly in connection with these models is the advance which was made from the merely quaint to the truly beautiful, and apparently almost at one bound; for the word beautiful can hardly be applied in its true sense to the early figures, either of Bow, Chelsea or Derby. Quaint they certainly are, and interesting, and many of them have a certain undefinable daintiness which has decided charm, but the work of beauty sounds a deeper note and demands a higher level of excellence. The Derby biscuit figures are well "drawn," well designed, and beautifully modeled.

Attention is called to Illustrations 621 and 622, showing two of the finest biscuit figures of the Crown Derby period. One is the figure of Virgins Awakening Cupid, modeled by John James Spengler. The paste is soft and white and not as dry as that of the Elements. It was modeled about 1790 and had the Crown Derby mark of a "D" with a superimposed crown and the crossed batons, which was the mark of this period. The incised star indicates that the repairer was Isaac Farsnworth. It also shows the pattern No. 195. The other figure is known as Bacchantes Adorning Pan. This figure is thought to date 1795 as it incorporates the improvements attributed to Kean. It has the No. 196 pattern mark, the star indicating that Isaac Farnsworth repaired it, and the Crown Derby mark impressed under the base. The well known "patch marks" are present on all of these figures, and the "soft polished glaze" is evident.

We show as Illustration 642 a mug decorated by Withers and having a border of the blue enamel referred to as "Derby blue" or "Smith's blue." The mark is a gold anchor and "D." Illustration 641 shows a cup with the "Smith's blue." The mark is a crowned "D" in blue, indicating that it was decorated at Derby, whereas the mug was decorated at Chelsea. Illustration 640 shows one of a pair of diamond-shaped platters in the "Smith's blue" with the early crown "D" mark in blue and painted in the style of Withers. Illustration 580 shows a handleless tea bowl and saucer in a typical Chelsea type of decoration of detached flowers and having the gold "D" and anchor mark. Illustration 637 depicts a deep plate in the popular Thistle design. The mark is the crowned "D" in violet, the earliest color. The plate is from the collection of Dr. and Mrs. Frank Mercer of Detroit, Michigan.

CROWN DERBY PERIOD (1784-1811)

We come now to the "Crown Derby" period, 1784-1811. The finest useful ware of the factory was made at this time, and the porcelain is considered to be the finest ever made in England with the exception of that of Nantgarw. The glaze is sometimes "crazed," and as this is not an uncommon fault of some of the best Chelsea pieces, it seems to suggest that the Derby body was improved upon Chelsea lines. The paste is a true pâte tendre, the fracture close, and it is not improbable that calcined bone was introduced into the mixture at this time, either in accordance with the Chelsea formula, or what is more probable, as a result of Duesbury's purchase of the Bow factory in 1776. Although he did not operate it separately, as he did with Chelsea, all the Bow formulae and other information were available to him. Whatever the reason, the Crown-Derby now shows an excellent translucency. A quite special feature is the exceeding softness of the glaze, resembling sometimes that of early Sèvres, the paintings having often the appearance of being under-glaze, so deeply have they sunk in. The glaze is frequently iridescent over the decorations. A light green wash on the bases of figures and a predominance of turquoise and pink on the cloaks of the figures were characteristic of this period. The mark was a crowned "D" with crossed batons, and it is said that Duesbury added the crossed batons so that he would also have a mark comparable to that used at Meissen. The new mark first appeared in blue, then puce or purple, and finally about 1795, a Chinese red. Unlike the practice in the early period, each piece now showed both the factory mark and the pattern number (in many cases the decorator's number also). Fortunately the old design books have survived.

At this time when Derby had absorbed practically all of the other leading English factories except Worcester, a large quantity of useful ware was made and many designs created. The old records reveal that twelve numbers were assigned to the gilders and that these numbers were placed at the foot-rim, while the pattern numbers were placed below the "D" in the factory mark. The following is the list:

Gilders

Thomas Soar	1
Joseph Stables	2
William Cooper	3
William Yates	4
Jonathan Yates	5
Not known	6
William Billingsley	7
William Longdon	8
William Smith	9
Jonathan Blood	10
William Taylor	11
John Duesbury	12
Joseph Dodd	13

Famous Modelers

Stephan, Spengler and Rossi

Famous Painters and Gilders

Edward Withers
William Billingsley
Richard Askew
Jockey Hill
Quaker Pegg
Duvivier
Zachariah Boreman
Moses Webster
John Brewer
George Complin
James Banford

Famous Repairers or Molders

James Hill
Isaac Farnsworth

While Worcester porcelain was invariably marked under the glaze, Derby (almost every specimen being marked) without exception was marked over the glaze in gold, blue or purple. Michael Kean, as previously stated, was taken into the firm in 1795, and some pieces have the mark with a "K" entwined with the "D," but this mark was seldom used.

There are in existence two sets of pattern books, one of plates and the other of cups and saucers, and each is in duplicate; in each set, one copy is evidently later than the other, though containing the same patterns with the same numbers. From No. 6 to No. 24, the patterns are all various borders with painted flower sprigs or sprays in the center, with the exception of No. 17, which is a blue Adam border with blue sprig in the center. In the early book, these sprays of flowers are beautifully painted in, and from the technique and grouping we are inclined to think that they are from the brush of Billingsley himself (this opinion was given by W. Moore Binns in his *First Century of English Porcelain*, 1906). In the older book, the first 120 patterns are beautifully executed. From this point to No. 450 they are still carefully executed, but not with the artistic touch of the previous ones. From 450 to 770, the execution becomes poorer. Patterns 1, 2, 3 and 4 are apparently the same and are plain white with gold dentil edge inside and out and a gold foot-band. It is believed that the majority of the rich patterns were never made in tea-sets at all, but were simply "cabinet cups."

We call attention to Illustration 639, which is a cup and saucer of octagonal shape, having the Duesbury or Crown Derby mark in puce. It has as a pattern mark the numeral I on both the cup and saucer. The gold work is superb, and it corresponds exactly to the pattern book above. At the foot-rim, also in puce, will be found the numeral 2 which indicates that the gold, which is the only decoration, was by Joseph Stables. Illustration 643 is from a large dinner service made for Lord William Frieth of Bristol, of which one hundred and thirty-five pieces have survived to the present time. The mark is the crowned "D" and crossed batons in Pomeranian red and has the pattern No. 9. It is one of the numbers that Moore Binns ascribes to the hand of Billingsley. The fact that the mark is in red would indicate the possibility of a date around 1795-1800. The paintings around each piece have a decided "halo" or "iridescence." The interesting point is that all the porcelain made at Nantgarw by Billingsley's formula and decorated in London have this same characteristic.

The porcelain produced during the Bloor period (1811-28) was of poor character and comprised a large number of defective pieces decorated in the Old Japan style to cover the defects. The colors of this period were heavy reds, browns, and blues which also changed the appearance of the figures.

CHARACTERISTICS OF DERBY

1. Very soft to the touch as a result of the lead content of the glaze.
2. Very translucent and slightly brown to green by transmitted light.
3. Under-glaze blue is very rare.
4. No mark until 1770; then "D" superimposed crown to 1784 on that made at Derby factory; blue, puce and Chinese red in that order; that made at Chelsea by Duesbury marked with anchor and "D" in monogram form, usually in gold.
5. From 1784-1811, the mark Crown "D" and crossed batons with dots; same order of colors.
6. Pattern marks and decorators' numbers quite usual in this period; also finest useful ware made at this time.
7. Has tendency to craze after 1770.
8. Figures invariably have "patch marks." Early period colors pale.

9. Figures usually have fixed stare.

10. Figures have cheeks painted flesh color.

11. Flowers frequently have bun centers with cross marks.

12. Dirty turquoise color typical.

13. Dry edge characteristic of Planché porcelain.

14. Original English designs characteristic.

15. Derby figures light in the hand.

17. Drapery on Derby figures deeply cut.

18. Pastoral Derby figures have large button-like flowers.

19. Very large moths, beetles, etc., characteristic, as well as flowers with stalks having thread-like appearance.

20. Swags, festoons, small detached flowers, wavy lines and charming monochrome painted urns and classical figures are typical.

21. White biscuit porcelain figures, finely potted, characteristic only of this factory in England, probably the factory's most noted achievement. When a soft sheen is present, the period 1795 is indicated; earliest ones are white and dry.

ENGLISH LOWESTOFT PORCELAIN

There has been probably more argument about Lowestoft china and the facts and fictions with regard to it than about any other of the early English factories. The fame enjoyed for so long by this modest factory was not due to any intrinsic merit of its productions, but was due to a colossal mistake made by William Chaffers, author of the comprehensive volume *Marks and Monograms on Pottery and Porcelain*, first issued in 1863 and running into several editions before his death in 1892. By means of circumstantial evidence and interviews with old workmen from the factory, Chaffers attributed that large class of Chinese porcelain properly known as "Chinese export ware" to this little English factory. As a result, many collectors filled their cabinets with what they thought was English porcelain, whereas in fact it was the product of China. Mr. Frederick Litchfield, the able reviser of this comprehensive work recognized the mistake made by Chaffers, but it has been impossible even to this day to separate the name Lowestoft from that large body of oriental porcelain made for export to England, France, Holland and the United States by the Chinese and decorated largely in Canton.

The English Lowestoft factory was founded in 1757 and the partners were Messrs. Walker, Browne, Aldred and Richmond. It closed in 1802 and never produced anything but soft-paste porcelain, whereas the controversial Chinese porcelain was always hard. One of the reasons for the mistake was that so much of the export ware was decorated in the armorial style with English coats-of-arms of many great families. There was much interest in Chinese porcelain at the time, and the East India company's ships took sketches of such coats-of-arms to Canton, where the Chinese reproduced the desired decorations on porcelain to be returned to England and elsewhere.

Robert Browne evidently took a leading part in the manufacture of porcelain at Lowestoft, a small town in Suffolk. According to tradition, Browne learned the secrets of Bow porcelain by taking a position there. The fact that the Lowestoft body contains bone-ash and is chemically the same as that of Bow lends color to this story. The factory was a small one, never hiring more than seventy workmen, but the many pieces of porcelain made there are accounted for by reason of its long existence. The Victoria and Albert Museum has a very large collection of Lowestoft. It is sometimes rather hard to distinguish it from Bow, particularly in the blue-and-white wares. No recognized factory mark was used. The most significant marks found on this porcelain are numerals and letters written in blue on the inner side of the foot-rim. The placing of these marks is peculiar to this factory. The workman's number most often encountered was the numeral 5, thought to be that of Robert Allen. The foot-rim is also unusual, an inverted broad-based triangle, not at all undercut. The paste is like that of Bow, but the glaze is usually thinner. The blue-and-white is generally of mediocre quality and in many cases its designs are copied from Worcester. A dark blue is characteristic, but on the best pieces, it is remarkably pure and luminous. As transfer printing in blue was not practised at Bow, all such pieces can be ascribed to Lowestoft.

The colored wares of the first twenty years of the factory are of a few types easily recognized. Chinese subjects inspired by Worcester are common. The favorite globular shape of Lowestoft teapots was a close copy of Chinese export ware. The Lowestoft teapot was more nearly spherical as a rule, and had a higher foot than the similar copies made at Worcester and Bristol. The Lowestoft jugs and coffee pots are usually of an easily recognizable form, with a handle that returns outwards with a knobbed "kick" at its lower end and is usually provided with a thumb-rest above. Small cylindrical mugs were made with flat glazed bases. The bouquets of pink roses and other flowers by one prolific hand are marked by a stiff shading of the petals sometimes in parallel lines. Certain diapers, mainly of a trellis pattern in red or pink, regularly dappled with darker spots, also help to identify the Lowestoft types. Hexagonal and other cell-diapers in red and blue were also favorites.

Illustration 634 shows a very typical English Lowestoft teapot. We show from the Colonial Williamsburg collection a garniture comprising six vases (Illustration 560) and from the same collection a very interesting coffee pot and cover (Illustration 545). The principal decorations on this last-named piece are the name of the original owner, John Ward Blofield, and a poem in under-glaze blue. Similar objects and inscriptions were not unusual at this factory, particularly one saying "A Trifle from Lowestoft."

PLYMOUTH, BRISTOL AND NEW HALL

These three factories are here considered together, since one is the outgrowth of the other. They represent the only true or hard-paste porcelain ever made in England and for that reason have an interest quite apart from other English porcelain. As Plymouth lies near the great beds of clay and feldspathic stone which have supplied English potters for centuries, it would seem proper that here for the first time in England true porcelain should be made. It is strange, however, that with the search and discovery of steatite these rich deposits of kaolin clay so necessary for the production of true porcelain were not sooner found.

As early as 1745, William Cookworthy, a Quaker chemist of Plymouth, is thought to have known the nature of the clay used by the Chinese, and it is further believed that as early as 1758, he had discovered the source of this fine white clay. The use of Cornish soapstone in the manufacture of soft-paste porcelain may also have been due to his discoveries.

In 1765, Richard Champion of Bristol, although only twenty-two years old, was interested in producing china and had received from his brother-in-law, Caleb Lloyd, of Charleston, South Carolina, a shipment of china-clay. This was the same "unaker" that had some twenty years earlier been used at the Bow factory. Champion wrote at this time about "new work just established" in the attempt to make porcelain with Cornish materials. The body is perfectly white *within*, he wrote, but not *without*, which is always smoky. Champion promised to try the American clay, but pointed out that without a fusible china-stone, it would be useless.

At a later date, a variety of granite or feldspar known in Cornwall as "moorstone" or "growan-stone," was discovered by Cookworthy. His first samples proved to have too much iron, causing reddish stains, but later, near St. Austell, he found a deposit showing greenish spots similar to that described by Père d'Entrecolles in his writings concerning the porcelain production in China. Accordingly, Cookworthy took out a patent in 1768 covering the production of porcelain, using these materials. A porcelain manufacturing company was formed, composed of William Cookworthy, Philip Cookworthy, Richard Champion, John and Joseph Harford, William Phillips, T. Were and Sons, John Bulteel, William Wolcott, Joseph Fry and Thomas Franks. The last-named was a son of a Bristol potter; the others were prominent Bristol men or relatives of Cookworthy.

Cookworthy's account of his discovery discloses his scientific methods and his diligent study of the letters of Père d'Entrecolles. The lime and plant-ash used in his glaze were prepared exactly in the same manner as was done by the Chinese at Ching-tê-Chên. The factory was located at Coxside, Plymouth, and was operated with the assistance of Thomas Pitt, afterwards Lord Camelford. As noted above, the partners were mainly Bristol men, and so it is not known exactly when the manufacture was transferred to Bristol; but it was probably around 1770. As Cookworthy was an old man, in 1773 he sold the business and his patent to Champion, a much younger man, who changed the name of the works to "Bristol China Manufactory" and employed John Brittan as his foreman. The patent expired in 1775 and this was a great blow to Champion, who was only successful in getting a modified re-issue of the patent because of the opposition of Josiah Wedgwood and other potters. His failure to get full protection from his patent was one of the reasons why he did not attain any commercial success in producing true porcelain. Financial difficulties obliged him to sell the patent rights in 1781 to a company of Staffordshire potters, who continued the manufacture of the more simply decorated wares at a factory opened the following year, called the New Hall, at Shelton.

On early pieces of Plymouth, we sometimes find as a factory mark, the symbol for tin, which is a combination of the numbers 2 and 4 conjoined, in under-glaze blue, gold, or enamel. Cookworthy, a chemist, probably adopted it in recognition of the ancient tin-mining industry of Cornwall. This symbol is also sometimes found on porcelain produced at Bristol, which is usually marked with a Maltese cross alone, or in combination with numerals, and some times a capital "B." Illustration 584 has the Maltese cross and the numeral 7. The cross swords mark, and a cross are not unusual and the presence of the "T" or "To" of Mr. Tebo, the repairer, are sometimes encountered. To distinguish Plymouth from Bristol is not always an easy task, but the specimen shown as Illustration 633 is probably a Plymouth plate. It is, in any event, more logical to divide the products into the early porcelain produced by Cookworthy and the later porcelain of Champion. It is not difficult, however, to distinguish either one from other English porcelains, as Plymouth, Bristol and New Hall are pâte dure, or hard porcelain, while all others are soft-paste. Both Plymouth and Bristol show a brownish smoky color which was never completely overcome. Illustration 496 depicts a good example of the Bristol manufactory. Technical shortcomings were never entirely eliminated, and the porcelain was extremely hard to the file, more so than Meissen or Chinese. Grit often adhered to the foot-rims and the glaze frequently has a tendency to collect in globules containing bubbles and black specks. As a result of the unskilful work of the potter, pieces thrown on the wheel invariably have spiral ridges, known as "wreathing." This is almost an identifying mark of the factories. Warping and fire cracks were usual at Bristol, which accounts for the fact that plates are rare, and the high temperature used in the kilns usually resulted in the figures leaning forward, a characteristic of this factory. Because of extremely hard-paste, the enamel did not sink into the glaze as in the case of soft-paste, but seemed to stand out as a superficial incrustation. A fused appearance resulting from difficulties in the firing, together with a common smokiness, usually indicates Plymouth. Bristol had the same faults, but to a less extent. The under-glaze blue of Plymouth usually has a blackish or greyish tone. For some reason not apparent, classical style borders were a feature in the blue-and-white and were quite attractive.

Shell salts were favorites of the unidentifiable repairer, Mr. Tebo, and we find his mark on salts ascribed to the Cookworthy period. It is surprising to find Longton Hall models used by Plymouth. The early Plymouth figures may be recognized and distinguished from Bristol by their scrolled rococo bases, often picked out in the distinctive Plymouth brownish-crimson. (Illustrations 269 and 591 show good examples of Plymouth figures and birds). On the other hand, the Bristol vases have indefinite rockwork also found at Sèvres during the Louis Seize period. The Bristol "Elements" show the same excellent lively movement as those made at Derby, and the "Seasons" are the work of the same modeler. The Shepherds and Shepherdesses, Children with Dogs, and Venus and Adonis are to be seen in the Schreiber collection. Some have the Tebo mark. Much more successful than the figures are the large hexagonal vases with painting on a white ground. The decoration usually showed birds in a distant landscape having a strong Sèvres influence. It may be said that the unusually fine Plymouth and Bristol painting goes a long way to compensate for the imperfections in the porcelain itself. Champion made a number of handsome china services for his friends, as well as "cottage china." Had he paid more attention to the latter, he would doubtless have enjoyed a greater degree of commercial success. Transfer printing was rarely used; the principal decoration included ribbon and festoon patterns, laurel and husk and grey camaieu painting in the style of Sèvres. Finally, Bristol made a number of biscuit plaques with portrait busts and coats-of-arms in relief as presentation pieces for Champions. The productions of the factory at New Hall do not come within the scope of this book and are of little importance from the standpoint of a collector.

LIVERPOOL

Very little has been written about the factories which made porcelain at Liverpool, but it has been thought that several operated there. Seth Pennington, one of three brothers, made porcelain at Shaw's Brow, but little is known of it. The principal factory, however, was Richard Chaffers' of Shaw's Brow. Chaffers was a delft manufacturer who secured the services of Robert Podmore, formerly a workman in the Lund Bristol factory and later at the great Worcester factory. This same Podmore, it will be remembered, was one of the workmen who received special payments as arcanists from the Worcester factory when it was formed in 1751. It is said that he was bribed by Wedgwood to enter his employ. He left Wedgwood in 1756 and furnished the technical knowledge which enabled Chaffers to start his Liverpool factory. Podmore died in 1765 and Chaffers soon thereafter.

The products of this factory followed closely that of the factories where Podmore had been previously employed. Chaffers became the licensee of a soapstone mine in Cornwall in 1756, probably at the suggestion of Podmore, who was well aware that soapstone was one of the principal ingredients used by Lund, and later at Worcester. The body of the porcelain made at the Chaffers' Liverpool factory was greyish in appearance, the glaze slightly blued, and the translucency green in color like that of Dr. Wall Worcester.

Sadler and Green, it is claimed, invented transfer printing in Liverpool as early as 1752, but this early date has been questioned. That they were doing this type of decoration about 1756, at which time Hancock was also producing it at Worcester, is certain.

Printing in under-glaze blue was also practised at Liverpool around 1779. Mugs seem to have been a favorite shape at these factories. Characteristic of the work at the Pennington factory was the use of a "sticky blue." A group of Chinese figures copied probably from Worcester and now in the British Museum have been assigned by W. B. Honey to Liverpool. Paintings in under-glaze blue distinguished by curiously lax clusters of circles representing a tree in a Chinese landscape, are undoubtedly Liverpool, and such a type is shown here as Illustration 570. It is green by transmitted light, has an undercut foot-rim, is painted in a spreading blue, represents a Chinese landscape including a tree, made of curiously formed clusters of circles or cells, and its glaze is bluish-gray. The shape of the handle is also characteristic of Liverpool. Illustration 535 shows a small milk jug painted with polychrome chinoiserie decoration and has the typical Liverpool handle, the translucency is green, and the paste soft. Illustration 543 is a most unusual cream jug in blue scale, and Illustration 594 shows a pair of wall vases decorated with chinoiseries, both from the Colonial Williamsburg collection.

Today more interest and research are being devoted to these hitherto neglected factories, and a very interesting paper will be found on the subject in the *English Ceramic Circle Transactions*, Vol. 4, Parts 1 and 2, page 71. by Dr. Knowles Boney. From the new information—and more which will surely follow—it may be that a good deal of the porcelain formerly attributed to Worcester will now be ascribed to Liverpool, in which event we may have a repetition of what occurred in the case of Longton Hall.

CAUGHLEY

Thomas Turner who had been in the employ of the Worcester manufactory started the production of porcelain at this new factory about 1772. It is believed that experiments were being made there as early as 1752, but what was produced is uncertain. Turner is given credit by some as the originator of the widely used "Willow Pattern" and other allied designs. This factory made much blue-and-white quite similar to that of Worcester. The factory mark was a "C" made to look like the Worcester crescent, thereby greatly confusing collectors of a later day. Worcester of the Wall period is greenish by transmitted light, whereas the Caughley has a browner translucency. The Worcester blue is usually clear, while Caughley is more often cloudy. This factory also made a great deal of white porcelain which was outside decorated by Robert Chamberlain and other enamelers.

COALPORT

John Rose started a porcelain factory about 1790 across the River Severn from the Caughley works, which he purchased in 1799 and combined with his own. This factory produced during the first quarter of the nineteenth century a great deal of useful ware of good commercial quality, but not of the types sought by collectors. In later days some good copies of the Sèvres ground colors, and many vases today are found which the owners consider are the products of that factory, but which are in fact Coalport with the pseudo-Sèvres mark. The best achievement of this factory, however, was the perfection around 1820 of a feldspar porcelain of very fine quality for which Coalport received a medal of award in England. The Coalport works were finally closed in 1959.

SPODE AND DAVENPORT

The Spode factory was founded by Josiah Spode the First at Stoke-on-Trent for the making of pottery. At the beginning of the nineteenth century, Josiah Spode the Second began to produce porcelain as well and is generally given the credit for having discovered the most satisfactory formula for bone-china, which remains the English standard to this day. The Davenport factory at Longport was established in 1793, but both of these factories are outside the scope of this book.

WEDGWOOD

While the name Wedgwood is known everywhere, many people fail to realize that its fame lies in its production of pottery and not porcelain. It is true that in 1804 and until 1815, the factory experimented with the manufacture of porcelain, though this had little to recommend it above that which was being made at the other contemporary Staffordshire factories. Before it abandoned the manufacture in 1815, the factory did make a tea set for Napoleon at St. Helena. During the last half of the nineteenth century, the factory again made and today still produces high quality bone china.

NANTGARW AND SWANSEA PORCELAIN

It may seem strange to the reader that so much prominence is given here to porcelain produced in the nineteenth century. The reason is explained in the following statement of John Haslem in his well-known book, *The Old Derby China Factory*, 1876: "The China made at Nantgarw was superior to anything which had then been produced. Many collectors and dealers, indeed, of our own day do not hesitate to say that it is superior to anything ever made before or since, and the extraordinarily high prices which genuine specimens realize seem to warrant this opinion." With this statement English authorities are in general agreement. Present-day prices further confirm this belief. With the possible exception of the pâte tendre of Vincennes and Sèvres, the writers concur in this opinion. It will be understood that William Billingsley was attempting at Nantgarw and Swansea to produce a porcelain equal to the French referred to above.

Any study of Nantgarw and Swansea must begin and end with the very colorful figure of William Billingsley, who invented the paste and glaze, and of his son-in-law, Samuel Walker, who made the kilns and later at Swansea created several modified types of porcelain, always trying to retain the beauty of that created by Billingsley and at the same time to secure a formula that was practical to use.

The story begins with Billingsley at the Derby Factory, 1774-96. There he became the leading flower painter, following Withers in 1790. He was the inventor of the "wiping-out process." The previous practice was to leave a portion of the white porcelain untouched as a highlight. Billingsley created a softer effect by painting the entire flower and then highlighting it by wiping off either with a dry brush or his finger.

In spite of his high standing as a painter, his real interest and fame reside in his creating a paste and glaze resembling, if not equaling, the world-renowned French pâte tendre. He left Derby in 1796, apparently because he could not persuade that factory to adopt his formula. No information is available as to whether the Derby factory ever tried it. Writing of his painting, W. Moore Binns in his *First Century of English Porcelain* (1906), says that "all floral designs from one to twenty-four were considered to be the work of Billingsley." The Derby dinner service (Illustration 643) has the number 9, and it is referred to here because of the fact that its floral painting has the halo of iridescence around each flower in the service. Mr. W. D. John in his authoritative book *Nantgarw Porcelain*, 1948, discusses the matter in great detail. The presence of this iridescence on early Chinese porcelain is not unusual, but is never found on Meissen or French hard-paste porcelain. John says: "It occurs too on the English soft-paste porcelains made at Bow, Chelsea and Derby, though limited to a slight sheen principally over the copper-green pigment colors."

The experience of the writers with the sole exception of the Derby service is in full agreement with the statement of W. D. John.

When Billingsley left Derby, he started a small factory in partnership with Mr. John Coke at Pinxton. Later he set up an enameling shop at Mansfield and finally at Torksey. Little of his work at these is known. A very interesting collection, however, may be seen at the museum at Lincoln in England.

In 1808, William Billingsley and Samuel Walker went to Worcester. This factory during the Dr. Wall period used soapstone or soap rock as one of its principal ingredients, but for some twenty-four years had been experimenting otherwise with its paste and glaze. While the porcelain made during the Wall period was the most famous in the life of this great English factory, yet it was never noted for its fine paste or glaze but rather for its potting, gilding and decorations. The ownership during these twenty-four years had been in the hands of the Flights and the Barrs, and one of the latter (Martin Barr) was interested in improving the formula during the time Billingsley and Walker were employed. The Worcester factory accordingly entered into an agreement to pay £200 for the exclusive use of the Billingsley formula but granted Billingsley the right to use it himself should he start a factory of his own. Records are available to show that Worcester did make some porcelain during the years 1808-1813 in accordance with Billingsley's formula. From a letter which Flight, Barr and Barr sent to L. W. Dillwyn the proprietor at Swansea complaining that Billingsley had broken his contract with Worcester, it appears that difficulty had been experienced there in producing a commercially satisfactory porcelain; but on account of its fine quality, Barr was afraid that some competitor might overcome these difficulties.

We show a part tea and coffee service as Illustration 588 which we believe, although we have no proof, is an example of the porcelain made at Worcester according to Billingsley's formula. When a piece from this service is placed alongside a marked Nantgarw specimen under an ultra-violet light, it shows a marked similarity and is certainly of the same family. This Worcester service is exceptionally translucent and the glaze is a brilliant white, comparing favorably with much of the Nantgarw. Certainly Worcester never made other porcelain during any period to compare with it, and had it been possible to make it commercially, then Worcester would, in our judgment, have produced it in quantity and probably Billingsley and Walker would never have gone to Nantgarw.

It must be assumed, however, that Flight, Barr and Barr decided against its use, and in any event, we know that Billingsley and Walker left Worcester in the fall of 1813 and went to Nantgarw, a little village on the Glamorgan canal near Cardiff in Wales, and there, with the very limited capital at their disposal, made the first Nantgarw porcelain. In addition to his son-in-law, Walker, Billingsley had two daughters, Sarah and Lavinia, who went with him, but his wife for some reason never left Derby. Their letters to her relate the many hardships and heartbreaks that he suffered in his efforts to make his porcelain a success. From the very first it was apparent that the paste and glaze were superb, and if he could only make it practical to manufacture, his success would be assured. Unfortunately, he was never able to do so.

Another man who had a great impact on the several attempts at Nantgarw and Swansea was William Weston Young. The great author and collector of Welsh porcelain, the late E. Morton Nance, describes Young as follows: "Of the many interesting personalities connected with the manufactures of Swansea and Nantgarw, none makes a stronger appeal to our sympathies than William Weston Young . . . He had the ability always to make money easily, yet he certainly lacked the faculty of keeping it. He was an artist who knew how to engrave, a writer of prose and verse, an antiquarian, a man of science with an eager interest in natural history, an architect, and an inventor. He knew everyone and was welcome everywhere." It was this man who supplied £600 to provide capital when the original investment of £200, collected from the Worcester factory, had been expended. When the experiment was moved to Swansea, largely as a result of his influence, he, without protest took his losses, and as a result, was himself thrown into bankruptcy. Again on the failure of the venture at Swansea, it was Young and others who subscribed a further £1,100 and later he induced 10 gentlemen of the County to advance a like sum. It was also Young who was left "holding the bag" when Billingsley and Walker secretly departed for Coalport, when the second period of manufacture at Nantgarw failed. In spite of all this, it will be seen from a letter of record that he held no resentment against them, and his only regret was that "so fine a discovery was to die for lack of capital." His letter concluded as follows: "So whatever loss individuals have sustained, the public is benefited and the general state of the manufacture of porcelain in this Kingdom had been advanced."

Young attempted to have the Board of Trade finance the manufacture of Nantgarw porcelain. This it politely refused to do; but Sir Joseph Banks, a member, did request L. W. Dillwyn, whose father in 1802 had purchased the well-established Cambrian Pottery at Swansea, to go to Nantgarw and investigate the merits of the new porcelain being made by Billingsley. He was much impressed with the beauty of the porcelain, but found that about 75 per cent. of each firing was lost in the kiln. He agreed, however, to have the production transferred to Swansea where, with new and better kilns and the experience of the Cambrian works, he hoped to strengthen the porcelain so that the excessive loss in firing could be reduced to a point that the manufacture would be a commercial success.

On October 8th, 1814, Billingsley and Walker reached Swansea where Walker stayed until September 1817, Billingsley probably not so long, then they returned to Nantgarw. We shall here relate briefly what occurred during the approximately three years at Swansea, and in so doing, we will draw upon the information set forth in great detail in the authoritative books, *The Pottery and Porcelain of Swansea and Nantgarw* by the late E. Morton Nance, and *Nantgarw Porcelain* by W. D. John. We will also refer to the most authentic record extant, now in the Victoria and Albert Msueum entitled "Notes of Recipes for porcelain bodies and glazes, dated 1815-1817 contained in a note book in the handwriting of Lewis Weston Dillwyn, chief proprietor of the Cambrian Pottery, Swansea." This record will be found here as Appendix No. 2. Readers interested in further information on the subject should read the books referred to above. L. W. Dillwyn promised Billingsley to give his formula a fair trial, but just how long he experimented with it is not known. Certainly as early as the autumn of 1815, Walker had turned over to Dillwyn certain formulae recorded in the note book. At an earlier date, it is thought he was given instructions to strengthen the Nantgarw body.

We have no actual record as to the Billingsley formula, as it was possibly known only to Walker, and of course, Billingsley. We do have an analysis of two marked pieces of Nantgarw, by H. Eccles, as follows:

	Specimen 1	*Specimen* 2
Silica	46·	38·9
Alumina ..	17·	18·1
Phosphoric acid	13·9	17·1
Lime	19·7	22·5
Magnesia ..	None	None
Potash	2·69	2·56

From the above analyses, it will be noted that there was a small variation between the pieces, which was to be expected. This may account for the slight variation in the translucency and color of known pieces. The porcelain was a true "frit," as was the case with the French pâte tendre. It will also be noted that no soap rock was used.

We call attention to the first three formulae shown in the note book which Dillwyn says are *variations* of the Nantgarw body. While no date is given in the book, their position at the beginning probably means that they were the first real departures from the Billingsley formula and that any experiments made before them were attempts to strengthen the Nantgarw body.

The first of the three formulae comprise equal parts of sand and feldspar fritted with a small quantity of pearl ash and then 1 part of soap rock mixed with 14 parts of this frit. The second one has 11 parts of sand and 9 parts of feldspar fritted with 6 parts of pearl ash and 3 parts of borax. To 26 parts of this frit were added 12 parts of lead and 1 part of soap rock. The third used 3 parts of sand, 3 parts of feldspar and 2 parts of pearl ash fritted together, and to 10 parts of the frit 1 part of soap rock was added.

The note book shows that in March 1817 a formula was used as follows: 8 parts sand, 6 parts feldspar, 1 part pearl ash fritted to a very high heat, and then 1 part soap rock added. This was the "glassy" china. It will be noted that it is somewhat similar to the first three formulae shown in the note book. All of these early soap rock variants were more or less glassy in appearance, the translucency varying from almost a pure white, which is the type usually referred to as "glassy," to a mellow ivory and to a pale cloudy smoky brown; but they were all distinct from, and superior to the trident china. They rarely, if ever, bore the Swansea impressed mark and probably on account of their beauty, Billingsley frequently used them for his personal decorations. Such examples are usually marked Swansea in over-glaze script in red and other colors and also in gold.

The "fully developed trident" Swansea body perfected in March 1817, was likewise similar to the "glassy" except that it had twice as much soap rock. It comprised a mixture of 12 sand, 10 feldspar and 2 pearl ash as a frit. To 14 parts of this frit, 2 parts of soap rock were added.

The note book also gives the formula for the "duck egg" Swansea, which is exactly the same as the Spode "bone china" formula. It is 3 parts china clay, 3 parts feldspar and 3 parts bone ash. This was not fritted and had no soap rock. The reason for its green translucency is not entirely clear. Several variations are shown, but Dillwyn says: "It is a beautiful body and in all respects answers."

It is also significant that Samuel Walker was familiar with the hard-paste porcelain formula used at Meissen and the French pâte dure factories. The note book records that in 1817 Walker produced this body by using equal parts of china clay and china stone, but a very high heat was required which his saggars would not stand. He further discovered only a glaze made of feldspar could be used as "all others craze." The Walker formulae for three glazes are noted in detail in the note book. They each use a high percentage of lead in the mixture, and this soft glaze was found to be impractical when used with true, or hard-paste porcelain.

From the note book, it will be seen that Walker was quite busy during his three years at Swansea, and his accomplishments may be listed as follows: (1) Attempts to strengthen the Nantgarw body; (2) Creation of "duck egg" porcelain; (3) Creation of "glassy" porcelain; (4) Creation of "trident" porcelain.

With regard to (1) it will be seen that these experiments extended for more than a year, or from the time that production of the Nantgarw body was abandoned until the Autumn of 1816, when the "duck egg" was perfected. During this period Walker undoubtedly experimented with the use of soap rock as shown by the first three formulae in the note book, but in all probability he experimented also with the use of additional amounts of china clay. The Nantgarw formula called for not more than 20 per cent china clay, whereas Walker apparently knew the practical hard-paste porcelains used about 50 per cent. More will be said about this possibility in our comments regarding three pieces of china in the tea and coffee services shown as Illustrations 44 and 45 in color in this book.

(2) This porcelain is called "duck egg," because of the pale green translucency associated with it. John attributes the green color to the maximum percentage of china clay in relation to the other ingredients. This green color is found in contemporary Spode but of lesser strength, also in Dr. Wall Worcester, Meissen, and other types and is there attributed to the addition of a small amount of cobalt blue, which combines with the iron oxide found as an impurity in the materials and gives the porcelain a white color. This bone ash porcelain varies to some extent as the earlier experimental pieces show an overall green translucency, while the improved body has a cloudy white translucency tinged with green, especially in the thicker portions. A considerable quantity of this china was made and a goodly proportion sent to London where it appears to have been well received, though it fell short of the Nantgarw body. The marks used were Swansea impressed and in red transfer: also Swansea in script, but much was not marked.

With regard to (3) the "glassy" Swansea, not very much of this type was apparently made. It is usually marked with a script Swansea in gold, green, or puce, and infrequently in black. John says that this porcelain was almost a hard-paste and Nance at p. 278 says: "Even an experienced collector, unless familiar with all the distinct types of Swansea china, might easily suppose these glassy specimens to have been of some fine French porcelain, possibly even a French hard-paste porcelain; but this would be a serious mistake . . . The impression that the body might be of French origin is strengthened by the similarity of Swansea shapes to those of Sèvres and other French hard-paste porcelain manufacturers of that day. French china was then more fashionable in England than any other, and was therefore imitated by Swansea." Confirmation of this statement will be found in the cabaret tea sets in the Empire style as shown in Mr. John's latest book, *Swansea Porcelain*, 1959.

With regard to (4) "trident" porcelain, it will be remembered that it is somewhat similar in composition to the "glassy," the principal difference being that it has twice as much soap rock. This porcelain is somewhat off-white in appearance and frequently has a "pigskin" or "orange-peel" finish. It is brownish by transmitted light, particularly so where the potting is heavy. The mark, when used, was Swansea impressed accompanied by one or sometimes two tridents.

Referring to the Swansea porcelain developed by Walker, W. D. John has this to say: "Apart from an extremely small amount of the earliest Swansea porcelain, it is impossible to recognize any close resemblance between the characteristic varieties of Swansea porcelain and the unvarying soft-paste porcelain produced by William Billingsley and Samuel Walker at Nantgarw."

Colored plates 10 and 11, Illustrations 44 and 45, show a tea and coffee service which includes several controversial pieces. These services are probably London decorated, as the beautiful gold shell design is quite like that on the MacIntosh dessert service, considered London work. However, the teapot especially is in the best style of Billingsley, whose personal work is usually characterized by the great depth of the painting, leaves never prominent, flowers "full" but never "overblown," the highlight "wiped-off," the flower arrangement showing the stems together at the bottom, and a fondness for painting roses from the back side, usually pink ones but sometimes white.

These services have an interesting history, as they were brought to Canada around the middle of the nineteenth century by a Welsh family who settled near Toronto. About twenty years ago we purchased them from the granddaughter of the original owner, who needed the money to finance a musical education in New York City. In the family tradition, all of these pieces were Nantgarw porcelain, and the family had always considered them very rare and fine. Certain of them, however, have a somewhat different paste and glaze from the rest, and several of the shapes were not found at the excavations and therefore have been questioned. There are several known services where the London decorators used pieces of white porcelain other than Nantgarw to fill out a set.

In these services there are eight tea cups with inverted heart-shaped handles and eight saucers without foot-rims and unglazed, six "coffee-cans" with cylindrical bodies and typical curved shaped handles, and six saucers like those above, an elegantly designed teapot with the "blunted oval outline," and two large round plates 9 ins. in diameter, which are rare. All these pieces are very characteristic, and no one can question that they are Nantgarw. Two cups and saucers of like design will be found in the National Museum of Wales, at Cardiff. The round sugar bowl to the tea set has been questioned as to shape. The lid fits down slightly further into the bowl than the usual one shown by W. D. John as Item 39C. The sugar bowl shown here is certainly more pleasing to the eye and goes very well with the round teapots like the one from the Duke of Cambridge service shown by W. D. John as 18B. In fact, it also goes very well with the oval teapot in this tea service. That this sugar bowl is in fact Nantgarw paste and glaze will hardly be questioned by anyone who has examined it. Three sizes of jugs are included. Two of them are alike except as to size, and none of them were known until very recently when the well known authority, Mr. Kildare S. Meager of Swansea came into possession of an unquestioned Nantgarw jug of exactly the same shape as the two in this service. This illustrates the danger of saying categorically that Nantgarw never made a certain shape, solely because none was found in the excavations or has been previously known to collectors. While this shape is certainly rare, it should now, it would seem, be added to the shapes made at Nantgarw. This shape is not unlike a design made in pottery at Swansea and shown by both E. M. Nance and W. D. John; it is more pleasing to the eye than the round Nantgarw cream jug 39B in the John book or 25B shown there. The third jug shown here with the coffee service is likewise a shape not heretofore associated with Nantgarw. Nance shows a somewhat similar shape in Swansea pottery as F on Plate XLVII. The color of this piece is quite unlike the other two jugs, which are of undoubted Nantgarw paste and glaze. It is soft and creamy in appearance, but this may be the result of long use with hot liquids. We come now to three pieces (coffee pot, sugar bowl and waste bowl), which differ somewhat from the characteristic Nantgarw paste and glaze. While the glaze is a brilliant white and these pieces are quite translucent, they appear to be slightly harder than the characteristic Billingsley formula. The coffee pot and sugar bowl are in the typically French Empire style and therefore suggest when first seen, Paris porcelain. When, however, one of the three pieces was placed under an ultra-violet light, alongside a piece of such porcelain it became quite clear that whatever else it might be, it was certainly not Paris. A marked example of Nantgarw was also included in the test and it too was not at all like the Paris piece. The marked Nantgarw varied to some extent from our specimen but was without question from the same family. The flower decoration on each of these three pieces shows the same iridescence as that found on the remainder of the services, and as it is never found on Paris or other hard-paste porcelain, it further supports our contention that these pieces were made by Walker at Swansea. Likewise it is improbable that they are Coalport. Mr. John in his *Nantgarw Porcelain*, at pages 73 and 74 says that Coalport porcelain is quite unlike Nantgarw, and the records show that Coalport porcelain is feldspar porcelain, which was in effect a type of hard-paste and consequently would not show the iridescence found in these pieces.

A careful review of the above facts would seem to justify the tentative conclusion that these three pieces were made at Swansea by Walker during his early experiments there. Tending to further confirm this belief is the presence under the base of the waste bowl of an incised script captial letter W, which certainly might stand for Walker, and E. M. Nance points out that such numerals and letters were also found on pieces dug out at Nantgarw. When the two services are viewed in a cabinet together, it would take a close inspection to notice that they were not all alike.

When the trident porcelain proved unacceptable to the London decorators in the fall of 1817, Dillwyn decided to give up manufacturing, and in September 1817 Walker returned to Nantgarw, where it is thought Billingsley had already preceded him. With the assistance of Young, manufacture at Nantgarw was resumed and a large quantity of fine porcelain was produced during the next three years. Mortlock was apparently willing to buy all the porcelain that the factory could deliver in the undecorated condition.

The name Mortlock, always associated with Nantgarw and Swansea, refers to a firm of selling agents in London. The firm was founded in 1746 not to decorate but to sell porcelain and had its show rooms at Number 250 Oxford Street, London, and at the beginning of the nineteenth century was the leading London dealer in fine pottery and porcelain. It was extensively patronized by Royalty and by many members of noble families, and later in the nineteenth century, was described as "John Mortlock and Co., Oxford Street, London, Artists and Designers in Porcelain and Glass to Her Majesty the Queen." The firm went out of business in 1933.

Illustration 649 shows a finely decorated Nantgarw plate having the impressed Nantgarw C.W. mark, and in gold, superimposed over the Nantgarw mark, is found the name Mortlock. The plate, Illustration 646, is from a service in Mr. and Mrs. Williams' collection and has an incised "B" mark. The sole object that Billingsley had in his several ventures was to make porcelain in the white and to sell it to Mortlock who in turn would have it decorated and sell it to his customers as equal in quality to fine pâte tendre Sèvres, which was greatly sought after at the time, and brought very high prices. Illustration 645 shows the "Three Rose" design and Illustrations 647 and 648 other London decorated pieces. While Billingsley was a fine painter, his principal interest from the time he left Derby and probably for a few years before that, was to make porcelain rather than to decorate it. He is known to have painted several services, however, for his landlord in order to pay the rent, and there are a few pieces (cf. Illustration 650 from the Prince Regent service) said to be his personal work. A few fine examples of his personal work too, will be found in the Glynn Vivian Gallery in Swansea. He apparently painted more on Swansea than he did on Nantgarw and taught other painters while there. In fact, from the evidence now available it seems that Billingsley painted a considerable proportion of the early soaprock china and to a much less extent on the china clay bodies. Up to the publication of Mr. Nance's book in 1942 Billingsley was generally regarded, apart from a few landscapes, as a flower painter only, and his work as then recognized was chiefly to be found on the china-clay porcelain. His paintings on the early soaprock china, except a few examples, had not then been identified.

The confusion became further aggravated by the belief that the white glassy china was made from one of the March 1817 formulae, as at that time many authorities believed that Billingsley was no longer at Swansea. So much was this the case that E. M. Nance writes in his book, "Whatever painting Billingsley did at Swansea should be looked for on the duck's-egg body."

Mr. Kildare Meager was the first to recognize and draw attention to the paintings by Billingsley on the early soap rock porcelain, where he painted shells, figures, etc., previously attributed to the hand of Baxter. For further information see *Swansea and Nantgarw Potteries*, by Kildare S. Meager, M.B.E. More recently, several important pieces mostly on the soaprock body have appeared and they have been now quite generally accepted as Billingsley's work.

The principal outside enameling shops which were used by Mortlock in London were Messrs. Robins and Randall, Simms, Muss, Powell, Cartwright and others.

In spite of the great demand for this white porcelain, by 1820 the factory was again in bad financial condition, with the result that Billingsley and Walker slipped away to Coalport, where John Rose, who had lost this London business, probably thought this the easiest way to get rid of his competition. The previous opinion seems to be that no Nantgarw porcelain was made there. We feel, however, that during the period of 1820-1828 while Billingsley and Walker were at Coalport some porcelain having the general characteristics of the Billingsley or Walker formulae was made there. Billingsley, in any event, died in 1828 and Walker, at that time or even before, went to America and opened a small pottery in New York State.

Young was left with full responsibility for the dying firm and he recouped what he could by having a painter named Thomas Pardoe to decorate such pieces as were found in the store room and selling them locally. Most of the porcelain that remained was in some degree defective, which accounts for its not having been sent to Mortlock, and some was unglazed. Pardoe did a very skilful job in so painting these pieces as to cover up the imperfections. Two such plates are shown as Illustrations 644 and 652. We also show a rare cruciform deep dish as Illustration 651. It has a typical Pardoe landscape scene with birds and insects. This dish and all the plates have the impressed mark. Color plate 22, Illustrations 103, 103A, 104 and 104A, show seven Swansea specimens painted by different local artists from the collection of Sir Leslie and Lady Joseph of Porthcawl, South Wales. Illustration 552 is a Swansea dish from the collection of Dr. and Mrs. Quincy Wolf, and Illustration 555 is a Swansea Trident plate from the collection of Mr. and Mrs. Sidney Farnsworth, Sr.

Thus ends the fascinating story of an inventor who created the most beautiful porcelain ever produced and yet could not make the manufacture of it a commercial success.

DISTINGUISHING CHARACTERISTICS OF NANTGARW PORCELAIN

1. The glaze is brilliantly white yet mellow and tight for soft-paste.
2. It has about 35 per cent. bone ash.
3. It is highly refractive with brilliant luster and rarely crazes.
4. The glaze did not sink into the biscuit.
5. No difficulty was experienced in making the glaze or the decoration; all the trouble was with the biscuit.
6. The porcelain is very translucent with remarkable clearness and usually a mellow ivory tint, which when once seen is never forgotten. This color, however, does vary to some extent.
7. Very characteristic is the presence of small cracks in molded specimens.
8. Potters had difficulty getting two halves to match on molded specimens; hence the presence of seams.
9. Coffee sets usually had "coffee cans," small cylindrical mugs with ear shaped handles; plates were not supplied except for two used to serve bread, butter and cake. Strangely enough coffee pots were not known.
10. Nearly all of the good pieces were sent to Mortlock in the white to be decorated in London.
11. Saucers are usually 5⅜ ins. to 5½ ins. in diameter.
12. Rims were generally finished with a plain gold line, often not quite reaching the edge: dentil gold edging indicates London decoration.
13. A very early service has in place of the usual marks incised numerals. Fragments similarly marked have been dug out at the works.

14. When Nantgarw is marked it is almost always with an impressed NANTGARW C.W. Also small incised stars and rather flourishing incised numerals and incised script capital letters have been found.

15. Nantgarw closely resembles Sèvres pâte tendre, and many of the shapes were based on Sèvres and Paris molds.

16. Approximately 75 per cent. of all pieces made were plates, and these are the shapes which are usually marked.

17. Tea services are quite rare, less than a dozen being known, the finest being oval in design and the others round. The most usual cup handle is the inverted heart, and the saucer is flat-backed, unglazed, and without foot-rim. The presence of annular grooves under the bottom is characteristic.

DISTINGUISHING CHARACTERISTICS OF SWANSEA PORCELAIN

1. "Duck egg" Swansea has green translucency, is more translucent than other types of Swansea, but not so translucent as Nantgarw; the surface somewhat rough, usually marked Swansea in red or impressed, often London decorated, but sometimes painted by Billingsley and more frequently by other Swansea artists.

2. "Glassy" Swansea is rare, surface smoother than "duck egg" or "trident," translucency better than "trident," although somewhat similar, not as good as "duck egg": almost hard-paste porcelain and usually marked with a script Swansea in gold, green or puce, infrequently in black.

3. "Trident" Swansea usually a poor white and by transmitted light, particularly when heavily potted, brownish in color, having frequently a pocked or orange peel surface; mark, when used is Swansea, impressed with one and sometimes two tridents.

CHAPTER 7

AMERICAN PORCELAIN

The authors are aware that nothing was produced in America that would add a great deal to the antique ceramic art. Arthur W. Clement, in his book *Our Pioneer Potters*, already referred to in connection with the Bow factory, has covered fully the work of Andrew Duche who did in all probability produce around 1744 at least a few experimental pieces of porcelain. Certain advertisements in a Boston paper of 1769 show that at least an effort was being made at the time to make porcelain in America, but it is equally certain that nothing concrete resulted from it. In 1769 in Philadelphia, Gousse Bonnin and George Anthony Morris, the former probably from the Bow factory, did make some porcelain, as is shown by a soft-paste bowl belonging to the Franklin Institute, which was a part of a dessert service and is now in the Philadelphia Museum of Art.

Nevertheless, the only factory that we can say with certainty made any considerable quantity of porcelain in America during the antique period was the Tucker factory in Philadelphia. It was started in 1825 and closed in 1838. From 1816 to 1822, Benjamin Tucker, a Philadephia Quaker, had a china shop in Market Street. His son, William Ellis Tucker, experimented with porcelain in the back of his father's premises. Having satisfied himself that he could make porclain, he enlisted the help of his brother Thomas in 1825, admitted Thomas Hulme to partnership in 1828, and in 1832 made Judge Joseph Hemphill a member of the firm.

The porcelain was hard-paste, quite similar to what is known as "Paris." The styles were Empire, and in many cases copied the Paris made pieces. The clay, however, which came from the United States, is of great help to collectors in distinguishing the Tucker from the Paris Porcelain. The French porcelain of the early nineteenth century was made from kaolin clay which was very free from the impurities which had plagued so many manufacturers in the past. The Paris porcelain, when viewed by transmitted light, had no color, whereas the Tucker porcelain showed a green color because it had become necessary to add a small quantity of cobalt blue to the mixture, as had been done with Worcester porcelain of the Wall period. Therefore, the best test known to collectors today, in an effort to say whether a piece of porcelain is Tucker or Paris, is to hold it to the light, preferably sunlight, and if the translucency is clear and white it is Paris, and if it is green it is in all probability Tucker. Another test is the gold decoration. The French gold is usually uniformly applied, whereas the Tucker is in nearly every case unevenly applied. The Tucker handles to jugs and the like are generally inadequate, but on the other hand this is likewise true of much of the Empire style pieces. The Philadelphia Museum has a large collection of the Tucker wares including a dinner service with the Tucker initials on some of the pieces, and a history showing that it was made for the Tucker family and was always in the family. This and other marked pieces are of great help in distinguishing Tucker from Paris. Also in the Museum will be seen the original sketches used at the factory. Some collectors think that these sketches fall far short of showing all of the designs made there. Illustrations 655 and 656 show two typical jugs of undoubted Tucker manufacture in the Metropolitan Museum of Art in New York. The colors used at this factory differ to some extent from the colors found on similar Paris pieces. Of especial note is the color of the pink in the roses and elsewhere.

We find in this country what we noted in connection with certain things made in unimportant Continental factories, that is, a tendency for collectors in America to value the Tucker porcelain far above its due worth from an artistic standard. It is regarded as "Americana," and unquestioned pieces bring high prices.

MEISSEN 1 and 2 (1722); 3, 4, 5, and 6 (1723); 7 and 8 (1724); 9 and modifications (1725-1763); 10 (1763-1774); 11 (1774-1800). 12 Vienna. 13 and 14 Höchst. 15 Fürstenberg. 16 Wegley. 17 Gotzkowsky. 18 Berlin. 19-20-21 Frankenthal. 22 and 23 Nymphenburg. 24 and 25 Ludwigsburg. 26 Copenhagen. 27 Marieberg. 28 Zürich. 29 Nyon. 30 Hague. 31 Mol. 32 Vezzi Venice. 33 Cozzi Venice. 34 and 35 Nove. 36, 37 and 38 Ginori. 39, 40, 41 and 42. Capo-di-monte and early Buen Retiro. 43 Buen Retiro. 44 and 45 late hard-paste Buen Retiro. 46 and 47 Naples.

48 possibly Rouen, usually unmarked. 49 17th cent. St. Cloud. 50 18th cent. St. Cloud. 51 Chantilly, red early, blue late. 52 Mennecy. 53 Vincennes rarely before 1753. 54 Vincennes or Sèvres any period. 55 and 56 Vincennes. 57 and 58 Sèvres. 59 Tournay. 60 and 61 Chelsea Triangle Period. 62 and 63 Raised Anchor. 64 Red Anchor. 65 Gold Anchor. 66 Bow. 67 to 72 Worcester. 73 Longton Hall. 74 to 76 Chelsea-Derby. 77 Crown Derby. 78 Plymouth. 79 to 81 Bristol. 82 Nantgarw. 83 and 84 Swansea.

APPENDIX I

EARLY BOW DATINGS

Some years ago we purchased a pair of interesting Bow porcelain plates. They were octagonal in shape and without foot-rims, creamy-white in color and ornamented with raised prunus flowers. The plates were badly warped and had elongated spurs under the bases. By transmitted light they showed large moons. The prunus flowers had six petals each in lieu of the usual five. (Similarly the sauce boat belonging to Mr. Aubrey Toppin, included in the recent British Museum Exhibition had six petalled prunus modelling, and was there dated c. 1748-50). The arrangement of the prunus decoration is typical of Bow, and as far as we know, no other English factory produced plates without foot-rims. One of these octagonal plates is illustrated here as No. 539: two views of the other as No. 657.

We believed the plates to be Bow of the period 1744-48 and on this point we sought the opinion of the late Mr. Sigmund Katz, certainly one of the most reliable and accepted authorities on the subject. He said that the plates were definitely early Bow, and probably of the period 1744-48.

Mr. Hugh Tait, F.S.A., Assistant Keeper of British and Medieval Antiquities in the British Museum, has also been shown one of the plates and stated that without doubt it was early Bow, not later than 1750.

A chemical analysis to determine the presence or absence of phosphoric acid was now of the utmost interest and Mr. Frank Tilley, an outstanding dealer in ceramics, recommended Dr. Reginald F. Milton, B.SC., PH.D., F.R.I.C., M.I.Biol., as having great experience in testing porcelain bodies, and he was authorized to determine the phosphoric acid content of the one Bow plate.

Dr. Milton took the greatest care to ensure that the testing samples, taken from the most heavily potted portion of the plate, were not contaminated with the glaze, and his report showed about 4% phosphoric acid. This result certainly justified further investigation and we asked Dr. Milton to make a complete chemical analysis, the results of which are as follows (Dated 26th August 1960):

Certificate of Analysis.

ALL WHITE PLATE WITH RAISED PRUNUS ON EDGE.

SiO_2	Silica		58·0 %
Al_2O_3 Fe_2O_3	Alumina & Iron Oxide		8·2 %
PbO	Lead Oxide		4·0 %
MgO	Magnesia		1·0 %
K_2O	Potash		2·5 %
Na_2O	Soda		1·2 %
P_2O_5	Phosphate		4·8 %
CaO	Lime		20·3 %
			100·00%

It is recorded that in 1744 when the first Patent was taken out that George Arnold and Edward Heylyn purchased land on the Middlesex side of Bow Bridge, and that Thomas Frye, one of the inventors was furnished ample funds to proceed with a porcelain manufactory. In November 1748 a further new Patent was issued to Frye alone, based on the use of about 40% Bone Ash, an ingredient never before used to make porcelain. About the same time a new factory was set up on the Essex side of the Bow Bridge and produced porcelain on a commercial basis of the type called for in the new patent. It traded under the name of "Alderman Arnold & Co." and made salts, figures, etc. in addition to useful wares.

For many years past collectors have asked the question "What did Frye produce during the four years between the first and second patents?"

The specimens and analysis referred to above seem to provide the answer—that he made a creamy porcelain having a much smaller percentage of bone ash than the 1748 patent recorded and that it was only in table ware.

Strong confirmation of this answer will be found in Samuel Richardson's fourth edition of Daniel Defoe's "Tour of Great Britain," made apparently in 1748, where he says "the first village we come to is Bow: where a large Manufactory of Porcelain is lately set up. They have already made large Quantities of Tea-cups, Saucers etc. which by some skilful persons are said to be little inferior to those which are brought from China." It will be noted that only table ware is mentioned.

Other factories such as Nantgarw and Swansea produced a large quantity of porcelain in a comparable time and with much less financial support: it is unreasonable to believe that Frye did nothing at Bow for four years.

Frye was the first to discover the benefits to be derived by the use of bone ash. It is unrealistic to think that he reached the 1748 formula of 40% at once, and undoubtedly he first used smaller proportions. These two octagonal plates prove this and they were probably made around 1745-46. Other pieces of useful wares, we feel, will now come to light having a bone ash content between that determined in the plate and the very much larger percentage which was finally attained.

The reason that it has taken so long to answer the question certainly lies in the fact that during past years we have been looking for porcelain with *no* bone ash instead of examples with a much lower percentage than the patent of 1748 considered the best proportion.

We hope that we have made a small forward contribution and that as a result of our efforts many additional specimens of early Bow porcelain with varying amounts of bone ash will be identified.

APPENDIX II

Notes of Recipes for porcelain bodies and glazes dated 1815-1817, contained in a note-book in the handwriting of Lewis Weston Dillwyn, chief proprietor of the Cambrian Pottery, Swansea.

(Published by kind permission of the Director of the Victoria and Albert Museum)

V.	Sand.	GX.	Arsenic.
KO.	Flint.	AX.	Lead.
LO.	Lime or Ch.	MX.	Borax.
YX.	Bone.	DX.	Glass.
B.	St. Steven's Clay.	LX.	Smales.
E.	Norden Clay.	SR.	Soap Rock.
FO.	Composition, China Stone.	NO. 157.	Sand Frit.
FX.	P. Ash.	343.	Comp. do.
EX.	Nitre.	MX.	Borax.

Body.

12V
1FX. } —fine.

10 FO.
1 FX. } —course.

7 fine.
7 course.
1 SR.

G. Frit. 11 V. 9 FO. 6 FX. 3 MX.

26.
12 AX.
1 SR.

or

3 V. 3 FO. 2 FX. fritted and
one tenth of SR.—
The above is a Variation from the Nantgarw body.

Common Body.

12 FO.	Compn.	4 cwt.	70 lb.
8 YX.	Bones.	5 Bone.	
8 B.	China Clay.	$3\frac{1}{2}$.	
1 E.	Blue Clay.	35 lb.	

Bisket rect. used Autumn 1815.
20 parts V.
1 — FX. in Water.

fritted in a *very* high heat.
140 lbs. of the above Frit.
110 — FO.
25 — SR.

must be fired very regularly and gradually or it will blister.

It was afterwards found that the blistering proceeds from an accidental mixture of Alabaster to prevent the possibility of which great care must be taken.

[133]

140 lb. Frit.
110 lb. FO.
35 lb. SR.

makes the above sounder, but the articles still continue occasionally to fly with hot water.

1817.

It was discovered that the B. and FO. when fritted together into one Mass with FX. make an equally good looking Body which stands well.

45 FO.   Composition.
10 LO.   Lime.
28 B.   China Clay.

makes a body which comes very near the Chinese Egg Shell and will take a hard Glaze but must be fired very high and is then apt to get out of shape.

9 parts   V.
1 —   B.
and a little   LO.
fritted in a very high heat.
3 above Frit.
3 FO.
1/10 S.R.
Very good.

B. of which half has been fritted and ground, glazed with FO. is the Dresden China. A *very* great heat is necessary and difficult to get Saggars to stand it. Equal parts of B and FO. is the very best French China, and will take an FO. Glaze. No other than an FO. Glaze will do, as all others craze.

12 B.   China Clay.
12 YX.   Bone.
9 FO.   Stone.
3 LO.   Lime.

is a beautiful China which stands well, but is rather too soft for the hard Glaze.

Autumn 1816.

3 B.
3 FO.
3 YX.

Is a beautiful body in all respects answers.

8 B.   China Clay.
7 FO.   Do. Stone
8 YX.   Bone.

is found to be an improvement.

9 B.
9 YX.
7 FO.

makes the body harder, but large pieces are more apt to fly.
Glazes well with Glaze No. 2.

March 1817.

12 V.
10 FO.   } Fritted together.
2 FX.

14 of the above Frit.
2 SR.

makes a beautiful and good Body—if only 1 SR. is used it makes the body whiter—but the Clay is more difficult to work. Afterwards the following alteration was made, but without much improvement.

8V.   } Fritted in a high heat.
6 FO. } which had better exceed
1 FX. } the Bisket heat.

This Body Glazes well with Glaze No.1

December 1817.

24 YX.	Bone.
8 KO.	Flint.
16 B.	China Clay.
5 E.	Pool Clay.
1 LX.	Smalts.

Makes a beautiful white opake body and with Glaze No. 3 is the finest Earthenware I ever saw.

Glaze No. 1.

Frit

10 FO.	⎫ run in the Glaze kiln or earthen-
6 LO.	ware Bisket Kiln which is
2 B.	about the same heat. I prefer
12 V.	the latter on acct. of its longer
14¼ AX.	continuance which makes the
8 MX. calcined	Frit run more thoroughly
4 EX.	⎭ throughout

——
56 ⎣
——

56 of the above Frit.
30 FO.
6 LO.
2 B.
14 AX.
½ GX.

Glaze No. 2.

24 V.	Sand.	⎫
12 LO.	Lime.	run in
6 AX.	Lead.	Glaze heat
16 MX.	Calcined Borax.	or as No. 1.
2 FX.	Pearl Ash.	⎭

28 of the above Frit.
40 FO. Composition.
28 AX. Lead.
6 LO. Lime.
4 B. St. Steven's Clay.

Glaze No. 3.

24 V.		⎫
12 LO.		
6 AX.		Frit in Glaze heat as No. 1.
16 MX.	Calcined	
2 FX.		⎭

48 FO. Composition.
6 LO. Lime.
4 B. China Clay.
30 AX. Lead.
40 above Frit.
½ GX. Arsenic.

To be dipped thick.

APPENDIX III

Reprinted from "Mitteilungsblatt" No. 43

Der Keramikfreunde Der Schweiz (Translation by Ralph Wark, Hendersonville, N.C.)

Höroldt's "Propositions" for the Re-Organisation of the Meissen Factory, dated February 24, 1731.

The number of painters and apprentices employed at the Factory now number: 25 painters and 11 apprentices, as well as two men who do the grinding of colors. When in 1720 I first came to the Factory from Vienna, I found no painters employed at all. I had to do all the painting and decorating alone. Shortly after my arrival I took into service a young apprentice by the name of Heintze, who now has developed into one of my best painters. I was also given for my assistance a man coming from the Eggebrecht Fayence Factory in the old part of Dresden, and from time to time additional workers and apprentices, who, owing to their poverty, could not make a living at that Factory. I trained these people so that today they are doing good work at our Factory. It becomes clear that, as the work in the Factory expands, additional help will be necessary and more painters and apprentices will have to be employed.

From various sources complaints have been made about my having employed men, who from profession were cloth-makers, carpenters, etc., instead of my having taken persons who had been painting on pottery and fayence. It was shown, however, that such painters are very difficult to train for porcelain painting, also there arose other obstructional difficulties. It proved to be much more satisfactory to employ men, who had no knowledge of painting and to train them, even if I did not test them as to their ability in advance.

At first it was my intention to employ painters from the Dutch Delft Factory, or men from other cities, but it was found that these men, having bad living habits, had bad influence on my men, their work was quite indifferent and poor, with the result, that I soon gave up this idea.

It will be best in the future for me to have a free hand in selecting men to be employed in accordance with the needs of the Factory. Also I must be left the authority to be able to correct the work of painters and apprentices, and to check on their behavior, because otherwise they will fall into ill repute and will not make good use of their time during working hours. There would be no proper relationship between production and wages.

If in future work is to be paid for by piecework instead of on the basis of a weekly wage, and his Majesty's interests are to be maintained, working hours should continue as at present, i.e. from Easter until Fall beginning as early as a workman wants to start, but not later than 6 a.m., and for the winter months starting as soon as it becomes daylight.

During the summer, work should be carried on until 8 p.m., and during winter until 9 p.m. since working hours are shorter during the winter. All employees must keep these hours and must not absent themselves without cause or without my special permission, nor may they go away on travel.

Only such a work-schedule can be of profit to his Majesty's treasury when painters and apprentices, who up to now have worked on a weekly wage basis, are now to be paid for their work by the piece. In order to maintain proper relationship in connection with their work, and in order to take care of possible future changes and additions of new lines of merchandise, I have made the suggestions listed as No. 1 in my re-organisation plan. This takes care of the prices to be paid for the different types of decoration in accordance with how they have been paid for by me in the past, and how payments should be handled in future to the various painters and apprentices as listed below. It takes into consideration the abilities of the workmen.

It will be seen that future prices and costs differ considerably from those of the past. If his Royal Majesty's treasury is to continue to pay me on the yearly basis of 600 Taler and the Factory is to operate with a good profit, it will be found, that existing prices will not be possible to be maintained. In the past I have been paying the workmen a weekly wage. As the Factory's production increased, however, I was compelled to let the men work overtime and had to pay them for this work by the lot or by the piece. The trouble was, however, that the men started to neglect their regular day-work on which they were paid a fixed wage and would either draw out this work over days, or neglected their work entirely in preference to doing overtime work where they could earn more money.

During the last years some of the men have worked the entire night and up to early morning and have made night into day, thus in some instances doing no wage work at all during the day, preferring to rest up so that they could work all night at over-pay by the piece.

In order to take care of this situation, I recommend that within the new re-organisation plan it become forbidden for any man to work late into the night, specially after the regular working hours as mentioned in paragraph 3, since, if a man has his proper rest during the night, he will be more alert and capable during the day. If he wants to earn much, he must work hard during the day and remain on the job. Should he still engage in overtime work, this work will be poor and in order to check this, I in future will not authorize payment unless the work has been passed upon by me.

Although some of the apprentices do as good a painting job as the regular painters, I would still have them paid but one half of the earnings of the regular painters. This would be to the best interest of his Majesty's treasury. By this method we will keep the apprentices under control as well as in obedience under the realisation that they are under strict supervision during their full six years of apprenticeship. At the end of this period when they pass their test, they will receive, as has been customary, a Sword as well as their freedom to become a painter.

It may be said that present regulations are in the best interest to his Majesty and it will be generally conceded, that all types of decorations listed under sub. til. 1 complying with present public taste, would not have been accomplished if not passed upon and approved of by me according to my best conscience and ability and also considering what the workmen have earned.

It is my intention in future, that inspections shall continue to be carried out by me and that I will prepare the gold color and all other colors, and that, as far as time permits, I will personally execute special orders for fine table-wares. I should be paid for such work and I will leave it up to the Management to consider the proper reimbursement I should be paid for such work.

It will not be possible to discontinue wage payments by the week in preference to payment by the piece for all workmen, because now and again special work comes along, which if paid by the piece, could not properly be calculated, and later on difficulties would result.

In order to take care of such cases I suggest that for the following employees only, the weekly wage be maintained. This wage is to be as follows:

1. Koch, who applies the gold and who is very good at this work must do many small applications on many pieces. When not doing gold work, he paints flowers or Services with "grodesco," or flowers on knife handles. Since he does his work very well, he has been earning a weekly 2 Taler 8 Gr. He now should receive 2 Taler 16 Gr. since he must discontinue his after-hours work.

2. Leutner, who, after the gold has been applied and fired does the burnishing and thus cannot be paid by the piece, single items having to be worked over at many spots. He should be paid for this work a weekly 1 Taler 8 Gr.

3. Petzold, who paints fine panel scrolls on Services, and who's time is fully occupied by this work, but who also does some flower painting, should continue to be paid his present weekly 2 Taler.

4. Stein, who paints flowers on Services, because those who paint fine figures and landscapes in gilt panels have nothing to do with flower painting, and who also has to paint small flowers on handles, or small Tea-Pots as well as lids, and because sometimes gets quantities of these items that could not be calculated on a piece time pay, should continue on a wage basis. He now receives 1 Taler but because he will lose his overtime pay should now get a weekly 2 Taler.

5. Lehre, who paints the brown edges around pieces decorated in the Japanese style has a full-time job. Sometimes I have had to give him an additional helper. No one likes this type of work and much of the work becomes defective in handling and must be re-done. This man who has been getting 1 Taler should receive now 1 Taler 8 Gr. and an agreement should be made with him that, if it becomes necessary for him to finish a job on overtime, he shall receive 2 Gr. for each hour.

6. Zimmermann, who is a blue painter and who must from time to time make models for pieces to be decorated later with gold, and who has a full-time job in decorating Tankards, Center-Pieces, Butter Dishes, Bowls and Platters is a painter of some skill. He has up to now received 2 Taler 4 Gr. Since he will lose his overtime pay, from which he has been earning well, he should now receive 2 Taler 16 Gr.

7. Zoellner, a color-grinder and

8. Burkhardt, likewise a grinder, who have been working for me several years so that I always have a supply of the necessary colors on hand, and because the work is too much for one man to handle alone, and because their work has steadily been increasing, have each been getting 18 Gr. but should now receive 21 Gr. to 1 Taler. They should be told, however that in future during the winter months, they must help in firing the stove in the Painters Room, something the apprentices have been doing up to now. They should also carry the painted pieces in blue to the Glazing Room and all otherwise decorated pieces to the Firing Room and return them. Also, they should bring from the Store Room the porcelains to be decorated and return them for storage when finished. Since these two grinders are fully occupied, another assistant will become necessary very soon.

9. Wittich, a firer and

10. Muller, also a firer have up to now been receiving Wittich: 6 Taler and Müller 5 Taler. Since their work is heavy, standing all day in front of the kilns, I should consider that Wittich get 8 Taler, the other man 6 Taler per week. For this, these two men must not only continue in their present occupation, but they must also stand by and assist the Foreman Stoeltzel in whatever he may need them for. It would also be advisable that these two men take the Oath of Loyalty to the extent that they carry

out their work of firing with greatest care and also that they watch their associations, specially when in company with other men in Beer-Halls and the like, and that they do not talk about their work to any one.

11. Loewenfinck and

12. Eschenbach, two beginners and apprentices in painting who at present, as the other apprentices do not receive full pay, but only one half of what regular painters get, should receive a weekly 16 Gr. since they must still work in blue and since they must be taken care of and must not starve, and must be properly supervised.

13. Keil, who by profession is a Huntsman, is a sensible goodhearted fellow, and because he is also my Brother-in-Law I have employed him for two years and have given him valuable instruction. He puts on the colored glazes, burnishes the gold on porcelains in the Japanese manner and is fully occupied. He is also supervisor over all painters and has proven very satisfactory after his predecessor Dietzen, to be followed by Schindler, had caused such great disturbances among the painters and apprentices. As soon as these men turned their backs the painters worked according to their own likes.

This man Keil has received from me a weekly 2 Taler 12 Gr. because of his shown ability. In future he should receive more, because during my absence he must remain continuously in the Painters Room and supervise the painters and apprentices and also I intend to pass on to him additional information relating to painting and the preparation of colors.

Besides these 13 persons, all other painters and apprentices should in future be paid piece-work and according to the work they turn out. From month to month, if I find it necessary, the staff should be increased. Also in the case of the painter Dietzen now discharged, should he be re-employed, he should be placed on a piece-work schedule just like all other workmen, even though behind my back he talks, and not only he, but also his spouse, claiming he knows the secrets of the Factory, the preparing of the colors, but not admitting, that all he knows, he learned from me. He should be made to state in writing that in future he will not foster intrigues within the Painters Room. He must also not continue to hide in any dark corner and smear a lot of paint on white porcelain he has somehow managed to get a hold of. This sets a bad example to the other painters and harms the Factory.

For these Services and any future additional work, I should receive the yearly salary of 600 Taler. For this I will take care of all of the work in connection with the Painters Room, prepare the colors and the gold, and now and again do some personal painting and correcting. I am also to receive from the Royal Treasury the necessary gold and Dukaten coins against my personal voucher, as well as the necessary funds, also against receipt, for the purchase of color materials unspecified and to forestall any future possible complaints or doubts, I am willing to take an Oath, that I will only use this gold and the Dukaten coins handed over to me for the sole purpose of decorating porcelains, and will not use any of the funds advanced to me for other uses but the purchase of materials for the Factory.

Since one of the finest and most treasured colors to be applied on porcelain is the underglaze-blue, and which is still being used in our decorating, I find it necessary to make a report in this connection. At no time has this blue not tended to run or "bleed," even at the time of the former Supervisor David Koehler. Also did it always blur when fired a second time, making it impossible to obtain sharp outlinings, specially if the design calls for very fine strokes of the brush. Still, at Koehler's time it was better than what it is now, and prepared by the Supervisor Stoeltzel. I have spoken at several times to Stoeltzel, and once when he was in a specially great difficulty, shortly after Koehler's death, and Stoeltzel could not produce a good blue at all. I gave him some suggestions by which at last this blue could be properly produced, however, in a costly and difficult manner. Just before the former Supervisor Koehler's death, so to speak on his deathbed, and because Koehler always had confidence in me, he confided to me, and told me how to prepare this blue at a low cost. After my instructing Stoeltzel, the blue painting improved during about six months to a year, but from then on not a single firing has produced a good blue. All turns out a gray-blue, a blackish-blue and lead-spotted, which, as can be readily understood, is quite detrimental to the Factory's reputation and treasury. Not only can it not be sold even at auction, but dozens of sets costing a great deal of money cannot be assembled into Services for deliveries. At several times the Supervisor Stoeltzel has claimed that all of these faults are not of his making, but has tried to blame the painters, saying that they have applied the blue color unevenly and without sufficient care.

This all is not true, because I have had samples made from time to time by my painters and apprentices picking the most adept ones. Personally I have also painted pieces, in order to find out what is the trouble, but we have found that these carefully executed paintings, when being fired at the same time in the same kiln, and also having been painted by the same person, using the same paint, have come out of firing with some of them gray or black or covered with lead spots. I therefore believe that this blue color, if it is to be used successfully in decorating, must be improved upon by the Arcanists by solving the problems of the relationship between the porcelain paste and the glaze. This is proven by the fact, that the painting and the firing are not at fault, since pieces decorated by one and the same hand come out in different conditions, good and bad. In order to make a saving for the time being, and to prevent loss to the treasury, it would seem advisable not to produce too much of this type of decoration now. When larger sets are made, where all pieces must be uniformly alike in quality, there is too much waste at present.

I do wish the Supervisor Stoeltzel a long life, but should by chance he die unexpectedly, or should other difficulties in preparing paste and glaze arise, I have enough courage to believe, that I can assist ably and overcome many of the difficulties to the best satsifaction of his Majesty.

The other two Arcanists, Schubert and Hoppe, although good and reliable men, lack experience and the know-how in order to increase their personal knowledge, I, however, have experimented a great deal, and have accomplished much. I only call attention to the time of the late Koehler, when it was impossible to fire plates that did not warp, and how I invented the capsul and gave further instructions, so that most of the plates now hold their shape.

Because the present blue color is extracted from domestic cobalt ore from the Obergebirge mountains, and I also use this color in connection with mixing other colors, which have turned out unsatisfactory, it seems advisable that the Supervisor Stoeltzel be instructed to obtain a better ore, or that he be sent to the Obergebirge to the cobalt mine, on Royal decree, so that he may personally select a better quality.

With regard to paragraph 1 of the report, stating that at present there are 36 painters and apprentices employed, it will be likely that in the future, when more persons are given work, the present Painters Room is insufficient and there will be no place to put them. Up to now I have them all working in this one room, since they work on a weekly earning basis. Thus they are more likely to work competitively and more conscienciously, being under my or Keil's supervision. This situation will now change, as painters and apprentices will be working on piece-time, and better and more efficient work should be turned out, each man earning more.

It therefore would be to advantage that workmen be placed better so that on one side they are not so crowded with their porcelains and colors, and on the other side get improved lighting. At present more than half of the men must sit away from the three windows of the room and have poor working light.

It will also be better to separate the painters, because it is unavoidable that quarrels come up, and that some cannot get along with others. If those who work in blue are placed by themselves, and those who paint in gold and burnish it are placed by themselves, as well as the painters in colors, are separated, the organisation to my mind could not be better. Painters doing one type of work together with their apprentices should be kept together.

So, as to carry out this suggestion, I am willing to give up the two rooms that are just across from the present Painters Room and which have served up to now as my living quarters. I will move into a private house within the Palace grounds. Thus a number of the painters and their apprentices could be moved into the so-called Corner Room, which has very good lighting by three large windows, and in which I now store models and porcelains to be decorated. Some painters could be placed in my present living room, although it only has one window. Communication among all workers would be maintained. Personally I would separate within one of these rooms a section for my use, a small Cabinet, where I can do my own work, and where I can keep on hand the necessary colors. When I am not preparing the gold or the colors, I must spend my time as much as possible, with the painters and apprentices and also must do some painting myself.

This suggestion, specially the one concerning the Corner-Room should not incur much expense. The laying of a wooden floor to cover the dusty tile floor, replacing of the quite ancient fire-place by a stove as well as re-leading of the windows would provide a most suitable workroom with good lighting, which would also be to the benefit of the Factory, specially when local or outside visitors inspect the premises. Now everyone inspecting the one and only Painters Room is in constant fear of knocking down the stacks of porcelains which would cause damage and loss.

By storing the decorated and gilded porcelains in my Cabinet, installed in my old living room, a better control will be maintained, then when the boys, and also the girl, who keeps my premises cleaned, entered the Corner-Room, where they have been stored up to now. Thus, under my lock and key, I would have all pieces delivered to me under control and no losses should be feared, as has been the case in the past, when anybody could enter the Corner-Room.

Also several work-benches, chairs for painters and apprentices, which were made up at my expense, also a stove, in the living room, should be properly appraised, and I humbly request, that a commission decide on a proper reimbursement to me for these items, which should become the property of the Factory, and should be taken into inventory.

In order that the new work-rooms are not left alone during the night where colors and porcelains will be stored, the above mentioned Keil should be instructed to remain on the premises, together with one apprentice. On the other side of the living room, there, where my Cabinet will be located, on the wall having no window is a proper place for a night watchman.

As I have already requested in paragraph 2, I would like to have complete disposition over all painters and apprentices, so as to be able to maintain order and discipline, as well as to encourage interest in the affairs of the Factory. For this reason the Comptroller Nohr should be advised that under no pretext whatsoever he mix into the affairs under my supervision, and that he must not listen to all the complaints made by painters or apprentices, when they have been scolded. He would only make my work more difficult.

It would be a great consolation to me, if I were given power in regard to the employment of new personnel, so that I would not have to depend on decisions made by the Royal Commission, at least when it concerns painters and apprentices. I would submit written reports, which should be counter-signed by the Commission. This would have as a result that quick actions are possible, much to the Royal Majesty's interest. No decisions would be made without my knowledge as is now the case.

Not withstanding this, I would remain in close cooperation with the Comptroller Nohr in such matters concerning the Painters Rooms, and in connection with finance matters such as the supply of polishing-teeth, oil, firing-tins, wooden vessels, etc., which have to be replaced from time to time. For these I would give him my receipt. I would also be willing to provide him with worksheets of weekly and monthly earnings of the painters and apprentices and the time they have worked so that when he pays them, he has at hand a proper record.

Finally I humbly ask from His Dukal Excellency, the Cabinet Minister Count von Hoym, that I be paid for the many models of fine Japanese porcelains I have made, and for which I paid for colors and material. Also for the purchase of a quantity of painted and glazed originals, which should remain as models in the possession of the Factory. For these I beg the Commission to make an appraisal value, so that I may be reimbursed. Further I request that the Comptroler, or who may be responsible in this matter to pay me in addition to my salary of 600 Taler, the monthly cost of three cords of wood agreed upon, against which I will give my receipt. I then promise to further the best interests of His Royal Majesty's Porcelain Factory to my best ability, and to supervise all personell under my jurisdiction, so that His Royal Majesty may find pleasure in His enterprise and the Factory's Treasury obtain profitable revenue.

Commentary

This extensive and precise re-organisation plan of Höroldt's dated February 24th 1731, is of such interest, reflecting the past and the future, since the year of 1731, in the history of the Meissen Factory, was one of its most consequential.

If an attempt were made to analyze the very extensive record material of this year 1731, and a history calendar only covering this short period were made, one would obtain a cross-section of an economic organisation of the early 18th century, warm blooded and full of liveliness hardly to be conceived with greater clearness.

With the exception of Boettger, the entire classic ensemble would appear on the stage of this Opera of the year 1731. We find Höroldt, Kirchner, Kaendler, Loewenfinck, Stoeltzel, Hoppe, Schubert, Nohr, Otto, Chladni, Le Maire, Augustus the Strong, Count Hoym, v. Wichmannshausen, Pflugh, all make their appearance, and finally no less than the parasites Meerheim, Mehlhorn senior and Hunger. Particularly the first three months of this year bring events of dramatic Dynamics. Its culmination lies between the months of April and May when the King assumed personal control and management over the Factory. A second highlight is given by the entry of Kaendler in June. The tensions between him and his forerunner Kirchner are no less exciting, then those between him and Höroldt. Höroldt in February of 1731 was promoted to "Inspector" with a yearly salary of 600 Taler (at that only on a trial basis for one year duration!)

Since he was given additional duties in connection with this advancement, he was asked to make suggestions for the division of painting according to styles, as well as to introduce a new schedule of wage payments starting March 1st. He therefore incorporated into his "Propositions" descriptions concerning current grievances and recommendations for their elimination (mainly in wage policies). For this reason his "Propositions" were submitted.

The most important of his suggestions was the change-over from a fixed wage basis to that of payments on piece-work for workmen doing overtime work.

That Höroldt thus obtained a more rigid control over his staff is clearly visible. If the quality of the work was to be improved, is another matter of debate. Also the strict allotment of working hours is of interest. We see at least that in those days it was not easy to earn money, specially since the wage schedule suggested by Höroldt was not adopted, but lowered by nearly 50%. Of this low rate the apprentices, who in many instances did as good work as their teachers (this is specially pointed out in the report), finally only received one half of what the regular painter was paid.

Most revealing for Höroldt's mistrust against the rising younger talents is his discrimination against Loewenfinck and Eschenbach who are excluded from all other apprentices from being placed on a piece-work basis, but who must continue to work on a weekly miserly 16 Groschen "so that they are taken care of and kept from starving and remain under close and better control".

The youngest Arcanist, the "Herr Court Painter Höroldt" thus began an iron rule over the Factory. He had been intrusted now with the full "Arcanum". His influence spread considerably.

It is not surprising that these "Propositions" suggest improvements in the still very unsatisfactory production of the underglaze-blue, and thus reveal also his strained relationship with Stoeltzel. He also makes a "bagatel" of the somewhat mysterious circumstance under which he obtained the secret from Koehler of making the blue color. Finally, he stands up with sound reason for the separation of the blue painters from the other painters, whereby the latter are given more and better lighted working space.

The active events of the spring of 1731 finally are reflected by Höroldt's withdrawal from Nohr, the Comptroller, and his demand that the Factory Comptroller mind his own business. No doubt, Höroldt was already aware of the fact, that Nohr's days of freedom were numbered.

Otto Walcha, Archivar, Meissen

SELECTED BIBLIOGRAPHY

GENERAL COVERAGE

Burton, William. PORCELAIN. Its Nature, Art and Manufacture. London, 1906.
Hannover, E. POTTERY AND PORCELAIN. English translation by B. Rackham. Vol. III. London, 1925.
Honey, W. B. EUROPEAN CERAMIC ART. Vols. I and II. London, 1949-1952.
Litchfield, Frederick. POTTERY AND PORCELAIN. Revised by Frank Tilley. London, 1953.

ORIENTAL PORCELAIN

Bushell, S. W. ORIENTAL CERAMIC ART. New York, 1899.
Hobson, R. L. CHINESE POTTERY AND PORCELAIN. Vols. I and II. London, 1915.
Honey, William Bowyer. THE CERAMIC ART OF CHINA. London, 1944; New York, 1954.

GERMAN PORCELAIN

Honey, W. B. DRESDEN CHINA. New York, 1946.
Honey, W. B. GERMAN PORCELAIN. New York, 1948.
Ware, George W. GERMAN AND AUSTRIAN PORCELAIN. Frankfurt am Main, 1951.

SWISS PORCELAIN

Ducret, Siegfried. DIE ZÜRCHER PORZELLANMANUFAKTUR. Vols. I and II. Zürich, 1958-1960.

FRENCH PORCELAIN

Auscher, E. S. FRENCH PORCELAIN. English translation by William Burton. London, 1905.

ITALIAN PORCELAIN

Lane, Arthur. ITALIAN PORCELAIN. London, 1954.
Frothingham, Alice Wilson. CAPODIMONTE AND BUEN RETIRO PORCELAINS. New York, 1955.

VIENNESE PORCELAIN

Hayward, J. F. VIENNESE PORCELAIN OF THE DU PAQUIER PERIOD. London, 1952.

ENGLISH PORCELAIN

Binns, W. Moore. THE FIRST CENTURY OF ENGLISH PORCELAIN. London, 1906.
Honey, W. B. OLD ENGLISH PORCELAIN. New York, 1946.
Hobson, R. L. WORCESTER PORCELAIN. London, 1910.
MacKenna, F. Severne. CHELSEA PORCELAIN. 3 vols. Leigh-on-Sea, England, 1948-1952.
Savage, George. EIGHTEENTH CENTURY ENGLISH PORCELAIN. London, 1952.
Gilhespy, F. Brayshaw. CROWN DERBY. Leigh-on-Sea, England, 1951.
Watney, Bernard. LONGTON HALL PORCELAIN. London, 1957.
Marshall, H. R. COLOURED WORCESTER PORCELAIN. Newport, Mon., England, 1954.
Bryant, G. E. THE CHELSEA PORCELAIN TOYS. London, 1925.
Catalogue of Special Exhibit. BOW PORCELAIN. British Museum, 1959.
Nance, E. Morton. THE POTTERY AND PORCELAIN OF SWANSEA & NANTGARW. London, 1942.
John, W. D. NANTGARW PORCELAIN. Newport, Mon., England, 1948.
Meager, Kildare S. SWANSEA AND NANTGARW POTTERIES. Swansea, Wales, 1949.
John, W. D. SWANSEA PORCELAIN. Newport, Mon., England, 1958.

AMERICAN PORCELAIN

Clement, Arthur W. OUR PIONEER POTTERS. New York, 1947.

CERAMIC CIRCLE PUBLICATIONS

TRANSACTIONS OF THE ENGLISH PORCELAIN AND CERAMIC CIRCLES. Vol. I and Vols. I - IV. 1928-1958.
KERAMIK-FREUNDE DER SCHWEIZ: Bulletin des Amis Suisses de la Ceramique.

COLORED ILLUSTRATIONS
WITH DESCRIPTIONS

2.

2. MEISSEN. BEGGAR WOMAN PLAYING HURDY GURDY OR BALALAIKA.   Modeled by Kändler.
c. 1735. 4$\frac{9}{16}$" h., 3$\frac{1}{2}$" w.   (Possibly pre Kändler).

3. MEISSEN. BEGGAR MAN PLAYING HURDY GURDY OR BALALAIKA.   Modeled by Kändler. Blue
crossed swords mark on unglazed bottom. c. 1735. 5" h., 3$\frac{1}{2}$" w.   (Possibly pre Kändler).

4. MEISSEN. SCARAMOUCHE AND COLUMBINE. Modeled by Kändler. Crossed swords in underglaze
blue. c. 1744. 8$\frac{3}{4}$" h., 8$\frac{3}{4}$" w.

3

5. MEISSEN. COLUMBINE. From the Italian Comedy. Modeled by Peter Reinicke. c. 1743. $5\frac{1}{4}''$ h.

6. MEISSEN. SITTING HARLEQUIN PLAYING BAGPIPE. From the Italian Comedy. Modeled by Kändler. Blue crossed swords mark. c. 1735. $5\frac{3}{4}''$ h.

7. MEISSEN. THE CAPTAIN. From the Italian Comedy. Modeled by Reinicke. Blue crossed swords mark faintly visible on unglazed botton. c. 1743. $5\frac{1}{2}''$ h.

8. MEISSEN. INDISCREET HARLEQUIN. Modeled by Kändler. Early flat type base with unglazed bottom. Applied flowers unusually large. Colors very intense, and modeling throughout exceptionally sharp. Crossed swords mark on unglazed bottom. c. 1740. $6\frac{3}{4}''$ h.

9. MEISSEN. THE PIPE SMOKER, also known as DUTCH BOY STUFFING HIS PIPE. Modeled by Reinicke. Blue crossed swords mark faintly visible on unglazed bottom. c. 1743. $5\frac{1}{2}''$ h.

10. MEISSEN. PANTALOON. Modeled by Kändler. c. 1744. $5\frac{1}{4}''$ h.

11. MEISSEN. PRINT SALESMAN. Modeled by Kändler. c. 1740. $5\frac{1}{4}''$ h.

12. MEISSEN. AFRICA. This figure very rare, possibly from a series of the continents. Blue crossed swords mark. c. 1745. $4\frac{7}{8}''$ h.

13. MEISSEN. GRIMACING HARLEQUIN. Modeled by Kändler, one of his best. Twelve in this series, consisting of 11 men and one woman. 1738. $7\frac{1}{2}''$ h.

14. MEISSEN. DRUNKEN FARMER. Modeled by Kändler. Vestige of blue crossed swords mark on unglazed bottom. c. 1736. $6\frac{1}{2}''$ h.

15. MEISSEN. STANDING HURDY-GURDY PLAYER. Modeled by Kändler. c. 1740. $8''$ h.

16. ANSBACH. TURK. Modeled after French series by Ferriol. Mark scratched into bottom: 5 "Geritzt N 6." c. 1760. $5\frac{1}{4}''$ h.

17. HÖCHST. BOY PLAYING VIOLIN. Blue underglaze wheel with crown. c. 1755. $5\frac{1}{4}''$ h.

18. HÖCHST. COLUMBINE. From Italian Comedy. Iron-red wheel mark with five spokes, iron-red painter's signature "C." c. 1755. $2\frac{3}{4}''$ h.

19. HÖCHST. BOY PLAYING BAGPIPE. Blue underglaze wheel and crown. c. 1755. $4\frac{3}{4}''$ h.

20. CAPO-DI-MONTE. SUMMER. Impressed fleur-de-lis mark under base. Soft paste. c. 1745. $5\frac{3}{4}''$ h.

21. 22. 23. HÖCHST. SULTAN, SULTANA, AND SULTAN. Modeled by Johann Melchior. Same marks on all. Blue underglaze wheel with three balls and cross. HM impressed. c. 1770. Each $7\frac{1}{4}''$ h.

29. VINCENNES. STRAIGHT SIDED BOWL, finely painted with Boucher cupids in blue monochrome on plain white ground, the rim with gilt dentil decoration. Pâte tendre. Royal cypher on underside with capital "A" between entwined "L's" to denote year 1753. Vieillard's mark immediately above. One of this great artist's finest pieces. $3\frac{1}{4}''$ h.

30. VINCENNES. JAM POT, COVER AND STAND. Painted with Boucher cupids in blue monochrome, by Vieillard on canary yellow ground (jaune jonquille). Royal cypher mark on pot and stand with capital "A." Vieillard's mark above. 1753. Pâte tendre. Barrel $3\frac{1}{4}''$ h., $2\frac{1}{2}''$ d. Stand $6\frac{7}{8}''$ l., $5\frac{1}{4}''$ w.

31. VINCENNES. SUGAR BASIN. Rich turquoise blue ground. Decorated with flowers and brightly colored birds. Part of a service which Louis XV gave to Benjamin Harrison, early Governor of Virginia, whose son and great-grandson became presidents of the United States. Royal cypher with no date letter. c. 1752. Pâte tendre. $4''$ h., $9''$ l.

32. SÈVRES. CUP AND SAUCER IN ROSE POMPADOUR, rare color, difficult to make and in use only few years. Pâte tendre. c. 1757. Cup $2\frac{1}{4}''$ h.

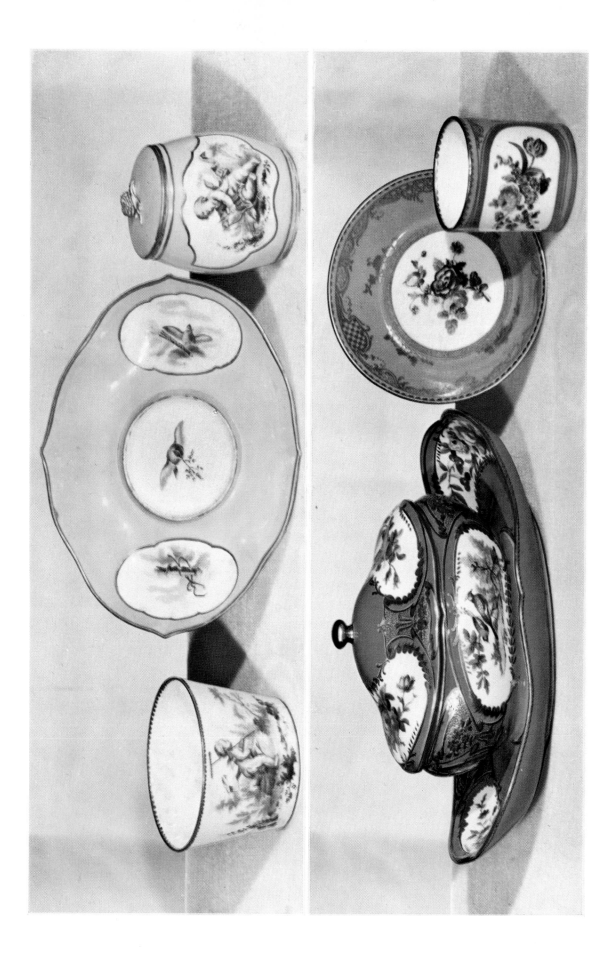

33. SÈVRES. CUP AND SAUCER. Royal blue ground with finest flower painting and gold ornament. Gilder's mark LG (LeGuay). Decorator's mark X (Micaud). Le Guay was the most renowned gilder of Sèvres. 1761. Pâte tendre. Cup $2\frac{3}{4}''$ h.

34. SÈVRES. LARGE CUP WITH TREMBLEUSE SAUCER. Interlaced handles. Panels painted in colors with exotic birds perched on branches on bleu-de-roi ground in oeil-de-perdrix pattern. Painted by Evans and Aloncle. 1763. Pâte tendre. Cup $3\frac{1}{2}''$ h.

35. SÈVRES. OVAL SHAPED DISH. Central panel in polychrome colors showing landscape. Bleu-de-roi ground. Border enriched with gilt laurel garland. Painted by Vieillard in 1765. Pâte tendre. $7''$ w., $9\frac{3}{4}''$ l.

36. SÈVRES. CUP AND SAUCER. Painted in colors with boy and girl catching birds and with reclining youth holding glass in landscape on bleu-de-roi oeil-de-perdrix pattern ground. Painted by Vieillard in 1761. Pâte tendre. Cup $2\frac{1}{2}''$ h.

37. SÈVRES. CUP AND SAUCER. Yellow ground with panels outlined in green. Figures in oeil-de-perdrix decoration. Mark: royal cypher without date letter. c. 1757. Pâte tendre. Cup $2\frac{7}{8}''$ h.

38. VINCENNES. BEAKER CUP. Boucher child in polychrome colors, with gold cartouche, on soft green ground. Date letter "D" for 1756, first year this color was used. Vieillard's mark. Pâte tendre. $3\frac{1}{2}''$ h.

39. VINCENNES. CUP AND SAUCER. Painted in colors with exotic birds holding branches within gilt foliage scroll cartouches, on a bleu-de-Vincennes ground. Mark: royal cypher and date letter "B" for 1754 and the decorator's mark of Mutel. Pâte tendre. Cup $2\frac{7}{8}''$ h.

40. MENNECY. SUGAR BASIN, COVER AND STAND. Decorated with rare colorful birds, edges outlined in characteristic claret color enamel. Pâte tendre. D.V. mark impressed. c. 1750. $9\frac{1}{2}''$ l., 6'' w., and 5'' h.

41. ST. CLOUD. CANE HANDLE. Decoration a combination of lambrequin design and chinoiserie. c. 1700.

42. MENNECY. MILK JUG AND COVER. Impressed D.V. mark. Painting in monochrome rose color. Pâte tendre. c. 1748. $5\frac{1}{2}''$ h.

43. ROUEN OR 17TH CENTURY ST. CLOUD. KNIFE AND FORK. Lambrequin design in underglaze blue. Pâte tendre. c. 1695.

44.   NANTGARW.   COFFEE SERVICE: coffee pot, sugar dish, six coffee cans with saucers, milk jug and large cake plate.   Coffee pot and sugar dish probably Walker's experimental porcelain made at Swansea.   Floral design, embellished with gold shells, probably London-decorated.   Iridescent halo on all pieces.   1815-1820.   Coffee pot 9″ h., sugar dish 7¼″ h., coffee cans 2½″ h., saucers 5⅜″ d., milk jug 5″ h., plate 9½″ d.

45.   NANTGARW. TEA SERVICE: teapot, sugar dish, large plate, hot water jug, milk jug, eight tea cups and saucers and waste bowl. (The waste bowl has incised W in base, probably to distinguish experimental porcelain made by Walker at Swansea). Floral design embellished with gold shells, probably London-decorated. Iridescent halo on all pieces. 1815-1820. Teapot $5\frac{7}{8}''$ h. to top of handle; sugar dish $4\frac{3}{4}''$ h., $7''$ w. over handles; plate $9\frac{1}{2}''$ d., hot water jug $4''$ h.; milk jug $4\frac{1}{8}''$ h.; cups $3''$ top handle; saucers $5\frac{3}{8}''$ d.; waste bowl $3''$ h., $6\frac{7}{8}''$ d.

46. CHELSEA. BEAKER CUP, inverted bell shape, no handle, molded in form of overlapping leaves. Painted in Japanese (Kakiemon) style with red tiger, flowering prunus tree, rocks, and bamboos, in red, yellow, blue, green and black. Triangle Period. 1745-1750. $2\frac{3}{4}''$ h.

47. CHELSEA. PLATTER. Molded form. Floral design with caterpillars and butterflies. 1750-52. $11\frac{1}{2}''$ l., $9''$ w.

48. CHELSEA. SMALL POMADE JAR WITH COVER, in claret color and embellished with unusually fine gold, probably decorated by itinerant French painter. Gold Anchor period. 1758-70. $3''$ h., $2''$ d.

49. CHELSEA. BASKET. Applied flowers and painted insects. Small red anchor on bottom. Also three round spurs. c. 1753. $3''$ h., $6\frac{3}{4}''$ l.

50. LONGTON HALL. VASE. One of a pair. Green translucency, large moons, typical Littler blue. c. 1753. $8''$ h.

51. BOW. OCTAGONAL BOWL. Partridge decoration in Kakiemon style. c. 1760 $3''$ h., $7\frac{1}{4}''$ w.

52. WORCESTER. CUP AND SAUCER. One of a pair. Egg shell porcelain. Imari type decoration. Small chinamen similar to work of "Fine Brush Painter" at Lund-Bristol factory. Early scale blue. A pair similar to these in Schreiber colletion. c. 1751. Cup $1\frac{3}{4}$" h., Saucer $4\frac{5}{8}$" d.

53. LUND-BRISTOL. MUG, inverted bell-shape with reeded loop handle. Chinoiserie decoration by "Fine Brush Painter." c. 1748. $4\frac{3}{4}$" h.

54. WORCESTER. CUP AND SAUCER. "Red Cow" design. c. 1760. Cup $1\frac{1}{2}$" h., saucer $4\frac{7}{8}$" d.

55. WORCESTER. MILK JUG, modeled with cabbage leaves and bearded mask spout, cylindrical neck, shaped panels painted in color with exotic birds among trees and with butterflies on a scale blue ground. Square seal mark. 1760-65. 7" h.

56. WORCESTER. HEXAGONAL VASE AND COVER. Imari style painting with phoenix bird among flowering plants issuing from rockwork and with sheaves of corn in similar panel, divided with blue panels reserved with flowers and foliage the shoulders with orange trellis ornament. Cover similarly decorated. Blue square mark. 1760-1765. $11\frac{1}{2}$" h.

57. WORCESTER. FLUTED PEAR-SHAPED COFFEE POT AND COVER. Interlaced handle and flower-spray finial. Vertical panels outside decorated with garlands of flowers on ruby ground, gilt with flowering foliage. Square seal mark. 1760-65. $9\frac{1}{2}$" h.

58. DU PAQUIER. TEA BOWL AND SAUCER, decorated in characteristic Japanese flowers, similar to frontispiece in J. F. Hayward's *Viennese Porcelain, Du Paquier Period*, and there described as in the manner of famille verte porcelain. c. 1725. No mark. Cup $1\frac{7}{8}''$ h., saucer $5\frac{1}{4}''$ d.

59. DU PAQUIER. TEA BOWL AND SAUCER. One of a pair. Chinoiserie decoration by J. G. Herold at Vienna in 1719. No mark. Cup $1\frac{5}{8}''$ h., saucer $5\frac{1}{4}''$ d.

60. DU PAQUIER. TEA BOWL AND SAUCER, beautifully decorated in early pastel colors, with characteristic chinoiserie decor by J. G. Herold at Vienna in 1719, expertized as such by the late Dr. E. W. Braun. No mark. Cup $1\frac{7}{8}''$ h., saucer $5\frac{1}{4}''$ d.

61. DU PAQUIER. TEA BOWL, decorated with putti in orange and puce colors. 1725-30. No mark. $1\frac{3}{4}''$ h.

62. DU PAQUIER. BEAKER CUP AND TREMBLEUSE SAUCER, decorated with Japanese flowers in monochrome red (Eisenrot) painted by J. G. Herold in 1719 at Vienna. No mark. Cup $3''$ h., saucer $5\frac{1}{4}''$ d.

63. DU PAQUIER. BEAKER CUP AND SAUCER, decorated with prunus flowers and birds similar to the lost one formerly in the Berlin Kunstgewerbe Museum, which was the only decorated piece having the date 1719 inscribed. No mark. Cup $3\frac{1}{4}''$ h., saucer $6''$ d.

64. DU PAQUIER. LEAF DISH. Decoration bird and flowers in early pastel colors, predominantly Eisenrot, probably decorated by J. G. Herold in 1719 in Vienna. No mark. $5''$ l.

67. MEISSEN. MASKED SPOUT TEA POT AND COVER. Colorful Dutch Harbor scenes showing clouds and birds, enclosed in cartouche of gold and picked out in puce only. Around top, lace work in gold. Oriental flowers on handle and spout. Crossed swords mark and 55 in gold. 1730-1735. $5\frac{1}{2}''$ h.

68. MEISSEN. LARGE BEAKER. On upper part a continuous decoration starting with ten men in colorful costumes, a small boat, larger boat, men of different nationalities and a castle in the distance. Bottom half divided into eight panels, every other panel painted in orange monochrome; the others in puce. Crossed swords mark and 7 in gold. 1730-1735. $5''$ h.

69. MEISSEN. BOUILLON, COVER AND STAND. Early type harbor scenes on all three, probably painted by C. F. Herold. Each scene enclosed in cartouche having copper luster and picked out in early red. Flowers in the oriental manner on underside of stand. Finial squirrel. Gold lettering on each piece. Crossed swords mark on cup and stand. c. 1725. $4''$ h., stand $7''$ d.

70. MEISSEN. TEAPOT WITH MASKED HEAD ON SPOUT. Decorations of polychrome chinoiseries belived to have been painted by J. G. Herold, each scene in cartouche with fine old copper luster Indian blumen in between. KPM mark used in 1723-1724; also crossed swords over glaze; gold number 20. $5\frac{3}{4}''$ h.

71. MEISSEN. COFFEE POT. Polychrome chinoiserie design. Cartouche in red only and including intense Böttger copper luster. No mark; number 14 in gold only. Probably painted by J. G. Herold in 1723. $8''$ h.

72. MEISSEN. OVAL SUGAR BOX AND COVER. Chinoiserie decoration showing the Emperor and Empress in the garden having tea. Colors: red, green, purple and brown, touched with honey gold Crossed swords mark; also 20 in gold. c. 1725. $3\frac{3}{4}''$ h., $4\frac{1}{2}''$ l.

73. MEISSEN. COFFEE POT in underglaze blue with early S shaped handle. No line between the fond color and the Indian blumen decoration. Lid of a later period. Unusual crossed swords mark used only in 1724. $7\frac{3}{4}''$ h.

74. MEISSEN. TWO-HANDLE CHOCOLATE CUP in deep purple called "vin." Unusually fine landscape painting by Heintze. Cloud effects pink and blue. Crossed swords mark widely spaced with curved guards. Also two concentric underglaze blue circles under the bottom. c. 1724. $2\frac{3}{4}''$ h.

75. MEISSEN. POWDER BLUE CREAMER in what Honey calls warm lilac blue. Early Watteau landscape on one side. On other side harbor scene. Wide lacy gold design around the paintings. Gold pineapple finial. Crossed swords mark. c. 1730. $4\frac{1}{2}''$ h.

76. MEISSEN. SMALL COFFEE POT in light puce fond color (pink purple). No outline between the fond color and the Indian blumen in the cartouche. S handle. Crossed swords mark. c. 1727. $6''$ h.

78. MEISSEN. PUNCH BOWL AND COVER in yellow fond. Decoration of fable animals. Pineapple knop. The porcelain by transmitted light very green and full of moons. The decorations attributed to Loewenfinck. Crossed swords mark. c. 1735. $11\frac{1}{2}''$ h.

79. MEISSEN. BEAKER CUP AND SAUCER, egg yolk yellow fond. Painting on saucer, monument with dolphin perched on top and Neptune with his trident atop the dolphin. Unusually fine specimen. Impressed crescent mark on cup. Crossed swords mark on both . c. 1725. $3''$ h.

80. MEISSEN. ONE OF PAIR OF AR VASES, beaker form, upper part beautiful yellow fond with Indian blumen in dark purple monochrome painted on fond. Watteau landscapes in lighter purple enclosed on either side within cartouches. Lower part white with oriental flowers. 1730-1735. $9\frac{5}{8}''$ h.

81. MEISSEN. TEA SERVICE: coffee pot and lid, tea pot (not original lid), sugar bowl and cover, four tea bowls and saucers. Decorated with Chinese bird in yellow, rock garden, Indian blumen in underglaze blue, yellow, green and the early red in Kakieman style. Roof of Chinese pagoda in early Böttger copper luster. Porcelain full of moons. Crossed swords of type used in 1724. Coffee pot $7\frac{1}{2}$" h., sugar box $3\frac{3}{4}$" h., tea pot $4\frac{1}{2}$" h., cups $1\frac{5}{8}$" h., saucers 5" d.

85. MEISSEN. PAIR OF CONDIMENT JUGS. Decor on each unusual oriental water scenes. Bird in center in early iron-red (Eisenrot). Other color used an underglaze Köhler blue (not used after 1725). Crossed swords mark. 1724. $7\frac{1}{2}$" h.

86. MEISSEN. OCTAGONAL DEEP DISH, unusually fine decoration of oriental flowers and a bird, attributed to Löwenfinck. On underside Indian flowers. Crossed swords; also this potter's mark ÷|÷ (same as found on similar Jersey service dish). c. 1735. 12" l., 11" w.

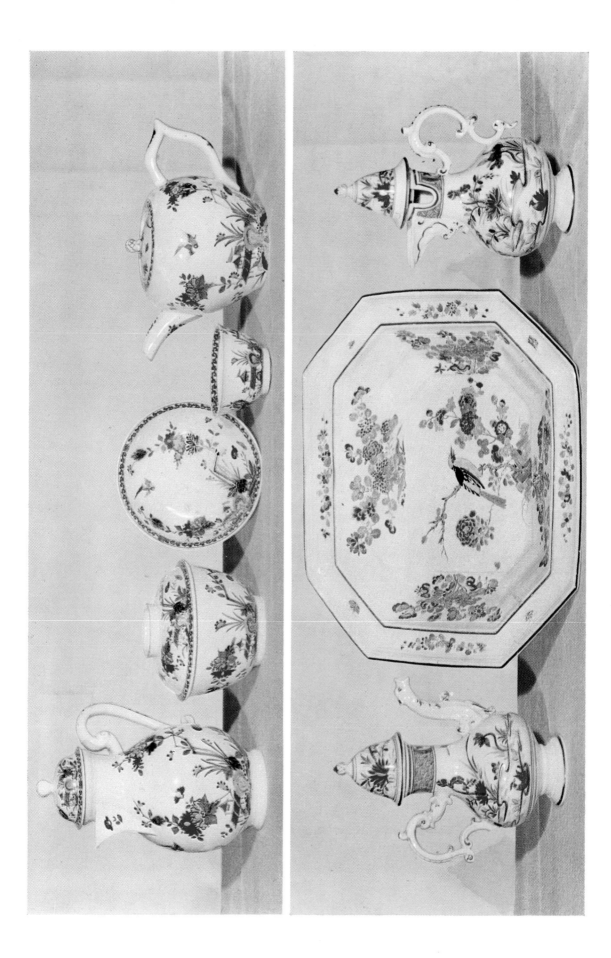

88. MEISSEN. TEAPOT. Large size figures after Comte Feriol known as "de la Levante," now called "Turks." Depth of painting exceptionally fine with blue clouds topped with yellow, all enclosed in eisenrot cartouche with the old copper luster. Painted by J. G. Herold. Lid not original. KPM mark used only in 1723 and 1724. 4″ h.

89. MEISSEN. TEA BOWL AND SAUCER. Decoration in polychrome chinoiserie. Tall figures. Mat underfoot a mottled green, which J. G. Herold used the year he was at Du Paquier and the first few years at Meissen. Oriental flowers, also early Böttger copper luster. On underside of saucer three concentric red circles. Gold Z mark on each piece. Date: before crossed swords mark. c. 1723. Saucer 5″ d., tea bowl $1\frac{3}{4}$″ h.

90. MEISSEN. TEAPOT. Earliest shape used by Böttger copied from the Chinese. Decorated with raised flowers and birds, partially covered with gold; figures in black and Pomeranian red monochrome by an unknown hausmaler. Potter's mark on the bottom; also the type crossed swords mark used in 1724. 5″ h.

91. MEISSEN. GENRE DECORATED WASTE BOWL. Painted by J. G. Herold with palette he brought with him from Du Paquier. Beautiful landscape enclosed in cartouche of red scroll work and the early Böttger copper luster. 1721-1722. 7″ d., $3\frac{1}{2}$″ h.

92. MEISSEN. TEA BOWL AND SAUCER. Design said to have been made for Augustus the Strong; shown in etching signed by Herold. Chinoiserie enclosed in cartouche having the early Böttger type luster and picked out in red only. c. 1722. Tea Bowl $1\frac{7}{8}$″ h., saucer 5″ d.

93. MEISSEN. TWO-HANDLED BOUILLON CUP, with earliest genre landscape decoration. Böttger shape. Painting extremely colorful and well done in "mother of pearl luster" paint, by the hand of J. G. Herold. 1721-1722. $3\frac{3}{8}$″ h., $4\frac{1}{2}$″ d., $6\frac{1}{4}$″ overall.

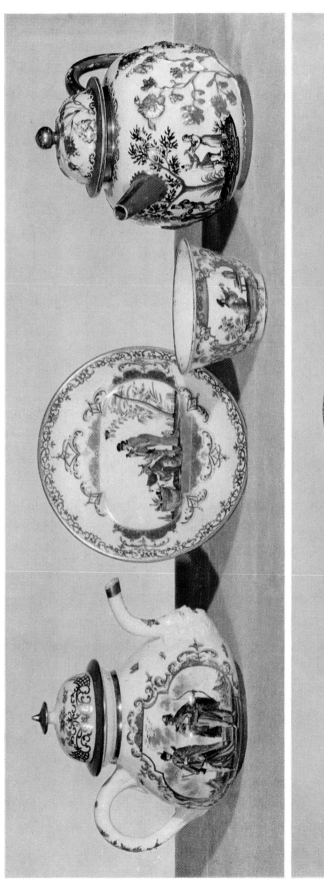

94. MEISSEN. TEAPOT AND LID, beautifully decorated in polychrome chinoiseries and bearing under the base the monogram of J. G. Herold, who probably personally decorated it. Mark similar to one found on a piece in the museum at Copenhagen and there described as signed by J. G. Herold. c. 1730. $3\frac{1}{2}''$ h.

95. MEISSEN. PAIR TEA BOWLS AND SAUCERS. Oriental scroll work $\frac{3}{4}''$ wide, extending around the saucers (same design inside cups). In center, polychrome chinoiseries beautifully painted. Background of flowers, trees and rocks in dark brown color, much of it early Böttger copper luster. On backs of saucers, early triple circles in red. On tea bowls chinamen in garden in brilliant yellow, blue, purple and gold. Early crossed swords mark. c. 1724. Saucers $4\frac{5}{8}''$ d., tea bowls $1\frac{5}{8}''$ h., $2\frac{13}{16}''$ d.

96. MEISSEN. OCTAGONAL SUGAR BOX AND COVER. Early Böttger shape. Polychrome decoration extending continuously around box. Cover decorated with miniature chinamen at tea. On box both KPM and crossed swords marks under the glaze. Cover crossed swords only, over the glaze. 1723 or 1724, only two years the KPM mark was used and then only on tea pots and sugar boxes. Gold mark 55 on each piece. $3''$ h., $4\frac{3}{8}''$ l.

97. MEISSEN. EXTRA LARGE CYLINDRICAL CHOCOLATE POT AND COVER. Paste and glaze of the early Herold period, green translucency with large moons. The design of fable animals in polychrome colors of the type brought from Vienna, plus the early type Böttger luster. No marks except some unusual potter's marks incised in the unglazed base. Also present is the "mottled" or "stippled" effect used by Gregor Herold at Vienna and also in his early years at Meissen. This piece unique, the personal work of Herold. c. 1722. $7\frac{7}{8}''$ h., $5''$ d.

98. MEISSEN. HEXAGONAL TEA CADDY. Concave vertical edges separating the six panels. Decoration polychrome chinoiseries in five of the panels representing Emperor, in sixth the Empress. Figures tall, undoubtedly by the hand of J. G. Herold. c. 1722. $4''$ h.

99. MEISSEN. SMALL TANKARD. Five Chinese figures, one very tall, grouped around drum type table. Mountains and lake in background. The inside cartouche of Köhler blue, and the entire design a modification by Herold of certain etchings turned over to him to copy. This painting by his hand. 1722-1723. The silver lid is not of the period. $5\frac{1}{2}''$ h., $3''$ d.

100. MEISSEN. TANKARD. Herold chinoiseries, large in size. Indian blumen, birds and insects. Diaper, Lambrequin style in Köhler blue top and bottom. Paste and glaze typical of period. Early copper luster, no mark. Painted by J. G. Herold. 1722-1723. $9''$ h.

101.   CAPO-DI-MONTE. ORPHEUS PLAYING TO THE ANIMALS, modeled by Guiseppe Gricci. Certainly among his best creations. Mark: blue fluer-de-lis. Only mark used during the first period. Soft-paste. c. 1743-1759. $13\frac{1}{2}''$ h.

21

102. MEISSEN. IMPORTANT COFFEE POT AND COVER in Böttger Red Stoneware. Color: the most desirable brown-red, ground to a mirror finish. Decoration incised on glass maker's wheel and extremely beautiful. Mint condition including silver-gilt hinge of the period. 1710-1715. 9″ h.

103. SWANSEA. TWO PLATES, of duck-egg porcelain: the left with scroll border and gold-green tracery decoration, the centre painted with wild flowers by William Pollard. Mark Swansea in red transfer, $8\frac{1}{4}''$ d. The right plate decorated with a wreath of garden flowers by David Evans. Mark *Swansea* in red script, $8\frac{3}{4}''$ d.

103A. SWANSEA. TWO CABINET CUPS AND SAUCERS: the left of soaprock porcelain, the cup on three paw feet, with a scroll handle terminating in a mask and the whole decorated with gilt tracery and briar roses by David Evans. Not marked. Cup $3\frac{3}{4}''$ h., saucer $5\frac{7}{8}''$ d. The right one, of duck-egg porcelain, painted with birds, flowers and butterflies on a stippled green ground by William Pollard. Not marked. Cup $3\frac{1}{4}''$ h., saucer $6\frac{1}{8}''$ d.

104. SWANSEA. Pot-pourri Vase with Cover in biscuit duck-egg porcelain with applied acanthus leaves and single beads. Decorated with garden flowers by Henry Morris. Not marked. $4\frac{7}{8}''$ h., $4\frac{1}{2}''$ d.

104A. SWANSEA. TWO PLATES of *glassy* porcelain: the left decorated with gilt scrolls, tracery and wreaths of roses in blue monochrome by William Billingsley. Mark *Swansea* in gold script. $9\frac{1}{4}''$ d. The right plate with a twig of oak leaves and acorns painted by William Billingsley. Mark *Swansea* in olive green script. $9\frac{1}{4}''$ d.

Sir Leslie and Lady Joseph Collection, Porthcawl, South Wales

MONOCHROME ILLUSTRATIONS DESCRIBED

146. MEISSEN. PAIR OF CUPS AND SAUCERS, Böttger style beaker shaped, decorated with raised prunus. Crossed swords mark. c. 1730. Saucer $5\frac{1}{4}$″ d., cups $2\frac{3}{4}$″ h.

147. MEISSEN. COFFEE POT, in style of Böttger decorated with applied acanthus leaves. Interesting as showing the continued use of the Böttger formulae as late as 1725. Crossed swords mark. 8″ h.

148. MEISSEN. TEA BOWL, with "cracked ice" glaze (crackle under the glaze). Exceedingly rare. Köhler under-glaze blue decoration. Pseudo-Chinese symbols. Formerly in the Royal Saxon collection. c. 1720. $1\frac{5}{8}$″ h., $2\frac{5}{8}$″ d.

39, 40 AN UNUSUAL COLLECTION of fine quality MEISSEN PAGODA FIGURES, of the period 1710-1725. Coll. Mr. Siegfried Kramarsky, New York, U.S.A.

149. Multi-colored. No mark. $3\frac{1}{2}$″ h.

150. Red stoneware. No mark. $3\frac{1}{4}$″ h.

151. White and gold. No mark. $3\frac{1}{2}$″ h.

152. White and gold. No mark. $3\frac{1}{2}$″ h.

153. White. No mark. $3\frac{1}{2}$″ h.

154. Multi-colored. Undergarment yellow and green stripes. No mark. $3\frac{3}{4}$″ h.

155. White. No mark. $3\frac{3}{4}$″ h.

156. White and gold. No mark. 2″ h.

157. Multi-colored. No mark. 3″ h.

158. Gold and black. No mark. 2″ h.

159. Multi-colored. Early crossed swords mark. Under-glaze blue. $3\frac{1}{2}$″ h.

160 and 161. White and gold. No mark. $2\frac{1}{2}$″ h., each.

162. Multi-colored. No mark. $3\frac{3}{4}$″ h.

41 163. MEISSEN. MUG of white Böttger porcelain with applied acanthus leaves and emblem of King Augustus the Strong of Poland. No other mark. c. 1715. Coll. Dr. Hans Syz, Westport, Connecticut.

164. MEISSEN. WHITE TURTLE SHAPED BOX, attributed to Georg Fritzsche. c. 1726. Crossed swords mark. $6\frac{1}{8}$″ l., $3\frac{1}{4}$″ h., $3\frac{7}{8}$″ w. Coll. Dr. A. J. Mourot, Alexandria.

42 165. MEISSEN. TEA BOWL AND SAUCER. Early Böttger period shape with gold chinoiserie decoration. Luster mark, YB on saucer; UI 203 on cup. 1709-1719. Tea bowl $1\frac{1}{2}$″ h., saucer $4\frac{5}{8}$″ d. Ex. von Born Coll.

166. MEISSEN. GLOBULAR-SHAPED TEAPOT. Domed lid with masked spout. Gold chinoiserie decoration. Luster mark c. 3. 1709-1719. 5″ h., $4\frac{1}{4}$″ d., $6\frac{1}{4}$″ w., including spout and handle. Ex. von Born Coll.

167. MEISSEN. TEA BOWL AND SAUCER. Applied strawberries, vines and leaves. Böttger porcelain, creamy in color with no moons. Crossed swords mark at right angles and having pronounced pommels and guards carefully drawn located at rim of cup. No mark on saucer. Tea bowl $1\frac{3}{4}$″ h., saucer $4\frac{13}{16}$″ d. c. 1722.

168. MEISSEN. TALL BEAKER CUP AND SAUCER. Gold chinoiseries. Charmingly fantastic design of silhouetted pseudo-Chinese scenes in plain soft-toned gilding with lightly tooled detail. Shape of cup like those Böttger made and presented to Augustus the Strong, 1710. Cross luster mark on cup. FW luster mark on saucer. Gold decorated at Meissen, according to some authorities. 1709-1719. Cup 3″ h., saucer $4\frac{3}{4}$″ d.

169. MEISSEN. BÖTTGER POLISH EAGLE TEAPOT. Eagle decorated in silver which has turned black through oxidation. Spout in shape of eagle's head. At top of handle, child's head in gold like rest of decorations. (It will be remembered that Augustus the Strong, in addition to being Elector of Saxony, was King of Poland, whose coat of arms included the eagle). Decoration believed to be factory work. 1710-1715. $5\frac{1}{4}$″ h., $6\frac{1}{2}$″ l. overall.

170. MEISSEN. FLUTED TEA BOWL AND SAUCER. Böttger porcelain. Gold chinoiseries on inside of tea bowl and saucer. S in luster on bottom of saucer. 1713-1719. Saucer $5\frac{1}{16}$″ d., tea bowl $1\frac{7}{8}$″ h.

43 171. MEISSEN. PAIR HEXAGONAL TEA CADDIES decorated in polychrome chinoiseries using the early palette of J. G. Herold. In each panel a chinaman in a different costume. Flat lids. c. 1723. 4″ h.

172. MEISSEN. OCTAGONAL SUGAR BOX AND COVER. Böttger shape. Herold's early palette. On one side of sugar box two Chinamen cooking in a large urn. On obverse side a Chinaman leaning over a fence and a Chinese woman playing a musical instrument. At each end of cover a miniature Chinaman very tall, also a dog, which is typical of the personal work of J. G. Herold. KPF mark. 1722. $2\frac{3}{4}$″ h., $4\frac{1}{4}$″ l., $3\frac{1}{4}$″ w.

173. MEISSEN. CANE HANDLE, molded in the shape of a woman's head and decorated with harbor scenes predominantly in puce color. c. 1740.

174. MEISSEN. HEXAGONAL TEA CADDY. Böttger shape. Each of six sides decorated as a panel showing a tall Chinaman, wide gold band separating them. Believed to be work of J. G. Herold. c. 1723. 4″ h.

175. MEISSEN. PIPE BOWL. Decorated with chinoiseries, flowers, urns, etc. c. 1760.

176. MEISSEN. OVAL SUGAR BOX. Lion or dog finial. Continuous river scene around box. Lid finely decorated with two harbor scenes and six small vignettes having miniature harbor scenes in puce monchrome. Gold mark 4. Early type crossed swords mark. 1725-1730. $3\frac{1}{2}$″ h., $4\frac{1}{2}$″ l.

177. MEISSEN. PAIR TEA BOWLS AND SAUCERS. Oriental scroll work $\frac{3}{4}$″ wide extending around saucers. Same design inside cups. In center polychrome chinoiseries beautifully painted. Background of flowers, trees, and rocks in dark brown which is early Böttger copper luster. Three red circles (early) on backs of saucers. On cups, Chinamen in garden. Colors: brilliant red, yellow, blue, purple and gold. c. 1724. Saucers $4\frac{1}{2}$″ d., cups $1\frac{5}{8}$″ h.

178. MEISSEN. OCTAGONAL SUGAR BOX with chinoiserie scenes. Mark on the lid under-glaze blue crossed swords and "54" in gold. On box crossed swords, "54" in gold, and letters KPP, until recently an unrecorded mark. c. 1724. $3\frac{1}{2}$″ h., $2\frac{1}{2}$″ w. Coll. Mrs. C. B. Stout, Memphis, Tennessee, U.S.A.

179. MEISSEN. CUP AND SAUCER, beaker type. Mottled under-glaze blue, the first fond color Meissen perfected. Decoration by Herold, a portrait of a single Oriental figure. Clouds in background light blue with pink sunset. Before the mark. c. 1722. Cup 3″ h., saucer 5″ d. Coll. Mrs. C. B. Stout, Memphis, Tenn. Similar one in Ralph Wark collection.

180. MEISSEN. ROOSTER TEAPOT. Crossed swords under handle. 1740-1745. 4″ h., 6″ l. Coll. Mrs. C. B. Stout, Memphis, Tenn.

44 181. MEISSEN. TEA BOWL AND SAUCER. Early shape. Decoration of polychrome chinoiserie. Flowers painted in the bottom of tea bowl. Three red concentric circles on under-rim of saucer. Gold X on each piece. c. 1723, before the crossed swords mark.

182. MEISSEN. CREAM BOWL AND COVER of squat circular form raised on three lions' paw feet and with scroll handle. Sides and cover painted with landscapes and various scenes, including a sportsman shooting duck by lake. Panels edged in gilt and red scrollwork and luster. Remainder enriched with Indianische blumen. No mark. Painted by J. G. Herold. 1721-1722. $4\frac{1}{2}$″ h.

183. MEISSEN. TEA BOWL AND SAUCER. Chinoiserie decoration in style of J. G. Herold, having unusual gold design around borders, which was copied later by hausmaler and used at Vienna on bases of figures. Crossed swords mark. c. 1725. $1\frac{3}{4}$″ h.

184. MEISSEN. SWAN SERVICE PLATE. Coat-of-arms of Count Brühl at angle of approximately

forty-five degrees when swans are in upright position. 1737-1741. 9″ d.
185. MEISSEN. CUP AND SAUCER FROM SWAN SERVICE. Coat-of-arms on cup only. Crossed swords on both. 1737-1741. Cup $1\frac{7}{8}''$ h., 3″ d. Saucer $5\frac{1}{8}''$ d.
186. MEISSEN. PLATE with coat-of-arms of Count of Munich, Marshal of Saxony. "Old Ozier" or basketweave border. c. 1732. $9\frac{1}{8}''$ d.
45 187. MEISSEN. TANKARD decorated by Löwenfinck. c. 1735. Coll. Miss Ilse Bischoff, New York, U.S.A.
188. MEISSEN. CONDIMENT POT decorated with chinoiserie figures and flowers by J. E. Stadler. c. 1725. Coll. Mr. R. H. Wark, Hendersonville, North Carolina, U.S.A.
189. MEISSEN. COVERED TALL BEAKER decorated in polychrome chinoiserie by J. G. Herold. No mark. c. 1724. Coll. Mr. R. H. Wark, Hendersonville, N.C.
190. MEISSEN. TANKARD. Decoration taken from etching by Engelbrecht. This scene found in Herold sketch book. Hence a documentary piece traceable to the hand of Herold. c. 1723. Coll. Mrs. C. B. Stout, Memphis, Tenn.
46 191. MEISSEN. HEXAGONAL TEA CADDY. Chinoiserie decoration. c. 1724. Coll. Mr. and Mrs. Herrick Norcross, Tyronza, Arkansas, U.S.A.
192. MEISSEN. BODKINS, decorated by von dem Busch. 1750-1775. Coll. Dr. A. J. Mourot, Alexandria, Va.
47 193. MEISSEN. KAKIEMON. DECORATED WASTE BOWL. Design known as "Chinesische Blumen." c. 1725. Crossed swords mark. $6\frac{1}{2}''$ d., $3\frac{1}{2}''$ h.
194. MEISSEN. SHELL-SHAPED TEA CADDY. Kakiemon Partridge decor, old intense hue of red. Also turquoise blue and a darker blue. c. 1730. $4\frac{1}{2}''$ h.
195. MEISSEN. KAKIEMON OCTAGONAL TEA BOWL AND ROUND SAUCER with slight decoration of flowering prunus tree with blue trunk and small blue bird in flight. Caduceus mark in blue and engraved Jöhanneum mark. c. 1723. Cup 2″ h., $3\frac{1}{8}''$ d.; Saucer $5\frac{13}{16}''$ d.
196. MEISSEN. MASKED SPOUT TEAPOT. Decoration Indianische blumen. Böttger shape and type porcelain. KPM mark and crossed swords. $4\frac{1}{4}''$ h. 1723-1724.
197. MEISSEN. PLATE from service known as the "Flying Fox." Decoration a fence fashioned of bamboo in iron-red with posts and stringers in blue. On fence a vine which has large red berries. Yellow bear perched on fence. Bright red fox (possibly a squirrel) high above in air. Crossed swords mark. c. 1730. 10″ d.
198. MEISSEN. CREAMER. "Flying Fox," from same service as plate No. 197. Incised cross in addition to crossed swords mark. c. 1730. $3\frac{7}{8}''$ h.
48 199. MEISSEN. RED DRAGON PLATE from service made in 1734 for the Elector August III. KHC stands for Royal Court Pantry at Dresden. Also crossed swords mark. $7\frac{3}{4}''$ d.
200. MEISSEN. RED DRAGON PLATE. Caduceus mark. c. 1723. $8\frac{3}{4}''$ d. Ex. coll. Lord Fisher.
201. MEISSEN. LARGE PLATE. Design in the Kakiemon style known as "Yellow Lion," actually a tiger with bamboos and plum tree. KHCW mark which was placed only on pieces made for the Warsaw Palace. c. 1728. $11\frac{3}{4}''$ d.
202. MEISSEN. PAIR OF PLATES. Decoration known as Tiger and Bamboos. Early paste (before 1724). c. 1728. Blue enamel crossed swords over glaze, Jöhanneum mark on both plates showing that they were in the Royal Saxon collection. $9\frac{1}{16}''$ d.
49 203. MEISSEN. AR VASE. Decor birds, flowers and rocks in Köhler blue, lid missing. $16\frac{1}{2}''$ h. c. 1723. Coll. Mrs. C. B. Stout, Memphis, Tenn.
50 204. MEISSEN. WASTE BOWL, polychrome chinoiserie scenes of a lion hunt, decorated by Herold. c. 1728. Crossed swords. Coll. Mr. R. H. Wark, Hendersonville, N.C.
205. MEISSEN. PAIR VASES decorated in Köhler blue, mark embossed "K." c. 1720. About 8″ h. Coll. Mr. R. H. Wark, Hendersonville, N.C.
206. MEISSEN. COFFEE POT. Harbor scenes in rouge-de-fer monochrome by Christian Herold. Crossed swords mark; gold number 4. c. 1730. Coll. Mr. R. H. Wark, Hendersonville, N.C.
51 207. MEISSEN. YELLOW FOND TEA BOWL AND SAUCER. The gold band at the fond outlining the design is also lightly outlined in black. c. 1740. Crossed swords mark, also gold letter H. $1\frac{3}{4}''$ h.
208. MEISSEN. OVAL TRAY, turquoise blue back. Inside painting in dark monochrome purple. Gold around the lip very fine. Decoration believed to be between 1730-1735, the porcelain older. In addition to crossed swords mark, there is an incised cross; also a gold h. $6\frac{3}{4}''$ l., $5\frac{1}{4}''$ w.
209. MEISSEN. TEA CADDY, turquoise fond. One side Dutch landscape scene, other side Dutch Harbor. A flower forms the knop. The crossed swords mark on the bottom has almost disappeared. c. 1740. $4\frac{3}{4}''$ h.
210. MEISSEN. CUP AND SAUCER. Apple-green fond. Gold band around the cartouche. c. 1735. Both have crossed swords; also gold mark B.K. 3″ h.
211. MEISSEN. BOUILLON COVER AND TREMBLEUSE STAND in deep purple fond. Applied flowers on raised rim. Cartouche formed with wide band of gold, outlined in black. Knop in form of strawberry. Crossed swords mark and a P and a 4 decorator's mark in purple. c. 1740. $4\frac{1}{4}''$ h., stand $5\frac{1}{4}''$ d.
212. MEISSEN. THREE-FOOTED CREAMER. Yellow fond. Decoration of Deutsche blumen. Cartouche enclosed with wide gold band outlined with black. Crossed swords mark. c. 1740. $4\frac{3}{4}''$ h.
213. MEISSEN. RECTANGULAR TEA CADDY, yellow fond, white top painted with beautiful butterflies. Harbor scenes on sides enclosed in single line cartouche of brown. Clouds touched with pink, flying birds. On ends, Indian flowers in red, blue and purple. Crossed swords, a 4 in gold, and a potter's mark. c. 1730. 4″ h., $3\frac{3}{8}''$ l., and $2\frac{1}{8}''$ w.
214. MEISSEN. TEA-BOWL AND SAUCER. Dead leaf-brown. Decor in under-glaze Köhler blue. Crossed swords. c. 1724. $1\frac{3}{4}''$ h.
215. MEISSEN. COFFEE POT. Olive-green fond. Decoration of harbor scenes in polychrome outlined with thin line of brown. Indianische blumen painted directly on the ground color. Crossed swords mark. c. 1735. $6\frac{5}{8}''$ h. under lid.
52 216. MEISSEN. VASE AND COVER. Kakiemon style decoration including lion, insects and flowers and birds in colors. AR mark. 14″ h. 1725-1730. Courtesy Smithsonian Institute, Washington, D.C., U.S.A.
217. MEISSEN. VASE AND COVER. Decoration of oriental flowers and figures. AR mark. 1725-1730. Courtesy Detroit Institute of Art, Detroit, Michigan, U.S.A.
53 218. MEISSEN. VASE AND COVER. Black ground. Chinoiserie decoration painted by J. G. Herold. AR mark. About 16″ h. c. 1730. Courtesy Berne Historical Museum, Berne, Switzerland.
54 219. MEISSEN. PAIR OF VASES AND COVERS. Rouge-de-fer (iron-red). Polychrome oriental flowers and insects. AR mark. 1730-1740. 28″ h. Courtesy Metropolitan Museum of Art. New York, U.S.A.
55 220, 223. MEISSEN. TWO BEAKER-SHAPED CHOCOLATE CUPS AND SAUCERS, painted with quay scenes in schwarzlot within gilt framework, with pink luster decoration, the borders with bandelwerk. Crossed swords mark. c. 1735. Cups 3″ h., saucers $5\frac{3}{8}''$ d.
221. MEISSEN. TEA BOWL AND SAUCER with schwarzlot decoration, consisting of quay scenes with chinoiseries and landscapes. All enclosed in cartouches having early copper luster. Flowers inside tea bowl. Three concentric red circles on underside of saucer. Gold mark 17 on both pieces. Also

early potter's mark incised in the foot-rim. Early crossed swords mark on saucer near the foot-rim. c. 1724. Tea bowl $1\frac{3}{4}$" h., $2\frac{5}{16}$" d., saucer 5" d.

222. MEISSEN. MILK JUG AND COVER, painted with quay scenes in schwarzlot, light puce and blue. Crossed swords mark and gold letter Z. 1725-1730. $5\frac{1}{4}$" h.

224. MEISSEN. LARGE PLATTER. Basket weave border. Flying Dragon and Phoenix with Indianische blumen. Crossed swords mark. 1732-1733. 15" d.

225. MEISSEN. NUT BOWL OR SAUCE BOAT, part of above service. Impressed potter's mark. Also crossed swords mark. 1732-1733. $4\frac{1}{2}$" h., $9\frac{7}{8}$" l.

56 226. MEISSEN. MODEL PLAQUE, decorated in polychrome harbor scenes by J. G. Heintze. Mark: 'Model' and swords mark. c. 1740. Coll. Mr. R. H. Wark, Hendersonville, N.C.

57 227. MEISSEN. TANKARD, decorated by Löwenfinck from the Earl of Jersey Dinner Service about 1735. This tankard signed with initials F.v.L. Crossed swords. Also embossed potter's mark. Coll. Mr. R. H. Wark, Hendersonville, N.C.

58 228. MEISSEN. OVAL PLATTER decorated by Löwenfinck from the Earl of Jersey Dinner Service. Crossed swords and embossed potter's mark. c. 1735. Coll. Mrs. C. B. Stout, Memphis, Tenn.

229. MEISSEN. OCTAGONAL DEEP DISH, decorated by Löwenfinck from Earl of Jersey Dinner Service. Crossed swords and embossed potter's mark. c. 1735. Coll. Mr. R. H. Wark, Hendersonville, N.C.

230. MEISSEN. OCTAGONAL DEEP DISH, decorated by Löwenfinck, from Earl of Jersey Dinner Service. Crossed swords mark and embossed potter's mark. c. 1735. Coll. Mr. and Mrs. Ben Williams, Highlands, North Carolina, U.S.A.

231. MEISSEN. OCTAGONAL LARGE DEEP DISH in polychrome decoration in the famille verte style. Crossed swords mark. c. 1730. Coll. Mr. R. H. Wark, Hendersonville, N.C.

59 232. MEISSEN. SMALL BEAKER. Decoration continuous harbor scenes. Beautiful cloud effects tinged with pink. Early type crossed swords mark. Gold mark 5. 1725-1730. $3\frac{1}{4}$" h., $2\frac{3}{4}$" d.

233. MEISSEN. BOUILLON WITH COVER AND STAND. Decoration quay scenes. Around border of cover a very fine gold C scroll. Sea serpent as knop. Gold number 2 on both pieces. Also crossed swords mark. 1730-1735. $4\frac{1}{2}$" h.

234. MEISSEN. SAUCER. Decoration of quay scenes. Cartouche of early Böttger copper luster picked out in red only. No mark. c. 1723. 5" d.

235. MEISSEN. LARGE COFFEE POT. Porcelain by transmitted light very green with large moons. Incised potter's mark, decoration of Indianische blumen of the best period. Crossed swords mark. c. 1725. $8\frac{1}{2}$" h.

236. MEISSEN. THREE CUPS AND SAUCERS. Decorration similar to that on coffee pot above. Potter's mark on cups and saucers. Red rings on underside of saucers. Also crossed swords mark. 1725-1730. Cups $1\frac{3}{4}$" h., 3" d.; saucers $5\frac{5}{8}$" d. Coll. Mr. and Mrs. R. H. Weaver, Jackson, Mississippi, U.S.A.

237. MEISSEN. EGG, colorfully decorated with naturalistic flowers and butterfly. c. 1760.

238. MEISSEN. RARE PLATE of unusual shape. Decorated in famille verte, with pseudo-Chinese seal mark in red enamel. c. 1723. $8\frac{1}{8}$" d.

60 239. MEISSEN. TEA AND COFFEE SERVICE, consisting of coffee pot with lid, waste bowl, teapot with masked spout and no lid, cream jug with cover, tea caddy with lid (rectangle shape) three cups, and five saucers. Dutch harbor and landscape decoration by C. F. Herold made popular by him. Scenes enclosed in cartouches, gold filigree, and picked out with red and a little lavender. Gold letters ii on all pieces. Also crossed swords. 1730-1735. Coffee pot $8\frac{3}{4}$" h., tea pot $3\frac{1}{4}$" h. (under lid), jug 6" h., caddy 4" h., cup $1\frac{5}{8}$" h., saucer $4\frac{7}{8}$" d., and waste bowl 3" h., 6" d.

61 240. MEISSEN. TEA BOWL AND SAUCER. Decoration in under-glaze blue with gold added later, probably by the mysterious F. J. Ferner. Early crossed swords mark. c. 1725. Bowl $1\frac{3}{4}$" h., $3\frac{1}{8}$" d., saucer $5\frac{1}{4}$" d.

241. MEISSEN. PLATE, painted outside factory at Pressnitz by F. F. Mayer. c. 1750. 9" d.

242. MEISSEN. EARLY TRAVELING SET of eight double-handled beaker cups and saucers, decorated in under-glaze blue with Chinese design of flowering plants and a bird. Gilding added later, probably by F. J. Ferner. Early crossed swords mark on all. Different early potter's mark on each. c. 1725. Similar pieces in the collections of Mr. and Mrs. Frank King, Sr., and Mr. and Mrs. Dunbar Abston, all of Germantown, Tennessee, U.S.A. 3" h., saucer $5\frac{1}{2}$" d.

243. MEISSEN. SUGAR BOWL AND COVER, decorated with fable animals in the style of Löwenfinck. c. 1735. 4" h.

244. MEISSEN. IMPORTANT BOWL AND COVER. Japanese Imari style of decoration, consisting of twelve panels around outer rim of cover, every other one having preponderance of under-glaze blue outlined in gold and set off with red. Alternate panels on white background with flowers, etc. in red and yellow. Center decorations of cover in the early Indianische blumen. Artichoke or pineapple in puce color for finial. Panel decoration repeated on outer rim of bowl. Sixteen panels. On bottom crossed swords of the period of 1725. $9\frac{1}{2}$" d., 7" h.

245. MEISSEN. BOUILLON AND COVER. Köhler under-glaze blue decoration. Crossed swords mark. c. 1724. 4" h.

62 246. MEISSEN. TUREEN, COVER AND STAND. Decoration lambrequin pattern in cobalt-blue, iron-red, purple, green, yellow, and gold. Sea-Serpent atop lid serving as handle. Mark: large under-glaze blue crossed swords. c. 1725. Courtesy of Dr. Schneider of Jägerhof Museum, Düsseldorf, Germany.

63 247. MEISSEN. ONE OF PAIR OF VASES from Swan Service. 1737-1741. Courtesy City Art Museum, St. Louis, Mo.

64 248. MEISSEN. INKSTAND, TRAY, INKWELL AND SANDER. Polychrome landscapes and harbor scenes, decorated by Heintze. Crossed swords mark. c. 1743. Coll. Mr. R. H. Wark, Hendersonville, N.C.

249. MEISSEN. PLATE. Unusual famille verte decoration. c. 1725-1730. Coll. Mr. R. H. Wark, Hendersonville, N.C.

250. MEISSEN. PAIR LEAF-SHAPED DISHES. Decoration naturalistic flowers. c. 1740. $8\frac{3}{4}$" l.

251. MEISSEN. TEAPOT. Schwarzlot decoration. Crossed swords mark. c. 1730. 4" h.

252. MEISSEN. CUP AND SAUCER. Naturalistic flower decoration. c. 1740. Cup $1\frac{3}{4}$" h., $2\frac{7}{8}$" d; saucer $4\frac{3}{4}$" d.

65 253. MEISSEN. RARE TEAPOT, with "bleu celeste" ground color having polychrome Oriental flowers on the ground. In panels polychrome chinoiserie in style of Löwenfinck. Crossed swords. c. 1740. Coll. Mr. R. H. Wark, Hendersonville, N.C.

254. MEISSEN. INVALID CUP AND SAUCER, pale lavender color with handle, spout and raised AR in white porcelain (Böttger). c. 1715. Coll. of Mrs. H. C. Isaacson, Sr., Seattle, Washington, U.S.A.

66 255. MEISSEN. FIGURES modeled by Kändler consisting of 12 Apostles and 12 candlesticks, only complete set in existence today. This set ordered by Augustus III in 1737 for the Empress Amalia of Austria. Austrian Imperial coat-of-arms in polychrome on the plinths. Figures in all-white except that mantles are trimmed in gold. 1737-1742. This set on display at Biltmore House, the Asheville, North Carolina, U.S.A., estate of the later George Vanderbilt. Illustrated here through courtesy of G. H. V. Cecil, grandson of the original owner.

67 256. MEISSEN. FIGURE IN ALL-WHITE OF JOSEPH FRÖHLICH, Court Jester of Augustus the Strong, probably modeled by Johann C. L. Lück. 1728-1729. Courtesy Detroit Institute of Arts, Detroit.

257. MEISSEN. FIGURE OF POSTMASTER "BARON" SCHMIEDEL, modeled by Kändler. c. 1737. Courtesy Detroit Institute of Arts, Detroit.

68 258. MEISSEN. BUST OF ST. THOMAS, modeled by Kändler. Crossed swords. c. 1743. 12″ h. Coll. Mrs. C. B. Stout, Memphis, Tenn.

69 259. MEISSEN. FIGURE OF AUGUSTUS III, Elector of Saxony and King of Poland, modeled by Kändler. c. 1740. Courtesy City Art Museum, St. Louis, Mo.

70 260. MEISSEN. WINTER, from the series of the Four Seasons, modeled by Eberlein. c. 1740. Crossed swords mark. 10″ h.

261. MEISSEN. RAPE OF A SABINE, modeled by Kändler (see English counterpart No. 485). c. 1745. 9″ h.

262. MEISSEN. FALL, from the series of the Four Seasons, modeled by Eberlein. c. 1740. 10¼″ h.

71 263. MEISSEN. SILVER MINER. From a series modeled by Kändler in which several of the figures resembled Augustus. c. 1740. 7⅞″ h.

264. MEISSEN. MAP SALESMAN. Modeled by Kändler. c. 1740. 6½″ h.

265. MEISSEN. TURKISH WOMAN MANDOLIN PLAYER. Modeled by Peter Reinicke. c. 1744. 6⅝″ h.

266. MEISSEN. SITTING MALE GARDENER. Modeled by Kändler. c. 1740. 8¼″ h.

267. MEISSEN. THE WALKING GARDENER. From the Handworker series, modeled by Kändler. Vestiges of blue under-glaze crossed swords at back near bottom. c. 1740. 7½″ h.

268. MEISSEN. SITTING WOMAN GARDENER. Modeled by Kändler. Mark: crossed swords. c. 1740. 8″ h.

72 269. PLYMOUTH. FIGURE OF GIRL PLAYING MUSICAL INSTRUMENT. Hard-paste. c. 1768. 6″ h.

270. BOW, SMALL CHILD WITH FLOWER BOCAGE. Decoration on plinth in claret. c. 1760. 4½″ h.

271. MEISSEN. BOY AS HARLEQUIN. Modeled by Kändler. Impressed 24X and crossed swords. c. 1745. 5″ h.

272. MEISSEN. COUNTRY DANCING GIRL. Crossed swords mark on back. c. 1745. 7½″ h.

273. MEISSEN. CLOTHES PRESSER. Modeled by Kändler. From the first Parisian Crier series. Mark: crossed swords. c. 1745. 7½″ h.

274. MEISSEN. THE COPPERSMITH. Modeled by Kändler. c. 1750. 7½″ h.

275. MEISSEN. FISH SALESWOMAN OR THE FISH-WIFE. From the first series of "Criers." Modeled by Kändler. c. 1745. Mark: crossed swords. 7½″ h.

73 276. MEISSEN. LADY AND MAN WITH BIRDCAGE, also called Passionate Lovers. Modeled by Kändler. c. 1736. Courtesy Wadsworth Atheneum, Hartford, Connecticut, U.S.A.

277. MEISSEN. GALLANT IN DRESSING GOWN AND LADY IN CRINOLINE WITH FAN, modeled by Kändler. c. 1736. Courtesy Wadsworth Atheneum, Hartford, Conn.

74 278. MEISSEN. SPANISH LOVERS. Modeled by Kändler. c. 1741. Mark: crossed swords. Coll. Mr. R. H. Wark, Hendersonville, N.C.

279. MEISSEN. LADY WITH CHOCOLATE CUP. Modeled by Kändler. c. 1737. Coll. Mr. A. Whittekind, Geneva, Switzerland.

75 280. MEISSEN. THE LOVERS. Modeled by Kändler. c. 1740. Courtesy Wadsworth Atheneum, Hartford, Conn.

76 281. MEISSEN. THE HEART SELLER. Modeled by Kändler. c. 1740. Courtesy Wadsworth Atheneum, Hartford, Conn.

77 282. MEISSEN. AFRICA, from the Four Continents. Modeled by Kändler. c. 1745. Crossed swords mark. 11½″ h., 9¼″ l.

282. MEISSEN. AMERICA, from the Four Continents. Modeled by Eberlein, 1745. Four such models made: in 1745 by Eberlein; in 1745 by Reinicke; again in 1746 by Reinecke, and in 1747 once more by Eberlein. Models different only in minor details and in scale. Crossed swords mark. 10⅝″ h., 12¼″ l.

78 283. MEISSEN. HARLEQUIN SEATED ON A STUMP. From the Italian Comedy. Modeled by Kändler. c. 1740. Courtesy Wadsworth Atheneum, Hartford, Conn.

284. MEISSEN. DANCING HARLEQUIN. From the Italian Comedy. Modeled by Kändler. 1740-1746. Courtesy Wadsworth Atheneum, Hartford, Conn.

285. MEISSEN. FRIGHTENED HARLEQUIN. From the Italian Comedy. Modeled by Kändler. c. 1740. Courtesy Wadsworth Atheneum, Hartford, Conn.

79 286. MEISSEN. SITTING HARLEQUIN PLAYING BAGPIPE. Modeled by Kändler. c. 1735. 5½″ h.

287. MEISSEN. PSYCHE AND CUPID. Modeled by Kändler. c. 1740. 6″ h. 5½″ l.

288. MEISSEN. SITTING HARLEQUIN PLAYING BAGPIPE. Modeled by Kändler. 1735-1740.

289. MEISSEN. NAKED CENTAUR. Modeled by Kändler. c. 1745. Mark on bottom KHCW. 8½″ h., 10″ l.

290. MEISSEN. THE THREE ARTS. c. 1750. Modeled by Kändler. 9½″ h.

80 291. MEISSEN. HARLEQUIN WITH JUG. From the Italian Comedy. Modeled by Kändler. c. 1738. Courtesy Wadsworth Atheneum, Hartford, Conn.

81 292. MEISSEN. TURK WITH THE JUMPING HORSE. Modeled by Kändler. c. 1750. 10″ h. Courtesy Antiquarian Society, Memphis, Tennessee, U.S.A

293. MEISSEN. COLUMBINE AND HARLEQUIN DANCING. Modeled by Eberlein. c. 1744. 8¼″ h., 7¾″ w. Coll. Mrs. C. B. Stout, Memphis, Tenn.

294. MEISSEN. ARDENT LOVERS. Modeled by Kändler. c. 1740. 6¾″ h. Coll. Mrs. C. B. Stout, Memphis, Tenn.

295. MEISSEN. CHINESE LOVERS. Modeled by Kändler. c. 1748. Crossed swords mark. 7¾″ h. Coll. Mrs. C. B. Stout, Memphis, Tenn.

82 296. MEISSEN. MOCKERY OF OLD AGE. c. 1745. 7″ h., base 7½″ × 4½″. Coll. Mrs. C. B. Stout, Memphis, Tenn.

297. DERBY. ENGLISH COUNTERPART OF MEISSEN MOCKERY OF OLD AGE. c. 1765. 9″ h. Large vent hole and three patch marks under base. Coll. Mrs. C. B. Stout, Memphis, Tenn.

83 298, 299. MEISSEN. HOOPOES BIRDS, one bird modeled by Kändler 1736, other by J. G. Ehder 1741. Coll. Mr. Irwin Untermyer, New York, U.S.A.

84 300. MEISSEN. TANKARD. Decorated by Löwenfinck. c. 1735. Original Danish silver mountings. Coll. Dr. Hans Syz, Westport, Conn.

300A. MEISSEN. TANKARD. Decorated by Löwenfinck. (From gold and black band service). c. 1735. Coll. Miss Ilse Bischoff, New York.

301. MEISSEN. TUREEN. Painted by Löwenfinck. c. 1735. Coll. Dr. Hans Syz, Westport, Conn.

301A. MEISSEN. TANKARD. Painted by J. G. Herold. c. 1722. Coll. Miss Ilse Bischoff, New York.

85 302. MEISSEN. EAGLE TEAPOT. Yellow ground. Painted by J. G. Herold. c. 1725. Coll. of Mr. Paul Schnyder von Wartensee, Lucerne, Switzerland.

303. MEISSEN. PLATE. Decor, chinoiseries and quay scenes. Probably decorated by Christian Herold. c. 1728. Coll. Mr. Paul Schnyder von Wartensee, Lucerne.

304. MEISSEN. SET OF THREE POWDER-BLUE VASES. c. 1730. Coll. Mr. Paul Schnyder von Wartensee, Lucerne.

86 305. Du Paquier. Cup and Saucer. Decorated entirely in silver, now oxidized to black. 1720-1725. $1\frac{3}{4}$″ h., saucer $4\frac{3}{8}$″ d.

305A. Meissen. Pagoda. Böttger porcelain in all-white. c. 1713. $3\frac{5}{8}$″ h.

306. Meissen. Tea Caddy. Puce ground. Decorated in schwarzlot. c. 1735. Courtesy Antiquarian Society, Memphis, Tenn. (Memorial to Mrs. Hiram Norcross), $4\frac{1}{4}$″ h.

307. Du Paquier. Cup and Saucer. Decorated probably by J. G. Herold at Vienna. c. 1719. $1\frac{7}{8}$″ h., saucer 5″ d.

308. Du Paquier. Cup and Saucer, one of a pair. Decorated in 1719 by J. G. Herold at Vienna. $1\frac{3}{4}$″ h., saucer $5\frac{1}{4}$″ d.

87 309. Du Paquier. Octagonal Sugar Box and Cover, decorated with putti in schwarzlot, probably painted by J. G. Herold in 1719. $2\frac{3}{4}$″ h., $4\frac{1}{4}$″ l., and $3\frac{1}{4}$″ w.

310. Du Paquier. Octagonal Sugar Box and Cover, with Japanese flowers and two tall Chinese figures, decorated by J. G. Herold at Vienna in 1719. 3″ h., $4\frac{1}{4}$″ l., and $3\frac{1}{4}$″ w.

311. Du Paquier. Tea Bowl and Saucer. Documentary specimen painted in 1719 at Vienna by J. G. Herold. Japanese rock and flower style with characteristic stippled "mat" also found on the earliest KPF and MPM teapots decorated by Herold at Meissen. Cup $1\frac{5}{8}$″ h., saucer $5\frac{3}{8}$″ d.

312. Meissen. Teapot, decorated in early chinoiseries (notice the stippled "mat") by J. G. Herold in 1723. Mark MPM. Coll. Mr. Ralph Wark, Hendersonville, N.C.

88 313. Du Paquier. Plate or Deep Dish. Decoration "Laub-und Bandelwerk." 1735-1740. 12″ d. Coll. Mrs. H. C. Isaacson, Sr., Seattle.

313A. Du Paquier. Rectangular Dish, decorated in colors with elaborate Baroque borders. 1735-1740. $12\frac{3}{4}$″ × $9\frac{1}{8}$″., $1\frac{3}{4}$″ d. Coll. Mrs. H. C. Isaacson, Sr., Seattle.

314. Du Paquier. Teapot with Cover. Baroque decoration. 1725-1735. 6.8″ h. Courtesy Bern Historical Museum, Bern.

314A. Du Paquier. Tureen and Cover. Imari design with eel handles and knop. Painted in polychrome. 1725-1730. 7″″ h., $12\frac{1}{2}$″ w. Coll. Mrs. H. C. Isaacson, Sr., Seattle.

89 315. Du Paquier. Tureen and Cover. "Mosaik" pattern. Polychrome decoration. Monkey as lid-knop. 1725-1730. Coll. Dr. Hans Syz. Westport, Conn.

316. Du Paquier. Tureen and Cover, from service made for Count Rohan, decorated in "Mosaik" pattern in iron-red with reserved panels of Japanese flowers in polychrome. 1725-1730. Coll. Mrs. H. C. Isaacson, Sr., Seattle.

90 317. Du Paquier. "Chimare" grotesque figure of animal with serpent tail decorated in red and purple. c. 1740. Coll. Dr. Hans Syz, Westport, Conn.

318. Du Paquier. Dual Candlesticks with Columbine Playing a Hurdy-Gurdy. 1730-1735. Coll. Dr. Hans Syz, Westport, Conn.

91 319. Vienna. Music. From the Arts series. Monkey on back. Base typical of period. c. 1765. $7\frac{1}{2}$″ h.

320. Vienna. Geography. From the Arts series. Monkey on back. Base typical of period. c. 1765. 8″ h.

92 321. Vienna. Tailor. Modeled by Johann Niedermeyer before 1767. Black shoes, short lilac trousers and vest, black three-pointed hat on his long hair. Blue mark. Red painter's number 26 (Christoph Driescharf). Gold painter's number 41 (Anton Mayer). $8\frac{1}{4}$″ h.

322. Vienna. The Hairdresser. From series of Vienna Criers, modeled by Niedermyer. Yellow shoes, lilac coat with dark strawberry-colored border stripes, lilac figured apron, blue bodice, scarf and white cap with lilac border. Marks: Blue shield under glaze, impressed R. C. 1760. $7\frac{1}{2}$″ h.

323. Vienna. The Wigmaker. From the series of Vienna Criers, modeled by Niedermeyer. Pale brown coat over white and lavender undergarments, yellow shoes, grey hair and wig on wig stand c. 1760. Marks: blue under-glaze shield, impressed P. $7\frac{1}{2}$″ h.

324. Vienna. Personal Body Guard of Maria Theresa. Modeled by Niedermeyer. Tight red trousers, similarly colored vest, white tunic and high cap. Drawn sword held in both hands. c. 1760. Blue under-glaze shield on bottom. $9\frac{1}{2}$″ h.

325. Vienna. Romulus and Remus with Wolf. Modeled by Niedermeyer. The Wolf stands on a Rococo base with purple and gold swirls. The two naked boys climbing around on base. Wolf's left paw on large vase, out of which water flows (clearly a personification of the Tiber). Above description written by Dr. E. W. Braun, Nurnberg, May, 1950. c. 1760. Mark: under-glaze blue shield, incised N. $4\frac{1}{2}$″ h., 7″ l.

326. Vienna. The Faint. Modeled by Anton Grassi. Her coat light purple, skirt yellow with light purple ruching, shoes dark blue with red eyelets. Her lover in black shoes with buckles, short trousers and coat, and gold trimmed light yellow vest. c. 1780. Blue under-glaze shield on bottom. $8\frac{1}{2}$″ h.

93 327. Vienna. Polish Musical Group. Modeled by Anton Grassi. Cap and coat of the man chocolate-colored, lilac inside. Shoes lilac and lemon green. Boy's garment light yellow and matching shoes. Standing girl in lilac skirt, yellow sleeveless coat, and similarly colored jacket with blue border. On reverse side, a kneeling boy in lilac suit and similarly colored jacket, iron-red shoes and turban, flowers in both hands. Mark: blue under-glaze shield. c. 1780. $12\frac{1}{2}$″ h.

94 328. Höchst. Lovers in an Arbor. Modeled by Simon Feilner. c. 1753. Red wheel mark. $8\frac{3}{4}$″h., $7\frac{1}{2}$″l.

95 329. Höchst. The Chinese Emperor. Modeled by Melchior. c. 1770. Courtesy Detroit Institute of Arts, Detroit.

96 330. Höchst. Disturbed Sleeper. Modeled by Melchior. c. 1770. Mark: blue under-glaze wheel surmounted by three balls and a cross. 6″ h., 7″ l.

331. Höchst. Children at Play. Modeled by Melchior. c. 1770. Mark: blue under-glaze wheel on bottom. $6\frac{1}{4}$″ h., 8″ l.

97 332 to 332E. Höchst. The Twelve Figures illustrated here are from the well-known collection of Mr. and Mrs. Edward M. Pflueger, New York, U.S.A. They are a part of the fourteen figures that were collected by Mr. and Mrs. Otto Blohm and shown in color in their catalogue. They were all probably modeled by Simon Feilner. 1750-1753. They represent characters from the Italian Comedy.

332. Höchst. Scaramouche. No mark: incised letters "IG" and one Gothic letter. $8\frac{1}{8}$″ h.

332A. Höchst. Ragonda. No mark. Incised letters "IG." $8\frac{1}{4}$″ h.

332B. Höchst. Isabella. Mark: wheel in iron-red; incised letters "INH." $7\frac{3}{4}$″ h.

332C. Höchst. Pantaloon. (Isabella's maid). No mark; incised letters "IGR." $7\frac{1}{2}$″ h.

332D. Höchst. Cynthio. Mark: wheel in iron-red. $8\frac{1}{8}$″ h.

332E. Höchst. Pantaloone. No mark: incised "YRG." $7\frac{7}{8}$″ h.

98 333 to 333E. Höchst. Captain. Wheel mark in iron-red; incised letters "PGS" and "PI." $8\frac{1}{16}$″ h.

333A. Höchst. Harlequin's Companion (Harlekine). Mark: wheel in iron-red; incised letters "RI." $8\frac{1}{4}$″ h.

333B. Höchst. Pierrot. No mark; impressed numeral "2." $7\frac{1}{8}$″ h.

333C. Höchst. Mezzetin. No mark; incised letters "PI" and a Gothic letter. $8\frac{1}{4}$″ h.

333D. Höchst. Harlequin. No mark; incised letters "LIG." 8⅛″ h.
333E. Höchst. Bagolin. Wheel mark in iron-red; incised letters. "PI." 7⅞″ h.

99 334. Höchst. Little Girl with Salt and Pepper. Modeled by Melchior. c. 1770. Mark: scratched on bottom: HS. 5½″ h.
335. Höchst. Girl with Scarf. Modeled by Melchior. c. 1770. Mark: blue under-glaze wheel on bottom, scratched underglaze No. 7 M24 R. 5½″ h.
336. Höchst. Boy Eating Apple. Modeled by Melchior. c. 1770. 4¾″ h.
337. Höchst. Seated Girl with Bird. Modeled by Melchior. c. 1768. Mark: blue under-glaze wheel, three balls and cross. 7″ h.
338. Höchst. Girl with Bird. Modeled by Melchior. c. 1770. Mark: under-glaze blue wheel with three circles and cross. 7″ h.
339. Höchst. Young Cavalier. Modeled by Melchior. c. 1770. Mark: under-glaze blue wheel, three balls, crown. 6½″ h.

100 340. Wallendorf. Vase with Cover. c. 1770. 12″ h. Coll. Mrs. H. C. Isaacson, Sr. Seattle.
341. Frankenthal. Sauce Tureen. c. 1765.
342. Höchst. Beggar Musicians. Modeled by Melchior. c. 1768. Mark: under-glaze blue wheel with six spokes. 8½″h. Coll. Mrs. C. B. Stout, Memphis, Tenn.

101 343. Frankenthal. Chinese Musician with Trumpet. Modeled by Karl Lück. c. 1775. Mark, surmounted by a crown, under-glaze blue. 6″ h.
344. Frankenthal. Chinese Musician with Large Sheet of Music. Modeled by Karl Lück. c. 1775. Mark, surmounted by a crown, under-glaze blue. 4½″ h.
345. Frankenthal. Chinese Musician with Small Sheet of Music. Modeled by Karl Lück. Mark, surmounted by a crown, under-glaze blue. 4½″ h.
346. Frankenthal. Chinaman Drinking Water. Modeled by Karl Lück. c. 1775.
347. Frankenthal. Chinese Woman with Basket. 1774. Mark: blue under-glaze crown 74. 5½″ h.
348. Frankenthal. Sitting Cello Player, modeled by Lanz. c. 1755. Lion mark and impressed PH (Paul Hannong). 6″ h.
349. Frankenthal. Chinese Musician. Modeled by K. G. Lück, 1775. Mark, surmounted by a crown and 75 (under-glaze blue). 5¾″ h.

102 350. Frankenthal. Shepherd and Shepherdess. Modeled by K. G. Lück, 1772. Mark, under-glaze blue, surmounted by a crown; under it: 72. 6½″ h., 9″ l.

103 351. Frankenthal. Boy Feeding Lamb, modeled by K. G. Lück. c. 1776. Mark, (Carl Theodor) surmounted by a cross and 76 (1776) in under-glaze blue. 5¼″ h.
352. Frankenthal. Sculptor. Modeled by K. G. Lück. c. 1775. Mark, crown and 75 (under-glaze blue) impressed 10. 5¾″ h.
353. Frankenthal. Winter. Modeled by K. G. Lück. 1779. Blue mark with crown and 79. 5¾″ h.
354. Frankenthal. Winter. Modeled by Link. c. 1765. Blue mark, under-glaze, and crown. 7″ h.
355. Frankenthal. Summer. Modeled by K. G. Lück. c. 1778. Blue mark: Carl Theodor with crown, N inscribed. 5¾″ h.

Figures in Plates 104, 105 and 106 are used here through the courtesy of the Berne Historical Museum, Bern.

104 356. Nymphenburg. Modeled by Bustelli. 1754-1763. Italian Comedy figure of Mezzetino. 7.8″ h.
357. Nymphenburg. Modeled by Bustelli. 1754-1763. Italian Comedy figure of Lalage. 8″ h.

105 358. Nymphenburg. Modeled by Bustelli. 1754-1763. Italian Comedy figure of Isabella. 7.8″ h.
359. Nymphenburg. Modeled by Bustelli. 1754-1763. Italian Comedy figure of Arlequina. 8.8″ h.

106 360. Nymphenburg. Modeled by Bustelli. 1754-1763. Italian Comedy figure of Octavio. 7.4″.
361. Nymphenburg. Modeled by Bustelli. 1754-1763. Italian Comedy figure of Columbine. 8.2″ h.

107 362. Nymphenburg. Modeled by Dominikus Auliczek. c. 1764. Representing St. Simeon Stylites and Asia from the series of the Continents. Mark: shield impressed on bottom. 7½″ h.

108 363. Ludwigsburg. Apple Vendor. c. 1755. Blue mark, and crown. 2½″ h.
364. Ludwigsburg. Turnip Vendor. c. 1755. Blue mark, and crown. 2½″ h.
365. Fürstenberg. Flute Player. c. 1770. Mark: F on bottom in blue, impressed Z on bottom 4″ h.
366. Fürstenberg. Hunting Horn Player. c. 1770. F in under-glaze blue on bottom. No. 2 F impressed. 4½″ h.
367. Fürstenberg. Milkmaid. c. 1770. Mark, under-glaze blue F on bottom and incised No.236 4″ h. LB
368. Ludwigsburg. Shepherdess. c. 1770. Mark: crossed C's in under-glaze blue on bottom. 4½″ h.
369. Ludwigsburg. Shepherd. c. 1770. Mark: crossed C's and crown in under-glaze blue on bottom, and incised M 03 III. 4½″ h.
370. Ludwigsburg. Hunting Group. c. 1765. Mark: double C with crown, impressed 3. 5½″ h.
371. Ludwigsburg. Man with Turkey. Modeler of the "Folk Type" figures. c. 1750. Mark: crossed C's with crown in under-glaze blue. 6½″ h.
372. Ludwigsburg. Woman with Turkey. Modeler of the "Folk Type" figures. c. 1750. Mark: crossed C's and crown in under-glaze blue. 6″ h.

109 373. Ludwigsburg. Satyr and Bacchante or Bacchus and Woman. Modeled by J. C. W. Beyer. c. 1765. Mark: blue under-glaze crossed C's with crown. 10″ h.

110 374. Berlin. April. Under-glaze blue scepter. "April" in relief on base. 1766-1767. 3¾″ h.
375. Berlin. March. 1766-1767. "Martins" inscribed on base. Mark: blue scepter. 4⅛″ h.
376. Kloster Veilsdorf. Mezzetino as a Painter. From the Italian Comedy. c. 1765. 6½″ h.
377. Wegely. Standing Farmer or Gardener. 1752-1755. Mark: blue W and three sets of numerals impressed with a stamp. 8″ h.
378. Gera. The Hun Family. c. 1772. Blue mark G. 7″ h.

111 379. Zürich. The Hay-Raker, modeled by Josef Vees. Standing bare-footed girl holding rake in her right hand, the left upholding her apron filled with hay. Hayrack supporting the figure. Round base covered with grass. Purple bodice, skirt striped in iron-red and blue, white apron and yellow straw hat with dark violet ribbon. Mark: embossed W 3. c. 1770. 5⅛″ h. Coll.: Dr. Siegfried Ducret, Zürich, Switzerland.
380. Zürich. The Building Contractor. Modeled by Josef Vees. Man holding a hammer in both hands with green hat, violet pants, blue coat, white shirt, yellow breeches. Round base with architectural implements. 1770-1775. Mark: embossed Q MO X E. 6.3″ h. Coll. Dr. Siegfried Ducret, Zürich.
381. Zürich. Hunter and Huntress. Modeled by Valentin Sonnenschein. On the base hunting prey of dead birds. Hunter kneeling on green base holding lady's hand. Huntress on tree stump turned towards hunter. Her bodice violet, black striped apron, gray skirt, and buckled shoes in iron-red. The hunter in short green jacket, gold-edged,

and green breeches. c. 1775. 6.3″ h. Coll. Dr. Siegfried Ducret, Zürich.

382. Zürich. Fisherman Couple. Modeled by W. Spengler. Woman standing against a high tree stump, next to a wooden bucket filled with fish. Man holding a fish in his hand removing the hook. Her skirt flowered white, white bodice edged with iron-red. He with a violet jacket, green breeches and barefoot. High grassy base. c. 1773. Coll. Dr. Siegfried Ducret, Zürich.

112 383. Gotzkowsky. Cup and Saucer. Decoration in puce monochrome popular during the 1760's. On both pieces the mark for Gotzkowsky. Cup $1\frac{3}{4}$″ h., saucer 5″ d.

384. Fulda. Cup and Saucer. Floral decor. Mark of factory on saucer, a deeply incised + c. 1770. Cup $2\frac{3}{4}$″ h., saucer $4\frac{7}{8}$″ d.

385. Hague. Cup, a rarity because so few pieces were produced. Border on cup a bleu-de-roi with rich gilding. Mark: in blue, a stork standing on one leg with fish in his mouth. 1775-1785. $2\frac{1}{2}$″ h.

386. Zweibrücken. Cup and Saucer. Mark: PZ in under-glaze blue. 1767-1775. Cup $2\frac{1}{2}$″ h., saucer $5\frac{1}{4}$″ d.

387. Worcester. Cup and Saucer. Decoration gilt with blue border. Crescent mark. c. 1765. Cup $2\frac{1}{2}$″ h., saucer $4\frac{7}{8}$″ d.

388. Worcester. Cup. Decorated in Kakiemon style. Fretted square mark. c. 1765.

389. Frankenthal. Cup, one of a pair, each marked with monogram of Carl Theodor. c. 1760. 2″ h.

390. Lassia. (French) Cup. Watteau landscape. Mark: L. c. 1784. $2\frac{1}{2}$″ h.

391. Tournay. Cup and Saucer. Decoration under-glaze blue and gold. Mark: crossed swords with dots. c. 1764. Cup $1\frac{5}{8}$″ h., saucer $5\frac{3}{8}$″ d.

392. Nyon. Plateau and Cremiers. Decoration colorful floral designs. Mark: under-glaze blue fish on every piece. c. 1785. Plateau 14″ l., cups $2\frac{3}{4}$″ h. Coll. Mr. and Mrs. Leland B. Dow, Jr., Memphis, Tennessee, U.S.A.

113 393. Du Paquier. Plate. Painted in polychrome and gilding after Oriental prototype. 1730-1740. 8″ d. Coll. Mrs. Harold Eggers, Seattle, Washington, U.S.A.

394. Ludwigsburg. Teapot on Little Legs. Landscapes painted in purple monochrome. 1765-1770. Mark: crown and double C. $6\frac{1}{2}$″ h. Coll. Mrs. DeWitt Williams, Seattle, Washington, U.S.A.

395. Cozzi Venice. Flower Pot, one of a pair. Open basket weave, pale yellow bands at top. Strands of basket outlined in green. c. 1765. $4\frac{1}{2}$″ h. Coll. Mrs. Kingsley Page, Seattle, Washington, U.S.A.

396. Frankenthal. Two-handled Covered Bowl. Pierced handles, diapered pattern with natural birds in polychrome. Mark: Lion in under-glaze blue and impressed PHF, for Paul Hannong on inside of foot-rim. 1754-1759. Coll. Mrs. W. L. Harnan, Seattle, Washington, U.S.A.

114 397. Capo-di-Monte. Beaker Cups and Saucers. All-white with raised prunus design. On both cups and saucers the fleur-de-lis mark in under-glaze blue which was used during first period. 1743-1759. Soft-paste. Cups $2\frac{7}{8}$″ h., saucers $5\frac{1}{2}$″ d.

398. Capo-di-Monte. Beaker Cup and Saucer. Decor early polychrome Watteau landscape. Gold quite different from that of other factories. Mark: under-glaze blue fleur-de-lis appearing on each piece. Soft-paste. 1750-1759. Cup $2\frac{3}{4}$″ h., saucer $5\frac{1}{4}$″ d.

399. Oude Loosdrecht (Holland). Cup and Saucer. Mark: MOL on each piece. 1772-1784. Cup $1\frac{1}{2}$″ h., saucer $4\frac{3}{4}$″ d.

400. Höchst. Jardiniere. Decoration, landscape in red monochrome. Mark: red wheel. c. 1755. $4\frac{1}{2}$″ d., $3\frac{5}{8}$″ h.

401. Höchst. Cremier. One of a pair. Floral decor. Mark: red wheel. c. 1755. 2″ h.

402. Buen Retiro. Cup and Saucer. Decoration: bull fight and Spanish landscape. Enamel paint and gold peculiar to this factory. (Gold heavily applied). Hard-paste. Mark: Interlaced C's surmounted by a coronet. c. 1788. Cup $2\frac{1}{2}$″ h., saucer $5\frac{3}{16}$″ d.

403. Doccia. Cup and Saucer. Copied from Meissen. c. 1750. Cup $3\frac{3}{4}$″ h., saucer 5″ d.

404. Le Nove. Plate. Hard-paste with tin glaze and brown color by transmitted light. Potting thin, glaze pitted, gold fine Italian. Incised + mark. c. 1765. $9\frac{3}{8}$″ d.

405. Cozzi Venice. Oval Sugar Bowl, Cover, Stand and Spoon, all original and perfect. Mark: large red anchor. 1765-1770. Tray $7\frac{1}{2}$″ l., $4\frac{3}{4}$″ h.

115 406. Cozzi Venice. Shell-shaped Dish. Typical under-glaze blue border. No mark. c. 1775.

407. Doccia. Cream Jug. No mark. c. 1775.

407A. Bourg-la-Reine. Bowl and Cover. Painted with large sprays of colorful flowers. Incised B.R. $3\frac{3}{4}$″ h. Coll. Mrs. G. W. Stoddard, Seattle, Washington, U.S.A.

408. Doccia. Tureen with Cover. c. 1775. Coll. Mrs. H. C. Isaacson, Sr., Seattle, Washington.

116 409. Rouen. Ewer or Water Jug. Soft-paste. Late 17th century. Courtesy Metropolitan Museum of Art, New York. (Gift of J. Pierpont Morgan).

117 410. St. Cloud. Cup and Trembleuse Saucer. Decoration of raised prunus. c. 1720. Cup $2\frac{7}{8}$″ h., saucer 5″ d.

411. Mennecy. Mustard Pot, Cover and Stand (barrel is part of the stand). Decoration polychrome flowers in colors typical of Mennecy of the best period. Edges in claret color. c. 1750. $3\frac{1}{2}$″ h., $6\frac{1}{2}$″ l.

412. St. Cloud. Beaker Cup and Trembleuse Saucer, one of a pair. Cups fluted and without handles. Lambrequin decoration in under-glaze blue. Sun mark. c. 1696. Cups $2\frac{7}{8}$″ h., saucers 5″ d.

413. Rouen. Beaker Cup and Trembleuse Saucer. Fluted cup without handle. Lambrequin design in under-glaze blue. Porcelain of greenish gray cast. No mark. 1675-1695. Cup 3″ h., saucer $5\frac{3}{4}$″ d.

414. Chantilly. Cachepot mounted on silver gilt. Kakiemon design. Dog head on each side. Mark: red hunting horn. c. 1740. $4\frac{5}{8}$″ d., $4\frac{5}{8}$″ h.

415. Mennecy. Teapot. Soft-paste. Impressed D.V. mark. c. 1750. 4″ h.

118 416, 417. St. Cloud. Chinese Figures. French pâte tendre. Courtesy The Metropolitan Museum of Art, New York. (Gift of R. Thornton Wilson in memory of Florence Ellsworth Wilson).

119 418. Mennecy. Group. Pâte tendre. 1735-1740. Courtesy Metropolitan Museum of Art, New York. (Gift of R. Thornton Wilson in memory of Florence Ellsworth Wilson.)

120 419. Mennecy. Grotesque Hawker. c. 1740. Courtesy Wadsworth Atheneum, Hartford, Conn.

121 420, 421. Mennecy. Music. From the Arts series. Exceptionally fine white glaze, quite like the Chinese (Fukien). Mark: DV incised. c. 1748. Both $6\frac{3}{4}$″ h.

122 422. Vincennes. Pair of Pot-pourri Vases. Glaze extremely white and brilliant, characteristic of this factory. Design found in the effects of Madame de Pompadour, who prepared sketches of pieces she wished Vincennes factory to make for her. Pâte tendre. c. 1745. 8″ h.

123 423. Vincennes. The Harvester. Biscuit figure modeled by Blondeau. Farm girl, La Moissonneuse" with scarf-like bonnet and sheaf of wheat in her arms. Behind her several other bundles of wheat. Pâte tendre. c. 1750. $5\frac{1}{2}$″ w., $7\frac{3}{4}$″ h.

124 424, 425. Vincennes. Pair of Figures in color, modeled by Blondeau in 1753. Pâte tendre. Courtesy Metropolitan Museum of Art, New York. (Gift of R. Thornton Wilson in memory of Florence Ellsworth Wilson).

125 426. VINCENNES. TEACUP. "Jaune jonquille" ground color. Decorated in monochrome blue. Pâte tendre. Mark: crossed L's (no date letter) also Vieillard's mark in blue enamel. c. 1753. $2\frac{3}{8}''$ h. Courtesy Victoria and Albert Museum, London. (Joicey Bequest).

427. VINCENNES. SUGAR BOX AND COVER. "Jaune jonquille" ground color. Decorated in monochrome blue. Pâte tendre. Vieillard's mark in blue enamel; also the crossed L's enclosing A, which dates it 1753. $3\frac{3}{8}''$ h. Courtesy Victoria and Albert Museum, London. (Joicey Bequest).

428. VINCENNES. TEAPOT AND COVER. White ground. Monochrome blue decoration, with elaborate gold framing. Pâte tendre. Vieillard's mark above the crossed L's, the letter B (1754) enclosed in the L's. $3\frac{7}{8}''$ h. Courtesy Victoria and Albert Museum, London.

126 429. VINCENNES. TEA SET (chocolate). "Jaune jonquille" ground color. White reserve painted with figures of clothed children and landscapes in monochrome blue, with elaborate gold framing. Pâte tendre. Crossed L's (no date letter) with painter's mark above (ш) for Vieillard. c. 1755. Tray $11\frac{1}{2}''$ l., 9″ w. Courtesy Wadsworth Atheneum, Hartford, Conn.

127 430. SÈVRES. OVAL POTPOURRI VASE. Apple-green ground decorated with cupids after Boucher. Lid decorated with modeled flowers, painted in colors. Pâte tendre. c. 1757. Reproduced by permission of the Trustees of the Wallace Collection, London.

128 431. VINCENNES OR SÈVRES. VASE with blue and apple-green ground, the former marbled in gold. Pâte tendre. Modeled by Duplessis. The bird painting attributed to Aloncle. 1755-1761. Reproduced by permission of the Trustees of the Wallace Collection.

432. SÈVRES. CANDLESTICK-VASE WITH ELEPHANTS' HEADS. Pale blue-green ground decorated with rich gilding and cupids. Pâte tendre. Modeled by Duplessis. Painted by Dodin after Boucher, about 1757. Reproduced by permission of the Trustees of the Wallace Collection.

129 433. SÈVRES. THREE-PIECE GARNITURE. Rose Pompadour. Pâte tendre. 1757-1763. Courtesy Metropolitan Museum of Art, New York. (Gift of R. Thornton Wilson in memory of Florence E. Wilson).

130 434, 435. SÈVRES. POTPOURRI VASES WITH COVER, representing fortified towers. Pâte tendre. Courtesy Metropolitan Museum of Art, New York. c. 1758. (Gift of R. Thornton Wilson in memory of Florence E. Wilson).

131 436. SÈVRES. TEAPOT AND LID. Decorator's mark for Dutanda. Hard-paste. Date letter for 1771. $4\frac{1}{2}''$ h.

437. SÈVRES. SAUCE BOAT, COVER AND STAND. Turquoise blue ground. Decoration flowers and birds outlined with gold. Part of Benjamin Harrison service described in No. 31 of this book. Mark: royal cypher with date letter F for 1758. $4\frac{1}{2}''$ h., $9\frac{1}{2}''$ l. (Pâte tendre).

438. SÈVRES. CUP WITH YELLOW GROUND. Decorated by Cornaille. Hard-paste. 1786. $2\frac{3}{4}''$ h.

439. SÈVRES. SHELL-SHAPED DISH. Hard-paste or pâte dure. c. 1780. 9″ l., 9″ w.

440. VINCENNES. PLATE IN BLEU-DE-ROI COLOR. Characteristic cupid in style of Boucher in center of plate. Mark: royal cypher, no date letter. c. 1752. $9\frac{7}{8}''$ d.

132 441. OLD PARIS. CREAMER. c. 1790. $3\frac{1}{2}''$ h.

442. SÈVRES. JEWELED DEEP SAUCER AND CUP. Turquoise blue ground color. Jewels representing rubies, pearls and other stones. c. 1780. Saucer 8″ d., $2\frac{1}{8}''$ h.; cup $3\frac{7}{8}''$ d., $3\frac{1}{2}''$ h.

443. SÈVRES. PAIR OF URNS of exceptionally fine quality. Empire shape. Mark: M. N. Le in red on glaze (used in 1804 only). It will be remembered that Napoleon Boneparte was crowned Emperor in 1804). $8\frac{1}{2}''$ h.

444. SÈVRES. CUP AND SAUCER. Deep rose ground color. Continuous band of chinoiseries around outer edge of both pieces, one in schwarzlot and the other in puce monochrome. Date letter 1794. Cup $1\frac{7}{8}''$ h., saucer $5\frac{1}{4}''$ d.

133 445, 446. OLD PARIS. PAIR OF FIGURES. Mounted on plynths bearing coat of arms. No mark. Style usually attributed to Jacob Petit. c. 1790. $23\frac{1}{2}''$ h.

134 447. FRANKENTHAL. PAIR OF FIGURES. Months: October and November. Modeled by Konrad Link. Mark C. T. c. 1765. Coll. Mrs. Donald Graham, Seattle, Washington, U.S.A.

448. HÖCHST. VENUS AND CUPID. Melchior model. Mark: blue wheel. c. 1770. 5″ h. Coll. Mrs. Donald Graham, Seattle.

449. DOCCIA. KNEELING WOMAN. White glazed porcelain. Probably from a model by Massimilano Soldoni-Benzi. c. 1770. 6″ h. Coll. Mrs. W. L. Harnan, Seattle.

450. HÖCHST. GIRL WITH MANDOLIN. Melchior model. Mark: blue wheel. 1770-1775. $6\frac{3}{4}''$ h. Coll. Mrs. Neil McDougall, Seattle, Washington, U.S.A.

451. MENNECY. FIGURE OF A GIRL. Flowing drapes. White glazed porcelain. 1750-1755. 6″ h. Coll. Mrs. S. A. Creighton, Seattle, Washington, U.S.A.

135 452. VINCENNES. BOAT-SHAPED DISH with "gros bleu" ground. Reserves painted with landscapes in crimson monochrome. Gilding thickly applied and chased. Mark: crossed L's. c. 1753. No date letter. 11″ l. Coll. Mrs. W. L. Harnan, Seattle.

453. MENNECY. BOWL WITH HANDLES. Polychrome painting. c. 1760. 5″ d. Coll. Mrs. G. W. Stoddard, Seattle.

454. CHANTILLY. VASE. Pierced and resting on a flower-encrusted base with tree trunk. White glazed porcelain. 1750-1755. 6″ h. Coll. Mrs. S. A. Creighton, Seattle.

455. CHANTILLY. VASE, bottle form. Kakiemon decoration. Mark: red horn. 1725-1750. 8″ h. Coll. Mrs. Robert Nichols, Seattle, Washington, U.S.A.

136 456. NYMPHENBURG. CUP AND SAUCER. Painted in schwarzlot with gilding. Deep lambrequin borders. On saucer an iconoclast king destroying Pan. Impressed shield mark. c. 1765. Coll. Mrs. Harold Eggers, Seattle.

457. BOURG-LA-REINE. TRIPLE SALT. Decorated with flowers in polychrome. Mark: B.R. incised. c. 1775. 3″ × 5″. Coll. Mrs. George W. Stoddard, Seattle.

458. MENNECY. FIGURAL SNUFF BOX in form of reclining woman with dog and cane. Underside of lid and base moulded with sprays of flowers painted in polychrome. Silver mounts. c. 1760. $3\frac{3}{8}''$ l. Coll. Mrs. Robert Nichols, Seattle.

459. COZZI VENICE. TEAPOT with twig handles attached to pot with beautifully modeled leaves and grapes in white. Scroll pattern in gold with flowers painted in dark lilac color. Mark: red anchor. 1767-1770. 4″ h. Coll. Mrs. Kingsley Page, Seattle.

460. VINCENNES. PLATE. Border molded in low relief with sprays of berries and leaves; bird painting in landscapes. Mark: crossed L's with date letter A for 1753. Crescent in blue for the painter Ledoux. 10″ d. Coll. Mrs. W. L. Harnan, Seattle.

137 461. CHELSEA. GROUP OF LOVERS. In all-white. No mark. Similar one in British Museum marked with crown and trident in under-glaze blue. c. 1745. $9\frac{1}{4}''$ h. Coll. Mrs. Sigmund Katz. Covington, Louisiana, U.S.A.

138 462. CHELSEA. AESOP shown as hunch-backed Ethiopian. Square base decorated with leaves and flowers. Around his neck the "freeman's chain"

with medallion attached bearing silhouette of man's head in gold. c. 1752. Mark: small red anchor at back of base. 10¼″ h. Coll. Mrs. Sigmund Katz, Covington, La.

139 463, 464. CHELSEA. PAIR OF BULLFINCHES. Black heads, purple beaks, red breasts, purple backs, black and white wings, and black tails; resting on stump with leaves and berries. Mark: on stump of each under tails, painted red anchor. c. 1755. 7⅞″ h., 8 1/16″ l. Courtesy Colonial Williamsburg, Va. (Ex collection: Sigmund Katz).

465, 466. CHELSEA. PAIR OF HEN-HARRIERS. One with rust head and back, yellow shading to brown on wings, and white with rust specks on breast. Mate has brown in place of rust and dark gray in place of brown. Mark: on base under tail of each: anchor raised in relief and painted red in applied oval medallion. c. 1750. 8″ h. Courtesy Colonial Williamsburg, Va. (Ex collection: Sigmund Katz).

140 467, 468. LONGTON HALL. PAIR OF LEOPARDS on scroll bases picked out in red, each with applied flowers and leaves. Seated leopard colored yellow wash with black spots. 3¼″ h., 4½″ l. Crouching leopard with tawny wash and black spots. 3⅜″ h., 6″ l. Unmarked. c. 1755. Coll. Mrs. Sigmund Katz. Covington, La.

469. CHELSEA. CRESTED BIRD with long tail perched on stump of tree with small fruit and leaves. Mark: anchor in relief painted in red on applied oval medallion. c. 1755. 8¼″ h. (Schreiber collection). Courtesy Victoria and Albert Museum, London.

470. CHELSEA. FEMALE HEN-HARRIER. Mark: anchor in relief painted in red on an applied oval medallion. c. 1755. 6¾″ h. (Schreiber collection). Courtesy Victoria and Albert Museum, London.

141 471, 472. BOW. PAIR OF PHOENIX BIRDS, modeled not molded. Only two examples of the hen recorded. The cock constituting the matching member of pair, unrecorded and hitherto unknown to collectors. c. 1750. 6½″ h. Coll. Mrs. H. C. Isaacson, Sr., Seattle.

473. CHELSEA. BIRD resembling one in Chelsea sales catalogue of 1755. Mark: raised anchor. c. 1752. 8 13/16″ h. Courtesy Museum of Fine Arts, Boston, Mass., U.S.A. (Gift of Mrs. T. O. Richardson, ex collection Mrs. Richard Baker).

474. CHELSEA. PLATE 66 from Vol. II of George Edwards' *Natural History of Birds*, London, 1743. "The Black and White Chinese Cock Pheasant with its Hen." Many Chelsea birds traceable to the four volumes of this series. Courtesy Museum of Fine Arts, Boston, Mass.

142 475. CHELSEA. MONKEY BAND FIGURE. Monkey dressed in pink coat with painted flowers, yellow vest and light blue breeches. Leader of set of ten monkeys, playing instruments or singing. 1755-1756. 8″ h. Courtesy Colonial Williamsburg, Va. (Ex collection: Sir Edward and Lady Baron; MacGregor Duncan).

476. CHELSEA. PERFUME POT. c. 1755. 14½″ h. Courtesy Victoria and Albert Museum, London. (Gift of Mr. W. King).

143 477. CHELSEA. COLUMBINE. From the Italian Comedy. c. 1755. No mark. 6¼″ h. Courtesy Museum of Fine Arts, Boston, Mass.

478. CHELSEA. HARLEQUIN. From the Italian Comedy. c. 1755. Courtesy Museum of Fine Arts, Boston, Mass.

479. CHELSEA. CRINOLINE FIGURE, perhaps from the Italian Comedy. Red anchor mark. c. 1755. 6″ h. Courtesy Museum of Fine Arts, Boston, Mass.

480. CHELSEA. From the Italian Comedy. c. 1755. Courtesy Museum of Fine Arts, Boston, Mass.

481. CHELSEA. From the Italian Comedy. c. 1755. Courtesy Museum of Fine Arts, Boston, Mass.

482. CHELSEA. RIVER GOD. Mark: red anchor. c. 1753. 5″ h. Courtesy Museum of Fine Arts, Boston, Mass. (Gift of Mr. Richard C. Paine).

483. CHELSEA. RIVER GODDESS. Mark: red anchor. c. 1753. Courtesy Museum of Fine Arts, Boston, Mass. (Gift of Richard C. Paine).

144 484. BOW. FORTUNE TELLER. From an engraving after Francois Boucher. No mark. 1750-1752. 6¾″ h. (Similar figure in Seattle Museum). Courtesy Museum of Fine Arts, Boston, Mass. (Gift of Richard C. Paine).

485. CHELSEA. RAPE OF A SABINE. Red anchor mark. 1750-1758. Courtesy Museum of Fine Arts, Boston, Mass.

486. CHELSEA. ISABELLA. From the Italian Comedy. Mark: raised red anchor. 1750-1753. 10″ h. Courtesy Museum of Fine Arts, Boston, Mass. (Gift of Richard C. Paine).

487. CHELSEA. BEGGAR WITH HURDY-GURDY. Mark: raised red anchor. 1750-1753. 5¾″ h. (See this book, No. 3, for Meissen original). Courtesy Museum of Fine Arts, Boston, Mass. (Gift of Richard C. Paine).

145 488. CHELSEA. CAULIFLOWER TUREEN AND COVER. Mark: painted red anchor on inside. 1755-1760. Courtesy Colonial Williamsburg, Va.

489. WORCESTER (Dr. Wall). PAIR OF BELL PULLS. Very rare. 1765-1770. 2″ h. Coll. Mrs. H. C. Isaacson, Sr., Seattle.

490. CHELSEA. TUREEN AND COVER. c. 1755. 11½″ w. from edge of handles, 9½″ h. to top of boy finial. Coll. Mrs. H. C. Isaacson, Sr., Seattle.

491. CHELSEA. BOWL. c. 1752. 8″ d., 3¾″ h. Coll. Mrs. H. C. Isaacson, Sr., Seattle.

146 492, 493. BOW. MUSE TYPE FIGURES. Tom Bowling and His Mate. Large vent hole, which is glazed. Greater portion of base without glaze. 6″ h. Mate 5½″ h. Coll. Mrs. C. B. Stout, Memphis, Tenn.

494. CHELSEA. THE BAGPIPER. No mark. 1753-1758. 9¼″ h. Coll. Mrs. C. B. Stout, Memphis, Tenn.

495. CHELSEA. THE CARPENTER. c. 1755. 8″ h. Coll. Mrs. C. B. Stout, Memphis, Tenn.

496. BRISTOL. FIGURE OF A WOMAN. c. 1770. 7½″ h. Coll. Mrs. C. B. Stout, Memphis, Tenn.

497, 499. CHELSEA-DERBY. FIGURES, typical of late gold anchor and Chelsea-Derby period. c. 1768. 8″ h. Coll. Mr. and Mrs. C. M. Gooch, Memphis, Tenn.

498. CHINESE. CUP AND SAUCER. Early egg-shell porcelain. Turquoise background. Medallion outlined in black. c. 1750. Coll. Mr. and Mrs. W. W. Deupree, Memphis, Tennessee, U.S.A.

147 500. CHELSEA. MASKED DUTCH DANCERS. Same figure modeled by Eberlein at Meissen. Mark: small red anchor. From the Schreiber collection. c. 1755. 7″ h. Courtesy Victoria and Albert Museum, London.

148 501, 502. CHELSEA. PAIR OF VASES. Summer and Winter of Seasons series. Summer: modeled figures of cherubs with strawberries and cherries. Winter: a cherub tending a brazier. Red anchor mark on Summer. 1753-1758. 13½″ h. Coll. Mrs. Wendell Black, Seattle, Washington, U.S.A.

149 503. CHELSEA. POTPOURRI VASE AND COVER. Decorated with gilding on mazarine-blue ground. On one side, Chinese man and woman in trellised pavillion with birds perched upon bushes. On the other, Chinese boy and girl playing with bird in garden. Mark: anchor in gold. c. 1770. 14½″ h., 10⅝″ d. Courtesy Victoria and Albert Museum, London. (From the Jones Collection).

504. CHELSEA. POTPOURRI VASE AND COVER. Decorated with mazarine-blue ground. On either side group of exotic birds among bushes. Although closely resembling No. 503, probably not made as pair, both on account of the disparity of subjects and also slight differences of detail in decoration. Mark: anchor in gold. c. 1770. 14⅛″ h., 10¼″ w. Courtesy Victoria and Albert Museum, London. (From the Jones Collection).

150 505. Chelsea. Potpourri Vase and Cover. Claret-colored ground. Mark: anchor in gold. c. 1770. 14½″ h., 10¼″ w. Courtesy Victoria and Albert Museum, London. (From the Jones Collection).

506. Chelsea. Potpourri Vase and Cover, with subject adapted from engraving after Jean-Baptiste Greuze and landscape painted by Zachariah Boreman. Mark: anchor in gold. c. 1770. 15¾″ h., 11½″ w. Courtesy Victoria and Albert Museum, London. (From the Jones Collection).

507. Chelsea. Potpourri Vase and Cover. Companion to No. 505. Paintings in manner of Berchem. Mark: anchor in gold. c. 1770. 14⅝″ h., 10½″ w. Courtesy Victoria and Albert Museum, London. (From the Jones Collection).

151 508. Tournay(?) Man Playing Bagpipe. All white of extremely soft-paste with bluish white glaze. Translucency green. c. 1750. 6¾″ h.

509, 510. Longton Hall. Snow Man Figures. Emblematic of the seasons. All-white Winter, stooped bearded man wrapped in greatcoat. Summer, a peasant girl holding sheath of wheat. 5″ h. Coll. Mrs. C. B. Stout, Memphis, Tenn.

511. Tournay(?) Lady Musician with Sheep. All-white of extremely soft-paste, with a bluish white glaze. Translucency: green. c. 1750. 7½″ h.

512. Girl in a Swing. Bird in all-white, chamfored base with six points. Alternative convex and concave beveling. Bottom has large cone-shaped opening, unglazed and not ground. No mark. 5″ h. Coll. Mrs. C. B. Stout, Memphis Tenn.

513. Girl in a Swing. This charming figure in white has given her name to a group of early English porcelains not yet definitely localized. A similar example is in the Victoria and Albert Museum, London, and shows a different arrangement in the application of the leaves. c. 1751. 6″ h. Courtesy Museum of Fine Arts, Boston, Mass. (Gift of Richard C. Paine).

152 514. Chelsea-Derby. Girl with Flowers. Candle holder attached. Early flat base. Patch marks of Derby on bottom. Also ground like Chelsea. c. 1770. 9½″ h.

515. Chelsea. Juno. The goddess with her favorite bird, the peacock. Underside of base is ground, no patch marks. Characteristics of Chelsea of gold anchor period. c. 1765. 8″ h.

516. Longton Hall. Candlestick, one of two. Paste and glaze very soft and glassy. Base ground and flat with small conical hole. So-called "scum edge," inferior gold, peculiar green with the yellow tone and mulberry color, all characteristic of this factory. c. 1750. 9¼″ h.

517, 518. Chelsea. Fisherman and Fisherwoman. Large flower bocage back of each, typical of gold anchor period. 1765-1770. 11″ h.

153 519. Bow. The Muse Polymnia. Decorated in enamel colors and gold. Column on which one arm rests veined to simulate marble. Inscribed at back—"Polymnie." c. 1750. 6¾″ h. Coll. Mrs. Sigmund Katz, Covington, La.

154 520. Bow. Kitty Clive. Modeled after engraving by Charles Mosley, published in London in 1750, based upon somewhat earlier drawing by Worlidge. 9¾″ h., 6½″ w. Courtesy Metropolitan Museum of Art, New York. (Coll. Mr. Irwin Untermyer).

521. Bow. Henry Woodward. Modeled from undated mezzotint by James McArdell, who came to London in 1746. and whose print follows the painting of Henry Woodward by Francis Hayman. No mark. Below the base, incised date-1750. Courtesy Metropolitan Museum of Art, New York. (Coll. Mr. Irwin Untermyer).

155 522. Longton Hall(?) Spring. Or possibly experimental piece made in Staffordshire by Enoch Wood. 1750-1800. 7¼″ h.

523. Bow. Summer. All-white porcelain. c. 1755. 5½″ h.

524. Bow. Old Man Winter. All-white. c. 1750. 5½″ h.

525. Bow. Fall. All-white. Wreath of grapes around head. c. 1755. 5½″ h.

526. Longton Hall(?) Summer. Or possibly experimental piece made in Staffordshire by Enoch Wood. 1750-1800. 7¼″ h.

527. Bow. Fire, from the series of the Elements. Blue tunic with red and gold flowers, lined with yellow. Burning bush in her hand. Typical four-footed type base. Mark: red anchor and dagger. At back near base, a triangular hole found only on Bow figures. c. 1765. 9″ h.

528, 529. Bow. Abelard and Heloise. Pair of figures standing, holding books inscribed "of confession," wearing black robes with white surcoats; Abelard with a biretta. Bases modeled with puce wave scrolls and flower sprays. c. 1752. 5¾″ h.

530. Bow. Water, depicting Neptune astride a dolphin. His helmet under left arm, which is decorated in red with bands of gold. Hair and long beard purple, wreath of green flowers on head, mantle decorated in dark puce and light green, with prunus blooms in gold outlined with red. From mouth of Dolphin and from helmet the blue-gray color found only on Bow. Base of footed type. Red anchor and dagger mark. Triangular hole to be used for mounting candle holders or bocages. c. 1765. 9″ h.

156 531. Bow. Three-piece Garniture. c. 1760. Small vases 5¾″ h. Large vase with bird on top, 12½″ h.

157 532. Bow. Cup, rare and early, of beaker form, with simple loop handle, finely decorated in early palette with large butterfly, a beetle, small insects and scattered sprays of flowers, including fine tulip. c. 1750. 3¼″ h.

533. Worcester. Cup in Imari style decoration No mark. c. 1765. 1⅞″ h.

534. Grainger Worcester. Scent Bottle. Ground color lighter than the Smith blue of Derby. Scene: "Malvern Abbey Church." c. 1810. 7″ h.

535. Liverpool. Jug with chinoiserie decoration. c. 1765. 5″ h.

536. Longton Hall. Leaf-shaped Sauce Boat. Characteristic mulberry and yellowish-green colors with inferior gold, and dark line where glaze meets body at foot-rim (called "scum line")' Green translucency, with moons. c. 1753. 9″ l.

537. Chelsea. Cup, Cover and Stand. Decorated with oval gold classical medallion heads, suspended by ribbons from green laurel festoons, in arch-shaped panels on claret ground. Gold anchor mark. c. 1768. 4⅝″ h., saucer 5½″ d.

538. Worcester (Dr. Wall). Scalloped Deep Dish. Black monochrome transfer print, invented by Hancock. c. 1760. 10½″ l.

539. Bow. Octagonal Plate. One of a pair. All-white with raised prunus on border. Porcelain very glassy. On the base elongated pontils. By transmitted light large moons. c. 1746. 8⅝″ d. See Appendix I for chemical analysis.

540. Bow. Large Plate. Partridge decoration characteristic of Bow, copied from Kakiemon. c. 1765. 10¼″ d.

541. Bow. Plate. One of a pair. Partridge decoration, scalloped edges, oriental flowers. c. 1755. 8⅝″ d.

158 542. Chamberlain Worcester. Dish decorated with fable-animals in the manner of A. F. von Löwenfinck. c. 1800. Vertical height 7¾″. Coll. Dr. Hans Syz, Westport, Conn.

543. Liverpool. Cream Jug, over-glazed in bright blue scale pattern on ground of lighter tone. This unusual decoration not known to have been used in any other English factory. The cake plate to this Liverpool service in Victoria and Albert Museum. c. 1765. Courtesy Colonial Williamsburg, Va.

544. Worcester (Dr. Wall). Pair of Vases with Covers. Under-glaze blue decoration showing

flowering plants, oriental bird and Chinese landscapes. Mark erroneously attributed to Frye, on base of each vase and collar of each cover. c. 1765. Courtesy Colonial Williams- burg, Va.

545. ENGLISH LOWESTOFT. COFFEE POT AND COVER. Blue decoration with name of original owner, John Ward Blofield, in cartouche on lid. Poem by Blofield in similar large cartouche on body. c. 1776. Courtesy Colonial Williamsburg, Va.

159 546. CHELSEA. HANS SLOAN BOTANICAL PLATE. Brown line on edges. Coloring very dull. Red anchor mark. c. 1755. $8\frac{1}{4}''$ d. Coll. Mrs. C. B. Stout, Memphis, Tenn.

547. BOW. HANS SLOAN BOTANICAL PLATE. Decorated with "Cotton Tree" (words "cotton tree" written on one of the leaves). c. 1755. $8''$ d. Coll. Mrs. C. B. Stout, Memphis, Tenn.

548. BOW. OCTAGONAL PLATE. No mark. c. 1760. $8\frac{1}{2}''$ w. Coll. Mrs. C. B. Stout, Memphis, Tenn.

549. LONGTON HALL. PLATE with raised strawberry decoration. 1753-1757. $9\frac{1}{2}''$ d. Coll. Mrs. C. B. Stout, Memphis, Tenn.

550, 551. WORCESTER. O'NEALE FABLE ANIMAL PLATES: The Stag Looking into the Water; and The Hanging Fox and Three Geese. Taken from Aesop's Fables. c. 1770. $7\frac{1}{2}''$ d. Coll. Mrs. C. B. Stout, Memphis, Tenn.

552. SWANSEA. OBLONG DISH. Floral decoration. c. 1816. Coll. Dr. and Mrs. John Quincy Wolf, Memphis, Tennessee, U.S.A.

553. PLYMOUTH. DEEP PLATE. Badly warped and with many black specks. No mark. c. 1768. $8\frac{3}{4}''$ d., $1\frac{5}{8}''$ deep. Coll. Dr. and Mrs. John Quincy Wolf, Memphis, Tenn.

554. CHINESE PLATE. Ch'ien Lung famille rose decorations. The cock in blue, yellow, black and rose. c. 1750. $9''$ d. Coll. Mrs. Carrington Jones, Memphis, Tennessee, U.S.A.

555. SWANSEA. PLATE with floral decoration. c. 1817. Coll. Mrs. Sidney Farnsworth, Sr., Memphis, Tennessee, U.S.A.

556. BRANCAS-LAURAGUAIS. PLATE. c. 1758. Coll. Mrs. W. T. Pride, Memphis, Tennessee, U.S.A.

160 557. BOW. VASE with decoration in scale blue. Exotic birds by Giles. Rare mark. c. 1760. $9\frac{1}{4}''$h. Coll. Mrs. T. V. Butler, Memphis, Tennessee, U.S.A.

558. CHAMBERLAIN WORCESTER. DISH, one from a large service. Blind Earl Pattern. c. 1795. Coll. Mr. and Mrs. J. P. Norfleet, Memphis, Tennessee, U.S.A.

559. WORCESTER (Dr. Wall). CHESTNUT BOWL AND COVER. One of a pair. One with crescent mark and other with red anchor. c. 1765. $5\frac{1}{2}''$ h., $10''$ l., and $8\frac{1}{2}''$ w. Courtesy Antiquarian Society of Memphis, Tenn.

560. ENGLISH LOWESTOFT. GARNITURE; white ground with border of sepia trellis pattern and floral garlands of green, sepia, red, and yellow above multi-colored bouquets of varied flowers. c. 1770. Courtesy Colonial Williamsburg, Va.

161 561. WORCESTER (Dr. Wall). TEAPOT. The decoration is known as "Long Eliza," evidently from the elongated Chinese figures. Mark: script W. c. 1760. $5\frac{1}{2}''$ h.

562. WORCESTER (Dr. Wall). JUG with "Long Eliza" decor. c. 1760. $3\frac{7}{8}''$ h.

563. WORCESTER (Dr. Wall). CHESTNUT BOWL, STAND, AND COVER. Translucency of this underglaze blue-and-white bowl very green. Mark: crescent. c. 1760. $6''$ h., $10''$ l., $8\frac{1}{2}''$ w.

564. WORCESTER (Dr. Wall). TRAY with Imari decoration. Handle formed with raised flower stem. Mark: several Chinese characters in under-glaze blue. c. 1760. $5\frac{1}{2}''$ d.

565. WORCESTER (Dr. Wall). FLUTED OBLONG DISH. Imari decoration. Mark: six Chinese symbols. c. 1760. $10\frac{1}{2}''$ l.

566. WORCESTER (Dr. Wall). TWO-HANDLED CUP AND SAUCER. Imari decoration. Mark: five Chinese characters. c. 1760. Saucer $5\frac{5}{8}''$ d., $2''$ h.; Cup $2\frac{3}{4}''$ h.

567. WORCESTER (Dr. Wall). CROCUS POT, one of three. Under-glaze blue decoration: Mark: crescent. c. 1760. Ex collection Earl of Jersey. $6\frac{1}{2}''$ h., $8\frac{1}{2}''$ l.

568, 569. WORCESTER (Dr. Wall). CUPS AND SAUCERS. Under-glaze blue decoration. Mark: crescent. c. 1765.

570. LIVERPOOL. EARLY MUG. Tit at top of handle. Runny under-glaze blue with tree made of balloons. c. 1755. $6''$ h.

162 571. WORCESTER (Dr. Wall). CUP with fluted shape. Blue scale around top. Mark: crescent. c. 1760. $1\frac{1}{4}''$ h.

572. BOW. TEA BOWL decorated in partridge pattern with transfer outline and enamel. c. 1755. $1\frac{1}{2}''$ h.

573. LUND-BRISTOL. CUP with unusual Chinese shape. Oriental handle and decoration. 1748-1750. $2\frac{3}{4}''$ h.

574. WORCESTER (Dr. Wall). CUP with floral decor. Mark: Oriental seal or square. c. 1760. $1\frac{3}{4}''$ h.

575. WORCESTER (Dr. Wall). LEAF-SHAPED DISH. Under-glaze blue-and-white decoration. Mark: crescent. c. 1760. $3\frac{1}{2}''$ l.

576. WORCESTER (Dr. Wall). TEA BOWL AND SAUCER. Not mates but both in Imari style. No mark. c. 1765.

577. WORCESTER (Dr. Wall). TEA BOWL AND SAUCER. Thumb scratch mark at foot-rim. c. 1755. Tea bowl $1\frac{1}{2}''$ h., saucer $4\frac{3}{4}''$ d.

578. WORCESTER (Dr. Wall). TEA BOWL AND SAUCER. Japanese style painting. Square mark. c. 1765. Tea bowl $1\frac{5}{8}''$ h., saucer $4\frac{3}{4}''$ d.

579. BOW. TEA BOWL AND SAUCER. Floral decoration. c. 1755. Tea Bowl $1\frac{3}{4}''$ h., saucer $3\frac{3}{4}''$ d.

580. CHELSEA-DERBY. TEA BOWL AND SAUCER. Floral decoration. Mark: D and gold anchor. c. 1770. Tea bowl $1\frac{3}{4}''$ h., saucer $4\frac{7}{8}''$ d.

581. PINXTON. CUP AND SAUCER. Landscape and gold decoration. 1796-1799. Cup $2\frac{1}{8}''$ h., saucer $5\frac{3}{8}''$ d.

582. LUND-BRISTOL. SAUCE BOAT, one of a pair. Oriental decor in famille verte color. c. 1748. $9\frac{1}{2}''$ l., $4\frac{1}{2}''$ w.

583. WORCESTER. SOUP PLATE. Pattern known as Queen Charlotte's Wheel or Royal Lily. From a service made for the wife of George III in 1788 in two tones of blue. $9\frac{7}{8}''$ d.

584. BRISTOL. MILK JUG. Oriental style decor. Mark: Maltese Cross in addition to numeral 7 with dot. c. 1770.

163 585. WORCESTER. SOUP BOWL from Duke of Clarence Service. Painted by John Pennington. Represents "Hope." Decoration blue and very fine gold. Mark: the word Flight with crescent and crown. c. 1790. $10''$ d.

586. WORCESTER (Dr. Wall). LARGE JUG. Decoration landscapes, flowers, and insects. Mark: crescent. c. 1765. $8''$ h.

587. WORCESTER (Dr. Wall). FLUTED PLATE with floral decoration. Mark: crescent in under-glaze blue. 1755-1760. $8\frac{1}{2}''$ d.

588. WORCESTER (possibly Billingsley porcelain). PART OF TEA AND COFFEE SERVICE. Gold on raised gadroon edges outside a bleu-de-roi section enclosing yellow ground with cartouches in white with floral decoration. Two plates, waste bowl, 12 tea cups, 12 coffee cups and 12 saucers. c. 1810.

164 589. LONGTON HALL. GOATHERD, on moderately high Rococo base. Decorated in enamel colors with hair on both goatherd and goat, finely delineated. Unmarked. c. 1755. $10\frac{1}{4}''$ h. Coll. Mrs. Sigmund Katz, Covington, La.

590. LONGTON HALL. POTPOURRI VASE. Rococo shaped body with scattered applied flowers. Lid covered with large applied flowers in blue, green,

yellow, pink and lavender. c. 1755. 7¾″ h., 4¼″ d. Courtesy Colonial Williamsburg, Va. (Ex collection Mr. L. V. Lockwood).

165 591. PLYMOUTH. PAIR OF PHEASANTS in all-white. c. 1770. 7¾″ h. Courtesy Colonial Williamsburg, Va.

592, 593. CHELSEA. PAIR OF DWARFS. A man and woman, the former adapted from an engraving by Jacques Callot in series published 1622 under title "Varie figure Gobbi." Mark: on man, anchor in relief; painted in red on an applied oval medallion; anchor in red on woman. Man c. 1750. Woman c. 1755. 6⅛″, 5⅛″ h., respectively. From Schreiber collection. Courtesy Victoria and Albert Museum, London.

166 594. LIVERPOOL. PAIR WALL VASES. Chinoiserie scene painted on white ground in sepia, green, yellow, blue and lilac. Third quarter of 18th century. 4¾″ h., 3¼″ w. Courtesy Colonial Williamsburg, Va.

595. DERBY. BOWL WITH COVER. 1760-1765. 7¾″ h., 7⅝″ d. Courtesy Colonial Williamsburg, Va. (Ex collection Mr. L. V. Lockwood).

167 This entire plate from the Schreiber collection, shown here. Courtesy of Victoria and Albert Museum, London.

596. DERBY. PUNCH-POT AND COVER. c. 1760. 8½″ h., 11½″ w.

597. CHELSEA. MUG. Mark: anchor in red. c. 1755. 5½″ h., 4½″ d.

598. DERBY. COFFEE POT. c. 1760. 8¾″ h., 4¼″ d.

599. DERBY. MUG. c. 1760. 4″ h., 3¼″ d.

600. DERBY. COFFEE POT AND COVER. c. 1760. 8¾″ h., 4¼″ d.

601. DERBY. JUG. c. 1760. 5¾″ h., 4⅛″ d.

602. DERBY. JUG. c. 1760. 6¾″ h., 4⅝″ d.

603. CHELSEA. CUP. Mark: red anchor. c. 1755. 3⅛″ d.

604. CHELSEA. BOWL. c. 1755. Mark: red anchor. 2⅜″ h., 4½″ d.

605. DERBY. JUG. c. 1760. 9″ h., 5¾″ d.

606. CHELSEA. FINGER-BOWL. c. 1755. 2⅝″ h., 3¼″ d.

607. CHELSEA. BOWL. Mark: red anchor. c. 1755. 2⅜″ h., 4″ w.

608. DERBY. JUG. c. 1760. 7¼″ h., 5″ w.

609. CHELSEA. PLATE. Mark: red anchor. c. 1755. 8½″ d.

610 CHELSEA. SUGAR BOX WITH COVER. Mark: inside, an anchor in red. c. 1755. 3⅞″ h., 3⅛″ w.

611. CHELSEA. TUREEN AND COVER. in the form of rabbit. Mark: red anchor on inside of both, also "No. 1" in red. c. 1755. 8⅞″ h., 14¼″ l.

612. CHELSEA. BOX AND COVER, in form of apple. c. 1755. 3″ h., 2⅝″ d.

613. CHELSEA. CREAM JUG, molded in relief. Mark: red anchor. c. 1755. 8⅜″ h., 3½″ w.

614. DERBY. PLATE. c. 1760. 8½″ d.

168 615, 616. DERBY. FIGURES DEPICTING MINERVA, goddess of plenty, and Mars, god of war. Colors typical of early period with very little gold. Mars heavy with small vent hole in ground base. No patch marks on base. Patch marks on base of Minerva, also large vent hole; lighter in weight. 1756-1760. Mars 13½″ h., Minerva 15½″ h.

169 617, 618, 619 and 620. DERBY. WHITE BISCUIT FIGURES OF FOUR ELEMENTS: Earth, Air, Fire, and Water. Modeled by Stephan and having the repairer's mark of Joseph Hill (△). Similar set sold at Christie's in 1772. Also under the base will be found an incised D, surmounted by crown, and patch marks. c. 1772. 8½″ h.

170 621, 622. DERBY. BISCUIT FIGURES: Bacchantes Adorning Pan and Two Virgins Awakening Cupid, both modeled by J. J. Spengler after paintings by Angelica Kaufman, molded by Isaac Farnsworth. Mark: Mold number 195 and 196 and Spengler's mark, (*). Also the Crown Derby mark, D, batons surmounted by crown incised, and patch marks. 1790-1795. 12½″ h.

171 623. DERBY. FIGURE. c. 1760. 5¾″ h.

624. DERBY. FIGURE. c. 1760. 5″ h.

625. DERBY. FIGURE. c. 1760. 4½″ h.

626. BOW. FIGURE. c. 1755. 5⅛″ h.

627. BOW. FIGURE. c. 1755. 4½″ h.

628. BOW. FIGURE. c. 1750. 5″ h.

629. WORCESTER(?) FIGURE. c. 1755. 5″ h.

630. DERBY. ASIA, one of the Continents series. "Vacant stare" typical of Derby. Patch marks and large vent hole under base. Typical "bun" effects on tops of flowers. Dry spot on camel where glaze did not stick. "Dry patch" period. c. 1760. 8½″ h.

631. STAFFORDSHIRE (?) NEPTUNE. Soft-paste, probably made by Ralph Wood Jr. around 1790. Similar specimens in Victoria and Albert Museum from Broderip bequest. 9″ h.

632. DERBY. FALSTAFF. Bottom has typical large vent hole and patch marks, also incised triangle, mark of repairer Joseph Hill. c. 1765. 9″ h.

172 633. PLYMOUTH. PLATE, badly warped. Rim decorated in oriental manner, a bow holding flowers together. Hard-paste. c. 1770. 7½″ d.

634. ENGLISH LOWESTOFT. TEAPOT AND COVER. Soft-paste. c. 1760. 5½″ h.

635. CHAMBERLAIN WORCESTER. PLATE, part of tea service, consisting of 6 cups, 6 saucers, cream jug, teapot, covered sugar, and waste bowl. Mark: Chamberlain Worcester on tea pot. c. 1790. Coll. Mr. and Mrs. Dunbar Abston, Sr., Germantown, Tenn.

636. CHELSEA. PLATE with scalloped edge in brown. Typical flower decoration. No gold. Mark: brown anchor. Red anchor period. 1750-1756. 8¾″ d.

637. DERBY. PLATE with thistle decoration. Mark: crowned D in early violet color. c. 1784. 9″ d. Coll. of Dr. and Mrs. Frank Mercer, Birmingham, Michigan, U.S.A.

638. CHELSEA. PLATE with typical Chelsea bird decoration. Mark: red anchor. c. 1756. 8½″ d.

639. DERBY. CUP AND SAUCER, fluted shape, decorated in gold only. The number 1 indicates it was first design made of the 770 used during this period. The numeral 2 indicates that gold decoration, finely executed, was the work of Joseph Stables. c. 1784. Cup 2¾″ h., saucer 5½″ d.

640. DERBY. DIAMOND-SHAPED DISH, one of a pair. Flowers painted by Withers. Smith blue border in over-glaze. Mark: crowned D c. 1770. 12″ l., 9⅝″ w. Coll. Dr. and Mrs. Frank Mercer, Detroit.

641. DERBY. CUP with decor of floral swags and Smith over-glaze blue. Mark: crowned D. c. 1770. 1¾″ h.

642. CHELSEA-DERBY. MUG with Smith over-glaze blue. Floral decor by Withers. Mark: (gold anchor and D). c. 1770. 4″ h.

173 643. DERBY. DINNER SERVICE, with floral decoration. An example of Crown Derby at its best, made for Lord William Frieth of Bristol, England. Of special interest is the presence of an iridescent "halo" around the painting on every piece. The service at present comprises the following: 2 large tureens with covers, 14″ l., 9½″ w., and 9½″ h.; 2 small sauce boats, covers and stand, 6½″ l., stand 8½″ l.; 2 oblong salad bowls, 13¼″ l., 8¾″ w.; 2 oblong vegetable dishes with covers, 10½″ l., 8½″ w., 7″ h.; 22 small plates 7¾″ d.; 69 dinner plates 10″ d.; 15 soup plates 10″ d.; 9 platters, varying from 13½″ l. to 19½″ l. Mark: D with crossed batons, surmounted by crown; also the numeral 9 (the factory had 750 designs). 1795-1800.

174 644. NANTGARW. PLATE with molded design, a floral decor painted by Pardoe. Mark: impressed Nantgarw C.W. c. 1820. $8\frac{3}{4}''$ d.

645. NANTGARW. PLATE with typical molded border. Three rose decoration. Mark: Nantgarw C.W. c. 1818. $9\frac{13}{16}''$ d.

646. NANTGARW. PLATE with typical molded shape. Design on rim: oeil-de-perdrix in green. Elaborate gold trim. Nantgarw C.W. impressed mark. c. 1818. $8\frac{5}{8}''$ d.

647. NANTGARW. PLATE with raised scroll molding repeated six times around border. Floral decor. Mark: impressed Nantgarw C.W. c. 1818. $9\frac{3}{4}''$ d.

648. NANTGARW. PLATE with raised scroll molding repeated six times around border. Floral painting in center. Dentil gold pattern around outer-rim. Impressed mark, Nantgarw C.W. c. 1818. $9\frac{5}{8}''$ d.

649. NANTGARW. PLATE with raised scroll molding repeated six times around the border. Floral decoration with gold bands around both sides of border. Impressed mark with "Mortlock" in gold over it. c. 1818. $9\frac{5}{8}''$ d.

650. NANTGARW. PLATE. One of a pair. Prince Regent service. Painted by Billingsley. c. 1818. $8\frac{5}{8}''$ d.

651. NANTGARW. CRUCIFORM DISH, painted by Thomas Pardoe. Decoration: landscape with birds, insects, etc. Impressed Nantgarw C.W. mark. c. 1820. $9\frac{1}{4}''$ d., $1\frac{7}{8}''$ deep.

652. NANTGARW. PLATE with molded design. Floral decor by Thomas Pardoe. Impressed mark: Nantgarw C.W. c. 1820. $5\frac{5}{8}''$ d.

175 653, 654. CHELSEA. SET OF MUSES, URANIA AND EUTERPE. Mark: gold anchor. c. 1765. $15\frac{1}{2}''$ h. Coll. Mr. and Mrs. Bertrand W. Cohn, Memphis, Tenn.

176 655, 656. TUCKER. Two JUGS, typical of hard-paste porcelain made at Philadelphia, U.S.A. by William Ellis and Thomas Tucker, Thomas Hulme and Judge Joseph Hemphill, from 1825 to 1838. $6\frac{5}{8}''$ h., $8\frac{3}{4}''$ h. Courtesy Metropolitan Museum of Art, New York.

177 657. BOW. TWO VIEWS OF A DOCUMENTARY PLATE. Showing arrangement of prunus and absence of foot-rim, each peculiar to Bow. The prunus petals are six in number rather than the usual five, the glaze is missing in areas around what would be the foot-rim.

178 658. MEISSEN. FIGURE OF CUPID WITH BOW AND ARROW, and inscribed Coup sur coup. One of a pair, the other one Cupid with Bird Cage is inscribed Fe le captive. The figures were modeled by Acier. The mark is a crossed swords with a star beneath. c. 1775. $5\frac{1}{4}''$ h. $4\frac{3}{4}''$ d.

659. SWANSEA. DISH. One of a pair. London decorated. Flowers have the iridescent halo peculiar to Nantgarw and Swansea when decorated in London. No mark. c. 1816. $8\frac{7}{8}''$ d. $1\frac{1}{2}''$ deep.

660. MEISSEN. RECTANGULAR TEA CADDY, turquoise fond, top decorated with gold. Sides decorated with landscapes, including colorful trees and animals. Ends decorated with harbor scenes. Decorations all enclosed by lacy gold cartouches. Crossed swords mark. c. 1730. $4''$ h., $3\frac{3}{8}''$ l., and $2\frac{1}{8}''$ w.

661. LUDWIGSBURG. LARGE PLATTER. Creamy white glaze decorated with flowers. Basket-weave rims with brown edges and badly warped. Mark two C's surmounted with a crown and above the crown the numeral 6, all in underglaze blue. c. 1760. $15\frac{3}{4}''$ d., $2\frac{3}{4}''$ deep.

179 662. NANTGARW. DEEP ROUND DISH from the MacIntosh service, London decorated with two exotic birds: the border richly gilded and with reserves of floral sprays. Mark: impressed Nantgarw C.W. (1818-1820). $9''$ d. Coll. Major G. N. Dawnay, Cardiff, Wales.

180 663, 664. WORCESTER. TWO BROTH BOWLS AND COVERS. First period: with double scroll handles and floral knop, decorated with flower sprays on a rich scale blue ground. Square marks. c. 1770. $4\frac{1}{2}''$ h. $7\frac{1}{2}''$ d. Coll. Major G. N. Dawnay, Cardiff, Wales.

MONOCHROME ILLUSTRATIONS

CHINESE   106   105   1·07
                                            (Scott)
                   108   108

Courtesy of the City Art Museum, St. Louis

110

111

113
109

112

111

CHINESE

CHINESE

114
Courtesy of The Walters Art Gallery, Baltimore
Mr. & Mrs. George Ware Collection

115   116

CHINESE
117
Courtesy of The Walters Art Gallery, Baltimore

CHINESE   120   119   118
                121   122   121

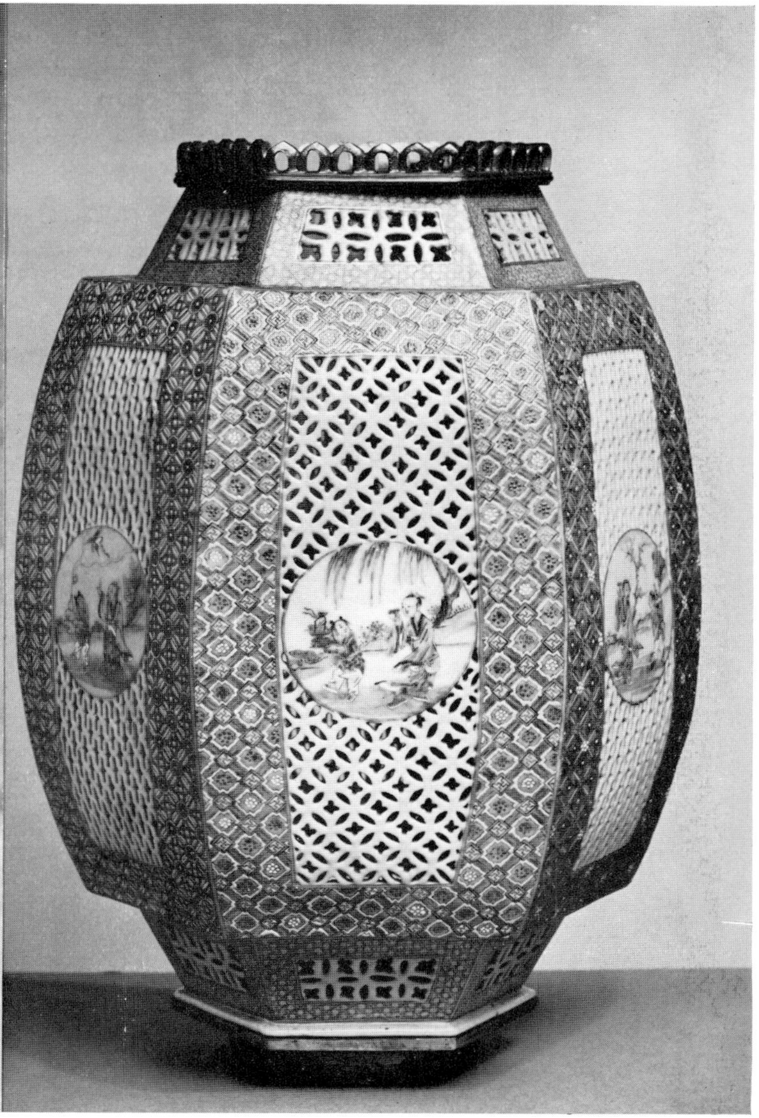

31

125
Courtesy of The Walters Art Gallery, Baltimore

CHINESE

124
Courtesy of the City Art Museum, St. Louis

CHINESE

Courtesy of Colonial Williamsburg, Va.

CHINESE   127   128   129
           130   131   132

JAPANESE

133
134
Courtesy of The Seattle Art Museum

JAPANESE   135   136

137   138

The British Museum, London

MEISSEN   141   *Dr. Mourot Collection*
                          142   *Dr. Hans Syz Collection*

145
146

148

144

147

143

146

MEISSEN

MEISSEN (1710–20)

149—155
Mr. S. Kramarsky Collection

156—162

Mr. S. Kramarsky Collection

MEISSEN (1715-25)

MEISSEN

163
Dr. Hans Syz Collection
164
Dr. Mourot Collection

165   168   169   166   170   167

MEISSEN

43

MEISSEN   171   172 (Scott)   173   171
     174   175   176 (Scott)   177
        178   179   180 *Mrs. C. B. Stout Collection*

44

183
186

182
185

181
184

MEISSEN

MEISSEN
187
Miss Ilse Bischoff Collection
189
Mr. R. H. Wark Collection

188
Mr. R. H. Wark Collection
190
Mrs. C. B. Stout Collection

MEISSEN

191

Mr. & Mrs. Norcross Collection

192   192

Dr. Mourot Collection

47

198   195

197

194

193   196

MEISSEN

200
202
199
201

MEISSEN (c. 1723)

203
Mrs. C. B. Stout Collection

205   204   206

Mr. R. H. Wark Collection

51

MEISSEN   211   207   212   208   213   209   214   210   215

MEISSEN 216
Courtesy The Smithsonian Institute, Washington, D.C.

217
Courtesy of The Detroit Institute of Art

MEISSEN (c. 1730)

218

The Berne Historical Museum, Switzerland

MEISSEN

219
Courtesy The Metropolitan Museum of Art, New York

55

223

225

222

221

224

220

MEISSEN

226
Mr. R. H. Wark Collection

MEISSEN

MEISSEN (c. 1735)

227
Mr. R. H. Wark Collection

MEISSEN

228
Mrs. C. B. Stout Collection
230
Mr. & Mrs. Ben Williams Collection

229
Mr. R. H. Wark Collection
231
Mr. R. H. Wark Collection

234
238

233   237

232   236

235

MEISSEN

61

240   243

241
244

242
245

MEISSEN

MEISSEN (c. 1725)

246
Dr. Schneider Collection

MEISSEN (1737-41)
247
Courtesy of the City Art Museum, St. Louis

MEISSEN

248   249   252

250   251

(Scott)   Mr. R. H. Wark Collection   (Scott)

MEISSEN

253
Mr. R. H. Wark Collection
254
Mrs. H. C. Isaacson, Sr. Collection

255

MEISSEN (1737-42)

"Biltmore," Asheville Collection, N.C.

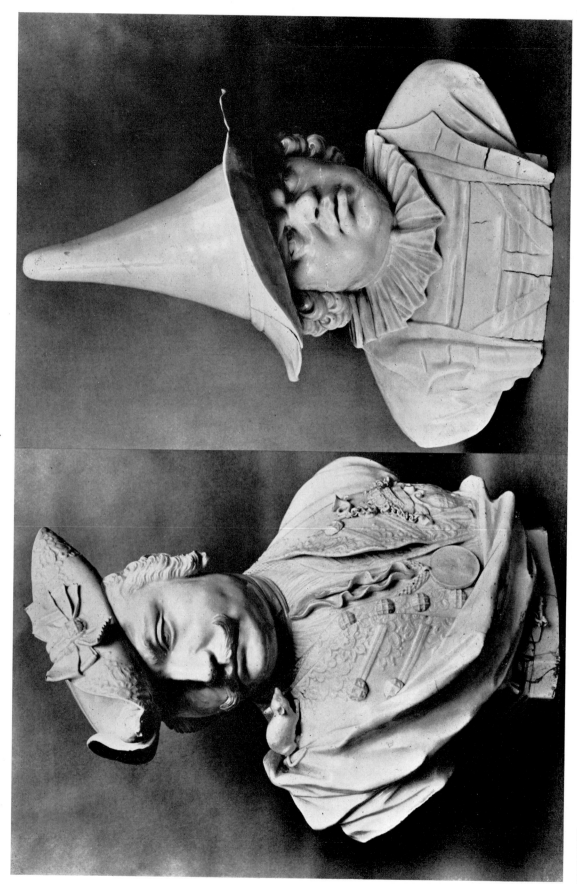

256

257

MEISSEN

Courtesy of the Detroit Institute of Arts

68

MEISSEN (c. 1743)

258
Mrs. C. B. Stout Collection

69

MEISSEN (c. 1740)

259

Courtesy of the City Art Museum, St. Louis

260 261 262

MEISSEN   263   264   265

                       266   267   268

MEISSEN   269 (Plymouth)   270 (Bow)   271   272
               273   274   275

73

276

277

MEISSEN (c. 1736)

MEISSEN

278
Mr. R. H. Wark Collection
279
Ex. A. Whittekind Collection

MEISSEN (c. 1740)

280
Courtesy Wadsworth Atheneum, Hartford

76

281

Courtesy Wadsworth Atheneum, Hartford

MEISSEN (c. 1740)

77

282

MEISSEN (c. 1745)

78

283   284   285

Courtesy Wadsworth Atheneum, Hartford

MEISSEN

MEISSEN   286   287   288

289   290

MEISSEN (c. 1738)

291

Courtesy Wadsworth Atheneum, Hartford

MEISSEN   292   293
     Memphis Antiquarians   *Mrs. C. B. Stout Collection*
                   294   295

82

MEISSEN (c. 1745)   295   297   DERBY (c. 1765)

Mrs. C. B. Stout Collection

MEISSEN   298   299

                        (July, 1736)   (August, 1741)

The Irwin Untermyer Collection

85

MEISSEN   302
        304   304   303
                    Mr. Paul Schnyder von Wartensee Collection   304

86

DU PAQUIER   (*Scott*) 305   (*Scott*) 305A (Meissen)   MEISSEN

DU PAQUIER   (*Scott*) 307   (*Scott*) 306   (*Memphis Antiquarians*)

(*Scott*) 308
(Du Paquier)

DU PAQUIER

309 (Scott)
311 (Scott)

310 (Scott)
312
Mr. R. H. Wark Collection

DU PAQUIER
MEISSEN

DU PAQUIER

313
314
The Berne Historical Museum

Mrs. H. C. Isaacson Sr. Collection

313A
314A
Mrs. H. C. Isaacson Sr. Collection

315
Dr. Hans Syz Collection
316
Mrs. H. C. Isaacson Sr. Collection

DU PAQUIER

317
318
Dr. Hans Syz Collection

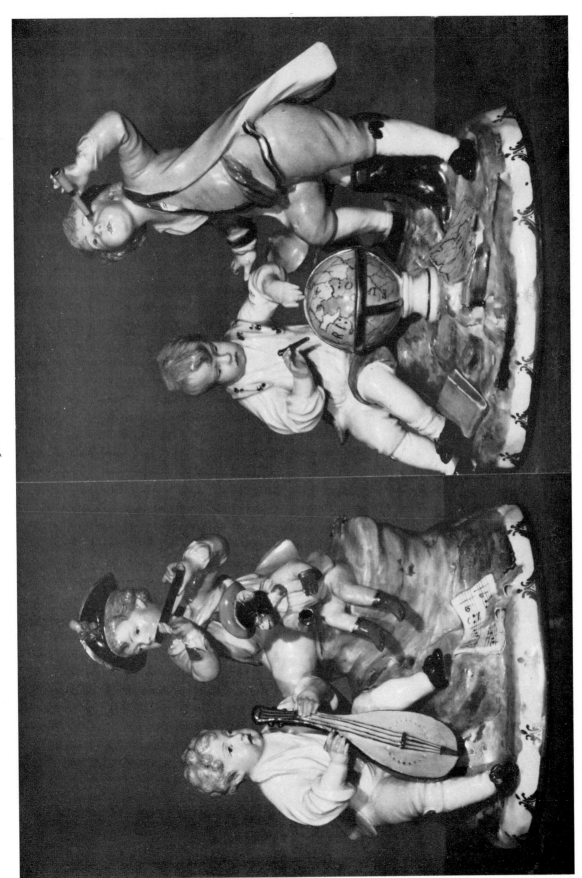

320

319

VIENNA (c. 1765)

VIENNA   321   322   323
          324   325   326

93

VIENNA (c. 1780)   327

94

HÖCHST (c. 1753)   328

HÖCHST (c. 1770)

329

Courtesy of The Detroit Institute of Arts

HÖCHST (c. 1770)   331
                                  330

HÖCHST 332 332A 332B
332C 332D 332E
Mr. & Mrs. Pflueger Collection, New York

HÖCHST   333   333A   333B
                      333C   333D   333E

Mr. & Mrs. Pflueger Collection, New York

HÖCHST (c. 1770)   334   335   336
                    337   338   339

100

WALLENDORF   340
Mrs. H. C. Isaacson Sr. Collection

341 *(Scott)*   FRANKENTHAL
342   HÖCHST
Mrs. C. B. Stout Collection

FRANKENTHAL 343   344   345   346
347   348   349

350

FRANKENTHAL

351
353

354

352
355

NYMPHENBURG (1754-63) 356
The Berne Historical Museum, Switzerland 357

NYMPHENBURG (1754-63)   360   361
The Berne Historical Museum, Switzerland

NYMPHENBURG (c. 1764)   362

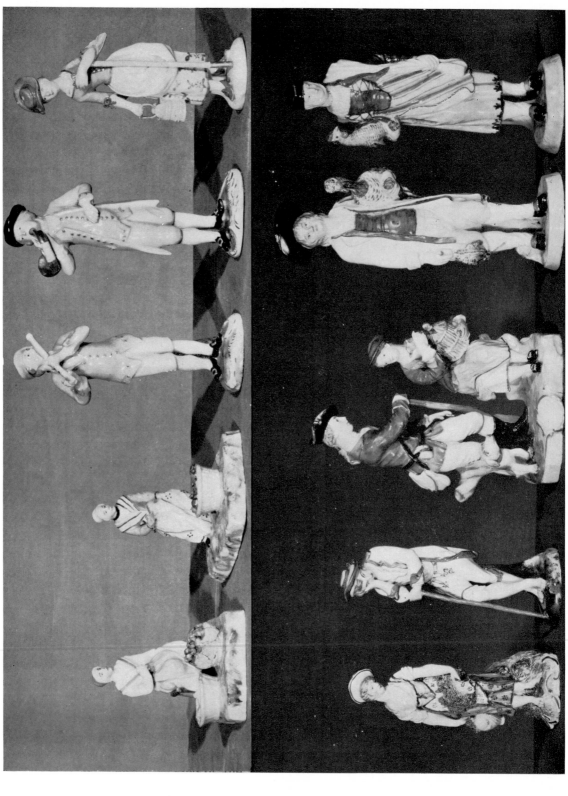

367

(Furstenberg)
372

366
371

365
(Furstenberg)
370

364

363
369

LUDWIGSBURG
LUDWIGSBURG 368

LUDWIGSBURG (c. 1765)   373

ZURICH 379
381

380
382

Dr. Siegfried Ducret Collection

NYON

383 (Gotzkowsky)   384 (Fulda)   385 (Hague)   386 (Zweibrücken)
387 (Worcester)   388 (Worcester)   389 (Frankenthal)   390 (Lassia) 391 (Tournay)

392

Mr. & Mrs. L. B. Dow Jr. Collection

DU PAQUIER   393   394   LUDWIGSBURG
      Mrs. H. Eggers Collection   *Mrs. De Witt Williams Collection*
COZZI VENICE   395   396   FRANKENTHAL
      Mrs. Kingsley Page Collection   *Mrs. W. L. Harnan Collection*

114

CAPO-DI-MONTE

397 (Mol-Holland)
399 (Doccia)
403

397 (Buen Retiro)
402 (Cozzi Venice)
405

398 401 (Höchst)
400 (Höchst) 404 (Le Nove)

COZZI VENICE   (*Scott*) 406   (*Scott*) 407 (Doccia)   407A BOURG-LA-REINE
DOCCIA   408   *Mrs. G. W. Stoddard Collection*
                    Mrs. H. C. Isaacson Sr. Collection

ROUEN (1675-95)   409
                 Courtesy of The Metropolitan Museum of Art, New York

117

ST. CLOUD
MENNECY

412
415

411 (Mennecy)
414 (Chantilly)

410
413

ST. CLOUD
ROUEN

416

417

ST. CLOUD

Courtesy of The Metropolitan Museum of Art, New York
(Gift of R. Thornton Wilson)

MENNECY (1735-40)
418
Courtesy of The Metropolitan Museum of Art, New York
(Gift of R. Thornton Wilson)

MENNECY (c. 1740)

419

Courtesy Wadsworth Atheneum, Hartford

MENNECY (c. 1748)

420

421

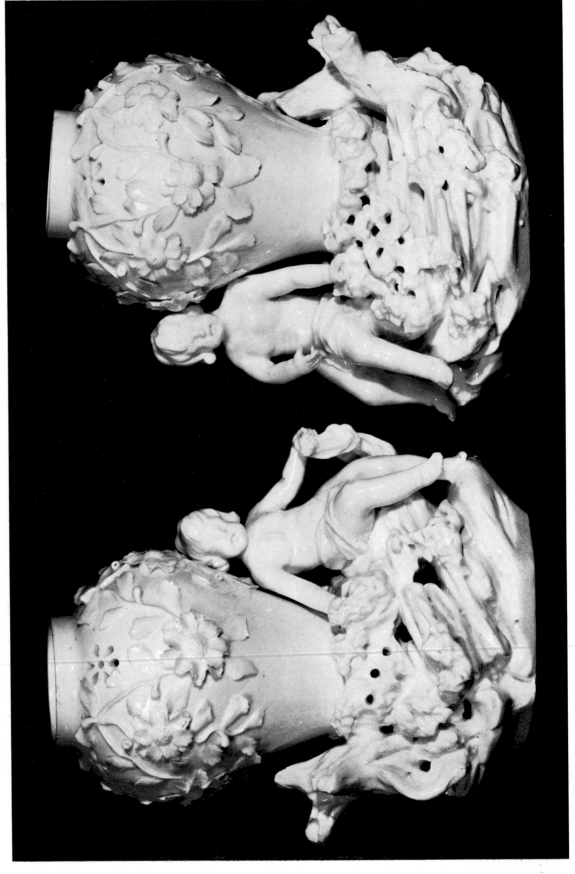

122

422

VINCENNES (c. 1745)

VINCENNES (c. 1750)   423

VINCENNES (c. 1753) 424

Courtesy of The Metropolitan Museum of Art, New York
(Gift of R. Thornton Wilson)

425

VINCENNES (c. 1755)

429
Courtesy Wadsworth Atheneum, Hartford

SEVRES

430
The Wallace Collection, London

432

The Wallace Collection, London

431

VINCENNES
OR SEVRES

129

SEVRES (1757-63)

SEVRES (c. 1758)　　　434　　　　　　　　　　　　　　435
　　　　　　　Courtesy of The Metropolitan Museum of Art, New York
　　　　　　　　　　(Gift of R. Thornton Wilson)

131

VINCENNES

438   440   437   439   436

SEVRES

OLD PARIS 441   442   SEVRES
SEVRES   443   444   443   SEVRES

OLD PARIS (c. 1790)   445   446

FRANKENTHAL 447   447   448   HÖCHST
DOCCIA   *Mrs. Donald Graham Collection*   MENNECY
    449   450 (Höchst)   451
Mrs. W. L. Harnan Collection *Mrs. N. McDougall Collection* *Mrs. S. A. Creighton Collection*

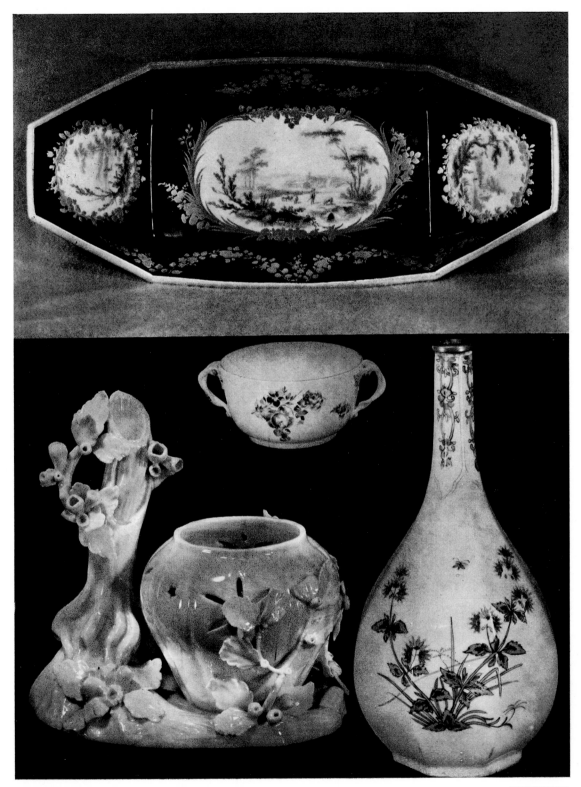

VINCENNES   452   453   MENNECY
CHANTILLY   454   455   CHANTILLY
Mrs. W. L. Harnan   Mrs. S. A. Creighton   Mrs. Stoddard & Mrs. R. Nichols Collections

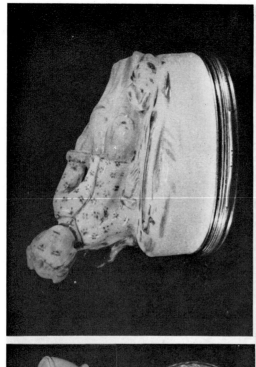

MENNECY
VINCENNES

458
460

Mrs. H. Eggers, Mrs. Stoddard, Mrs. R. Nichols, Mrs. K. Page and Mrs. W. L. Harnan Collections

(Bourg-La-Reine)   457

NYMPHENBURG   456   459
COZZI VENICE

CHELSEA (c. 1745)

461
Mrs. Sigmund Katz Collection

CHELSEA (c. 1752)

462
Mrs. Sigmund Katz Collection

CHELSEA (c. 1750) 465
CHELSEA (c. 1755) 463

466
464

Courtesy Colonial Williamsburg, Va.

LONGTON HALL (c. 1755)   467   468
Mrs. Sigmund Katz Collection

CHELSEA (c. 1755)   469
The Victoria & Albert Museum, London   470

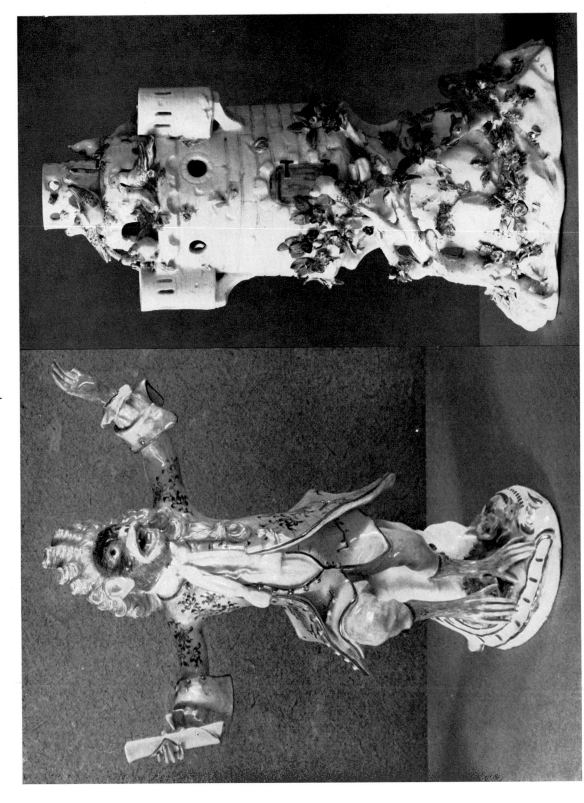

142

CHELSEA (c. 1755)

475.
Courtesy Colonial Williamsburg, Va.

476
The Victoria & Albert Museum, London

CHELSEA   477   482   478   479   480   483   481

Courtesy The Museum of Fine Arts, Boston
(Gift of Mr. Richard C. Paine)

BOW
CHELSEA

484
486

485
487

CHELSEA

Courtesy Museum of Fine Arts, Boston

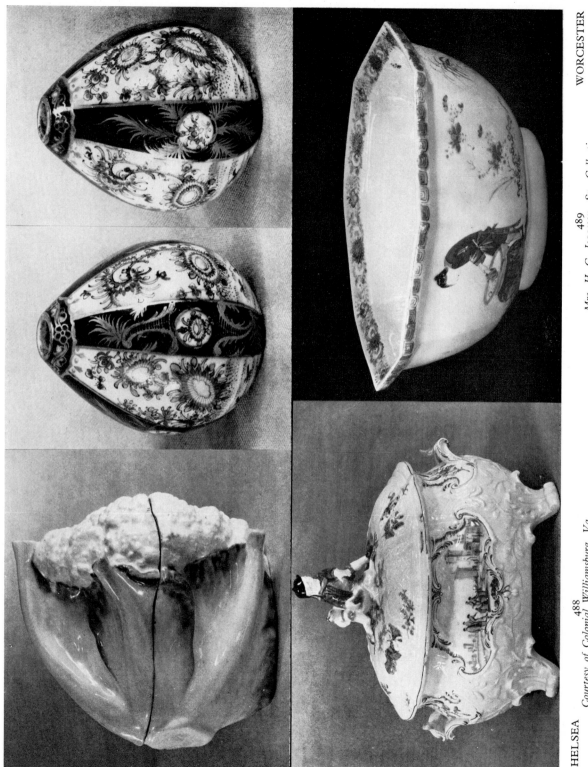

145

CHELSEA
CHELSEA

488
490

Courtesy of Colonial Williamsburg, Va.

WORCESTER
CHELSEA

489
491

Mrs. H. C. Isaacson, Sr., Collection

Mrs. H. C. Isaacson, Sr., Collection

146

BOW 492   493   494 (Chelsea)   495 (Chelsea)   496 BRISTOL

Mrs. C. B. Stout Collection

499 CHELSEA-DERBY

CHELSEA-DERBY 497   (Chinese) 498   *Mr. & Mrs. C. M. Gooch Collection*

Mr. & Mrs. C. M. Gooch Collection   *Mr. & Mrs. W. W. Deupree Collection*

CHELSEA (c. 1755)

500

The Victoria & Albert Museum, London

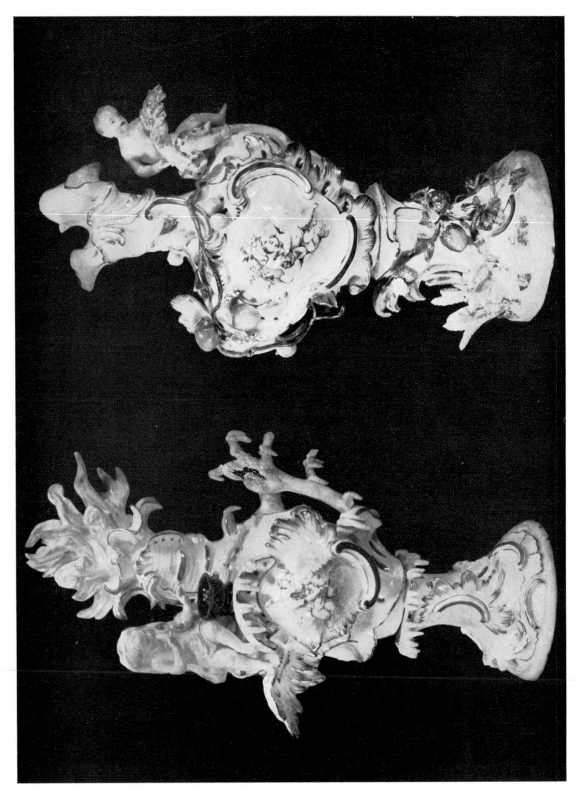

CHELSEA (1753–58)   501   *Mrs. Wendell Black Collection*   502

503   504

CHELSEA (c. 1770)   *The Victoria & Albert Museum, London*

150

The Victoria & Albert Museum, London

506

505

CHELSEA (c. 1770)   505

507

TOURNAY   508 (Scott)   509 (Longton) 510   511 (Scott)   TOURNAY
            512   (Mrs. C. B. Stout)   513   GIRL IN A SWING
GIRL IN A SWING   Mrs. C. B. Stout Collection   Courtesy The Museum of Fine Arts, Boston

CHELSEA DERBY 514 515 516 LONGTON HALL
(Chelsea)

CHELSEA 517 518

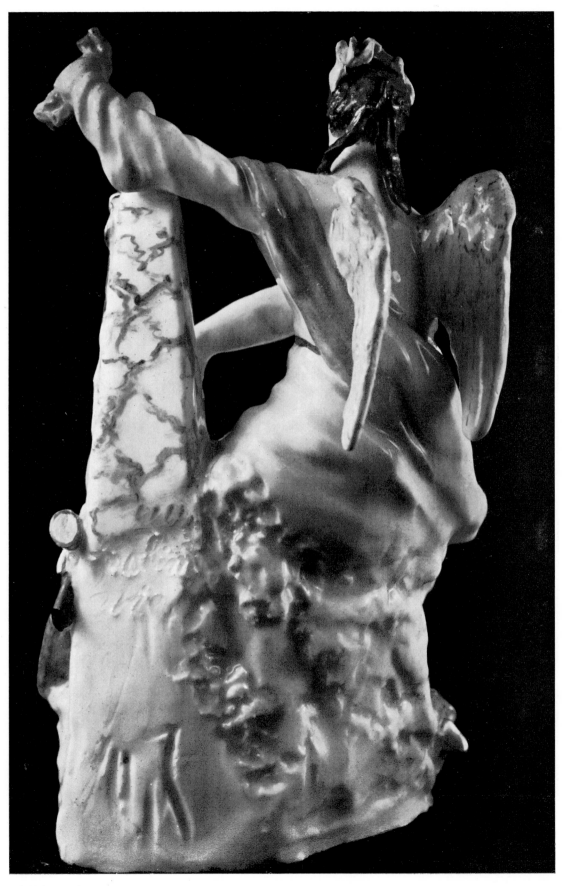

BOW (c. 1750)

519
Mrs. Sigmund Katz Collection

154

BOW (c. 1750)   520   521 (Bow. Incised 1750)

The Irwin Untermyer Collection

LONGTON HALL (?) 522   523 (Bow)   524 (Bow)   525 (Bow)   526
                                                           LONGTON HALL (?)
BOW   527   528   529   530   BOW

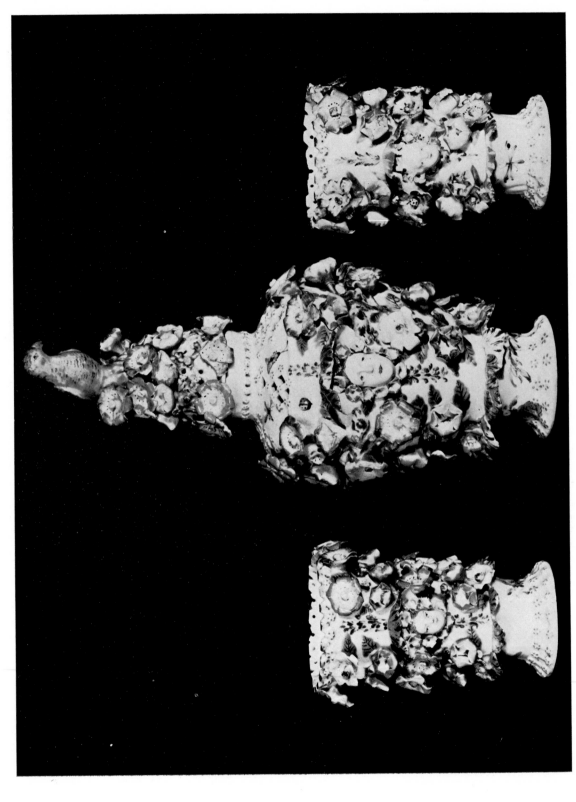

531

BOW   532   533 (Worcester)   534 (Grainger)   535 (Liverpool)   536   LONGTON

CHELSEA   537   538   WORCESTER

BOW   539   540   541   BOW

158

WORCESTER   542
            Dr. Hans Syz Collection
WORCESTER   544
    Courtesy of Colonial Williamsburg, Va.

            545   LOWESTOFT

            543   LIVERPOOL
    Courtesy of Colonial Williamsburg, Va.

VARIOUS   546   547   548 *Mrs. C. B. Stout Collection*
549   550   551 *Mrs. C. B. Stout Collection*
552   553 *Dr. & Mrs. Wolf Collection*
554   555   556
Mrs. C. Jones, Mrs. S. Farnsworth & Mrs. Pride Collections

559
Memphis Antiquarians

558 (Chamberlain)
Mr. & Mrs. Norfleet Collection
560
Courtesy of Colonial Williamsburg, Va.

557
Mrs. Butler Collection

BOW
ENGLISH LOWESTOFT

ENGLISH   571   572   573   574   575
(18th cent.)   576   577   578
                579   580   581
                582   583   584

585

586
588

587

WORCESTER

LONGTON HALL (c. 1753) 589
  Mrs. Sigmund Katz Collection

590
Courtesy of Colonial Williamsburg, Va.

PLYMOUTH   591   591

Courtesy of Colonial Williamsburg, Va.

CHELSEA   592   593

The Victoria & Albert Museum, London

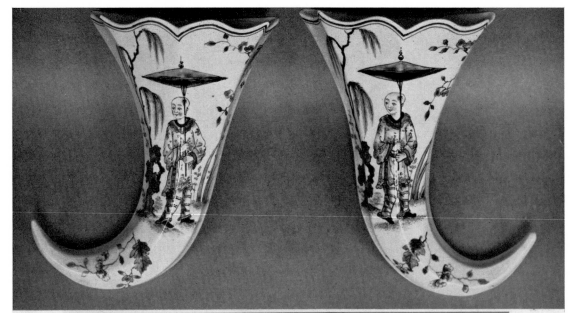

LIVERPOOL (c. 1765)   594   594
DERBY (1760-65)
                                       595
                        Courtesy of Colonial Williamsburg, Va.

167

CHELSEA (c. 1755)   597   598   596   599   600   601
   AND   602   603   604   605   606   607   608
DERBY (c. 1760)   609   611   614
                        610   612   613
The Victoria & Albert Museum, London

615

619

DERBY (1756-60)

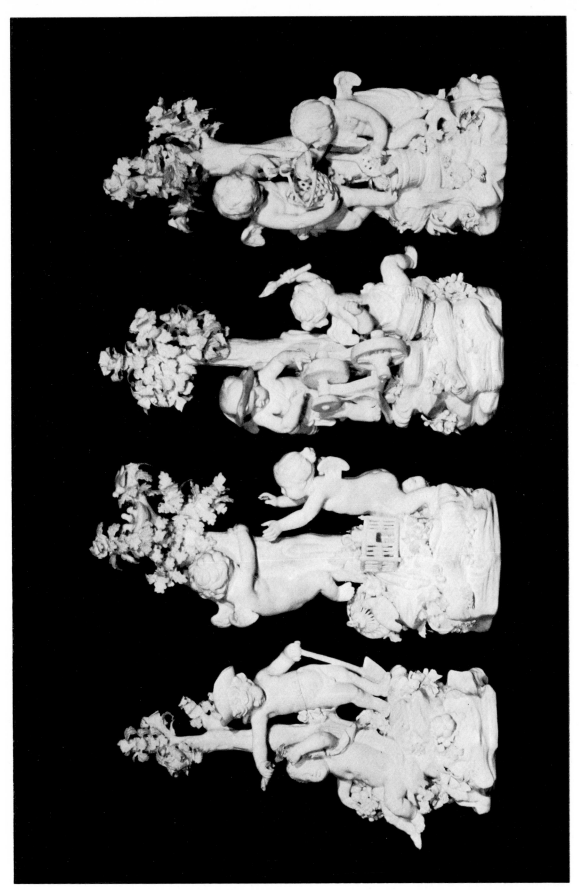

169

DERBY (c. 1772)   617   618   619   620

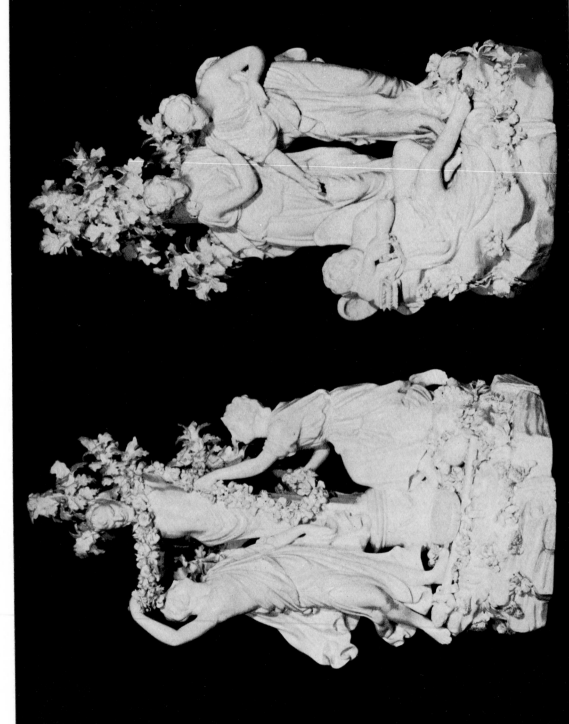

170

622

621

DERBY (1790-95)

DERBY 623   624   625   626 (Bow) 627 (Bow)   628 (Bow) (Worcester) 629

DERBY   630   631 (Staffs.)   632 (Derby)

ENGLISH 633   634   635
(18th cent.) 636   637   *Mr. & Mrs. Abston Collection*
        Dr. & Mrs. Mercer Collection   638
    639   640   641   642

DERBY (1795-1800)

643
(Dinner Service)

NANTGARW   644   645   646
                              647   648   649
                              650   651   652

CHELSEA (c. 1765)   653

Mr. & Mrs. Bertrand W. Cohn Collection

654

176

AMERICAN-TUCKER (1825-38)   655
                                   656
              Courtesy Metropolitan Museum of Art

MEISSEN 658   659 (Swansea)   660 MEISSEN
661 (Ludwigsburg)

NANTGARW (1818-20)

662
Major G. N. Dawnay Collection

WORCESTER (1770-75)
663
664
Major G. N. Dawnay Collection